BRAVE MEN *and* GREAT CAPTAINS

BRAVE MEN *and* GREAT CAPTAINS

R. ERNEST DUPUY, *Colonel, U.S.A., Ret.*
and
TREVOR N. DUPUY, *Colonel, U.S.A., Ret.*

HARPER & BROTHERS, PUBLISHERS, NEW YORK

973
D
COPY 7

"Niagara River Region" map, page 76, by permission from
Military Heritage of America by R. Ernest Dupuy and
Trevor N. Dupuy. © 1956 by McGraw-Hill Book Company, Inc.

*The Library of Congress catalog entry for
this book appears at the end of the text.*

To

Cadet Trevor Nevitt Dupuy, Jr., who, in common with his comrades of the United States Corps of Cadets, must be prepared to assume the responsibility of leadership in the years to come

ACKNOWLEDGMENT

To Laura Nevitt Dupuy, Army wife and Army mother, the authors join in tribute for her keen insight, logical reasoning and literary guidance which has kept this work on the rails, checking every impulse to wander from the chosen frame of reference.

FOREWORD

It has been said by others that America is entering the decade of decision. This is true. It is also coming into an age of full maturity. It is attaining a stature in the world that brings with it a responsibility for wise and able leadership. Part of this leadership is military, and a very significant part it may be.

It would be well for us to understand our past military leadership. It has not all been good, but on the whole it has been more than adequate. American military leadership has been different from that of others as our people are different from others. That it will be different in the future goes without saying. Undoubtedly, however, we will develop military leadership of a breadth and ability to grasp effectively global and space problems.

Colonel Dupuy and his son have written a book on our past military leadership, beginning with military leaders in the early days of the Republic and continuing through the Korean War. They have analyzed and presented men of varied background and ability. The Dupuys are well qualified to do this, both because of their military background and because of their combined insight into military thinking and their ability to present their ideas in written form. I have known both of them for a number of years and I respect their military judgments and ability.

Brave Men and Great Captains is thorough; it is a comprehensive treatment of its subject, covering the good leadership as well as the bad. It is well worth reading by military and civilian alike. Besides this, it is entertaining reading. It should provide a basis for understanding the peculiar qualities of American leadership and thus for projecting those qualities into the future to meet the challenge that will certainly be ours in the coming decade.

JAMES M. GAVIN
Lt. General, U.S.A., Ret.

CONTENTS

LIST OF MAPS

PREFACE

What Is Leadership?

Military leadership is *multum in parvo*; it embraces many things. Through good leadership men can be galvanized into performance of acts transcending the norms of their individual reactions and capabilities. Poor leadership, on the other hand, confuses; it stifles initiative; it can bring panic on the battlefield to the most stout-hearted soldier.

The very mention of the word "leadership" creates in the American mind a succession of images bridging nine score and more of our nation's history. Leading all will be a big man in blue and buff, mounted on a great white charger. Prominent also in the procession will be a group of men in Confederate gray and Union blue. The final figure is that of a man in modern khaki, wearing a visored cap, wading through island surf. But, varied though their uniforms and superficial appearance may be, all of these apparitions share two common characteristics: they are in the forefront of action, and their slogan is "Follow me!"

How does one define leadership?

Definitions, paraphrases and synonyms can be found literally by the hundreds. The authors of this book prefer a definition used at West Point:

"Leadership is the art of influencing and directing people to an assigned goal in such a manner as to command their obedience, confidence, respect and loyal co-operation."

But no definition can tell us the essential ingredients of leadership. In the analysis of this book we have endeavored to distill the essence of leadership, as demonstrated in American military history, to provide a yardstick against which the accomplishments of individual leaders can be measured.

The Yardstick of Leadership

The requirements of the yardstick were in fact established by the failures of command in our first national battle, Bunker Hill, on June 17, 1775. The standards by which later leaders could be judged were etched indelibly by the achievements of George Washington. And the pattern of leadership—the record of actual accomplishments against the high standards of the yardstick—has been woven continuously throughout our history by the successes—and the failures, too—of Washington's subordinates and his and their successors. So, in reading the following pages, it may be helpful to the reader to bear in mind the essential measures on that yardstick of leadership, as the authors envisage it.

First, and perhaps most important, is *professional military skill or competence,* comprising knowledge of military history, judgment in the flexible application of theoretical principles, and the ability to take positive, energetic action in applying knowledge and principles to specific situations.

Second is the need for thorough *understanding of the human tools of the leader;* i.e., a knowledge of the capabilities and limitations of his men.

Here it might be advisable to digress briefly to consider what qualities in the American soldier have most concerned our military leadership. It is interesting to note that the major personal characteristics of the colonists who fought at Bunker Hill, and who followed Washington to Yorktown, were to be revealed by Americans in all of the subsequent wars of our history.

Most of these men were individualists, quite dissimilar in character to the bovine peasantry providing the bulk of the the soldiery of Europe. And this individualism, as all American leaders have since discovered to their frequent annoyance and frustration, led to a pervading suspicion of authority, and thus to resistance of the discipline which is the catalyst of an army.

These men combined imagination with intelligence. The leader who failed to recognize these qualities in his men, and who was unable to keep one mental jump ahead of them, could not succeed. These were qualities, too, which enabled the men to perceive more readily than their European counterparts the immediate and potential dangers of a situation; a perception which would often impel them to avoid such dangers—even if this meant running away in battle.

On the other hand, the colonists at Bunker Hill, like their descendants, possessed the qualities of self-reliance and initiative to a degree hitherto and elsewhere unknown in private soldiers. Related to these, and strikingly exemplified by colonial marksmanship at Bunker Hill, was precision in the use of tools and weapons. These were characteristics, when properly controlled and utilized, that were to make the trained American soldier the finest in the world.

Which leads directly to another measurement of leadership on our yardstick: *insistence upon high standards of training and discipline,* whereby the leader, knowing his men, their strengths and weaknesses, capitalizes on their capabilities and minimizes their limitations.

Then there must be, inherent or acquired, *inspirational ability;* men must recognize their leadership and respond to it confidently.

Other necessary qualities for the leader are *personal courage,* which is related to inspirational ability, and *perseverance and determination in adversity.*

There is one more measure of leadership, but one which can be applied only to men who attain the top level of command of their nation's forces. This is *the ability, in peace and war, to understand the relationship between military strategy and national policy,* and to contribute, without transcending the limits of a soldier's authority, to the formulation of a nation's defense policy.

Selecting Examples for a Pattern of Leadership

The story of combat leadership in the United States Army is, on the whole, an inspiring one. Stemming from the almost haphazard achievements of a few individuals of natural or acquired military talent, it has progressed to a national military manner and system. While perhaps differing little in basis from that of other nations— for neither courage nor military ability has national bounds—nevertheless, as we have noted, military leadership in these United States does face certain problems and does have certain characteristics peculiar to the American people.

Here, then, to prove the thesis, and to evaluate against our yardstick, are narratives of selected highlights in the careers of certain of our Army leaders from revolutionary times to the present. These are case histories of American military leadership, most of them encouraging, some disheartening. The scope of the actions involved, and the restricted canvas of presentation, forbid fuller coverage.

The task of selection of these case histories has been fascinating, stimulating and provocative. Even in our first national war it was not simple. For instance, Nathanael Greene was Washington's principal lieutenant in the Revolution. Reluctantly we have had to omit him from our examples of leadership in that war because we feel that as an army commander he was far surpassed by his commander in chief, and we believe that Wayne, Morgan and Steuben are more representative of diverse aspects of the birth of the American tradition of leadership in subordinate roles.

Selection became more difficult as the Civil War was reached. Almost ruthlessly we limited our case studies to a few examples of incompetence and of excellence. Our purpose was to show the pattern of leadership, not to prepare a biographical dictionary of the leaders. Reluctantly again, therefore, we were forced to dismiss such capable leaders as James Longstreet, Joseph E. Johnston and George H. Thomas—only three of many we have perhaps slighted.

In World War I the problem of selection was compounded. Robert L. Bullard, Frank R. McCoy and a number of other men also left their indelible stamp of leadership upon our Army during that period; part of a very definite pattern, whose details must be suppressed in focusing upon Pershing and Summerall.

By 1941 the pattern was indeed unmistakable. Military education, past experience, and tradition had combined to develop within the United States Army a systematic but flexible methodology in the practice of the art of war. Leadership, as defined in our frame of reference, had become the rule rather than the exception.

So it was that in World War II, as in the Korean War that followed, the names and exploits of a host of qualified and proven leaders of whom both the Army and the American people are proud necessarily became subordinated to the general pattern of Army leadership.

There was, for instance, Omar N. Bradley, whose farsighted planning, strategic judgment and velvet-gloved tactical control led troops to victory from North Africa to the Elbe. Eisenhower's tribute tells it best: "I unhesitatingly class General Bradley's tactical operations . . . as equal in brilliance to any that American forces have ever conducted." Similarly, we can but point to the ability of Jacob L. Devers to control in battle such diverse army commanders as loyal, competent American Alexander McC. Patch and unpredictable French De Lattre de Tassigny.

We can only list senior commanders like brilliant Albert C. Wedemeyer in China; keen, professional Walter Krueger, direct-acting Robert L. Eichelberger and stout Simon Bolivar Buckner in the Pacific; and dependable Courtney H. Hodges, philosophic William H. Simpson and indomitable Lucian K. Truscott in Europe. The records of all these men speak for them.

The corps and division commanders, and the airmen flying above them, whose leadership dovetailed into the mosaic of successful command, were so many that—save for the examples we have selected for our pattern—it would be both impractical and invidious to single out a few at the expense of the others.

Out in Korea later, the leadership of Matthew B. Ridgway and James A. Van Fleet, whose mettle had already been proven as corps commanders in World War II, fashioned in the flame of a fantastic war one of the most efficient fighting machines of history: the U.S. Eighth Army.

All these men and many other contributed to a saga, from the elements of which we have endeavored to present in bold strokes the essence of United States Army leadership.

The reader will get from these pages a summary view of our nation's wars. One of them alone—the Spanish-American War—is missing; and that by design. It was barren ground insofar as our theme was concerned. In our opinion there was in that war almost no opportunity for demonstration of leadership in its highest phases, and what little existed was deplorable. The troop leadership in lower echelons was everything that might have been expected from our tight little self-reliant Army, just graduated from Indian fighting. That was all. It is well to recall that more American soldiers were killed by Indians in one day in Custer's Battle of the Little Big Horn than were killed in action during the entire Spanish-American War.

This book is neither a history of our Army nor a definitive narrative of our wars. The historical framework upon which it is based is as accurate as honest research plus personal experience can make it. While footnotes—the delight of the pedant and the bane of the average reader—are lacking, the selected bibliography will, it is hoped, make easy the task of those desirous of verification or further information.

The choice of examples, and the opinions expressed herein, are the responsibility of the authors alone—two American soldiers proud of their Army and solicitous for the future welfare of their country. Neither the examples nor the opinions should be construed as necessarily representing the viewpoint of the Department of Defense, the Department of the Army, or the services at large.

R. ERNEST DUPUY
TREVOR N. DUPUY

BRAVE MEN *and* GREAT CAPTAINS

CHAPTER I ☆ ☆ ☆ *The Battles of Bunker Hill*

Proud, Cocky, and Confident

"It's getting too hot around here for me! Let's get out!"

In panic the young lieutenant fled from the earthworks. For as long as he could, he had tried to be an example to the confused and frightened soldiers who cowered with him behind the parapet, seeking protection from the vicious whine of bullets flying overhead. But the earthen wall was shuddering constantly now as hostile artillery fire pounded the hillside, and he was terrifyingly aware of the steady, implacable advance of the enemy infantry up the hill. It was more than flesh and blood could stand.

The lieutenant's shriek was the signal to the men nearby. Out they dashed, in mad flight, following him down Bunker Hill toward safety.

Bunker Hill! But with a difference.

This was Bunker Hill, Korea, separated by 7,000 miles and 176 years from the Battle of Bunker Hill, Massachusetts, for this took place shortly before midnight on May 17, 1951. It was separated, too, by an indefinable atmosphere lacking in the earlier battle. Because, three hours after he had run away, this young lieutenant, thrice wounded in the process, had fought his way back to his post. A crisp, familiar voice in the night had turned him; the voice of leadership; the voice of his battalion commander, Lieutenant Colonel Wallace Murdock Hanes.

"Get back on the hill," Hanes said scathingly. "We don't give up

1

a position until we're beaten. And dammit, we're not beaten and won't be if every man does his share."

This and no more. He strode back to his command post. The frightened lieutenant and the score of panic-stricken soldiers who had accompanied him in the mad flight couldn't see his face, but they could well imagine his expression as he halted them, and the fugitives turned sheepishly to climb back up into the storm of fire on the top of "Bunker Hill." They were back in business—soldiers all.

There lies the difference between the Bunker Hills. Our frightened boys of 1775 didn't come back, once they had fled. There had been no one to lead them.

On the western side of Korea, late in April, 1951, the Chinese Communists had launched the first of their two massive spring offensives, which United Nations forces had been able to bring to a halt at the outskirts of Seoul, Korea's capital, after surrendering a great deal of valuable ground to the enemy. By mid-May it was obvious that the enemy had brought in many reinforcements from Manchuria, and was about to strike a second blow before the defenders could recover from the first. The main effort of this attack, it became clear, would be in the center of the peninsula, in the general region defended by the 2nd Infantry Division.

The extreme western portion of the wide division front was held by the 3rd Battalion, 38th Infantry, commanded by Lieutenant Colonel Hanes. *

Virginia-born Wallace Murdock Hanes had assumed command on the 2nd of April 1951—just twelve days after his thirty-fifth birthday. The 38th Infantry—the "Rock of the Marne" regiment—was a part of the 2nd Infantry Division, whose proud record of combat in two world wars had been enriched by its recent months of incessant combat in Korea. It had borne the brunt of the Chinese Communist main effort in western Korea the previous November and December, and it had been in the thick of the winter fighting in the X Corps sector of central Korea ever since. The 38th, like the rest of the "Indianhead" Division, had suffered many casualties, and so there were lots of replacements now mixed with

* See map of Korea, p. 323.

those veterans who had arrived in Korea in August, 1950. A few of the newcomers, like the newly appointed commander of the 3rd Battalion, were battle-wise soldiers who had seen action with other units in Korea; some were hastily recalled reservists who had had no refresher training since their active-duty days in World War II; many were recruits who had never before heard a shot fired in anger.

Hanes took advantage of a period of relative quiet in the X Corps sector to learn everything he could about his new command, and to impress his personality on the battalion. Officers and men alike quickly came to respect the energy as well as the businesslike, impersonal attitude of the short, slight lieutenant colonel. They soon discovered that the steely glint in his eye was a better indication of his character than was his deceptively mild, Southern manner of speech. They learned, too, that he had an uncanny knack of appearing on the scene when things were going wrong. The Indian-head veterans were not long in realizing that Hanes, who had a fine record of combat in Italy in World War II, was also just as experienced as they were in the peculiar problems of combat in Korea. The new arrivals were perhaps more impressed by his splendid physical condition, by his immaculate appearance, his unfailing courtesy in dealing with officers and men, and by his unyielding insistence on perfection in military fundamentals.

The key to Hanes's extended sector, four miles in width, was Hill 800—so called from its elevation as shown on the map—a sprawling hill mass, rising to a bald, pointed peak.

The battalion had occupied its position during the first week in May. The men grumbled as, day after day, Hanes made them keep digging and cutting down trees to build up thick log and dirt protection over their first skimpy foxholes. "Dammit," he is reported to have told the grumblers, "I want bunkers with cover to protect you from artillery fire."

So bunkers they gave him—deep, roomy bunkers, each covered with logs and several feet of earth, and all camouflaged as completely as the scant vegetation would allow. On the bald peak of Hill 800 one platoon alone of K Company built twenty-three bunkers. And as they sawed, and dug, and hauled sandbags, land mines, barbed wire, ammunition, and other supplies up to the top

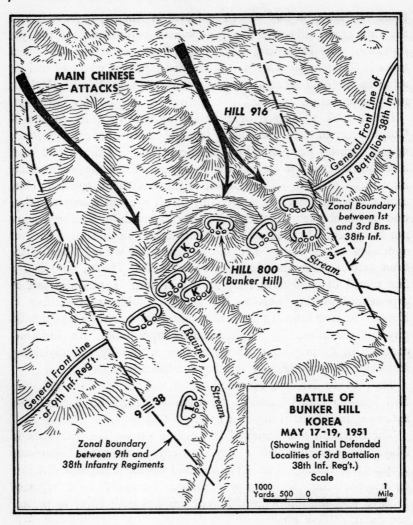

MAIN CHINESE ATTACKS

HILL 916

General Front Line of 1st Battalion 38th Inf.

Zonal Boundary between 1st and 3rd Bns. 38th Inf.

Stream

HILL 800 (Bunker Hill)

General Front Line of 9th Inf. Reg't.

(Ravine) Stream

Zonal Boundary between 9th and 38th Infantry Regiments

BATTLE OF BUNKER HILL KOREA MAY 17-19, 1951
(Showing Initial Defended Localities of 3rd Battalion 38th Inf. Reg't.)
Scale
1000 Yards 500 0   1 Mile

of their rocky inaccessible peak, the men of the 3rd Battalion began to call it "Bunker Hill."

Finally the bunkers were good enough to satisfy Colonel Hanes, and his men expected to get some rest before the expected enemy attack. But their perfectionist commander would not allow them to relax. Now more barbed wire and more mines had to be carted up the mountain footpaths, to create barriers across the most likely avenues of enemy approach, and particularly along the ridge line which formed a saddle connecting Hill 800 with slightly higher Hill 916, three-quarters of a mile to the north.

The three rifle companies of Hanes's battalion—I, K, and L from left to right—were disposed each on a two-platoon front with the third platoon in reserve. His heavy weapons (machine guns and re-coilless rifles) company, M, was covering the entire front, prepared to give supporting fire.

Hanes had no doubt K Company, holding the center on Hill 800 itself, could easily repulse any attack on that key point. He was more concerned about the flank companies, particularly I on the left, which lay in a deep depression between K Company's "Bunker Hill" and high ground held by a neighboring unit. It was thus par-ticularly exposed to an attack slicing off of Hill 916.

To offset this potential weakness, Hanes directed Captain George R. Brownell, commanding K Company, to place his reserve platoon behind I Company's right flank, and earmarked it as battalion re-serve. Brownell, then, could not use this platoon without Hanes's express sanction.

By evening of May 17 it was obvious from the build-up of enemy strength around Hill 916, and from their probing against the units to the right and left, that the 3rd Battalion would be attacked that night.

The attack came, sure enough, at about 10:00 P.M. It struck across Hanes's entire front, but—true to the uncertainties of war —it was not on either of his flanks but in K Company in the center that things first went wrong. Brownell's telephone line to the sup-porting artillery went out, cut by enemy mortar or artillery fire, as did his lines to his platoons. When he tried to get through over the battalion headquarters line from his first platoon, where his com-mand post was, that too went dead. Finally, when he reached the battalion commander by radio, a direct hit on his command-post bunker put his transmitter out of business.

All Hanes knew was that Brownell and K Company were in trouble and he could not communicate with them by normal means. Nor did the arrival at this time of that little handful of panic-stricken fugitives add to his comfort.

But Hanes had another trick up his sleeve. He had insisted on alternate phone communications—lines from each platoon to his command post, and lines to each of his four recoilless rifles. He could thus speak directly to the commander of K Company's third platoon on the western slope of the hill, and to the crews of the two recoilless rifles emplaced on the crest. They reported a confused situation, with enemy troops all around them, but stated that the bulk of K Company was still holding firm.

Confident, then, that Brownell and his platoon commanders could hold until dawn, Hanes contented himself with putting artillery fire in front of K Company to cut off enemy reinforcement.

Not long after this a call came from Brownell himself, who had worked his way through the enemy milling about the west slope of the hill to reach the command post of his third platoon. The company commander wanted to counterattack with his second platoon, which as we know had been placed in battalion reserve. Hanes, approving, at the same time refused Brownell's further request that artillery fire be placed on the top of the hill itself, as preliminary.

There were still many Americans holding out on the hilltop, according to the reports of the recoilless riflemen, and Hanes felt that normal artillery fire, which was being directed by these riflemen through the battalion switchboard, was sufficient to check further enemy reinforcement.

Having thus expended his reserve, the battalion commander at once ordered I Company on his left, which was doing all right at the moment, to shunt its reserve platoon over to the right, replacing the one he had given Brownell. That weak spot between I and K Companies still worried him.

Shortly after midnight Brownell, jubilant, called in to report his counterattack had been successful. He had driven the Chinese completely off the hill, with few casualties to his second platoon. By 1:30 phone and radio communications were completely re-established and concentrated artillery fire on the saddle leading to Hill 916 apparently discouraged any renewal of the attack.

It was the calm before the storm. At 4:15 a powerful Chinese assault came smashing against I Company, to overrun its right flank and the extreme left of K Company—exactly through the depression that had worried Hanes before the fight started.

Thanks, however, to his foresight, his new reserve platoon, just arrived to backstop his line, met the enemy in the gap and halted what otherwise might have been a clean breakthrough.

All along the battalion front, now, the pressure continued, with L Company on the right also hotly engaged. Fortunately—for Hanes now had no reserves left to influence the action—the line held, and at dawn the enemy, as usual with the Chinese, melted back under cover.

Hanes, inspecting his defenses, was satisfied with what he found, except for the break between I and K Companies. Here several hundred Chinese had crowded into the bunkers which his men had dug.

This was serious. Left to themselves under cover, the intruders would be in position to spearhead a major breakthrough that night —an eventuality that Hanes felt sure would come.

Taking advantage of the daylight lull, the battalion commander gathered up a platoon each from I and K Companies, under his own personal command, to root out the peril.

The men were exhausted from the fighting of the previous night, but they were fired to a fever pitch of enthusiasm by Hanes's words and example. Before jumping off against the much larger enemy force, Hanes ordered an intensive mortar preparation, while artillery fire covered the approaches from the north to prevent reinforcements and to seal off the enemy escape route. In a few minutes more than a thousand 4.2″ mortar shells landed on the Chinese positions. The thunder and concussion of this massive concentration of fire were more than the closely packed Chinese could stand. As they fled in panic, they ran into his planned artillery concentrations while heavy machine-guns from the flanks poured fire into them as they tried to clamber over the barbed wire through which they had infiltrated the night before. Hanes's counterattackers, cheering madly, reached the old positions without a casualty, while only a few of the Chinese were able to get away.

Meanwhile, the remainder of the battalion had been repairing damage done during the previous night, and putting in new phone wires—this time digging them into the ground as Hanes had told them to do before. Thus by nightfall, though his men were tired, the position was re-established, and Hanes was confident that it was even stronger than before.

The Chinese attack was renewed as expected, but this time there was perfect co-ordination between the infantry and their artillery support. Communications worked without a hitch. Several times the enemy was thrown into confusion and their attacks halted by artillery fire placed on their assembly areas and the avenues of approach. One determined assault, however, finally broke through to the top of Bunker Hill.

Up through the barbed wire and onto the bunkered earthworks of K Company's sector the shouting Chinese poured. This time not a man of the defenders left his post, and as the enemy reached the bunkers, Captain Brownell asked the artillery to fire right at his position. Without hesitation, Hanes gave the order. Once again the men were thankful that he had insisted on protected bunkers.

In an eight-minute space two thousand 105-mm. high-explosive projectiles swept the summit with an inferno of searing blasts. Safe in the bunkers they had sweated to build, Brownell and K Company crouched, while above their heads thudding projectiles exploded and the screams of their enemies caught in the open drowned the whine of deadly shell fragments. After the fire lifted, all was silent. Not an enemy remained alive on the hill.

Though the Chinese mounted several more attacks, the position was never again in danger, and the men of K Company had little to do except to stay back from the openings of their bunkers, to avoid fragments of friendly or enemy artillery bursts. By daylight the enemy had withdrawn completely.

But the 3rd Battalion was now a bulge in the United Nations line, since troops on both sides had been forced back during the violent attacks of the two previous days. Despite Hanes's bitter protests, he was ordered to move back to a new position. There was nothing to do, of course, but to carry out the order. He made sure that his company commanders explained to every man why they were leaving, and assured them that higher commanders knew that they had not been beaten. Then he marched his men back by companies.

Proudly they strode past their regimental commander. As one historian has written of the scene: "Their horseshoe packs were rolled tight, their heads were high, their shoulders were thrown back. They had proved they could beat an all-out enemy attack, and they looked proud and cocky and confident."

They had proven themselves to be fit successors to the men who had won the regiment its nickname "Rock of the Marne" thirty-three years before in France, repelling simultaneous German attacks on front and both flanks to write, as General Pershing then reported, "one of the most brilliant pages of our military annals."

In retrospect certain elements stand out in this Korean action. We see first a capable commander, preparing his men and his position to get the utmost possible results. Second, we see this commander maintaining personal control of the action at all times. He knew his men and they knew him; a mutual confidence dissolving incipient panic, inducing teamwork. This was leadership.

It had not been thus at the earlier Battle of Bunker Hill.

Blueprint and Mirage

British-held Boston town blinked out of its sleep at dawn on June 17, 1775, to the roar of a lively cannonade, punctuated by roll of drums, blare of British fifes, and the hurried clumping of soldiery on its cobbled streets. Across the harbor on the slopes of Charlestown Heights, less than a mile away, something new had been added since the sun last went down. A squatty earthwork gashed the green banks with a smear of brown. Around and behind it men were clustered, and British warships in the anchorage were blasting away at it.

For two months British General Thomas Gage and his troops had been bottled up in Boston by a swarm of hornets in homespun, spontaneously aroused. Some fifteen thousand New Englanders in patchwork array held the countryside; a force, however, too disorganized to storm the town. On the other hand Gage well knew that his seven thousand trained soldiers could not subdue an inflamed population; Lexington and Concord had taught him that.

So until that morning uneasy stalemate had reigned. Now, it seemed, the rebels had forced the issue. From this new position at Charlestown they might be able to bring artillery fire upon the harbor shipping, might make the town untenable.

Gage huddled in hasty council of war with his subordinates— Generals William Howe, John Burgoyne, and Henry Clinton. Clinton pointed out that the rebels had actually outsmarted themselves. A small force, landed at Charlestown Neck behind their position and supported by the fire of the warships, could cut their communications with the mainland. Without water, food, or ammunition, the rash effort must fall in a day or two, with practically no loss to the British.

But Gage overruled him. A full-strength attack would be made at once by the elite of the British garrison, with Howe commanding. Five regiments of foot, a battalion of marines, and all the shock troops in Boston—ten companies each of light infantry and grenadiers—were mustered and by early afternoon embarked for the Charlestown side.

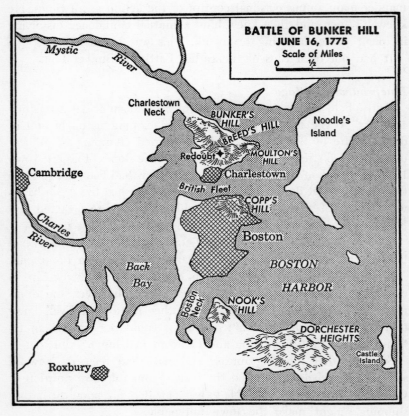

Let's look at this pear-shaped peninsula, where Colonel William Prescott, sixty-year-old farmer from Pepperell, Massachusetts, who had done some campaigning in King George's War, found himself that morning with twelve hundred nervous, untried men, looking down into the lion's mouth from his new-built earthwork fort on Breed's Hill.

Springing from a narrow, thirty-foot-wide neck lying just above high-water mark, Charlestown peninsula jutted for a good mile from the mainland into Boston harbor. Three hills ranged from north to south in successive downward steps to the confluence of the Mystic and Charles rivers.

Bunker's Hill, the northernmost, lifted sharply from the Neck to a 110-foot crown, beyond range from Boston of all but the most powerful ordnance of the day. A ridge led to Breed's Hill 600 yards to the south and slightly lower, with Charlestown village on its western waterfront, a half mile from Boston across the Charles and within fair cannon range of the harbor. At the eastern tip of the peninsula lay Moulton's Hill, the flattish bottom step. The surface of the bulbous peninsula, which was about a mile at its widest, was mostly pasture land, its high grass still unmowed.

Why Prescott was where he was requires some explanation, for he was supposedly carrying out the orders of the Committee of Safety of the Massachusetts Provincial Congress. And those orders were that Bunker's Hill—not Breed's—be fortified by "a strong redoubt . . . with cannon planted there, to annoy the enemy coming out of Charlestown, also to annoy them going by water to Medford."

This whole business, it must be remembered, had started as Massachusetts' war, and, under the Committee of Safety, her men were commanded by Major General Artemas Ward, a colorless individual with some slight military experience gained in Abercromby's disastrous campaign against the French at Ticonderoga in 1758. But Massachusetts had called on her neighbors for help, and they had responded—New Hampshire, Rhode Island, and Connecticut—in typically New England fashion; that is, each colony retained liberty of action to control its own men.

As John Adams would later write: "These four Armies met at Cambridge and imprisoned the British Army in Boston. But who was the Sovereign of this united or rather congregated Army and who was its commander-in-chief? It had none. Only Ward was Subject to the orders of the Massachusetts Provincial Congress. . . ."

This heterogeneous mass had little ammunition; the entire camp

supply consisted of eleven barrels of powder and some lead melted
down from the pipes of a church organ. Its small arms were those
which each individual had been able to snatch up, and its few
cannon were manned by men ignorant of even the rudimentary
gunnery of those days.

As for the men themselves, who came and went as they saw
fit, they were levies coaxed from the militia rolls to replace the
"Minute Men," those momentary warriors of Lexington and Concord, most of whom by this time had departed for their homes
and farms. Their officers, commissioned for the most part solely
because of popularity with their men, were, as one diarist of the
period noted, engaged in "a Strugling . . . which shold be the hiest
in offist."

Under such conditions one can well imagine that General Ward
was in no mood to take any offensive action against Gage's regulars.
On June 15 he received the Committee of Safety's order to fortify
Bunker's Hill. At once he gloomily discussed it with his so-called
council of war—really a debating society composed of all the higher
commanders of the four colonial forces.

A vocal majority, headed by Brigadier General Israel Putnam
of Connecticut, voted down Ward's objections. They were spoiling
for a fight, it seemed, and Putnam's voice—he had had more military
service than any other man present—was the voice of experience.
Reluctantly, Ward ordered out a task force under Prescott to obey
the committee's directive.

Prescott's own regiment—three hundred men from Groton, Pepperell, and Acton—who knew their leader and respected him, formed
the core. Other Massachusetts regiments contributed quotas, and
Connecticut was represented by two hundred men from Putnam's
force under Captain Thomas Knowlton. Carrying with them "all the
entrenching tools in camp," Prescott's troops moved out in the
dark of June 16, bound for Bunker's Hill.

On crossing the causeway at the Neck, Prescott detached a com-
pany to occupy Charlestown village and protect his right flank.
At this time Putnam joined the force, which moved up and over
Bunker's Hill. There it was halted and Prescott disclosed their job.

At once argument arose. An "unnamed" general officer (Putnam, who had no command status there, was the only general officer present) urged that Breed's Hill, not Bunker's, was the vital spot. While precious minutes passed, the debate continued, until old Colonel Richard Gridley, chief engineer of the Massachusetts Army, whose job it was to lay out the proposed fortification, bluntly told them to make up their minds else dawn would find them bare to the enemy.

They did. They chose Breed's Hill, in direct violation of the committee's order. And by that decision, itself a hiatus in leadership principles—since Bunker's Hill was the assigned goal—they changed a precautionary measure into a brash threat which the enemy could not tolerate.

By dawn they had thrown up a respectable redoubt some 130 feet square on the hillside. Prescott, now taking stock as the British began their shelling from the warships and from a battery on Copp's Hill on the Boston side, realized his vulnerability. His right flank, should the British attack, was protected by his detachment in Charlestown, but the left-hand slopes of the hill mass were bare.

So, while cannon balls bounced and bounded, Prescott pushed his workers to new effort, extending his square fortlet by a breastwork running down the hillside to the eastward for some three hundred feet. He did it under difficulties. Although most of the British guns were outranged, sufficient fire was falling close to terrify his amateur soldiers. One man was killed, and a trickle of deserters began to leave that hot, noisy spot.

The Americans had been digging since midnight. They were tired, hungry, and hot under a now blazing sun. They were thirsty, too; a spent ball had smashed their two hogsheads of water.

But Prescott, hat and wig doffed, bald head gleaming with sweat, kept driving them, holding the greater part of his men by sheer will power. By eleven o'clock the work was done and they could rest. Meanwhile he had sent to Ward at Cambridge for supplies (which he never got) and for reinforcements.

Ward at first refused to further deplete his main body, but the Committee of Safety, in session at his headquarters, thought differently. Again reluctantly, Ward ordered out the two New Hampshire regiments in camp. Since they had no ammunition, flints, powder, and sheet lead were doled out. It would be noon before they could melt and pound sufficient lead into bullets.

It was noon, too, before Prescott's men on the hill glimpsed the British barges, crammed with red coats and twinkling bayonets, rowing across the river. Brass fieldpieces poked their snouts from the two leading craft. At Moulton's Point, out of range from Breed's Hill, the British disembarked and Howe drew up his line of battle. The plan was to march up the Mystic side of the peninsula, out of musket range, outflank the redoubt, and attack it from the rear.

Howe, noting the extension of the American earthworks and the presence of more troops on Bunker's Hill behind, delayed advance until he should be reinforced. Meanwhile the troops were drawn up in three lines—light infantry, grenadiers, and line regiments in that order. His eight small cannon were disposed to support his right, the main effort, which he would lead himself. Brigadier General Sir Robert Pigot would lead the left, nearer Charlestown.

American musketry from that village began harassing Pigot's grouping, so Howe called for artillery fire from the ships and the Copp's Hill battery. As a result Charlestown village—now a deserted hamlet—soon blossomed into flame from incendiary projectiles.

While all this was going on, the roads and lanes between Prescott's position and Cambridge grew dusty with misdirected activity. Freelance Putnam, the only mounted man on the field, raced back and forth, importuning Ward again for reinforcements. So several Massachusetts regiments moved gingerly from Cambridge toward the Neck, there to halt in fear of the fire from two British gunboats sweeping the causeway.

Putnam got some of his own Connecticut men to the top of Bunker's Hill. He begged Prescott to send back entrenching tools. Prescott at first demurred; the men would not return, he feared. "They shall," swore Putnam, "every man!" So from the redoubt volunteers raced, eager to carry picks and shovels back to the safety of the far ridge and, as Prescott had feared, stay there. Nor was any entrenching done.

By now it became obvious to Prescott that the British intended to force his left, so he detached from his dwindling garrison Knowlton's two hundred Connecticut men, to oppose the threat. Knowlton found a rail fence some eight hundred feet in rear of the breast-work, paralleling it and running down almost to water's edge. Here he lined his men.

It was about this time that Colonel John Stark, experienced soldier who had been second-in-command of Rogers' Rangers in the French and Indian War, came striding down to the Neck with his New Hampshire men, their bulletmaking completed. The Massachusetts rabble milling there willingly made way for the newcomers to pass.

Stark reached the tip of Bunker's Hill, saw the British formation, and estimated that Knowlton's men at the rail fence were not strong enough to man that line. On his own initiative, then, he rushed his troops down to reinforce them and also built a hasty barricade of rocks on the narrow strip of beach between the fence end and the Mystic.

The American position thus consisted of three independent groupings. From right to left they were the original Charlestown detachment, now scattered behind a barn and along a roadway back of the blazing village; Prescott's troops manning the redoubt and its breastwork extension; and Stark's and Knowlton's men along the rail fence and the beach barricade. Lacking over-all direction, these three groupings would, as it turned out, fight as many isolated, unco-ordinated fights.

Howe moved to the attack, his reinforcements having arrived. His first line, the light infantry, filed off to their right, to advance in close column along the shore. Theirs would be a bayonet attack, to turn the rebel flank and roll it up against the two remaining lines pressing slowly up the hillside. The British light guns, pushed between the light infantry and the main body, fired a few rounds, then stopped. Some idiot, it seemed, had supplied twelve-pounder shot for six-pounder guns, and Howe had to send back for more ammunition.

They came slowly, the redcoats, burdened by full packs, through the tall grass in that blazing sun. They kept their ranks dressed and as they came within musket range the grenadiers and line regiments halted several times to fire volleys that spattered harmlessly on or below the earthworks.

Stark at the rail fence, Prescott in the earthworks, and the bouncing Putnam—he was all over the field that day, chasing stragglers at saber point, and urging newly arrived and most reluctant artillerymen into the line—managed to keep the trigger-happy farmers in restraint. That is, those of them who stayed; Prescott's redoubt was emptying fast now of all but his own regiment.

The British light-infantry column down on the beach was the first to close. At less than fifty yards' range Stark's stone barricade flamed and the leading company was torn apart. The next came pushing through, and the next, melting, as historian Christopher Ward puts it, "like a wax candle against a hot plate." The survivors turned and ran.

Committed thus to a frontal attack, Howe led his main body against the fence, where they met a searing discharge from Stark's and Knowlton's men. The grenadiers staggered, halted; the second line came barging through them to be greeted by another hail. For a few moments the British milled in confusion, then fell back beyond musket range. Red coats lay thick in the tall grass; every officer on Howe's personal staff was either killed or wounded.

On the British left, Pigot—his role was one of demonstration—tested Prescott's redoubt and received the same medicine. But the disciplined British infantry was made of stern stuff. Howe and Pigot reformed their commands, while across the way Putnam galloped back to Bunker's Hill, trying vainly to urge the men idling there to reinforce the line. Prescott, whose redoubt defenders had shrunk by now to about 150, praised his remaining men and exhorted them to stand.

For the second time Howe's troops started up the hill. This time Prescott's redoubt and its breastwork were their objectives. The light infantry, by now rallied, was merely to demonstrate in front of Stark's deadly rail fence.

Once more the American fire was held until the red-coated assault came close; once more its point-blank destruction shattered it. Putnam, back again, cursing and raving at the stream of skulkers fleeing the defense, manhandled an abandoned cannon himself, spooning powder into its muzzle because the cartridges were too big.

The second British attack reeled back beyond musket range, where Howe rallied it once again. He was going to dare it a third time, this stubborn soldier, who knew his men and knew how to lead them. They had lost almost 50 per cent casualties. In some companies but a half-dozen men remained of the thirty-odd who had started.

But the survivors shuffled into ranks again, dropped packs, and fixed bayonets. This time it would be cold steel, and in column instead of line; Howe against the breastwork, Pigot against the redoubt. All in all it was a remarkable demonstration of troop leadership and discipline.

The leading files were shivered by the blast of American fire, but the columns kept coming while British artillery—once more in action—raked the breastwork. Pigot leading, the left column reached the redoubt ditch, crossed it, and climbed the parapet. As they did, the firing died away. Their powder horns empty, the defenders clubbed muskets and threw stones.

That was the end. Some thirty Americans were bayoneted and Prescott ordered a retreat. The survivors crowded through the rear gateway while the British, now coming around the fort on both sides, held their fire lest they shoot one another. The fugitives from redoubt and breastwork flowed back in disorderly stream across the ridge and over Bunker's Hill.

There was some sporadic resistance to the further advance of the almost exhausted victors; hedge fighting by the Charlestown flank group and a few fresh fragments coaxed from the people who had stood as spectators on Bunker's Hill. The rail-fence garrison—Knowlton's and Stark's men, who had permitted the British attack to skirt their position—now withdrew in fair order, taking their one field gun with them.

But there was no thought of another stand until the Americans had retreated over the Neck and up to the mainland hills beyond. There they began to dig in again, while the British were well content to halt and organize a strong point on Bunker's Hill.

That's the tale of a battle fought at the wrong time and in the wrong place. The fighting was all over in less than two hours. Physically it decided nothing; at its end the British were still beleaguered in Boston, the Americans still incapable of driving them out.

But psychologically this battle created a proud tradition which will not die so long as patriotism remains an American attribute. The name of Bunker Hill—where the battle did not take place—has come down in history as a synonym for American valor; the Minute Man —who as such took no part in the fighting—has become a symbol: the shibboleth of the citizen-soldier. In such curious fashion is folklore woven.

The men who stood and fought and died in that battle have rightly become forever shining examples to a grateful nation. There was indeed much cause for honest pride. American farmers, a rabble in arms with a hodgepodge of weapons, had met, held, and thrown back many more than their number of disciplined, well-armed, well-accoutered British regulars led by experienced officers. They had checked them until their ammunition was exhausted and the enemy closed in with cold steel against which they could not stand.

There was cause for pride too in the fact that these Americans were, almost to a man, marksmen who within the limited range and accuracy of their flintlocks could call their shots and drop a redcoat as neatly as they had been accustomed to drop deer and other game. They had had—at least a few of them—the fortitude to await, behind their breastworks, the fearsome, cadenced advance of their enemy until—legend credits Putnam with the injunction, and certainly someone made it that day—they could "see the whites of their eyes."

And, at thirty yards or less, these New Englanders, behind cover, were deadly indeed with fowling piece or musket (there were no rifles there; New England didn't know the rifle). The box score tells the tale; 1,054 British casualties out of some 2,200 men in action (226 killed, 828 wounded). Above all—shining marks in their white crossbelts, glittering gorgets, and gold lace—89 of these were officers (19 killed, 70 wounded); a loss, as British General "Gentleman Johnny" Burgoyne remarked, "uncommon among the officers, considering the number engaged."

All this carnage was inflicted with cost to the Americans of but 140 killed, 271 wounded, and 30 taken prisoner.

Still more remarkable, it is doubtful if more than 1,500 of the Americans were ever actually engaged in any part of the fighting.

The nub of the matter is that the Battle of Bunker Hill was brought about, insofar as American objectives, intentions, and operations were concerned, through the valor of ignorance, and was waged without co-ordinated leadership.

Prescott and Stark did show some qualities of leadership, but each exercised an independent command, and neither made any attempt to support the other. As for Putnam, doughty whipper-in though he was, all his frenzied effort went for naught. And Artemas Ward, sitting back in his Cambridge headquarters, influenced the action in no way other than by a halfhearted reinforcement which he could not or would not control.

As for the untrained rank and file, who doubted, many of them, both the ability and the good faith of their leaders and of their own comrades, self-preservation loomed ever larger in their minds as the fury of the battle increased.

The only mystery about Bunker Hill is that so much was accomplished under such adverse circumstances by men unaccustomed to war.

Bunker Hill, then, furnished the nation with a yardstick by which to measure the respective capabilities and limitations of both regular and amateur soldiers; a balance in which to weigh emotion versus discipline and patriotism against leadership. It was a priceless gift, this blueprint which the men who died at Bunker Hill had paid for.

Instead, the patriotic Homers of the period evolved the nation's most-treasured fable: through some mysterious dispensation of the Almighty the American amateur soldier was a better man than the British regular. (Later the boast would be enlarged to cover the entire world.)

Therefore, they chimed, training and discipline were unnecessary falderal and preparation for war was unessential. It was an illusion which would plague us right down to the opening of World War I. One of its most fatuous exponents was William Jennings Bryan with his silver-tongued cry that in time of danger to America "a million men would spring to arms overnight."

Fortunately for the United States, despite the incantations of successive generations of starry-eyed Fourth of July orators, we have found from time to time in our hours of need leaders who, welding discipline and training to patriotism, have preserved the nation.

Even as Bunker Hill was being waged, the first and greatest of such leaders, picked by the Continental Congress two days previously, was pounding north to take command.

CHAPTER II ☆ ☆ ☆ *Laurels on the Delaware*

Rare indeed is the leader who, without resources, can inspire a disorganized and dispirited soldiery to snatch victory from seemingly inevitable defeat.

Such a one was General George Washington.

By mid-December, 1776, the eighteen-month-old struggle for American liberty was apparently in its last gasp. Evacuation of Boston by the British in March had been followed by Admiral Lord Richard Howe's arrival in New York harbor, bringing from Halifax in his fleet the largest expeditionary force ever up to that time sent overseas by England.

From August 22, when his brother, General Sir William Howe, moved into Long Island, the British advance had been irresistible. For four long months disaster followed disaster. Washington's army, whittled by casualties, sickness, and desertions from twenty thousand effectives to sixty-six hundred—more than half of these green Pennsylvania militia—had escaped the British clutches by a hair's breadth in its flight across the Delaware River.

The Continental Congress, scampering from Philadelphia to Baltimore to escape the expected British onrush, had left Washington to his own devices, granting him authority almost dictatorial. An empty gesture was this; for what use authority without the army they had failed to provide?

What remained of the Continentals—one-year regulars still not the equal of British and Hessian grenadiers—would evaporate on

December 31, when their enlistments were up. Coaxing, cajoling, appeals to patriotism could not move them to re-enlist in a hopeless cause. And the militia could not be depended upon. Militia had fled at Long Island, at Kips Bay, at Harlem Heights, and at White Plains.

No one knew better than Washington to what pass things had come. He told the Congress on December 17, ". . . If [speedy enlistment of a new army] fails, I think the game is up." And on December 20 he bluntly added: ". . . ten more days will put an end to the existence of our army."

Despite all this gloom Washington had not abandoned hope. Intelligence reports indicated that the British were going into winter quarters awaiting the dissolution of the Continental Army. Scattered around New Jersey, their garrisons were beyond immediate supporting distance one from another. Washington envisaged a desperate plan to surprise and destroy the nearest British post; at Trenton, across the Delaware where a Hessian brigade was quartered.

These Hessians—fifteen hundred well-trained, disciplined mercenaries—were commanded by valiant but impetuous Colonel Johann Rall, known to be contemptuous of the fighting qualities of the American "provincials." Counting on a hard-drinking German Christmas, Washington planned his attack just before dawn on December 26.

If successful, the blow would electrify the country, at the same time gaining supplies of clothing and ammunition for his men, and would also inspire them to believe that the eventual success of their cause was possible. Failure, of course, as Washington well knew, would mean the end of the Revolution, death for himself, and disgrace for his family.

His plan was to cross the Delaware River Christmas night at McKonkey's Ferry, nine miles north of Trenton, with the bulk of his effective Continentals—twenty-four hundred strong. This would be the main effort. About a thousand Pennsylvania and New Jersey militia, under General James Ewing, were to cross south of Trenton just before dawn, to seize a bridge across Assunpink Creek, cutting off enemy retreat to the south toward Bordentown, where there was another Hessian brigade of fifteen hundred men. To confuse his foe, and to keep the Bordentown Hessians from interfering at Trenton, Colonel John Cadwalader, with some two thousand mixed Continentals and Pennsylvania militia, was to cross the river still further south.

The river crossing was to be completed by midnight. This would give plenty of time to organize the columns for the advance on Trenton, and to reach the town well before dawn.

He had the boats—for in his retreat from New Jersey he had swept the further bank clean to delay pursuit—and they were suitable, sturdy "Durham" flats especially built for Delaware River ferrying work. They could carry up to fifteen tons each. Glover's Marblehead regiment, those amphibious New England fisherfolk who had handled the evacuation of Long Island, would man them.

Washington's main body assembled in a sheltered valley by the ferry on Christmas afternoon—with forty rounds of ammunition per man, one blanket each, and carrying cooked rations for three days. In the pitch dark of a cloud-shrouded bitter night the embarkation began. The river was roaring swift; filled with ice cakes that bumped and crunched against the boats and sent chilling spray over their shivering occupants. About eleven o'clock a stiff wind whipped up, with rain and sleet. Under such conditions the timetable fell apart. Instead of midnight, it was after three o'clock in the morning when the last drenched man scrambled ashore on the New Jersey bank.

"This made me despair of surprising the town," Washington wrote later, "as I knew well we could not reach it before the day was fairly broke. But as I was certain there was no making a retreat without being discovered and harassed on repassing the river, I determined to push on at all events."

By four o'clock the little army was on the march. About four miles from Trenton the troops were halted to eat. Despite alternating snow, sleet and freezing rain, many men fell asleep beside the road, and could be roused only with difficulty to resume the march. At a road fork Washington divided his army; one division, under Greene, took the road to the left, the remainder, under Sullivan, continued along the river road.

Cloak-wrapped, scornful of the sleet lacing Birmingham crossroads, Washington watched his troop sliding and slipping on the

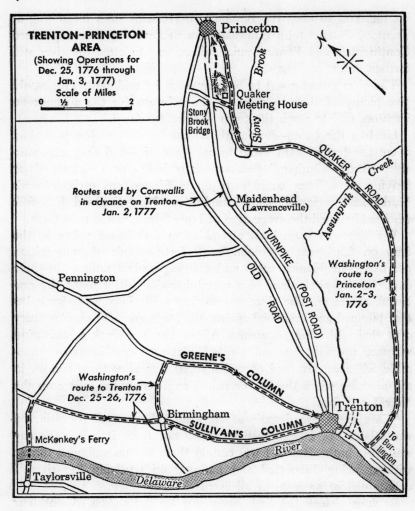

icy road, the monotonous plop-plop-plop of feet punctuated by the rumbling of wheels and the grunting of horses straining in gun harness.

As he stood at the junction, an aide approached. General Sullivan reported that the storm was wetting the muskets, and that most were now unfit for firing.

Was this indeed the end? Had he brought his thin-clad, freezing, ill-shod men to battle across an ice-packed river on a stormy Christmas night only to find they could not use their firearms?

"Tell General Sullivan," Washington firmly told the aide, "to use the bayonet. I am resolved to take Trenton." Then, as the first dim light of morning lightened the clouds to the east, the General, swinging into the saddle, rode into the dawn to join Greene in the forefront of his assault.

The march was painfully slow. It was almost eight o'clock, an hour after dawn, before the troops were close enough to deploy for the attack. But if the storm had delayed the American advance, it equally had discouraged the Hessians from patrolling the roads. As the two divisions came simultaneously to the outskirts of town —Greene to the north, Sullivan to the northwest—enemy outposts were completely surprised. They fired a few shots, then ran back into Trenton followed by cheering Americans.

Trenton was a compact little settlement whose two narrow main streets—King and Queen—ran north and south, their northern tips converging at the junction with the Pennington road. It was down this road that Greene's column struck, with Washington up in front with its commander.

At the southern end of town skirting Assunpink Creek, which emptied into the Delaware, several cross streets cut east and west across both King and Queen. The Hessians were quartered mainly in this portion of the close-huddled community, into which the river road debouched. Here the head of Sullivan's corps came barging in simultaneously with the northern assault.

The Hessians might have had a collective hang-over from their Christmas celebration, but they were soldiers. They came dashing out of the houses arms in hand. There was no time, in that confusion, for much of an orderly assemblage, but in rapidly formed detachments Rall's men drove promptly up King and Queen streets to meet the northern attack.

But American artillery—its ammunition had been kept dry—swept the narrow streets, the guns jammed wheel-to-wheel. Hamilton's battery poured canister down King, Forrest's down Queen, smashing the resistance. Shouting Americans came leaping down to close on the bewildered Hessians, who recoiled, only to be hit from the south by Sullivan's troops.

Some time earlier in the fighting Washington realized that neither Ewing, who was to seize the Assunpink Creek area, nor Cadwalader below him, was on the field. But Sullivan's troops, overlapping the fight in the town itself, had corked the southern bottleneck, while he directed Greene to push part of his corps well eastward beyond Trenton. It was an almost perfect envelopment.

So Rall's Hessians were squeezed to the southeast, beyond the edge of town, with the creek at their backs. He rallied them with beating of drums; he even tried a counterattack to force his way back into Queen Street, played in by his band. But by this time the still-falling rain had put their muskets out of business and his men had no heart for the bayonet.

The Americans were rushing them on three sides. Rall went down, mortally wounded, and the Hessians threw in the sponge. Twenty-two of them had been killed, 92 wounded. There were 948 prisoners, and only about 400 refugees had escaped. Of booty there was plenty —small arms, cannon, horses, wagons, and other munitions. Four Americans had been wounded; not a man killed, though two men had frozen to death during the bitter night.

Perhaps General Howe's reaction to the news best tells the story. He was, according to Washington Irving, simply stupefied "that three old established regiments of a people who made war a profession, should lay down their arms to a ragged and undisciplined militia."

But the most amazing thing is the accomplishment brought about by Washington's personal leadership, sparking both his subordinate commanders and his men to superhuman effort. Two points stand out; the military judgment that planned the affair, including the placing of the artillery well up in Greene's column; and the personal direction of the Commander in Chief on the spot, influencing the battle by his movement of part of Greene's men on the left of his pincers, and Sullivan's on the right, to correct the absence of Ewing's militiamen.

The battle was over by nine o'clock and Washington faced another decision. The British were in force in New Jersey. If their fresh troops at Bordentown and Princeton were to move against him, he realized that he could not hold them off with twenty-four hundred tired men, particularly since the whereabouts of Cadwalader and Ewing were unknown.

So, booty- and prisoner-laden, the indomitable little army retraced its steps through the storm to its boats. By the morning of December 27 they were all in their old bivouacs, tired as only men could be after marching more than forty miles in abominable weather, and as happy as men can be who have tasted victory after months of defeat. They well deserved the rest which, as the cards would fall, they would not get. So they fell asleep, lulled by the protecting roar of the angry Delaware, all unwitting that two days later they would be crossing it again.

We have indicated that the failure of Ewing and Cadwalader to carry out their share of the Trenton battle jeopardized Washington's plan. The lapse was what might have been expected from inexperienced leaders handling inexperienced men. Ewing, after one look at the Delaware that Christmas night, shrugged and marched his men back to camp. Cadwalader, metaphorically dipping his toe in the icy waters at his designated crossing point and not liking it, moved his troops further down-river, made a halfhearted try that momentarily put a handful of his men on the other bank, then he called them back and quit. Back in his quarters at Bristol on the morning of December 26—while Washington's troops were gaining their victory without him, Cadwalader wrote the Commander in Chief his misadventures, adding, "I imagine the badness of the night must have prevented your passing as you intended."

Stung later by the news of the victory, and hoping to share the glory, Cadwalader plunged across the river on December 27 and pushed inland. Discovering that the Hessian garrison at Bordentown had withdrawn into central New Jersey, he now urged Washington to cross again. The Commander in Chief was thus placed on the horns of an entirely new dilemma.

To recross and support Cadwalader would be to put his head in the lion's mouth. His men, without rest or tangible reward for their magnificent effort, might well still refuse to re-enlist. And even if they did, he would still have insufficient force to oppose the strong effort which an indignant and powerful enemy would now be likely to make.

Yet to order Cadwalader to withdraw now would undo much of the psychological effect of the Trenton coup. It would be considered as an ignominious retreat on the heels of a brilliant victory. It might well wreck the future of the Continental cause.

That was the deciding factor. Having given his men one more day of rest and good meals, Washington crossed the Delaware for the third time on December 29, reoccupied Trenton, and organized a defensive position south of the town on Assunpink Creek's further bank.

A last-minute plea for re-enlistment, including an offer of ten dollars bounty—entirely without authorization from Congress, incidentally—and one more appeal to patriotism brought some results. Approximately half of his able-bodied men, buoyed by their Trenton victory, signed up. On January 1, 1777, Washington found himself with a hard core of some sixteen hundred veterans; his militia swelled his effectives to almost five thousand.

That very day he learned the British reaction. Lord Cornwallis, with eight thousand British regulars, had reached Princeton, a bare dozen miles away. A brigade of Continentals was dispatched to delay the British advance along the Post Road from Princeton, while the defensive position was strengthened. Washington had acted just in time. Cornwallis advanced energetically on the 2nd. Despite effective delaying tactics by the Americans, and despite roads muddied by a thaw, the efficient British regulars had pushed down the Post Road through Trenton, to reach the Assunpink defensive line by dark.

Here, then, was immediate crisis. Confronting Washington's gaunt, footsore, exhausted veterans and his unreliable militia, Cornwallis had fifty-five hundred regulars in hand, with two additional brigades, twenty-five hundred in all, disposed in reserve at Maidenhead (now Lawrenceville) and Princeton, forty-eight hours away. Under the circumstances any effort to oppose the "flower of the British army" must result in the destruction of the Americans boxed in by the Delaware River behind them and the Atlantic Ocean.

Washington's calculated risk had become a gambler's lost chance. So felt Cornwallis, comfortable in his bivouac on the north side of

Assunpink Creek on the night of January 2. He had ordered his reserves to join him next day. Across the way American campfires flickered; the clatter of spade and pick told of hasty last-ditch entrenchment.

"We've got the old fox safe now," Cornwallis told his staff. "We'll go over and bag him in the morning."

He woke at dawn to the noise of distant cannonading behind him, to find a deserted camp in front of him.

Washington, his baggage train sent safely south to Burlington, had slipped away, screened by those fires and the simulated activity, and struck at Cornwallis' line of communications at Princeton in a move of calculated audacity every bit as brilliant as his Trenton operation nine days earlier!

Only his brigadiers knew the Commander in Chief's decision, divulged in a hasty conference at nightfall. But by midnight, with gun wheels muffled in rags and strict silence enjoined on every man, the American army had filed out of its trenches to move around the British left and north over rough, unused roadways, Princeton-bound. Men and horses skidded and stumbled on boulders; guns jammed between stumps were literally manhandled free. Five hundred men had been left behind to keep the fires burning and hold the one Assunpink bridge against British surprise; this crust would scamper at dawn.

Fortune, which had smiled steadily on Washington for over a week, still favored the brave. The weather turned cold just before midnight, stiffening the muddy roads. Tired, but surprisingly cheerful, the Americans marched steadily on, the head of the column reaching Stony Brook, about two miles south of Princeton, about dawn. After a short rest the march was resumed, over the old road following the course of the brook for about a mile, to Quaker Meeting House. Here the old road was within half a mile of the new Post Road, Cornwallis' line of communication, and the two roads thence ran parallel into Princeton.

Here Mercer's brigade of Continentals was detached, to throw a double block protecting the left flank. He was to destroy the Stony Brook bridge on the Post Road, not only to thwart any return move of Cornwallis, but also to cut the line of retreat of the British troops in Princeton. The main body of the army, headed by Sullivan's division, pushed on along the old road toward Princeton.

Meanwhile, the efficient Lieutenant Colonel Charles Mawhood, British commander at Princeton, had obeyed Cornwallis' order to join him. With two of his three regiments plus a cavalry detachment —some eight hundred men, all told—he was already on the move south along the Post Road. The third regiment—some four hundred men—he left in town to guard the military stores.

Mawhood's van had crossed the Stony Brook bridge when Mercer's column approaching from the south appeared. At almost the same instant the Americans saw the British. Both sides dashed to gain the high ground east of the brook and between the two roads.

Washington, who had been observing the march of his ragged troops past the Quaker Meeting House, heard the resulting rattle of musketry and galloped up the road a few hundred yards to observe the developing action through the trees. Seeing that Mercer was outnumbered, he sent back for the next unit on the road, which happened to be Cadwalader's nine hundred militia—the Associators of Philadelphia.

Mawhood had promptly mounted a co-ordinated infantry-artillery attack on Mercer's brigade. The exhausted Continentals stood their ground briefly, but when the British charged with the bayonet and Mercer fell mortally wounded, his brigade disintegrated, the remnants fleeing back toward the Meeting House. The British began to pursue, but Mawhood ordered a halt when they received some artillery fire from two American guns which had gone into position on their right flank, and he saw the advance elements of Cadwalader's militia emerge from the woods near the Meeting House.

Although shaken by the sight of Mercer's fleeing men, Cadwalader's militiamen advanced on the British position. But after one volley from Mawhood's men, the Pennsylvanians took to their heels. Once again harassing fire from the artillery pieces on their flank, combined with the arrival of more American reinforcements, kept the British from mounting a pursuit.

These new men were the American rear guard, Colonel Daniel Hitchcock's brigade of New England Continentals. Ordering these veterans to deploy to the right of the fugitives, Washington dashed into the mob of militia to help Cadwalader, who was vainly trying to reform his men. Raising his voice, Washington shouted:

"Parade with us, my brave fellows. There is but a handful of the enemy, and we shall have them directly."

Almost miraculous was the effect. Mawhood's force, established firmly now behind a fence and ditch, saw the men they had just routed turn and begin to re-form beside the newly arrived fresh troops. They saw that imposing figure, the big man on a big horse, gallop between the two bodies and wave them forward with his hat. Across the field his stentorian voice carried:

"Follow me! Hold your fire!"

As though drawn by a magnet, militiamen and Continentals advanced behind their imposing commander in chief. Less than 30 yards from the British line Washington drew rein and cried: "Halt!" His men raised their muskets, awaiting his command to fire. But before he could speak, a volley rang out from the British troops, spontaneously answered by the ready American muskets.

Washington, between the fires, was swallowed in billowing smoke. But frantic aides, dashing forward, found their chief untouched and unruffled.

"Bring up the troops!" he called. "Bring up the troops, the day is ours!"

And right he was. The American line overlapped the British position. Mawhood, abandoning his guns, pulled his men out. A desperate bayonet charge cleared the way back to the bridge, and he retreated toward Trenton in what rapidly became a rout.

Washington quickly ordered the British baggage to be collected and the bridge destroyed. Then, with a troop of the Philadelphia Light Horse, he pursued Mawhood, shouting to his aides as he left: "It is a fine fox chase, my boys!"

But the responsibilities of command weighed too heavily for him to continue the pursuit for long. Realizing that Cornwallis would soon be coming up from Trenton, he turned back toward Princeton, where Sullivan was now engaged. On the way he took time to comfort a wounded British soldier lying on the battlefield, personally chasing away a thief who had started to rob the helpless redcoat. Then galloping on to Princeton, he found that Sullivan had routed the third British regiment, chasing it east toward New Brunswick.

Quickly Washington ordered his troops to collect what they

could carry from the British stores and destroy the rest. Most of his ragged, barefoot men were able to refit themselves with new shoes and blankets, and gorge themselves on British rations. Then, just as fuming Cornwallis' advance guard reached the ruins of the Stony Brook bridge, Washington led his tired but happy men northward toward Morristown, safely inland of the enemy.

The Battle of Princeton, which lasted less than a half hour, was only a skirmish insofar as numbers engaged and casualties were concerned. The British loss was approximately a hundred killed and wounded and 200 taken prisoner; the Americans some forty-odd killed and wounded. Actually, however, it was the magnificent conclusion of one of the most brilliant military campaigns in history. Frederick the Great, and later von Moltke, would both sing the praises of that ten-day campaign.

Strategically and politically the effect was enormous. The dying embers of an almost lost cause flamed; the War of the Revolution would continue. Five years later, Cornwallis, surrendering to Washington at Yorktown, would put it all in proper perspective when he told the victor "fame will gather your brightest laurels from the banks of the Delaware rather than from the Chesapeake."

First In . . . Leadership

Eighteen months would pass before Washington again faced his enemies in pitched battle in New Jersey. Meanwhile his strategic leadership had shown itself in many ways. It was essentially defensive, as he well realized that so long as England held the seas she also held the initiative and would be able to attack the colonies not only from any selected point along the seacoast, but also from her Canadian bases on the St. Lawrence River.

The successes at Trenton and Princeton had won sufficient time and enthusiasm for the collection of an army respectable in numbers but still incapable of meeting British regulars on equal terms. As long, however, as he could maintain his army in the field, and retain control of substantial inland areas, Washington felt he might prolong the conflict until Britain wearied of the expense of keeping large forces in America.

His strategy, then, was one of constant harassment, but of avoiding battle if possible except where the British might be at a disadvantage,

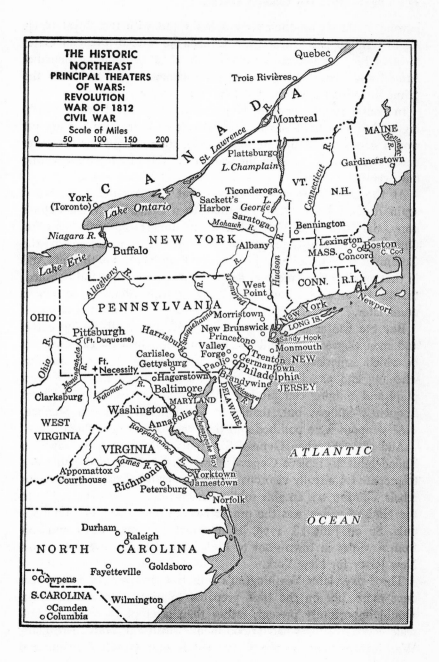

THE HISTORIC
NORTHEAST
PRINCIPAL THEATERS
OF WARS:
REVOLUTION
WAR OF 1812
CIVIL WAR
Scale of Miles
0   50   100   150   200

beyond contact with their seaport bases and with the Royal Navy. Against Burgoyne's threat from Canada he sent to General Gates most of his best troops and ablest subordinates including Benedict Arnold and Daniel Morgan and his riflemen. These had been the prime factors in the victory at Saratoga.

In consequence, opposing Howe with a weakened army, Washington lost two hard-fought but strategically indecisive battles, yet won a campaign of utmost significance, since Burgoyne's surrender encouraged France to enter the war on the side of America, ensuring our eventual success.

At the time, however, it seemed that the American effort had again reached bottom as 1777 drew to a close. For Washington's army, that winter at Valley Forge was almost indescribably grim. Only the inexhaustible perseverance and determination of the Commander in Chief held his starving Continentals with him. And in that crucible the American regular was being ground and polished, thanks to amazing Prussian drillmaster von Steuben, of whom more later.

But the winter did pass, with its snow and chill. Spring came, and men thawed out. And the hot June sun beat on cantonments in which American soldiers were marching and countermarching, wheeling and parading, with the lilt and cadence that only discipline and training can produce. They were ragged, still; and were frequently hungry, but, thanks to Washington and von Steuben, their weapons were polished and they knew how to use them.

And this was when General Sir Henry Clinton, newly arrived in Philadelphia to replace General Howe, decided the time had come to prepare for a really vigorous campaign against these presumptuous rebels. Clinton was an able soldier. In his opinion New York, key to the Hudson valley, was the proper base of operations, not Philadelphia. So on June 18, 1778, he marched his army—sleek and soft from a winter in town—out of Philadelphia, bound overland across New Jersey for New York.

Three days later Washington's lean troops crossed the Delaware once more, hot on the trail, prepared to nibble at Clinton's rear, should opportunity present, rather than attempt to bring on full-scale action. Clinton had 13,000 men, British and Hessian regulars, Washington some 11,000 Continentals and twenty-five hundred militia. Not unless by good fortune the British rear guard should first be overwhelmed did Washington intend to bring on a pitched battle.

Clinton moved in two parallel columns, each capable of supporting the other, should American attack materialize. Because of the intense heat—temperatures approached 100° each midday, the English marches were slow and short.

For about a week the American army hung on the inland flank of the British. To take advantage of the hoped-for opportunity, Washington built up his advance guard to almost 6000 men, under the command of General Charles Lee, his senior subordinate. But because of the British march formation in parallel columns, it was not till June 27 that Washington saw a chance to fall on a detached portion of the British army.

That day the British had encamped near Monmouth Courthouse (now Freehold). Clinton was more eager to get to New York than to fight a battle in the intense heat, and Washington's advance on his northern flank was threatening to block the direct route to New York.

Clinton decided, therefore, to march to Sandy Hook, and move thence by boat to New York. Intelligence reports brought Washington word of this change in British plan. Here was the long-sought opportunity: there was but a single road to Sandy Hook; consequently the British would be strung out in one long column, with their advance elements a half day's march from the rear guard.

Washington at once directed Lee to attack the British rear guard just as soon as it was in motion on the road next morning. He assured Lee that he would bring up the main body of the army promptly, to assist in defeating the enemy detachment, if this should be necessary.

Lee accepted his orders from Washington without question, but —whether coward or traitor never has been established—apparently had reached a predetermined conclusion that his attack would be unsuccessful.

He was slow in advancing to attack. He issued no co-ordinated orders to his brigade commanders, nor did he even suggest to them that he had any plan. Nevertheless, several of them closed vigorously on their own initiative. When the enemy turned on these poorly timed and unco-ordinated thrusts, Lee promptly ordered a general retreat, but made no effort to see that the order was disseminated to his scattered subordinates. The upshot, after only a few sharp, but scattered, exchanges of fire with the enemy, was that almost half of the American army was routed. Clinton, who had called up reinforcements from his advance guard, at once pursued, having almost 10,000 confident veterans close at hand, with 3000 more available a few hours' march away.

Meanwhile Washington, with about seventy-four hundred men, was moving rapidly to join Lee in overwhelming—so he believed— the British rear guard. He was flabbergasted, therefore, when he found refugees of Lee's force fleeing down the road. It was obvious from the sounds of sporadic firing he had heard that there could have been no serious engagement, and thus this confused retreat was incomprehensible. Putting spurs to his horse, he galloped through the thickening crowd of stragglers, until he met Lee, riding calmly to the rear with a group of staff officers.

"What, sir," asked the angry Washington, "what is the meaning of this? Whence come this disorder and confusion?"

"Sir, sir?" stuttered Lee, embarrassed and disconcerted by the glint in his commander's eye. Washington repeated his questions, his voice icy.

Lee's stammering excuses caused the usually calm Washington to explode, for the first and last time in the memory of his close associates. What words the General used matter little; the records are vague. One witness speaks of hearing the words "damn poltroon"; another tells of "a terrific eloquence of unprintable scorn"; a third related simply that Washington "swore like an angel from Heaven." What does matter are his actions as, leaving the cowering, spluttering Lee behind him, he plunged into the motley retreating mob. An officer reported the British to be only fifteen minutes away.

Hopeless seemed to be the word for such a situation. Half the army was in flight, the other half still in march order behind him all unaware of impending doom.

But hopeless was a word and a concept which the big man on the great white charger refused to accept.

"I never saw the General to so much advantage," wrote Alexander Hamilton. "His coolness and firmness were admirable. He instantly took measures for checking the enemy's advance, and giving time for the Army, which was very near, to form and make a proper disposition." Lafayette has also given a description of Washington during these critical minutes: "His presence stopped the retreat . . . his fine appearance on horseback, his calm courage, roused to animation by the vexations of the morning, gave him the air best calculated to excite enthusiasm. . . . I thought then, as now, that never had I beheld so superb a man."

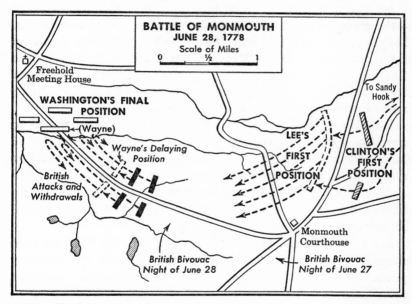

He rallied the two rearmost regiments with the enemy but 200 yards away. This covering force he then turned over to stouthearted Brigadier General Anthony Wayne. He began to organize the remainder of his army on a low ridge, a few hundred yards to the rear. But before this could be completed the main British army drove back the covering force, and advanced against the ridge. Here, however, heavy and accurate fire from those American troops in position halted the British. While Clinton brought up his reserves the two lines engaged in the most intensive musketry and artillery duel of the war.

Now Washington and von Steuben—who was helping the Commander in Chief direct arriving units to their posts—could see the results of the months of training at Valley Forge. The troops in line, though greatly outnumbered at first, stood steady as they returned the British fire and threw back one attack after another. And as the succeeding regiments marched up, under the hail of iron and lead, they marched with parade-ground steadiness and coolness, wheeling into line like seasoned veterans. Later Alexander Hamilton wrote that not until this time had he really "known or conceived the value of military discipline."

All afternoon, despite the stifling heat, the tough British troops —the cream of England's army—kept up the pressure. By 5 P.M., however, as the last of Washington's main body arrived, and most of the morning's refugees had been organized, it became evident to Clinton that he could not drive the Americans from their positions. So he broke off the fight, pulling his men back to a strong position, a few hundred yards from the Americans.

Washington, having tested the mettle of his army, wished to carry the fight to the enemy. But it was after six; his troops had been marching and fighting all day under the blazing sun and were simply incapable of further offensive effort. So he too went into bivouac and prepared plans for an assault the following morning. Night fell with both sides, undefeated, on the field; neither could claim victory.

But Clinton, too, had tested the mettle of this new American army; had discovered, to his alarm, its amazing new powers of recuperation. When dawn came the British army had vanished, having quietly marched from their positions at midnight. The Americans took up pursuit, but the British made good their escape to Sandy Hook and New York.

So ended the Battle of Monmouth. The Americans had suffered 360 casualties, of whom 40 were deaths from sunstroke. The British had lost 358 men, 59 being sunstroke deaths. Washington was half-satisfied, half-disappointed at the results of this indecisive battle; had it not been for Lee, he knew, he would have won a decisive victory.

But the outstanding feature of the Battle of Monmouth was that it marked the coming of age of the American regular. Washington's leadership had at long last produced an army as good as the British best.

From the Trenton-Princeton and Monmouth campaigns one can detect a pattern—the pattern for American military leadership. George Washington has been idolized, and he has been "debunked." The facts are these: as an amateur soldier in the early years of the Revolution, Washington made mistakes—some serious—yet at the same time demonstrated a natural leadership ability almost unique in history. Through experience, study, and reflection, by the end of the Revolution he had developed into one of the great captains of history. No better example of inspirational qualities, or of personal bravery, can be found than the attack at Princeton, or his rallying of the troops at Monmouth.

His grasp of the significance of seapower was phenomenal for his day, as evidenced by his seizing the one short two-month period of the entire Revolution when British seapower was momentarily eclipsed by France, to smash and capture the only British field army operating outside of besieged New York. A French fleet and a French army contributed to the victory at Yorktown; but the genius which seized the opportunity and controlled the allied forces to gain his objective were Washington's.

All great soldiers have had to face disappointments. Few, however, have been confronted so constantly, and for such a long time, with well-nigh hopeless situations. None has ever displayed greater patience, or will power in overcoming difficulties—and then persevering through to "impossible" victory.

But there is one more measure of leadership which must be applied to the top levels of military command. This is the ability, in peace as in war, to understand the relationship of operational strategy to national policy, and to be able to contribute, within the proper sphere of the soldier, to the formulation of a nation's defense policy.

In his magnificent biography of Washington, Freeman frequently notes Washington's "unshakable regard for civil authority," and lists his rules for dealing with Congress. These included—among other things—keeping Congress informed, acknowledging Congressional authority at all times, and assuming that the delegates were as sincerely concerned with the country's welfare and security as he was himself.

But how did Washington contribute to the development of military policy in peacetime?

At the close of the Revolution, in response to a request from a committee of Congress, Washington wrote a paper entitled *Sentiments on a Peace Establishment.* No document in American history reveals greater foresight, wisdom, or soundness in fundamental principles than did this blueprint for American military policy. In essence these *Sentiments* proposed the following fundamentals:

First, a small, regular, professional defense establishment, no larger than necessary to "awe" possible aggressors, "prevent encroachments, guard us from surprizes." In other words, he advocated what we today refer to as adequate deterrent force.

Second, a well-organized reserve force (militia) uniformly established on a national pattern (unlike the haphazard, motley State aggregations which so plagued him during the Revolution), trained for prompt and efficient mobilization in time of emergency.

Third, adequate war reserves from which the standing forces and the mobilized reserves could be maintained and supplied at the outset of a war.

Fourth, the development in peacetime of an adequate industrial mobilization base—he called this "Manufactories of some kinds of Military Stores"—to assure uninterrupted supply of our fighting forces after the war reserves had been consumed.

Fifth, he believed fervently in the need for military school systems for the training of leaders. He had learned, by bitter experience, that courage, intelligence, and ardor were not sufficient equipment for commanders who had to lead troops in combat, and had to bear the responsibilities of caring for them in the long, dreary days between battles.

These were Washington's *Sentiments on a Peace Establishment.* At first they were ignored by Congress. But over the years the validity of these principles was gradually recognized, until they have become the essentials of American military policy today, as sound in the nuclear age as they were in the days of the flintlock.

From the example of George Washington—his successes, his failures, the character of his leadership, his understanding of the American fighting man, and his evaluation of the nation's military needs —our soldiers and citizens today can learn the essential lessons of the role of the armed forces of a democracy, in peace and in war.

CHAPTER III ☆ ☆ ☆ *Soldiers Three*

Behind the heroic figure of George Washington in the War of the Revolution three men stand, close-knit in history's warp; reliable lieutenants. They were vastly dissimilar, these three, in background and in breeding. There was Daniel Morgan, Virginian backwoodsman. There was Frederick William von Steuben, Prussian baron and professional soldier. And there was Anthony Wayne, Philadelphia dandy and gentleman farmer. Yet all possessed one thing in common: the spark of leadership.

Daniel Morgan

Down in Quebec's Lower Town, where the overhanging houses nod to one another across the narrow streets, a fantastic dream was ending. Backed in a corner of the Sault du Matelot in freezing dawn, a whistling wind swirling snow and sleet about him, a deep-chested, broad-shouldered 38-year-old six-footer stood, sword in hand, facing a crowd of English and Canadian soldiers.

Tears of rage ran down his cheeks to mingle with the blood from a head wound as he scorned the shouted commands to surrender or be shot. But a clerical cassock in the crowd caught his eye.

"A priest? Then I give my sword to you. But not a scoundrel of these cowards shall take it out of my hands!"

Thus Captain Daniel Morgan, Virginia rifleman, on January 1, 1776; magnificent in initial defeat, as he would later be in victory on two other battlefields.

It was the end of an epic; the anabasis of Benedict Arnold and a handful of determined men across uncharted wilderness from the Maine coast to Quebec in the heart of winter. Of the eleven hundred starting from Gardinerstown on the Kennebec in this, one of the most amazing military treks in all history, but 600 half-starved souls had reached their goal. Joined by young General Richard Montgomery's force moving down from Montreal, they had stormed Quebec's fastness in the teeth of a howling blizzard.

Montgomery, leading one column, was killed in the assault, and his men were repulsed. Arnold, leading the other, fell, grievously wounded. His able lieutenant Morgan, whose backwoodsman's skill had guided Arnold's van throughout that long march, assumed command. Trapped in the maze of old Quebec's streets by the aroused garrison, the end came after a three-hour-long fight, Morgan being the last man to yield.

We must look closely at this man Morgan, natural leader of men, from Virginia's northern Blue Ridge country. He was a self-made man who, from the humblest of beginnings, had become a land-owner and person of some wealth and consequence in his Virginia community when war called him from peaceful pursuits. Without formal schooling, he had taught himself to read and write, and by 1775 his self-study had progressed to an appreciation of classical literature.

When the Continental Congress, on June 14, 1775, voted its first call for national troops—that "six companies of expert riflemen be immediately raised, two in Pennsylvania, two in Maryland and two in Virginia"—Morgan, ten days after he received the word, had recruited a company, and twenty days later was marching them into Washington's command at Cambridge, Massachusetts; no slight feat of organization and movement.

After the first few days in front of Boston, and after the British had learned to take cover from the, to them amazing, ability of the newcomers to pick them off at twice the range of the military musket, Morgan and his turbulent backwoodsmen found the war extremely boring. They had come to fight; in fact Morgan himself was no novice; he had been a soldier in the Virginia contingent accompanying Braddock's ill-fated expedition in 1755.

So for excitement the riflemen turned to drinking New England rum, picking fights with New England men, and flirting with New England girls. They became one of Washington's major headaches during this period.

To the satisfaction of all concerned, Morgan and his men were then picked to take part in the Quebec expedition to be led by brilliant young Colonel Benedict Arnold. Morgan commanded all the riflemen, his own outfit and two companies of Pennsylvanians, making up almost a quarter of Arnold's command.

A prisoner for several months following the Quebec disaster, Morgan was exchanged in late 1776, after contemptuously refusing the offer of a colonel's commission in the British Army. Rejoining Washington, he was made colonel, commanding a select regiment of riflemen. His next great opportunity came when "Gentleman Johnny" Burgoyne began his invasion of the Champlain-Hudson valley. Washington ordered Morgan's command to reinforce General Horatio Gates in northern New York.

And as the dice of war fell, it would be another Arnold-Morgan affair.

It was late in August, 1777, that Morgan's men commenced a forced march from the vicinity of Philadelphia to the upper reaches of the Hudson River. Hardly two weeks later he arrived with some 370 men at General Gates's headquarters near Saratoga at the junction of the Hudson and Mohawk Rivers. To these Gates added another picked group of 250, bringing Morgan's command to about 600 men.

On September 19 General Burgoyne—who had about 6,000 men—began to move around the position which Gates had fortified on the west bank of the Hudson River, near Stillwater. Gates, with over 7,000 men, had no plan to meet the British maneuver. It became evident to Arnold, commanding the American left wing, that the enemy would soon be in a position to envelop his flank and cut the American line of communications. Since Gates would do nothing, Arnold on his own initiative advanced his wing to halt the British near Freeman's Farm. He ordered Morgan to protect his exposed left flank.

For several hours the conflict was in doubt. Early in the afternoon

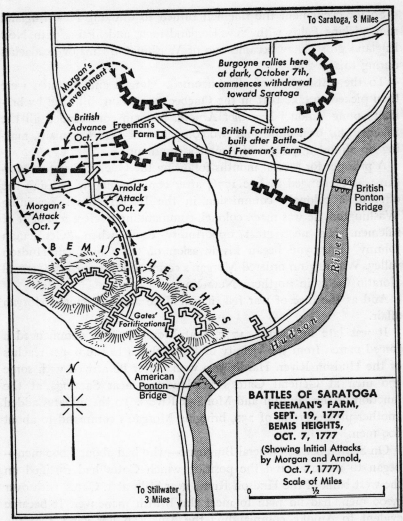

To Saratoga, 8 Miles

Burgoyne rallies here
at dark, October 7th,
commences withdrawal
toward Saratoga

Morgan's
envelopment

British
Advance
Oct. 7

Freeman's
Farm

British Fortifications
built after Battle
of Freeman's Farm

British
Ponton
Bridge

Arnold's
Attack
Oct. 7

Morgan's
Attack
Oct. 7

B E M I S   H E I G H T S

Gates'
Fortifications

Hudson River

American
Ponton
Bridge

N

BATTLES OF SARATOGA
FREEMAN'S FARM,
SEPT. 19, 1777
BEMIS HEIGHTS,
OCT. 7, 1777
(Showing Initial Attacks
by Morgan and Arnold,
Oct. 7, 1777)
Scale of Miles
0   ½

To Stillwater
3 Miles

the riflemen got out of hand, as they recklessly chased a small British detachment back to Freeman's Farm, only to be halted and thrown into confusion by a well-organized counterattack. But Morgan's calmness and steadfast presence saved the day. As he was alternately shouting and blowing on his turkey call—a Morgan idiosyncrasy— his men quickly rallied to the weird, gobbling sound and joined their voices to his in rolling oaths that echoed through the trees. Deadly aimed rifle fire halted the British advance and forced the enemy back to the farm.

Arnold now sensed that a vigorous counterattack would clear the field, but he had no reserves, and Gates refused his pleas for more men. So, as dark came on, with the entire British army now arriving on the field in overwhelming force, Arnold reluctantly withdrew, having suffered 320 casualties out of about 3,000 men engaged. The British, who had actively employed a like number, had lost over 600 men, most of them victims of Morgan's riflemen.

Eighteen days later Burgoyne's army again advanced, once more hoping to envelop the American left flank. Arnold no longer commanded this wing. He had been relieved by Gates as the result of a bitter exchange of recriminations over the outcome of the battle of September 19.

By this time Burgoyne's effective strength had dwindled to five thousand, while reinforcements had swelled Gates's army to eleven thousand. Yet, despite his great superiority, Gates could not make up his mind what to do. Morgan urged an immediate attack in strength against the British right flank. "Granny" Gates gave halfhearted approval, but would allow only two brigades to join Morgan in the attack.

Hastily Morgan ordered an advance, fearful that the vacillating Gates would call off even this faint effort. He was far from sure that he would get effective support from the two brigades Gates had promised. But just as his own men emerged from a woods near the British right flank, those two brigades received an unexpected and galvanizing lift. Benedict Arnold, defying Gates's order to remain in camp, rode out to assume command and lead an impetuous charge against the center and left flank of the first British line, just as Morgan struck the right. The British line collapsed.

Gates now ordered Arnold and Morgan to halt. Ignoring the order, they advanced against the British entrenchments near Freeman's Farm. While Morgan led his riflemen in a wide flanking movement through the woods, Arnold assaulted the center of the British line. This time the fire of the British regulars, delivered calmly from behind their entrenchments, drove back the Americans, leaving Arnold wounded on the field.

Just at this critical moment, the enemy heard the feared turkey call to their flank and rear, and found themselves once more under the murderous fire of Morgan's riflemen. That ended the battle. As Arnold sat on the ground, cheering them on, his men joined Morgan's in sweeping through the entrenchments. Not till after dark was Burgoyne able to rally his shaken men, back near the riverbank.

Burgoyne at once ordered a retreat. Gates was timorous in pursuit, but Morgan, on his own initiative, kept hard on the heels of the disorganized British and Hessians. Following his example, other American units pushed after the slow-moving enemy. By the 13th the British were completely surrounded, and on the 14th Burgoyne surrendered.

Thanks to Benedict Arnold and Daniel Morgan the decisive campaign of the Revolutionary War had been won. The pair, thus united on two memorable occasions, would not meet again as comrades on the battlefield. But one might meditate a moment upon their future, for there was another parallel in the fortunes of these two men, so similar in their combat leadership. Both received shabby treatment from the Congress. In Arnold's case, as we know, resentment led to treason; his lack of integrity blotting out all the qualities of leadership he possessed.

But Daniel Morgan, although embittered by the failure of Congress to grant him the promotion George Washington had recommended, merely resigned in 1779 and returned to his Virginia home, his health shattered by the rigors of the Quebec campaign. Less than a year later he would take the field again.

Down at Camden, South Carolina, fumbling, inefficient Gates was smashed on August 16, 1780, by able Cornwallis. On Washington's appeal Morgan, at long last appointed brigadier general, emerged as right-hand man to Nathanael Greene, sent south to replace Gates.

Greene was well aware of the natural military genius of Morgan. He entrusted to him an independent command—almost half his entire army—to cover the possible inland route of advance of the British from central South Carolina toward North Carolina and Virginia. Whether or not Greene was wise in making the strategic decision to divide his weak army need not concern us. Fortunately for the American cause, in Morgan he had chosen a commander with sufficient tactical skill to make any strategic decision appear sound.

As a preliminary to a general British advance northward, Cornwallis now sent his most able subordinate, young Colonel Sir Banastre Tarleton, with a picked force of eleven hundred men, to drive Morgan from South Carolina. Of these troops, five hundred were British regulars, horse and foot; five hundred were Tarleton's own British Legion, half of whom were cavalry—American Tories trained and equipped on a par with the very finest regulars—and a hundred more were picked Tory militia.

Learning of Tarleton's advance, Morgan prepared for battle. He took up a position in a bend of the Broad River, in a sparsely wooded region which was locally called the "Cowpens" because it was a roundup area for cattle. Morgan had 320 Continental infantry and 600 raw militiamen, a few of whom he mounted and joined to a troop of 80 Continental dragoons under Colonel William Washington.

Some historians have criticized Morgan for his choice of battleground, with a river at his back; others have praised it as "unorthodox" but "masterly." Only in recent years, however, have military analysts noted an amazing parallel to one of the renowned battles of ancient history. Morgan, as we have mentioned, had had no formal education in his youth, but in subsequent reading it is possible that he had learned about, and been impressed by, Hannibal's great victory over the Romans at Cannae in 216 B.C. Whether the resemblance of the battles of Cannae and the Cowpens was coincidental or not, both were tactical masterpieces.

Morgan drew up his men in three lines. In front were a few carefully selected sharpshooters, some undoubtedly veterans of his earlier rifle commands. These were to slow down the British advance, and force them to deploy. Behind the sharpshooters were the bulk of his militia, under the command of Colonel Andrew Pickens, spread out in an irregular line in a thin growth of trees. Behind them, on high ground, were the Continentals, under Morgan's personal command. In reserve, near the river, were Colonel Washington's cavalrymen.

Morgan knew his militia could not and would not stand against the British regulars. Consequently he told them that they need only wait till the enemy closed to within fifty yards, fire two volleys, then withdraw. He did not expect that this would be an orderly withdrawal; in fact he was sure they would run away. They were so placed, however, that they could run most easily past the left flank of the Continentals, and he knew the psychology of untrained fighting men well enough to know that they would flee along the easiest

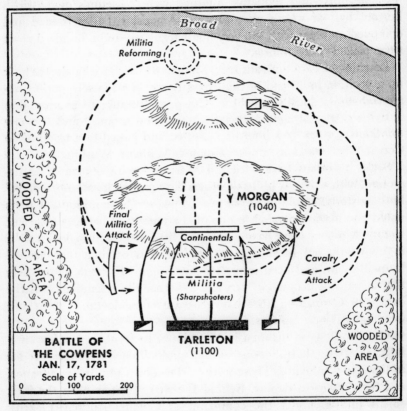

route. Furthermore, with an unfordable river close behind, they could not run far.

The battle went exactly as Morgan had anticipated.

Eager Tarleton had pushed eight miles that morning to bag his game. Discovering the Americans, his dragoons galloped confidently forward to flush them out. Fifteen saddles were emptied by the first volley of the sharpshooters, and the British horsemen reeled back to reform on the flanks of their line of battle. Two small guns accompanied this.

The British cannon blazed and the whole line started forward, Morgan's second line of militia waiting until they were in close range. The American leader had gauged the temper of his militia well; they fired two successive volleys, well aimed, with telling effect. Then they broke and ran around the hill to their own left.

The dragoons on Tarleton's right went dashing in for the kill, to meet Colonel Washington's small troop, riding compactly around the height to hit them and drive them back in disorder. Meanwhile the main British line, seeing the militiamen fleeing, went shouting up the rise to be confronted by the Continentals of the third line.

For thirty long minutes—just long enough for the scampering militia to get behind the hill and reform along the river, the thin Continental line held. Then it slowly fell back, in good order, as Tarleton's reserve deployed to the left to flank them.

Tarleton, seeing the retirement, called up his Legion cavalry. Horse and foot mingled, the British went cheering in disorder, their ranks broken in their haste. They topped the rise to be met by the Continentals with musketry and bayonet, just as the reformed militia coming around the hill on their right, hit them on the flank. Into the melee came the American dragoons on the other flank, and in the rear.

It was a complete double envelopment—the dream of every professional soldier. Tarleton's force unraveled. Bagged were 600 prisoners; 100 more had been killed and 229 wounded, and the entire baggage train was captured. Tarleton himself, with some 140 of his horse, made good his escape. The American losses were 12 killed and 60 wounded. In all the history of warfare one cannot find a more brilliant example of tactical leadership. The most exceptional feature of the battle, of course, was the ingenious manner in which Morgan got a full measure of fighting out of the unreliable militia.

The Cowpens was doughty Daniel Morgan's last battle. His recurring attacks of rheumatism made it impossible for him to continue active campaigning and so, reluctantly, he retired again to his home in Frederick, Virginia. There—save for leading the Virginia militia in the suppression of the Whisky Rebellion of 1794—he remained until his death in 1799.

Baron von Steuben

During the first three years of the War of the Revolution General Washington learned that the American citizen-soldier possessed some splendid inherent qualities. In marksmanship, in forest skirmishing, in the defense of fortifications and in guerrilla warfare, the Continentals were more than a match for the British and Hessian regulars. Even the militia could be useful under such conditions. But no American troops—not even Morgan's riflemen or Wayne's picked brigade of Pennsylvanians—had been able to meet the British on even terms on the battlefield. Inevitably the well-drilled precision, steadiness, and discipline of the enemy regulars would bring final tactical victory in battle, regardless of the brilliance of Washington's strategy.

The nature of the deficiency was clear; the American combat teams, from squad up, lacked coaching. Their officers, although a surprisingly large crop of individually brave and potentially capable young officers was available, knew no more of the details of discipline, drill, or other military routine than did their men. It was a case of the blind leading the blind.

How, then, could this be corrected?

Washington himself did not have the time to devote to the details of training an army, nor, indeed, did he have the experience necessary to give his subordinates detailed guidance in this task.

His first thought had been that instructors could be found among the horde of foreign volunteers flocking to America now that Europe was momentarily at peace. The motives inspiring these men ranged from the self-seeking of soldiers of fortune like the infamous Conway, to the love for Freedom's cause that urged the noble young Marquis de Lafayette overseas.

But while a few of these people were unselfish volunteers with ability, knowledge, and skill enabling them to serve the Revolutionary cause with distinction, most of them were more trouble to Washington than their military contributions warranted.

And so, in January, 1778, Washington read with mixed emotions a letter from Benjamin Franklin introducing Lieutenant General Baron Frederick William von Steuben of Prussia, who offered his services as a volunteer, with no claim for rank or pay beyond his immediate expenses, and who was prepared at once to impart to the American army his experience as a trusted subordinate of that greatest of generals, Frederick the Great. Here was a man who *should* be able to do the job. He was seeking no preferment that would arouse the indignation and jealousy of the hard-fighting American officers who looked so suspiciously on ambitious foreigners. But Washington had been disappointed often by well-advertised Europeans, and he was inherently cautious by nature, so that, welcoming von Steuben cordially, he met him also with courteous restraint and keen appraisal.

There is more myth than truth in the commonly accepted history of Steuben as one of the leading subordinates of Frederick the Great in the Seven Years' War. As Steuben's most authoritative biographer —Brigadier General John M. Palmer—has pointed out, he had never risen above the rank of captain in the Prussian army, certainly not lieutenant general, as averred by Benjamin Franklin in his letters introducing the German officer to Washington and the principal leaders of Congress. And evidently Franklin was as well aware of this as Steuben himself. But so impressed was our ambassador to France with what he had learned and seen of the Baron (and in truth he *was* a baron) that the discerning Franklin was convinced that this man could make a unique and vital contribution to the Colonial cause. And Franklin was right. Palmer—who exposed the hoax of Steuben's rank—has this to say of the Baron's importance to the American Revolution:

. . . Two men only can be regarded as indispensable to the achievement of American independence. These men were Washington and Steuben. . . . Each of them contributed something essential to final victory, that could not have been contributed by any other man then in the American Army. Brilliant as Greene's services were, it is conceivable that Lafayette or Wayne or some other general might have commanded the Southern army successfully. But it is not conceivable that any other man could have given the technical assistance, essential to military success, that Steuben gave to his chief. Washington was the indispensable commander. Steuben was his indispensable staff officer.

When he first met von Steuben, Washington's initial reaction was favorable. So he asked the Baron to look over the army in its miserable encampment at Valley Forge, and to give his frank opinion as to how its deficiencies could be corrected. In order to help Steuben —who spoke no English—in these inspections, Washington loaned him the assistance of two of his own aides-de-camp, John Laurens and Alexander Hamilton, both of whom spoke French. No doubt these two young men had also been directed to report to the Commander in Chief about the Baron.

Evidently Steuben's reports and recommendations impressed Washington favorably. So too did the glowing terms in which Hamilton and Laurens spoke of the newcomer. Furthermore, Major General Nathanael Greene, Washington's most trusted subordinate, immediately became a devoted friend of the Baron's. Finally, Steuben, with his martial bearing, his superb horsemanship, his gracious manner, and his keen sense of humor, won the liking of the officers and men of the army, while the incisiveness of his observations won their respect. Washington was satisfied. This *was* the man. He appointed Steuben as Inspector General, and commissioned him to retrain the army.

This was a formidable task. There were no drill regulations. There was no uniform drill procedure or system of handling weapons, nor even a commonly accepted method of marching. As was the British custom, the officers relied upon noncommissioned officers to conduct and supervise the drilling of the troops, but unlike the British army, the Americans had no experienced, veteran sergeants who could do this competently, nor were there any precedents. So, for all practical purposes, there was no drill. The problem, in its essence, was threefold. A system of drill must be devised. This, then, would have to be formulated into clear drill regulations which could be understood by inexperienced officers and men. Finally, a group of qualified instructors must be trained who could do the drilling. After all, no one man, no matter how able, or how loud his voice, could drill an army—particularly if he could not even speak the language of the soldiers!

First the system. The perceptive Baron quickly realized that the drill regulations of Frederick's army could not be transplanted bodily to America. To begin with, there was not time to practice the intricate movements which made the Prussian army the envy of Europe. Secondly, he recognized immediately that American soldiers could not be trained by the methods then in vogue in Europe. As he later wrote to an old German comrade in arms: "The genius of this nation is not in the least to be compared with that of the Prussians, Austrians or French. You say to your soldier, 'Do this,' and he doeth it; but I am obliged to say, 'This is the reason why you ought to do that'; and then he does it."

So he based his training program on a simple series of movements which would appeal to these Americans who were so properly suspicious of rigid military pedantry. He developed a manual for the musket, for instance, based upon the Prussian system, but from which more than half the movements had been eliminated.

Then he began to write out a new drill regulation, based upon this system he had devised. He wrote this in French, to facilitate translation. He could not afford to delay training until the entire regulation was complete and then translated, or the spring campaign would open before he had a chance to teach it to the army. So, as one day's lesson was written he had it translated, and then required Laurens and Hamilton to teach him the commands in English, which he promptly memorized. Night after night this continued, following a full day's labor on the drill field.

And it was on the drill field that the stout, jovial, and shiny-domed soldier completely won the hearts of the men, and—after some initial grumbling—the enthusiastic support of the officers. Washington authorized him to select 120 men from different regiments, who were to become the commander-in-chief's bodyguard—but more immediately important, were to be Steuben's model drill company. In addition he selected one officer from each of the brigades of the army, who was to become a brigade inspector. These men—bodyguard and brigade inspectors—he drilled personally, giving his commands "in a curious mixture of German, French and English." For a week this continued, with almost the entire army—at that time a bare five thousand men—gathered around the drill field. They were fascinated by the spectacle of this proud foreign general drilling squads, platoons, and the company; convulsed when things went wrong, and the Baron's voice rolled across the field, rich with multilingual oaths; impressed by the remarkable results, the precision, the self-confidence, and the soldierly attitude of this company when it paraded at the end of the first week.

The brigade inspectors were then sent back to their commands, to carry the Baron's training system to the entire army. And as they did their jobs, Steuben galloped from company to company, correcting here, praising there, and generally impressing on the entire army the same force of his personality which had so magically transformed the model company. Having seen a distinguished lieutenant general— at least so they thought—and an unquestionably bona fide baron personally drilling troops, the junior American officers now saw no reason why it should be beneath their dignity to drill their men personally. So they threw themselves into the task.

All day long, rain or shine, the army drilled under the eagle eye of the Baron. In the evenings he continued the instruction of the brigade inspectors, correcting their mistakes, offering suggestions based upon his observations. Then, till the early hours of the morning, he would write out another chapter of his drill regulations, to be translated, copied, and distributed the following day.

It was not merely in the external training and disciplining of the men that Steuben introduced regularity, precision, and efficiency. He began a system of inspections which he was to develop and improve during the course of the war, in which the welfare of the men and of the army as a whole were equally his objectives. In these inspections every man had to be accounted for, all articles of clothing and equipment had to be laid out to be checked for serviceability and against the property account records which Steuben insisted be maintained in each company. Companies and battalions, regiments and brigades vied with one another to see which could make the best impression on the keen-eyed Baron. And in all this he taught the United States Army a lesson which it has never forgotten; the welfare of the soldiers must be the first concern of every officer.

Perhaps the most remarkable thing about Steuben's theory was this humanitarian slant, so different from the abasing Prussian system of its time that degraded the individual soldier to the status of an automaton kicked about at the whim of a superior.

The company was the basic combat team; its officers, Steuben stressed, were responsible for the care of their men and the condition of their equipment. The captain, who "cannot be too careful of the company the state has committed to his care," must also "gain the love of his men by treating them with every possible kindness and humanity." He must inquire into their complaints and redress them "when well founded." He must know the name and "character" of every man; visit the sick and make sure they were well tended, because "the attachment that arises from this . . . is almost inconceivable." It would, he sagely reminded them, also "be the means of preserving the lives of many valuable men."

The junior officers, charged also with gaining the affection of their men, were invited, too, to "discourage them from complaining on every frivolous occasion" and to ensure that the noncommissioned officers "support a proper authority, and at the same time do not ill treat [the men] through any pique or resentment."

In short, Steuben was instilling the double loyalty, flowing downward as well as upward, which is the keynote of team spirit: the will to win.

As spring came along, and recruits began to stream into Valley Forge, Steuben's methods and systems whipped them into shape as soldiers. Washington observed with approval, and gave the Baron his full support. By the end of May the General had an army of more than twelve thousand men, trained, disciplined, confident, and proud. But how would they do in battle?

The answer was not long delayed. At Monmouth, as we have already seen, the American Army, despite General Charles Lee, proved itself at least the equal of the finest units of Europe. Thanks to Steuben, from 1778 on, Washington had an army that was a fitting instrument of his exceptional strategic genius.

Anthony Wayne

A fight in the night coined his nickname, to follow him down through the pages of history; thirty short minutes of savage combat, in which the unobtainable was obtained.

"Mad Anthony," they called him, saying that only a crazy man would have dared to storm Stony Point, or could possibly have had the luck to get away with a feat manifestly impossible. Was this a petty comment of lesser men, jealous of a courage and skill they dared not, or could not, emulate? Or was this a sound evaluation of a reckless, foolhardy spirit, ever bent on risking the lives of his men and himself in quixotic ventures? Let's look at the record.

At the age of twenty-eight, in 1773, young Anthony was elected to take his father's place as representative of the county of Chester in the Pennsylvania General Assembly. Two years later he was commissioned by that assembly to recruit a battalion of Pennsylvania Continentals for General Washington's army. On January 1, 1776, the young colonel had his battalion assembled and organized, as ready as any to fight for liberty.

Sent north by Washington to reinforce the sad remnants of Arnold's Quebec expedition, now retreating to Montreal, in June, 1776, Wayne's was one of four battalions sent to halt the British pursuit at the village of Trois Rivières, on the banks of the St. Lawrence. A mixed force of British regulars and Canadian militia had been reported there, and it seemed to General Sullivan—who had replaced the wounded Arnold—that this gave a chance to carry out General Washington's directive to stabilize the situation as far down the St. Lawrence as possible.

What Sullivan didn't know was that General Burgoyne, with an army of eight thousand British and mercenary Brunswick regulars, had arrived at Quebec three weeks earlier, and that by June 8 the bulk of this army was encamped at Trois Rivières. Certainly Wayne and the other battalion commanders—one of whom was a fellow Pennsylvanian, Colonel Arthur St. Clair—had no inkling of this fact as they landed from river boats at 3 A.M. that morning, a few miles from the encampment. They planned to attack at dawn.

Misled by an incompetent—or traitorous—guide, however, Anthony Wayne led his battalion into his first battle, against staggering odds.

His men displayed a relatively workmanlike efficiency which had impressed all observers. Wayne had led them with valor and determination—and a veteran's skill could hardly be expected of a commander in his first battle. Further, when the enemy strength became apparent, and the hopelessness of the situation evident, he extricated his command with relatively light losses and brought them back to Montreal in reasonable order and good spirits.

The Americans were soon driven from Canada by the British, being forced to fall back to Crown Point, New York. Wayne's performance during these terrible months of retreat, and the standards of discipline he maintained in his regiment while the rest of the army was disintegrating into a "rabble in arms," brought him to the attention of Generals Arnold and Schuyler. The latter placed Wayne in command of Fort Ticonderoga. Reports of Wayne's conduct reached Washington and the Congress, and in February, while still at Ticonderoga, he found himself appointed brigadier general. A few months later—April of 1777—Washington sent for the young brigadier to join the army at Morristown, there to take command of the Pennsylvania Brigade of the Continental Line.

At the Brandywine, September 11, 1777, Wayne's brigade held Chad's Ford, the main crossing, until Howe's professionally skillful envelopment made the general situation hopeless. Reluctantly, and in good order, Wayne withdrew to avoid being cut off by the advancing British.

Near Paoli Tavern nine days later Wayne was sent to ambush the British rear guard and baggage train during Washington's retreat from the Brandywine. Wayne's brigade, bivouacking in the woods, was itself surprised by a British night attack. Led by Tory spies, who had reported the hidden American brigade, a force of four British regiments rushed his camp.

Major General Grey, commanding the enemy, to make surprise doubly certain had ordered the flints removed from the British muskets (they dubbed him "No-Flint" Grey for that) and they came slashing in with the bayonet.

Had Wayne not posted his guards, and kept them constantly alert, his entire command probably would have been wiped out. As it was, the hastily aroused Americans fought manfully against the British bayonet charge, and Wayne was able to withdraw his brigade, with all four of his artillery pieces, having lost only about 150 men. A valuable lesson had been learned by the young brigadier. He took note not only of the enemy tactics, but of the skill and discipline of the British regulars, which had enabled them to perform a difficult night operation as though it were a simple parade-ground exercise.

But his education was not yet complete. At Germantown, on October 4, in Washington's ambitious, overcomplicated dawn attack,

Wayne's brigade, already engaged on front and right, was hit by a flank attack on its left. Quickly he reformed to try to drive off this new foe. At first he seemed to be successful, but his tired men, under fire from three directions, had had enough. They began to pull back, just as the new assailants also started to withdraw. Too late Wayne discovered that he had been fighting part of Greene's division, which had been lost in the fog. Heartened by the slackening American fire, the alert, disciplined British promptly counterattacked. Sullenly, slowly—too tired to run—the Americans pulled back. The Battle of Germantown was over, but General Wayne had learned another lesson about training, discipline, and the control and co-ordination of units.

Small wonder that Wayne became one of the first and most enthusiastic supporters of the new drill system established by Baron von Steuben later that winter. As a result, of all the Continental Line which took part in the Monmouth campaign in June, 1778, the Pennsylvania Brigade was the best trained and best drilled. Wayne, his officers and men had become regulars, confident that they could meet and defeat the finest regulars in the world.

And they proved it!

Wayne's brigade was the only major element of General Charles Lee's advanced guard at Monmouth which survived the early, disastrous hours of the battle without losing their cohesion or confidence. With one of his regiments and a nearby Maryland regiment, Wayne established a delaying position and held off most of Clinton's army for over an hour, while Washington rallied the fugitives and brought up reinforcements. Having successfully carried out the mission, Wayne then withdrew in good order, despite repeated British attacks, and rejoined the remainder of his brigade, which Washington had established as the anchor fixing the center of the new American line.

Here Wayne, his brigade now reinforced by a Virginia regiment as well as the Marylanders, bore the brunt of repeated British assaults for more than two hours. The first time the British approached, Wayne ordered his men to hold their fire. "Steady, steady," he is reported to have cried. "Wait for the word, then pick out the king birds!" Not a shot was fired, and not until the enemy came within forty yards did he give the word. Then a volley rang out which staggered the attackers—cavalry and infantry—and drove them back in confusion. This was repeated three or four times before the stubborn British regulars finally gave up.

Although Washington deserves the credit for bringing success out of sure defeat at Monmouth, he would have failed without the intrepid Wayne and his reliable brigade.

One realizes why Washington later picked Wayne to take Stony Point.

During June, 1779, British General Henry Clinton had seized and fortified Stony Point as a springboard for planned later operations

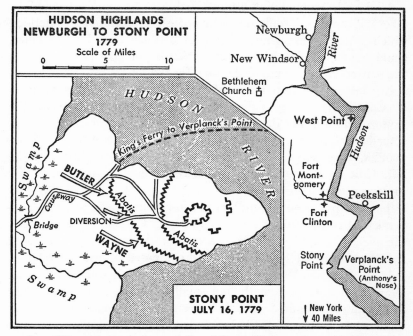

against West Point, whose fall might well have been fatal to the American cause.

Stony Point, whose bare rocks gave it its name, sticks out from the frowning, forested Dunderberg on the Hudson River's west bank toward Anthony's Nose on the other side. It is the key to the southern gate of the Hudson Highlands.

Impregnable from the water, Stony Point was seemingly so from land also. Its citadel of earthwork batteries connected by trenches was further protected by two outer rings of abatis (sharpened tree trunks and timbers interlaced into a barricade) thrown across the base of the promontory just short of the broad stretch of marshland which, at high tide, made Stony Point an island. A single narrow causeway across the marsh on its northern sector was the sole access route.

The garrison consisted of tough, seasoned troops, mostly regulars; a battalion of the 17th (Leicestershire) Foot, a grenadier company of the 71st (Fraser's) Highlanders, a detachment of the Loyal Americans, and some artillerymen.

All in all, Stony Point was a tough nut to crack. It could be taken, it appeared, only by a major siege operation, something which Washington's army, interposed between it and West Point, could not undertake. But General Washington had other ideas on the matter, and felt he had the man for the job.

In consequence, near midnight, July 15, 1779, two dense columns of Continental troops debouched from the mainland across the swamp before Stony Point. On the right near the river's edge and actually wading waist-deep in swamp water, the American commander, Brigadier General Anthony Wayne, was leading. On the left, Colonel Richard Butler headed the men hurrying over the causeway leading to the fort.

The troops, run-of-the-mill in origin—from Massachusetts, Connecticut, Pennsylvania, Virginia, and North Carolina—were actually the pick of the Continental Army. For this was Wayne's Light Infantry Corps, lately organized, and composed of selected veterans led by the smartest disciplinarian in Washington's command. Wayne's troops, in strength four small regiments of two battalions each—thirteen-hundred-odd in all—were roughly double the number of the defenders snug behind their formidable ramparts.

Always meticulous in his own appearance, from jaunty tricorn hat to polished boots, Wayne was equally insistent that his men be smartly turned out, clean, and neat. A small thing, this, perhaps, but important from the viewpoint of a leader who recognized the psychological value of personal grooming.

When Washington had placed him in command of the Light

Infantry Corps, Wayne's first reaction, as he wrote, was that he had "a prejudice in favor of an Ellegant Uniform and would rather risque my life at the Head of these same men clothed and Appointed as I could wish, with a single charge of Ammunition, than to take them as they appear with sixty rounds of Cartridges." So he set to work on them.

They had turned out that morning at Sandy Beach, "fresh shaven and well powdered," to make the thirteen-mile march skirting the Dunderberg to their jump-off point, about a mile away from Stony Point. There they were told their task, and final instructions issued.

They would march to the attack with bayonets fixed and arms shouldered. Except for one battalion which had a special mission, not a musket was to be loaded. That, it would seem, was the lesson learned from Paoli. Any man taking his piece from his shoulder during the advance, or trying to fire it, or attempting to "Skulk in the face of danger" was to be "instantly put to Death by his proper Officer."

Until the final assault, absolute silence was imposed. Then they would begin shouting—and keep shouting—"The fort's our own!" In each man's headdress a piece of white paper was stuck, for recognition in the night.

Ahead of each of the two columns went 150 men with muskets slung, carrying axes to chop through the abatis. And with each went, too, an additional officer and twenty men—picked, dauntless souls who should dash through the axmen's openings and rush on the foe. To the first man inside the fort would go a tangible prize—$500; to the next four in order sums ranging down to $100.

An alert British picket, hearing the confused shuffle and squashing in the night, gave the alarm; a disciplined garrison turned out. The first flashings of musketry and cannon disclosed the awesome sight of close-ranked infantry marching in silence through the mud toward the southern flank barrier. At almost the same moment alarm sounded from the northern side: more silent, marching men.

Then, as the axmen reached the outer barricade and their blades thumped deep into the timber, a continuous roar of musketry rose from the blackness between the two assaults. Small wonder that

Lieutenant Colonel Henry Johnson, the British commander, felt that the greatest threat lay in his center front, and rushed six companies —the bulk of his force—to repel it. Actually, this firing was a diversion, carried out by the one battalion of Wayne's troops whose muskets had been loaded.

Meanwhile gaps opened in the outer abatis, through which the Americans began to pour toward the second ring. Men were falling fast now, as the British fire increased, but sufficient axmen remained to hew at the new obstacle. Through the crevices they wrenched, the suicide squads of both columns dashed toward the inner works. And still the main bodies of the attackers kept silence as they clambered and pushed up the slope.

Wayne went down, momentarily stunned by a glancing bullet. Other officers were down, too. But Wayne regained his feet and, propped by one of his men as he walked, urged the troops on. Through the sally port and over the parapet the Continentals came, first in a trickle, then a tide. Their muskets were off their shoulders now, their bayonets ripping as they closed with the defenders, and their tongues unloosened.

Bewildered British soldiers, attacked on two sides, their ears ringing with the din of that monotonous, repeated "The fort's our own!" began to give ground. Some threw down their arms; others followed suit. Colonel Johnson, with his center group, hearing the noise behind him, tried to turn them back into the fight. But his men, hemmed in this swirling, shouting attack, lost heart and surrendered. He, too, had to drop his sword. A fragment of the 17th Foot, penned in the log barracks, held out for a few more minutes, then they also cried for quarter.

In a half hour Stony Point had been won and Anthony Wayne's intrepidity had gained for him forever the nickname of "Mad Anthony." Entirely undeserved was this sobriquet, for it was a victory coldly calculated and planned to the last detail, and carried out by an elite body of trained, highly disciplined men.

The fort had been carefully reconnoitered by a responsible officer, and its details studied by Wayne and his troop leaders. The actual assault had been rehearsed in camp. And that right-hand column had wallowed in the high tide not through oversight, but because

Wayne had studied his almanac and knew, as he explained to General Washington, that to wait for low tide would mean a daylight attack and complete loss of surprise.

Here indeed was leadership.

One last aspect of the fight at Stony Point deserves consideration; the behavior of the American troops when the fort was won.

"No instance of Inhumanity was shown to any of the unhappy Captives," writes one British historian of the period; "No one was unnecessarily put to the sword or wantonly wounded. Writes another: ". . . The rebels . . . showed at this moment a generosity and clemency, which during the course of the rebellion had no parallel."

Considering that grave allegations were made after the Paoli surprise that the attackers butchered a number of Wayne's men in wanton slaughter, this chivalrous conduct at Stony Point must be credited to Wayne's control—no mean feat of leadership in the heat of combat under any circumstances.

Wayne's further career in the Continental Army included such things as setting up Cornwallis for the knockout blow by an impetuous charge at Jamestown Ford, Virginia, July 5, 1871, when he took on the entire British force. He had to retire, but Cornwallis was through, too; he retreated to Yorktown.

The war over, Wayne returned to private life. But another chore was in the cards for him; none other than a complete revamping of a tiny United States Army unraveled by mishap. In 1791 Arthur St. Clair, onetime commander of Wayne and a fellow-Pennsylvanian comrade in arms, met defeat in Ohio in an attempt to curb the Maumee Indians. It was one of the worst misfortunes ever to befall our arms; half of St. Clair's little force of two thousand regulars and militia—most of the U.S. Army—was destroyed.

The newly organized Constitutional Congress rushed to enlarge the Army to some five thousand men, which would be organized as the Legion of the United States. Horse, foot, and artillery were to be components of each of four Sub-Legions—actually the forerunner of the combat team of today. It was all very nice on paper; the puzzle was to find a capable commander to make soldiers out of raw recruits.

President Washington, who had been shocked by St. Clair's disaster, called on Wayne. And out from his retirement came "Mad Anthony." He arrived at Pittsburgh in June, 1792, to join his assembling Legion. But that boisterous frontier city was no place to train soldiers; Wayne's encampment was situated twenty miles away from its temptations. Legionville he called it, this second Valley Forge, and there during the winter of 1792–1793 Anthony Wayne, a combined Steuben and Washington, built an army.

Wayne's detractors — and there were many among the disgruntled —said he was getting old, crotchety, and gouty. Perhaps he was (he was only forty-seven, then). But his ill temper fell only on the unfit and the obstreperous. He drilled, marched, and hardened them in rigorous grind.

That summer he moved his little army—now a disciplined force— to a new base at Fort Washington in Ohio (now Cincinnati, appropriate name), and pushed his outposts into the wilderness between the Ohio River and Lake Erie. But he wasn't ready yet; at Greenville, some eighty miles north of Fort Washington, he established a winter camp, and another period of rigorous training ensued. All the while he was attempting negotiations for peace. Spring came, with the Indians still spurning overtures.

Then Wayne moved. He was ready.

He had taken almost two years to build it, but when at last he struck into the wilderness his Legion was comparable to the legions of Rome. It could march and it could fight. Its camps each night were entrenched and fortified; no Indian raid could surprise them or disturb their cool confidence. This army was tailor-made for its task—to fight Indians in the wilderness.

Irresistibly Wayne marched back over St. Clair's ill-fated route, driving the Indians before him. The climax came on August 20, 1794, near present-day Toledo, at a place the Indians called Fallen Timbers, where a slashing of trees uprooted by some long-past tornado had formed an almost impenetrable thicket. Hidden here, the Indians awaited the American advance, in sight of a British fort illegally and impudently sited on American soil. The Indians attacked the Legion from ambush as they had struck St. Clair— this time to be met by a blasting volley. Wayne's infantry then charged, forcing the enemy from their wooded hide-outs with the bayonet. At the same time his cavalry circled around the enemy flanks, spreading confusion in the enemy rear. The remnants of the Indians scattered or surrendered, and their villages were burned under the eyes of the amazed British garrison, while Wayne waited grimly, ready for any overt move. But what they had seen gave the Britishers no taste to meet the Legion.

For some time to come the Indians lost interest in England's plan to organize them into a buffer nation within United States boundaries. In 1795 they agreed to Wayne's strict terms of peace in the Treaty of Greenville. Thanks to "Mad Anthony" Wayne the Northwest Territory was safe—at least while he and his Legion were around.

Trois Rivières, Paoli, Germantown, Monmouth, Stony Point, Yorktown, Fallen Timbers. Defeats as well as victories. But the lessons of the early defeats were to assure the victories that crowned the career of an intrepid, stormy, gallant, persistent, meticulous officer, of whom all Americans can be proud.

CHAPTER IV ☆ ☆ ☆ *Shadow and Substance*

Barren Ground

Rarely has any nation been as barren of military leadership as was the United States in 1812, when greedy politicians, beguiled by the mirage of an easy conquest which would add Canada to the Union, plunged the nation into war.

It is all the more remarkable, then, that out of this slough of despond in which our land forces floundered so disgracefully, three great leaders would emerge—two of them later to become Presidents of the United States, the third (who surpassed, we believe, the others in military ability) also to be a candidate for that high office of national leadership.

The Army in 1812 consisted of something less than three thousand regulars scattered in little packets along our wide frontier, and headed by an officer presenting the very antithesis of leadership— James Wilkinson of Maryland, tarnished warrior.

A sinister individual with a benevolent façade was this fluent-tongued trimmer, who by clever shifting of personal and political allegiance through the years had managed not only to hold his commission but to rise to command the Army. Actually, at this time, he had probably longer military experience than any other living American.

He had been with Arnold in the retreat from Montreal, with Washington at Trenton, Gates at Saratoga, and later, with Wayne at Fallen Timbers. He had betrayed the trust of the many people to whom he had previously sold himself by his ingratiating manners. Above all, he betrayed his nation's trust. For years he had been in the pay of Spain as a confidential agent, a traitorous connection frequently charged but never proven until long after his death, when Spanish archives revealed payment to him of large sums of money.

As might be imagined, Wilkinson, engrossed in his own personal projects and finaglings, had little time or inclination to attend to the personal wants of his troops. When Wilkinson was in command of troops near newly acquired New Orleans in 1808–1809, conditions in the military cantonments became so horrible as to lead a fiery young captain of artillery named Winfield Scott to publicly proclaim his commander to be "a traitor, liar and scoundrel."

Violations of all principles of hygiene and sanitation vied with the spoiled beef, rotten pork, and musty flour provided by rascally contractors, to bring disease and death to the unfortunate soldiers. Terre aux Boeufs, a cantonment below New Orleans, was a swampland in which they sweltered and steamed in semitropical heat. Wilkinson's indifference made matters worse. Finally, after the affair had become a national scandal, the troops were removed to Natchez and Wilkinson was temporarily relieved by Brigadier General Wade Hampton.

Allegations of his connection with Don Esteban Miró, Spanish governor of Louisiana; his affiliations with a group of conspirators including Aaron Burr; and charges of neglect of duty in the care of his troops, had brought about Congressional investigation and court-martial—out of each of which he managed to wriggle with "not proven" verdicts.

This was the man permitted from 1800 to 1812 to command, as senior brigadier general, the United States Army. It was small wonder that President Madison, in his first frantic effort to find men to lead the hodgepodge of militia, volunteers, and new-made regulars hastily called to the colors by Congress, now hesitated to entrust the national fortunes to Wilkinson. So he was left in his southern command in Louisiana, while for more than a year misfits from civil life and ex-Continental Army crocks stuffed back into uniform brought about disaster after disaster along the northern front.

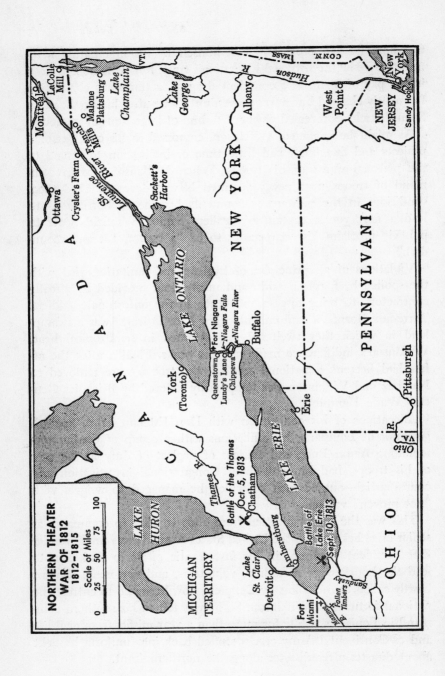

NORTHERN THEATER
WAR OF 1812
1812–1815

Scale of Miles

0 25 50 75 100

It was summer, 1813, when a frantic Administration, appalled by the situation, called Wilkinson up from the South to lead a new and by far the most imposing attempt yet to invade Canada. Masterminded in person by John Armstrong, Secretary of War—erstwhile political general with some Revolutionary War background—it consisted of a two-pronged affair. Brigadier General Wade Hampton, next senior regular to Wilkinson, would push north from Lake Champlain, to be joined by the main effort under Wilkinson, moving down the St. Lawrence River from Sackets Harbor on Lake Ontario. United, they would take Montreal.

But Hampton soon bungled his troops into a swamp where a tiny enemy force was waiting. The British commander, a latter-day Gideon, scattered his three buglers in as many directions and had them simultaneously sound the charge. Hampton's men panicked and that ended that part of the invasion.

Wilkinson, with eight thousand men—regulars in name only—started down the river in bateaux, strong advance and flank guards moving on foot on each bank.

At Crysler's Fields (or Farm), on November 11—halfway to Montreal, with three brigades ashore and his advance guard fifteen miles down the river, Wilkinson attempted to give battle to a British force some eight hundred strong—regulars and Indians. But true to the Wilkinson character, his orders to his subordinates were muddy and contradictory.

As result the two thousand troops ashore were defeated and forced to withdraw. "Never have so many Americans been beaten by such inferior numbers on foreign soil," comments James R. Jacobs, Wilkinson's biographer.

The entire expedition then retreated overland to French Mills, between the St. Lawrence and Lake Champlain. While his troops spent the winter under conditions as rotten as those at Terre aux Boeufs five years earlier, Wilkinson, ensconced in a comfortable house at Malone, New York, was writing excuses and dreaming of future conquests.

The army was finally evacuated to Plattsburg and Sackets Harbor, and from the former place Wilkinson in March, 1814, made what would be his final campaign. Crossing the frontier with four thousand men, and determined, as he published to his troops, "to return victorious or not at all," he attempted to attack a small stone Canadian fort at La Colle Mill, thirty miles north. Its six hundred defenders successfully stood him off and that night Wilkinson marched back to Plattsburg in utter demoralization.

On April 12, 1814, he was summarily relieved from command, his active duty ended. He would be court-martialed later, charged with a multiplicity of offenses ranging from neglect of duty to scandalous drunkenness and willful lying. Pleading not guilty, this remarkable individual—as elusive as a blob of quicksilver—talked his way out to an acquittal on all counts.

On June 15, 1815, James Wilkinson, the general who never won a battle nor lost a court-martial, was honorably discharged. Meanwhile, other men worked hard to clean up the wreckage and demoralization he had left behind. The first bright spot of leadership relieving the drab northern campaign had already come.

From Tippecanoe to Thames

William Henry Harrison of Virginia, newly made brigadier general, U.S. Army, was given an impossible task in the late autumn of 1812: to proceed, with all the regular troops in the Northwest and contingents of volunteers and militia from Kentucky, Ohio, Virginia, and Pennsylvania, to retake Detroit. The catch to this was that for the moment there were no troops available.

Fortunately for the United States, forty-year-old Harrison was a soldier who, two years earlier, had faced a somewhat similar situation. A transplanted Virginian, Harrison at that time was governor of Indiana Territory. He had entered the Army in 1791. He had campaigned with Wayne in the Legion, taken part in the Fallen Timbers battle, and by the time he resigned as a captain of infantry in 1798 to become a civilian official on the frontier he had a pretty thorough knowledge of discipline and training as taught by a master—"Mad Anthony."

In 1811, Harrison in his role of governor and head of the territorial militia had been ordered to wipe out the Indian menace to the Ohio River valley. Tecumseh, a Shawnee chief reviving with British aid Pontiac's dream of a confederacy which would unite the red men from Canada to Florida to resist American encroachment on their lands, had taken the warpath.

His headquarters were at "Prophet's Town," an Indian communal grouping ostensibly devoted to sobriety, industry, and peace, near Tippecanoe Creek (not far from the present city of Lafayette, Indiana). Here Tecumseh, a man of tremendous organizational ability as well as a great orator, ruled. His brother Tenskwata, known as the "Prophet," was meanwhile arousing the Indians' superstitious reverence.

Harrison's available troops consisted of one small regiment (three hundred strong) of regulars—the Fourth Infantry—and such local troops as he could raise. These Harrison trained for a month at Vincennes, his capital, then moved to an advance base, Fort Harrison, now Terre Haute. Here, following Wayne's example, he instituted another stiff course of practical instruction, much to the disgust of the militia, who resented the arbitrary discipline enforced by the regular infantry commander, Colonel John P. Boyd. Indignation meetings and loud complaints threatened possible mutiny.

Harrison gathered his troops together and harangued them. Explaining the task before them and the trouble they would face, he staked his future on his knowledge of America's part-time soldiers. Weaklings, he told the militia, might as well go home at once, to claim from their families the rewards of desertion. The strong would carry on and do the job. A roar of applause followed, stimulated later by his orders that an extra ration of whisky be issued. There was no further disorder, nor would there ever be any more in his command.

By the time Harrison moved his force, a thousand strong, up the Wabash toward the Indian capital, in September, 1811, he had a compact little combat group of horse and foot that could march and maneuver. He moved in battle readiness, his volunteer dragoons as advance and rear guards, his infantry filing on both sides of the trail, with his baggage train sandwiched between the whole. Bivouacs followed the same general square formation. Protected by hasty entrenchments, his troops were alert to turn out against surprise.

It was November 6 when they reached the vicinity of "Prophet's Town" and made their usual entrenched four-square camp, on a cold,

rainy night. Shivering men lay on the ground, their muskets protected, bayonets fixed, and cartridge boxes ready. The horse herd
and train were secure in the center of camp, a ten-acre area surrounded by marsh and thickets, bordering Tippecanoe Creek.

At dawn next morning the Indians attacked, urged on by the
"Prophet" (Tecumseh himself was absent). Warriors daubed with
black paint cloaking them in the half-light, came surging in through
the left rear of the bivouac. But Harrison's men, accustomed to
stand to at the break of dawn, sprang to their arms in the routine
they had practiced so long.

Despite the fact that some few braves actually got through into
the center of camp, there was, apparently, no panic; the attack, the
first of three, was repelled.

By this time Harrison's soldiers had shaken down and Harrison
himself was circulating the camp area on his horse, unperturbed, con-
trolling the defense. Twice more the Indians charged, only to be
thrown back. Now there was sufficient light to maneuver. Harrison
counterattacked from both flanks, driving the Indians in complete
rout, his little troop of dragoons riding down fugitives the infantry
could not reach.

"Prophet's Town" was destroyed, after a quantity of powder and
good rifles recently come from England had been captured, and—
for the time being—Tecumseh's power was broken. The price was
high—37 Americans dead, 150-odd wounded—almost one-fifth of
the force engaged. The Indians lost probably at least as many, for
of their 700 warriors they left 36 dead on the field.

Harrison's new problem, in 1812, was interesting.

On August 16, 1812, American Brigadier General William Hull,
Governor of Michigan Territory, supposedly leading an invasion of
Canada, had abjectly surrendered his entire command at Detroit,
without a shot being fired, to a Canadian force inferior in number
to his. So what Harrison was now being asked to do was to scrape
up spilt milk without a spoon.

British General Thomas Proctor, with British regulars, Canadian
militia, and a strong Indian contingent under Tecumseh—the Shawnee chief was now holding the king's commission as a brigadier
general of the British Army—controlled the area. Against him Har-

rison must assemble, train, and lead what bits and pieces of soldiery could be gathered, from any source.

Harrison, with his background of experience against Tecumseh the year before, refused to be stampeded into action. For eight months, operating in the area between the Miami and Sandusky Rivers below Lake Erie, he held off the enemy in a series of inconclusive actions while he trained a heterogeneous mass of Ohio and Kentucky militia and some newly raised regular outfits.

By August, 1813, his fighting force was ready, seven thousand strong. So, too was Oliver Hazard Perry's little naval squadron on Lake Erie. Perry, arriving at Put-in-Bay, conferred with Harrison, who furnished a detachment of soldiers to augment the Navy man's marines. On September 10, Perry, winning his brilliant naval victory over Barclay, rushed to Harrison his famous message—"We have met the enemy and they are ours—two ships, two brigs, one schooner and one sloop. Yours with greatest respect and esteem."

Command of the inland sea was assured; the stage set for an offensive. Harrison embarked his infantry on Perry's ships and put his Kentucky mounted riflemen in motion on the long hundred-mile march around the western end of the lake. British General Proctor, fearing for his communications, retreated northward.

Landed on the Canadian shore at Amherstburg, the army marched on Detroit; Perry's squadron, close offshore, keeping touch. The town was recaptured September 29. Three days later the mounted riflemen came riding in and Harrison pushed northeastward into Canada, up the Thames River in pursuit of Proctor. For fifteen miles Perry kept pace with three of his lightest ships. Then, the water shoaling, he went ashore to mount a horse. As a volunteer aide to Harrison he would be in on the kill.

Proctor was brought to bay October 5, at Chatham. Harrison, who had thirty-five hundred men to dispose against Proctor's eight hundred British regulars and more than a thousand of Tecumseh's Indians, went about his business in his usual methodical fashion. The enemy defensive position was taken under frontal attack, while from the west the Kentucky mounted riflemen came whirling in headlong charge against the enemy flank. The entire British line collapsed, and Proctor led a fraction of his force in hurried flight.

Only the Indians held firm, under Tecumseh's magnetic leadership, until the great chief, in the red and gold trappings of a British general, fell dead.

The majority of the British regulars—600, including 25 officers—were captured in this brief battle; 12 were killed, 22 wounded. The Indians left 33 dead on the field. American casualties were but 29.

The Battle of the Thames ended further Indian participation in the war. It might have had an even more decisive effect, but the cold dead hand of inept and jealous overlordship now fell on Harrison. The Secretary of War ordered his militia disbanded and sent home, his regulars to be concentrated in the Niagara area. "Old Tippecanoe," obeying, at the same time threw up his commission in high dudgeon and returned to civil life.

In 1840 the joyous slogan of "Tippecanoe and Tyler too!" would usher in his final mandate to the highest command of all: the Presidency of the United States.

These Are Regulars

It was spring, 1814; on the northern front the last whiffs of the Wilkinson miasma lifted to disclose the rise of a new star of leadership—a magnificent specimen of virility, with a fiery temper, a facile and vitriolic pen, and a profound compassion for his soldiers. This man's personal daring was as unlimited as his jealous sense of personal honor was razor-edged. For almost a half century to come he would dominate the American military scene. In three wars he would play major parts; a fourth would be won when his original plan for victory was put in effect, three years after his retirement.

This man gloried in combat, yet through his own personal efforts he would peaceably avert one attempt at secession as well as three potential wars. He would do more than any other one man to ameliorate the condition of the American regular soldier. He would be offered, in a perfectly legitimate manner, the presidency of Mexico only to turn it down. Thrice he would seek, and once win, nomination as a Presidential candidate. To the nation in general he would be a shining hero throughout his career, although during his military life he would be at loggerheads most of the time with his superiors and peers.

His name was Winfield Scott.

Spectacular was this man Scott, in every action of his long career, beginning with the time he publicly announced that his commander, Brigadier General James Wilkinson, was a traitor, a liar, and a scoundrel. Such language from a brash young captain with less than two years' service was, to say the least, imprudent, even if history confirms the truth of the allegations.

Tried by general court-martial for this—and other things—in 1810, Scott was convicted and sentenced to "be suspended from all rank, pay and emoluments for the space of twelve months." The sentence is remarkable in itself, for the charge was "conduct unbecoming an officer and a gentleman," for which the allotted punishment was dismissal. The court even recommended clemency—"remission of nine months of Captain Scott's suspension," which, perhaps naturally, the department commander, who was Wilkinson himself, did not see fit to approve.

The trial ended, Scott challenged his accuser, Surgeon William Upshaw, 7th Infantry, to a duel. Scott missed his man; Upshaw's bullet grooved Scott's scalp. Aside from this episode, Scott's year of suspension was mainly employed in the study of military history and tactics.

Scott had been restored to active duty in time to cross to Queenstown Heights on the Niagara as a volunteer in one of our early disgraceful abortive invasions of Canada. Major General Stephen Van Rensselaer, aging commander of the New York State militia, had 2,270 militia and 900 regulars.

On October 13, 1812, part of the American force—mostly regulars —crossed the river and established themselves on Queenstown Heights, driving off the local enemy troops. But able British General Isaac Brock, who had forced Hull's surrender at Detroit, hurried up reinforcements and the outnumbered invaders found themselves in a jam.

At this moment, with the roar of battle in their ears, the New York militia on the American side of the river, who until the actual assault had been clamoring to be led against the enemy, changed heart. Standing on their constitutional rights as militia not to leave the territorial limits of the United States without their own consent, they absolutely refused all Van Rensselaer's orders, pleadings, and exhortations to cross.

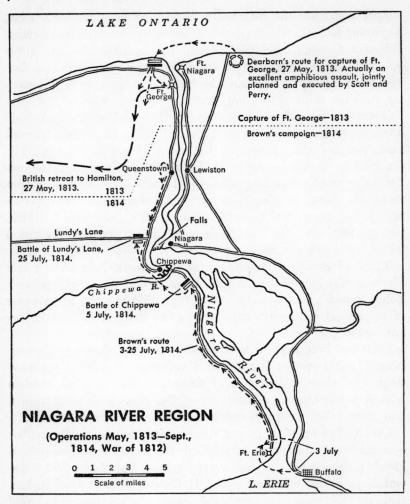

NIAGARA RIVER REGION

(Operations May, 1813—Sept., 1814, War of 1812)

So some 2,000 men in American uniform stood idly on the river-bank watching their comrades across the water being overwhelmed by Brock's 600 British regulars and 400 additional Canadian militia. American losses were 250 killed and wounded and 700 prisoners; the British lost only 14 killed and 96 wounded. But among their dead was brilliant General Brock, picked off by an American rifleman while he was leading his men; a loss indeed for the British, although fortunate for us.

Scott, who had fought furiously with the trapped troops, was among the prisoners. Exchanged in early 1813, he got back to the northern front to become General Henry Dearborn's adjutant general. With young Oliver Hazard Perry he planned and led the amphibious attack at Fort Niagara which was the sole bright spot in Dearborn's sorry adventures of that year.

Now, it seemed, President Madison, trying to wipe the slate clean of the incompetents in the north, had put stout Jacob Brown, erstwhile New York militiaman, in command and sent newly promoted twenty-seven-year-old Brigadier General Scott to join him with instructions to initiate a camp of instruction; something which the loquacious Scott had urgently recommended.

Brown's little army was a sorry affair. The comparatively few veterans had been chivvied about in four inglorious attempts to invade Canada. True, some of the men now joining had made part of Harrison's command at the Battle of the Thames. They had tasted of crusty "Tippecanoe's" vigorous leadership and training. But they had seen victory later frittered away by others and their leader throw up his commission in righteous indignation. Their morale was far from high.

Brown's newer elements were regulars in name only; regiments just raised by Congress, with both officers and men ill trained and poorly disciplined. All were badly uniformed, poorly fed, and much dispirited. Even their environment, Buffalo, partly destroyed by a British raid earlier that winter, was depressing.

Scott threw himself into his task with his usual verve. Brown, happy to see his men trained and confident in Scott's ability, stayed at his headquarters at Sackets Harbor and gave him full rein.

The new broom swept clean. Scott gathered into his own control all the quartermaster and ordnance stores in the area, put his men in tents, and, remembering the horrors of Terre aux Boeufs, insisted on a sanitation surprising to the army doctors of the day. One of them penned his amazement that "even the demon diarrhoea appeared to have been exorcised by the mystic power of strict discipline and rigid police."

All the officers were turned out en masse to learn the school of the soldier and squad drill. Like von Steuben before him, Scott was his own drill sergeant—his bible the one tattered military textbook in camp, a copy of French Napoleonic infantry drill regulations. Then the officers began drilling the men. It was a ten-hour grind each day, for three months, under Scott's all-seeing eye. Some men took it hard; but after four deserters had been shot to death before the eyes of the rest of the camp, desertion became unpopular. Officers, too, became aware that a new order had dawned, brooking no compromise.

The army by this time had been divided up in brigades, one of which was Scott's very own—"a handsome little army," as he wrote a friend, "of about 1,700 . . . the 9th, 11th, 21st and 25th regiments and two companies 2nd artillery. . . . The men are sober, cheerful and docile. The officers highly respectable; and many of the platoon officers are decent and emulous of improvement. If, of such materials, I do not make the best army now in service, by the 1st of June, I will agree to be dismissed the service."

Like Wayne, Scott believed that a well-dressed soldier was a self-respecting soldier. His biting rage descended on quartermasters and contractors when they informed him that blue cloth was lacking for the uniforms his men needed to replace their tattered garments.

As result he got them into new uniforms, all right. But they were gray—the hue worn by the militia of that period. That mattered not one whit to Scott, although as it turned out it would matter to some other people, later on. His 1st Brigade was clad. They looked like soldiers and they *were* soldiers. They could shoot, they could maneuver, and they could use their bayonets.

So it was that in June, with the arrival of General Brown to assume command, the army, as Charles Winslow Elliott, Scott's biographer, writes, "threw out its chest and began to sniff the breeze that blew from across the broad Niagara."

On the night of July 2–3, 1814, the army crossed.

It was late afternoon, July 5. Brown's army, with Scott's brigade in the lead, was bivouacked on the south side of Street's Creek. About a mile downriver, on the far side of the unfordable Chippewa, lay the main body of British troops in the area, behind entrenchments. Brown planned to throw a bridge across the Chippewa River, well to the west—a matter of at least one more day's labor—and outflank them.

Between the creek and the Chippewa lay an expanse of open field land bordering the Niagara on the right and flanked by a dense clump of woods to the left. Here was, concluded Scott, a natural parade ground. He had taken some trouble to feed his men a plentiful—if belated—Fourth of July dinner. Why not close the day with a dress parade, a metaphorical nose-thumbing toward the enemy lying safe behind his earthworks on the other side of the Chippewa?

It was an excellent idea. The enemy, having entrenched himself, certainly would not be stupid enough to throw away his advantage by crossing the river and offering battle.

That, however, was exactly what British General Phineas Riall, pugnacious Irishman, was doing. Riall, not unnaturally from his past experience along the Canadian frontier, held Americans in low esteem. So he marched his regulars over the bridge and moved onto the northern edge of the flat plain in compact columns just as Scott's leading regiment was crossing the Street's Creek bridge on the south.

American militia and Indians, skirmishing through the woods on the left towards the Chippewa, came smack up against the measured British advance and after receiving a smart volley scampered away. This, so far as Riall was concerned, was merely history repeating itself. So too would the troops he now perceived moving onto the field scamper, when his serried formations hit them.

These newcomers debouching across Street's Creek wore gray uniforms. "Why," quoth the delighted Riall, "these are nothing but Buffalo militia!"

On the river flank a battery of twenty-four pounders unlimbered and began to shell the Street's Creek bridge. But the gray column of Americans, unmindful of either cannon ball or musketry, kept pouring on; moving precisely by the flank to right and left, to form line. A battery of twelve-pounders came galloping through, swung to the right, and dropped trails to open a hot fire. Scott, at the bridge, kept hustling them on, by voice and gesture; a fight was even better than a parade.

His infantry, in perfect calm, formed their line, dressed their ranks, and marched forward as if they were back on the Buffalo parade ground.

And Riall, reversing his opinion, made his second recorded remark of the day:

"These are Regulars, by God!"

It was storybook battle, this; both sides advancing, each stopping from time to time to fire a volley, while cannon roared on the river flank. At seventy-yard distance, both fixed bayonets.

Storybook, too, are Scott's action and words then. Galloping in front of the 11th Infantry, the imposing brigadier, sword flashing high, bellowed a peroration:

"They say that the Americans are good at long shot but cannot stand the cold iron! I call on you instantly to give the lie to that slander! Charge!"

That is what Scott says he said. Perhaps he did; he was always an orator. But the words matter not. Here was their leader out in front, leading, and ordering a charge. His men responded, and the enemy recoiled.

Riall, personally bold, attempted vainly to hold his shattered ranks. One unit only, the King's Liverpools, sullenly covered the rout long enough to enable the entire British force to get back across the Chippewa and into its trenches.

Historian Henry Adams has summed up the action well: "The battle of Chippewa was the only occasion during the war when equal bodies of regular troops met face to face, in extended lines on an open plain in broad daylight, without advantage of position; and never again after that combat was an army of American regulars beaten by British troops."

The opposing forces were approximately equal in number. The British lost 148 killed, including 6 officers; 221 wounded of whom 27 were officers; and 46 missing or taken prisoner. Scott's brigade lost 44 killed and 224 wounded.

The news of victory at Chippewa electrified the entire nation, dispirited by the succession of shameful disasters. The soldiers, too, held high their heads in the realization that they could not only stand up to the British regulars but beat them. Later, in perpetual token, the War Department would order that the U.S. Corps of Cadets be thereafter uniformed in garb identical in pattern and cut with that worn by Scott's brigade July 5, 1814.

Twenty days after Chippewa the two armies met again in bloody stalemate at Lundy's Lane, opposite Niagara Falls. Both Brown and Scott were wounded, as was the British general Sir Gordon Drummond, now commanding the enemy. Riall, acting in subordinate capacity, was not only wounded but captured. But Lundy's Lane, indecisive in itself, was in fact clincher to the evidence of Chippewa: the American regular, well led and trained, need fear no foe.

It was, alas! a lesson still to be learned elsewhere. For the blackest, most shameful smudge of all, upon both the Army and the nation's escutcheon, would come one month after Lundy's Lane.

Little Tin Soldiers

Overseas, Napoleon had been overthrown in April, 1814, freeing Wellington's veterans of the Peninsular War for use on this side of the water. Yet, despite the harrying of the Chesapeake Bay area by British Admiral George Cockburn in 1813 and the continuous blockade of our ports, no steps were even started to protect the city of Washington until July, 1814. On August 18, Cockburn's ships, escorting newly arrived transports, stood in to land fifty-four hundred battle-tried veterans under Major General Robert Ross at Benedict on the Patuxent, not forty miles from the nation's capital.

President Madison and Secretary of War Armstrong, recently returned from his inept meddling in Wilkinson's northern campaign, belatedly got busy. A motley mass of untrained militia was called to arms. To lead it they selected Brigadier General William Henry Winder, politically prominent Baltimore lawyer whom Madison had appointed to generalship earlier in the war. Winder was given the responsibility for defending Washington because, as Armstrong wrote later, "being a native of Maryland and a relative of the governor," he would be "useful in mitigating the opposition to the war, and in giving an increased efficiency to national measures within the limits of the State." Truly it was the misfortune of war that Winder, who had promptly gotten himself captured during Dearborn's footless Niagara fizzle, should have been exchanged and now be available for this position.

Gathering in a camp reeking of county-fair atmosphere, Winder and his levies marched out to Bladensburg August 24, to do battle with the British advance guard. He had sixty-five hundred militia from Maryland, Virginia, and the District of Columbia, a handful of regulars, and some four hundred sailors and marines under Commodore Joshua Barney—the personnel of our little naval flotilla

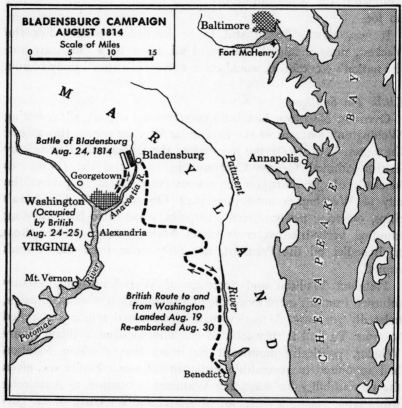

**BLADENSBURG CAMPAIGN
AUGUST 1814**

Scale of Miles

0   5   10   15

Baltimore

Fort McHenry

M A R Y L A N D

*Battle of Bladensburg
Aug. 24, 1814*

Georgetown

Bladensburg

Annapolis

Anacostia R.

Patuxent

Washington
(Occupied
by British
Aug. 24-25)

Alexandria

VIRGINIA

Mt. Vernon

*British Route to and
from Washington
Landed Aug. 19
Re-embarked Aug. 30*

River

Potomac River

Benedict

CHESAPEAKE BAY

on Chesapeake Bay, who had destroyed their ships to prevent them from falling into enemy hands.

The British commander, without waiting for his main body to come up, attacked at once with fifteen hundred men. The militia fired a few volleys, then fled. Barney's contingent and the few Regular Army men, standing their ground, forced Ross to bring up reinforcements, with which, of course, he overwhelmed them. American losses were 100 killed and wounded and approximately the same number made prisoner; the British, who had only 4,000 men on the field, had 294 casualties.

Watching the entire performance, and for a while actually meddling in the command, were President Madison, Secretary of State James Monroe, Secretary of War Armstrong, Secretary of the Navy William Jones, Secretary of the Treasury George W. Campbell, and Attorney General Richard Rush—all breathing down the neck of futile General Winder. It is improbable if there be any other occasion in our history where the titular commander in chief and his cabinet took such active part in a military operation.

It would seem that the President finally did take some cognizance of the ridiculous situation, for shortly before the action started he told Armstrong, who was trying to give orders to Winder, that "the military functionaries should be left to the discharge of their own duties, on their own responsibility."

The Attorney General's later comment on the Battle of Bladensburg is short and sweet: "To me it appeared plain," he told a Congressional investigating committee, "that entire ranks of our men, in front, were dispersed by the shock of the enemy, before any order for retreat was given by the commanding general." It was a mild way of putting it.

President, cabinet, commanding general, and army all took to their collective heels. They didn't draw rein until sixteen miles the other side of the capital, where they could watch on the horizon the smoke curling from Washington's public buildings as the invaders leisurely sacked the city before returning to their boats.

Had it not been so pitiful and so shameful, one might well laugh at this display of military mismanagement and lack of leadership. But people were not laughing in Washington. Angry mobs later greeted Armstrong when he ventured back. He was "hissed and hunted" to Baltimore, whence he sent in his resignation.

We turn now to a Southern battleground, where the last of our three leaders would combine cannon balls, cotton bales, and shrewd character analysis to bring victory in most unexpected fashion.

CHAPTER V ☆ ☆ ☆ *A Man from Tennessee*

Where There's a Will

Crisis spawns combat leadership. With the exception of George Washington, no American soldier learned this lesson harder, or put it to better use, than Andrew Jackson of Tennessee. The comparison ends there. For where Washington made subservience to civil authority his religion, Jackson flouted it when he saw fit. It was part and parcel of the man's turbulent spirit, so frequently demonstrated in his personal and private quarrels. But, although Jackson, himself a lawyer, a one-time judge of the supreme court of Tennessee, and for a short year a United States senator, showed time and time again an amazing disregard for constitutional authority and legal process, his sins—if one can call them that—were always committed in what he believed to be the best interest of the nation.

Jackson's hair-trigger temper and ruthless determination early molded him into the shape of an incipient dictator—in which character we would later see him as President of the United States. The unfortunate circumstances of his marriage, leaving him open to the slurring barbs of his enemies, quite naturally further hardened his heart; he would, it seemed, be perpetually carrying a chip on his shoulder. A psychologist, perhaps, might have a word for it; the soldier is interested merely because on one vital occasion Jackson the battler emerged from his narrow rigidity to demonstrate all the qualities of a real leader.

The conditioning which brought this about, the tempering, so to speak, of the steel, is important.

84

It was in 1813 that Jackson the soldier first emerged. Then a major general of militia, he led a mixed force of Tennessee militia and volunteers against the Creek Indians, Britain's allies who had fallen on the Southern settlements with fire and sword. The massacre of some five hundred men, women, and children in a surprise attack on Fort Mims, Alabama, August 30, aroused Jackson's ill-trained soldiers to fury.

In two sharp conflicts—Tallasahatchee and Talladega in the Alabama forests—Jackson crushed his enemy. Then his force dissolved. His part-time soldiers simply quit. They had revenged Fort Mims. Starved and destitute now—the supply system was atrociously incompetent—his men wanted no more campaigns. So Jackson had to lead them back to his base, Fort Strother.

There, all his importunities and appeals to patriotism failing, Jackson was faced by the fact that his militia regiments were determined to go home. The volunteers still kept some semblance of order. Deploying them across the path of the disgruntled militia, Jackson quelled the mutiny. Next day the volunteers tried the same stunt. This time the militia, the mutineers of the previous morning, barred the way!

But both militia and volunteers now claimed their enlistments were up. The dissidents milled and rioted. Of his twenty-five hundred men, only a round hundred stout souls could be found to answer Jackson's appeals and his rage. He had to let the volunteers go; to Tennessee's governor's recommendation that he disband the militia, he simply answered: "I will hold the posts I have established until ordered to abandon them by the commanding General [Armstrong, then Secretary of War], or die in the attempt."

He meant it, as the mutineers found out; on one occasion he barred their way alone, musket in hand. Meanwhile he called on the governor again for another draft of militia.

While this bit of *opéra bouffe* dragged on, the Indians, urged by British agents, took the warpath again. Most of Jackson's original force had simply evaporated by this time, but the new levy of nine hundred raw militiamen did report, and with these troops, officered by some experienced men, Jackson, amazingly, checked the Indians in January, 1814.

In February the command was stiffened by the arrival of the 39th U.S. Infantry (now the 7th) and additional Tennessee troops, and Jackson definitely took the offensive. At the Horse Shoe Bend of the Tallapoosa River, March 27, he ended the Creek War. With a loss of 201 men out of 2,000 engaged, he practically wiped out the Creek nation's war potential. Of 900 Indians, 700 warriors were killed.

Here, it seemed to President Madison, was a man who could fight. Jackson was commissioned, first, brigadier and, almost immediately after, major general in the Regular Army and put in charge of the Seventh Military District, which included the Gulf coast; Wilkinson's old command.

In the South no better springboard for future enemy operations existed than Spain's Pensacola, nominally neutral, but actually long used as a British base. From here came the arms and supplies for the Creeks. Jackson, well aware of the significance of Pensacola, several times reported to the War Department his recommendations that steps be taken against it. But the Administration had no desire to add Spain to the nation's enemies at this moment. Jackson was, in effect, told to be a good boy and contain himself.

Fuming, Jackson watched and as the days dragged on couriers brought him shocking news from the nation's capital. The British had come, indeed, bringing fire and sword to the very heart of the young nation.

Jackson, noting all these things, redoubled his vigilance along his coastal defense. But when a British-Indian attack was launched from Pensacola, upon Fort Bowyer, the American post commanding the entrance to Mobile Bay, he sprang. The garrison beat off the attack before Jackson and his reinforcement arrived. But Jackson didn't stop. Openly and flagrantly invading Spanish territory, he took Pensacola by force of arms November 7. The British there were driven back onto their ships, the Spanish fortifications razed.

His work completed, Jackson marched back to Mobile, calmly leaving to the State Department the chore of answering the King of Spain's screams. Loud as they might be, the matter was settled. Pensacola, when Jackson's troops left, was no longer in any condition for use as a British base. The enemy must look elsewhere.

That, of course, was just what the British were doing. The Gulf coast soon rang with rumors of British sail in the offing, of British intrigues with the Baratarian pirates nestled in the Mississippi delta wastes. That, Jackson felt, indicated New Orleans as the target, a rich prize; and New Orleans was part of his responsibility.

How the enemy would come remained to be seen. Jackson took up a position in readiness. Keeping his regulars—he had two small regiments now—at Mobile, he sent Coffee's brigade of Tennessee mounted riflemen and Mississippi dragoons up to Baton Rouge. Jackson in person pushed on to New Orleans, to stir the well-meaning but weak Governor William C. C. Claiborne into mobilizing the Louisiana militia.

There's a Way

Volatile New Orleans, sprawling along the Mississippi bank, was seething as Jackson rode in, December 2. The British were coming! Committees of safety chattered, banks were closed, hand-wringing merchants wheezed. In the coffee shops rumors flared. Gay blades in gaudy uniforms of the various Creole volunteer militia companies boasted of their intention to do or die. Sad-faced civilians shivered and whispered of a merciless sacking should any resistance be offered; "Beauty and booty!" was a redcoat slogan, they pointed out.

Governor Claiborne fluttered aimlessly with the other solons in the Cabildo, while down in the Place d'Armes below the population flocked and gabbled. In the cathedral the pious prayed; in the riverside slums the drums throbbed; *"Dansez Calinda! Badoum! Badoum!"*

A distracted city, verging on panic, was ripe for mass hysteria. It needed the face slap one gives a hysterical patient. The slender, gray-eyed, grim-lipped man in weatherbeaten Army blues, whose graying sandy hair topped high-templed, tanned features as he doffed his leather cap that morning in the Cabildo, was just the one to give such a slap.

The wonder is not that he did it, but that in the doing he made New Orleans like it. The people of New Orleans, predominantly Latin in origin, notoriously dilettante in character, were foreign in almost every fashion to Jackson's strait-laced North Ireland forebears or his rural upbringing.

Furthermore, New Orleans, although an established community for almost a century now, lacked any deep-rooted patriotic allegiance—it had been under the American flag for only eleven years. During that time it had witnessed the double-dealings of a military governor—Wilkinson—the uproar of the Burr "conspiracy," and the forcible imposition of the English language and of English customs. There was every reason why its Creole population should distrust and misunderstand this harsh, hard-bitten soldier who rode in now from

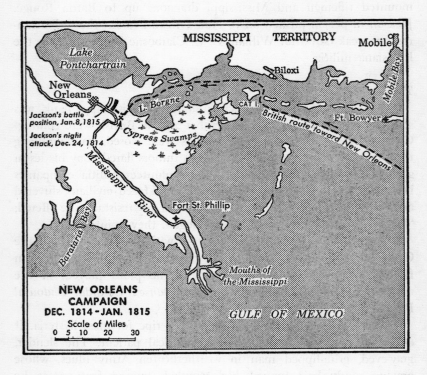

the border bickerings of that still-nebulous and frequently resented overlord, *les États Unis.*

But the man in the long blue Spanish cloak was making himself known. While Claiborne and the legislature were still arguing about calling out the territorial militia, Jackson reviewed and inspected the existing New Orleans volunteer militia companies with a gracious word of praise now and then for their equipment and drill.

His selection of a local militia officer, Major La Carrière Latour—

a competent engineer—to strengthen the old fortifications, was another happy stroke of public relations.

The hot-blooded Creoles drank this sort of thing up. Here, after all, was a general who knew war; who had met successfully both Indian and British. Jackson was here, there, and everywhere, listening to the clacking tongue of both Creole patriot and distracted merchant. He was, it seemed, bent on selling himself to New Orleans, and he knew that time was ticking away.

Actually, he was to have but twelve days beofre the blow fell. The British fleet materialized off Biloxi, and a flotilla of ship's boats crammed with soldiery went paddling up Lake Borgne. On December 14 the expedition overwhelmed the five little gunboats defending the closest sea approach to the city. This was it.

Jackson's reaction was instantaneous. Proclaiming martial law, he sent Claiborne and the legislature packing. "The district's safety must and will be maintained with the best blood of the country." The suspension of the writ of habeas corpus would ensure the separation of "the country's friends from its enemies." Meanwhile couriers rushed to Mobile and Baton Rouge to summon his troops.

From now on the U.S. Army, in the person of Major General Andrew Jackson, was running the city. Movement in or out would be by pass only—neither coward nor traitor would have opportunity to traffic with the enemy.

The slap, resounding, was also galvanic in results. Volunteers come pouring in. Jean Laffite, offering the services of his Baratarian pirates, those "hellish banditti," as Jackson had called them only a few days before, was welcomed; Jackson needed artillerymen. New volunteer units included Lacoste's battalion of "free men of color," and a battery of St. Domingo "men of color."

By December 23, Jackson's concentration was completed. From Mobile had arrived his 7th and 44th Infantry and a detachment of artillery; the regulars who with a handful of marines would constitute the hard core of his troops, just seven hundred strong. Down from Baton Rouge in forced march were the men of Coffee's brigade; the Tennessee mounted riflemen and Mississippi dragoons, nine hundred of them. He had trained them, and fought with them; they could be relied on but not too far. From Natchez had come Carroll, with perhaps a thousand more Tennessee riflemen, sharpshooters but undisciplined and untrained for formal warfare. The New Orleans volunteer militia companies, for what they might be worth, added another five hundred men. On the way, but definitely of doubtful value, were some two thousand additional Louisiana and Kentucky militiamen—a rabble in arms not all of whom would even have arms.

Waiting now for the enemy's next move, the man from Tennessee knew that for the first time in his short but violent military career he would have to go on the defensive, for rumor had it—and rumor was right—that those tall ships off Cat Island in the Gulf were carrying some fourteen thousand troops. Against them, the cream of England's regulars, battle-hardened and flushed with victory against Napoleon's best, he held fifty-one hundred men, 80 per cent of whom had never fought before; the remainder accustomed only to border fighting in the wilderness. Nor, for that matter, had he, their leader, ever encountered regulars in force. But one thing he knew, from hard experience and from the news that had come down from the North; no scratch team such as his could ever stand in open battle against these British regulars.

The vexed question, then, was where and how he could elect to make his stand; or even if the election could be his. Certainly it should be behind entrenchments; in some fixed position, whose flanks could not be readily turned, and from which his artillery and riflemen, protected from bayonet charges, could make their firepower felt. Everything depended upon the direction of the enemy's advance.

And that same day the British not only gave him the clue, but surrendered to him the boon that every good commander hopes for: the choice of battleground. Their advance element, Keane's division, twelve hundred strong, pushing from Lake Borgne into the Bayou Bienvenue, generally east of New Orleans, worked its way south and west to debouch on an open plain skirting the Mississippi, seven miles south of the city.

Actually, had Keane been willing to take the chance, he might have had New Orleans that same day, for he had captured the American militia patrols along the bayou, and the surprise was complete. But luck works both ways. The Creole part-time soldiers he had bagged told their captors there were eighteen thousand Americans in the city. Keane's men were exhausted from their strugglings through the marshy bayou land. So he bivouacked and waited reinforcement.

Just below the city, athwart the direction the enemy must take to enter, ran the Rodriguez Canal, an abandoned waterway from three to five feet deep that cut from the Mississippi across the thousand-yard-wide area of level, cultivated land and into the dense cypress swamp masking the rest of the terrain all the way east to the tip of Lake Borgne. There it was; a defensive position made to order, complete with moat, unturnable flanks, and in front a clear field of fire.

Jackson, concentrating his forces behind the canal, issued orders for an immediate strengthening of the position. Not that he intended for a moment to await the enemy's convenience. That night, even while the rest of his troops and enthusiastic city folk were hustling every bit of material they could lay their hands on to construct ramparts behind the canal, he hit the British bivouac, hoping that surprise and swamp-fighting ability at night would make up for the otherwise overwhelming disciplinary supremacy of the enemy. If lucky he might rock them off their feet before they consolidated their position.

Coffee's riflemen, fighting on foot, pressed through the swampy tangle on the British right, while the regulars, led by Jackson in person, hit across the plain. A gunboat sneaked down near the levee on the enemy left to add its bombardment to the surprise. For a few moments the attack was successful, but Peninsular War veterans were not men to stampede easily. Keane's troops rallied and their counterattack drove the Americans back. That was that.

But the American assault convinced the enemy that an enterprising commander opposed them, so no further advance was attempted until their strength could be built up for a crushing blow. The respite Jackson used to good advantage. Earth, timbers, and cotton bales were piled helter-skelter behind the canal. Across the river a battery of naval guns was emplaced to sweep the open plain in flanking fire. Behind the ramparts back of the canal the defenders were aligned in an enlacement of regulars and amateur soldiers calculated to give the best results, both physical and psychological.

Adjacent to the river on the levee were the Orleans Rifles—militia

—stiffened by a battery of artillery manned by Mississippi dragoons. Next came the 7th Infantry and a battalion of Creole volunteer militia companies picturesque in name and uniform—Carabineers, Dragoons, Louisiana Blues, Francs, and Chasseurs. In their midst lay two big long twenty-four pounder ship's guns, manned by artillery-men who had served them well before—Laffite's swarthy Baratarian pirates, commanded by his lieutenants Dominique You and Beluche.

The New Orleans volunteer battalion of "free men of color" and the St. Domingo mulattos came next, together with a battery manned by gun crews from the U.S. schooner *Carolina*, and on their left, as leaven, stood the 44th Infantry and a regular artillery detachment.

This line reached more than halfway across the front. Next came Carroll's Tennessee riflemen, seasoned by another regular artillery detachment and a handful of marines, with a clear field of fire before them. The left of the line, in the tangled cypress swamp morass, was held by Coffee's Tennesseans, dismounted; well used to fighting as they would have to now, knee-deep in water behind their log emplacements.

One lingers on this alignment, as evidence of a leadership definitely aware of the respective strengths and weaknesses of the force available. The local militia and volunteers, comparatively safe behind their shelters, would be spiritually bolstered by knowing they had trained soldiers beside them. In any event, the most unreliable troops were placed where they could do the least harm if they broke and fled; the Kentuckians far behind the main position, the Louisiana militia on the west bank.

Let's look southward now, where Major General Sir Edward Pakenham's expeditionary force was slowly building up to do a job rapidly becoming more and more confused. In the first place, the British were unable to obtain accurate indications of American strength or positions. Their patrols were shot down by the accurate fire of the American riflemen, whose balls carried twice as far as their own muskets. What garbled information they could receive from the few frightened countrymen they captured was, as usual in such cases, highly exaggerated. Even the elements were against them; the miasmic fogs of the season frequently blanked visibility.

Tentative operations to develop Jackson's position were repulsed; Pakenham, who came ashore December 24, found his troops in a plain locked in by rivers and swamps, without adequate communications and unable to maneuver. To get information he would have to fight for it.

It was the irony of fate that while Pakenham was taking his first glance at the field, American and British commissioners in Ghent were signing a treaty of peace.

On December 28, Pakenham tried a reconnaissance in force, moving up the plain in two columns. Such heavy fire was encountered that he withdrew, with the meager knowledge that he faced an entrenched position too strong to be carried by immediate assault. Certainly, to be successful an attack would first have to reduce that battery on the west bank whose galling flank fire raked the plain. He decided to make the effort.

His plan was to bring his artillery forward into earthwork batteries, then to make a frontal assault. A secondary effort would cross the Mississippi by boat, attacking simultaneously, to capture the flanking battery. The main attack, by Keane's brigade, would strike straight up the levee at the right flank of the American position, while Gibbs's brigade would drive along the edge of the swamp to turn the American left. His third brigade, Lambert's, he held in reserve.

No attempt was made, apparently, to probe the swamp by any preliminary reconnaissance.

No one, of course, will ever know exactly what went through Pakenham's mind. He was an experienced officer, had been one of Wellington's most trusted subordinates (he was also his brother-in-law), and had played a gallant part in the victory of Salamanca, leading his division in a series of impetuous charges against the best troops of France.

One might conclude, then, that despite Wellington's canny admonition (made just before Salamanca) not to fight a battle "unless under advantageous circumstances," Pakenham had become imbued with the spirit of the offensive, and was so confident in the ability of his veterans to whip Americans that he permitted himself to give battle under the most disadvantageous conditions.

Meanwhile, of course, the defenders' spirits rose every day the

British delayed attack. Soldiers and townsfolk delved to make the fortifications stronger, while the Mississippi dragoons made almost daily harassing dashes across the front of the British outposts.

The assault was set for January 8, the boats for the British cross-river attack being brought up from Lake Borgne, through the bayous and an additional canal, hastily cut. Actually, this was so difficult that only a fraction of the boats necessary got through. As a result only one third of the flanking force ever crossed the river that morning, and that too late, as it turned out, to affect the issue.

The impatient British commander would wait no longer, however. His assault columns moved out into the wet, slippery plain through a clinging mist. Along the levee three companies dashed up to the American position, actually got across the canal. But they were unsupported, and the 7th Infantry drove them back over the cotton-bale ramparts (which explains the cotton bale now borne on the coat of arms of the 7th to this day).

Behind a cloud of skirmishers Gibbs's brigade advanced in column —three regiments, echeloned, skirting the swamp, while another— the West Indian—supposedly capable of negotiating such terrain, worked through the cypress. But the West Indians failed dismally when they reached Coffee's Tennesseans, while the rest of Gibbs's brigade, caught between the cross fire of the artillery in front and the battery across the river, were badly shaken even before they came under the sights of the long rifles of Carroll's men. The British artillery was speedily dominated by the accurate fire of American guns.

To make matters worse, scaling ladders and fascines for filling the canal were slow in coming up and the attack faltered. The Tennessee riflemen laid the redcoats down in swaths, and Gibbs's brigade recoiled. Pakenham, a shining mark on his big black charger, came galloping up to rally them and lead a second charge. A rifle bullet spilled him from the saddle, mortally wounded. Gibbs, the brigade commander, went down beside him. Only a handful of men —the Royal Scots—ever reached the American ramparts. Keane, on the British left, led one more regiment diagonally across the field to support the advance, but he too went down and the entire assault collapsed.

It was all over in forty-five minutes. Some twenty-one hundred

British were down, killed or wounded; the remainder fled beyond range. As the American fire died away, five hundred more Britishers caught helplessly under the guns threw down their arms in surrender. And as the battle on the plain ceased, a flare of musketry from far across the river ironically heralded the British capture, all too late, of the battery there; its militia supports were streaming up-river in head-long flight.

There was, of course, no counterattack; no pursuit. Jackson's iron hand kept his troops behind their breastworks. He knew all too well what happens to raw troops launched in pursuit of a disciplined foe. He had saved New Orleans; he had broken the back of the flower of the British army. Its cost: seven Americans dead and six wounded. A week later the British army sullenly retraced its steps through the marshland to its boats on Lake Borgne.

If there is to be an epilogue to this, it should also answer a question: Why did not the British fleet simply sail up the Mississippi River and take New Orleans under their powerful guns?

The answer lay sixty-five miles downstream from New Orleans; at Fort St. Philip, just completed. There two little companies of regular artillery and two of infantry blocked the river approach and withstood for eight days a bombardment by all the light ships the Royal Navy could bring up: a sloop of war, a brig, a schooner, and two bomb-ketches. They did not pass. Jackson's confidence in his regulars had again been justified.

CHAPTER VI ☆ ☆ ☆ "*Old Rough and Ready*"

The enemy was twice his strength; so he attacked. Having driven the foe back decisively, he attacked again next day and this time won a complete victory. In so doing he was accomplishing the Administration's objective.

But Brigadier General Zachary Taylor, in his victories at Palo Alto and Resaca de la Palma, May 8–9, 1846, was doing more than that. He was furthering both a tradition and a legend; the proud tradition of the Regular Army's combat efficiency, and his own personal legend. The first he accomplished on a shoestring; the second, unfortunately, has become blurred.

For no good reason other than his nickname and his personal idiosyncrasies, Taylor has come down in history as a Kentucky backwoodsman and country bumpkin. His victories (he had no defeats) have been credited to the skill of his subordinates and his later election to the Presidency of the United States chalked up as the political thimble-rigging of smart politicians seeking a figurehead.

Even in his own times, according to Army lore, Taylor's informality of attire was sometimes misleading. Two young second lieutenants just out of West Point, arriving at Fort Smith, Arkansas, then a department headquarters, during the early 1840's, met a nondescript individual whom they mistook for a local farmer, and spent a pleasant half hour joshing the "old hayseed." They parted from him with a merry admonition to "Give our love to the old woman and the gals."

Having reported to the post adjutant, the youngsters then donned full dress to make the prescribed formal call on the commanding general at his quarters. There their acquaintance of the afternoon, now in full-dress uniform also, received them politely, and gravely presented them to Mrs. Taylor and his daughter with the introduction: "Here are the old woman and the gal."

It is not surprising, then, that against such a rustic backdrop the real Taylor has been overlooked by many historians. Actually, "Old Rough and Ready," or "Old Zach," as he was also dubbed, who was the antithesis of the spit-and-polish officer and who preferred rumpled civilian clothing to an epauleted dress coat, was throughout his career a stickler for training and discipline. So far as he was concerned, the soldier had but one objective: success in battle. To that end Taylor took advantage of every opportunity that garrison and camp life afforded, to drill and instruct his officers and men.

Taylor was born in Virginia on November 24, 1784, of a respected colonial family of the Old Dominion; his first cousin was patrician James Madison, fourth President of the United States. After his family moved to Kentucky—then part of Virginia—young Zachary's formal schooling was sketchy, but there is clear evidence, including his personal and official correspondence, that he was a well-read, literate man, educated at least to the level of most men of good family of his time.

Commissioned a lieutenant in the Regular Army in 1808, Taylor's active military career would run, with but one brief interruption, through thirty-nine years and four wars. He won the first brevet promotion for gallantry ever awarded in the United States Army, for his successful defense of Fort Harrison, near the site of Terre Haute, Indiana, in September 1812. Although he had no opportunity to take part in any of the principal battles of the War of 1812, by this victory and by his success in commanding expeditions against the British along the Mississippi River, young Major Taylor contributed greatly to American success in retaining the Northwest Territory.

His military career prior to the Mexican War was typical of the officers of his time. After one year of civilian life, immediately at the close of the War of 1812, he returned to the Army he loved. Most of his subsequent service was spent at lonesome, often dreary, frontier posts. When not engaged in drilling, or in occasional expeditions into the Indian country, he spent his spare time in reading and gardening. When opportunity offered, he visited his family property in Kentucky, or the plantations he later purchased in Louisiana and Mississippi.

In 1832 he commanded the only Regular Army regiment participating in the Black Hawk War and delivered the final blow in the Battle of the Bad Axe. In that affair Taylor led his command to the attack through water up to his chest.

A little more than five years after the Battle of the Bad Axe, Colonel Taylor was again fighting Indians, this time the Seminoles in Florida. On Christmas Day, 1837, he led his brigade of volunteers and regulars through the swamps to attack the Seminole stronghold near Lake Okeechobee. His experiences in the War of 1812 and the Black Hawk War had caused Taylor to doubt the steadiness of non-regulars, and so he decided to adapt Morgan's Cowpens tactics to his situation. He advanced in two lines, and when the volunteers in front had had enough, they fell back, allowing the steady, disciplined regulars to press home the climactic attack of the last pitched battle of the Seminole War. Though it dragged on for several more years, the Indians never forgot the lesson taught them by Taylor and his regulars, and never again risked a full-scale engagement.

The end would have come sooner, if Taylor had had his way. Breveted to the rank of brigadier general as a result of his victory at Lake Okeechobee, he had been placed in command of all forces in Florida. Dividing the territory into districts, he began the systematic elimination of resistance. In little over a year the end of our longest, bloodiest, and costliest Indian war was in sight. But the War Department, attributing the peaceful conditions to Indian docility rather than to the effectiveness of Taylor's military control, ordered him to cease all active operations and to withdraw his district garrisons. The Indians rose at once. Two years of toil and strife having gone for naught, Taylor had to start once more the painstaking pacification of the country. When he came down with fever, the War Department reluctantly approved his request for relief from the Florida command on the grounds of ill health, in 1840.

The next five years were spent quietly by General Taylor in the southwest. After a short tour of garrison duty at Baton Rouge, Louisiana, he was placed in command of the frontier district comprising the present states of Arkansas, Oklahoma, and parts of Louisiana and Missouri. His fairness in protecting the Indians from unscrupulous frontier hoodlums won him the respect of the red men, and the resulting peaceful conditions made easier his duties of safeguarding the border settlements.

At the age of fifty-nine, Taylor found himself ordered to Texas in July, 1845, with the vaguest of instructions and a force of fifteen hundred regulars to carry them out. The United States, annexing the new Republic of Texas, had with it inherited a long-drawn-out boundary dispute. Mexico claimed the Nueces River as its northern frontier. But Texas—and the United States—asserted the Rio Grande River, a hundred miles further south, was the boundary. Taylor was ordered to establish himself "on or near the Rio Grande," in a position favorable to the health of his command, and was told to "avoid any acts of aggression."

Not wishing to prejudice his nation's claim to the disputed territory or, on the other hand, to precipitate war unnecessarily by a provocative advance, Taylor selected as his base the village of Corpus Christi on the south bank of the Nueces, where it empties into the Gulf of Mexico. The spot, just within the debatable zone, was healthy. It was far enough from the Rio Grande to prevent the possible envelopment of his small forces before reinforcements could arrive. Here he waited orders and developments, while reconnoitering the zone and drilling his troops.

Reinforcements were not long in arriving, and by October, Taylor's little army comprised more than thirty-five hundred men—almost exactly two-thirds of the entire active strength of the United States Army at that time! Taylor was also authorized—but only if the Mexicans initiated hostilities by crossing the Rio Grande "with considerable force"—to call for volunteers from Texas and the other Southern states. In such an event he was also authorized, at his discretion, and should he "have sufficient force," to cross the Rio Grande into Mexico to "disperse or capture the forces assembling to invade Texas."

Obviously much was expected of him, and large-scale and long-

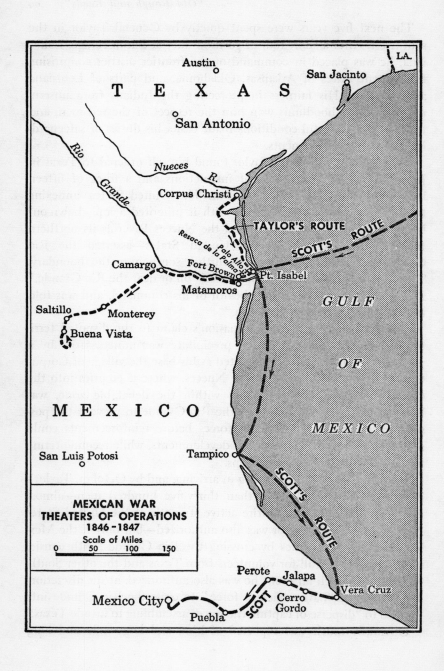

MEXICAN WAR
THEATERS OF OPERATIONS
1846-1847
Scale of Miles
0   50   100   150

range operations were contemplated by the government if war should break out with Mexico. Yet while Taylor was authorized to obtain volunteers *after* the initiation of hostilities in order to carry out such operations, he was not permitted to increase his puny force in order to make reasonable preparations in organization and training. All that he could do, therefore, was to try to increase the already high state of training of his regulars. And so for six months at Corpus Christi, as young Lieutenant George G. Meade—later hero of Gettysburg—wrote, activities were "nothing but drill and parades, and your ears are filled all day with drumming and fifeing."

Early in 1846, diplomatic negotiations with Mexico having failed, Taylor was ordered to move to a position closer to the Rio Grande. In March, therefore, ignoring Mexican threats, Taylor marched his little force to the north bank of the Rio Grande, opposite the Mexican town of Matamoros, where a Mexican army was gathering. Here, on the riverbank, he built a fortified camp, establishing a supply base a few miles away on the Gulf of Mexico at Point Isabel.

On April 24 a large Mexican raiding party crossed to the north bank of the river and ambushed an American cavalry detachment. Taylor considered this an act of war and immediately sent to the governors of Texas and Louisiana asking each to furnish him with four regiments of volunteers. But he was forced to fight before these reinforcements could arrive.

On April 30, Mexican General Mariano Arista led his army of six thousand men across the river about five miles below Matamoros, threatening Taylor's line of communication with Point Isabel. Leaving a portion of his force in the fortified camp, Taylor moved quickly with the remainder to protect and entrench his threatened base. Arista, confident of his superiority in strength, took up a position between the river and Point Isabel, near a little place called Palo Alto, in front of the forest area bordering the river. To lure Taylor into battle, he began a bombardment of the camp.

Having replenished his supplies and being sure of the security of his base, Taylor accepted the challenge. On May 8, with some twenty-two hundred men available for battle, he moved against Arista, who had about four thousand men at Palo Alto.

Taylor's troops moved in the early afternoon sun across a level, high-grassed plain, dotted with thickets, chaparral, bogs, and ponds; the infantry in regimental columns, the artillery between them. Arista, confident, waited them, his infantry drawn up, his guns in the intervals between regiments, and his cavalry on both flanks. The Mexican guns opened while the Americans were still out of range.

Taylor advanced to a half-mile distance from his enemy, then deployed his infantry into line. The guns, going into battery, like the Mexicans, in the intervals between regiments, opened fire with stunning accuracy on the dense masses of Mexican infantry. Arista hurriedly attempted several unco-ordinated attacks, both by infantry and cavalry, only to be repulsed each time. First he tried the American right, then shifted to the left flank. Each time Taylor's artillery cut swaths in his masses, while the steady musketry of the Americans then brought the disordered attackers up short.

Taylor, whose intention was to close with the bayonet, now advanced his right flank, covering the road to his base. But the sun was going down and he decided to wait till morning to push his attack home. The Americans bivouacked on the field, while the Mexicans pulled back into the chaparral.

Only five Americans had been killed, and forty-three wounded. Arista's losses were estimated at four hundred in all, mostly caused by artillery fire. It was far from being a crippling loss, but psychologically the steadiness and discipline of the American infantry had shocked the Mexicans, while the artillery marksmanship terrified them. Arista, now convinced his troops could not stand up against the Americans in the open, withdrew in the night to take up a defensive position in a wooded area five miles to the south.

Here Taylor's reconnaissance found him next day, at Resaca de la Palma, where the Rio Grande in former times had gashed the terrain into several ravines, now dry. One of these, the Resaca de Guerrero, lay athwart the road. Behind this breastwork provided by nature, Arista had skillfully emplaced his infantry and artillery. The position was good, his guns were well sited.

Taylor, who had never had any doubts as to the capabilities of himself and his highly trained regulars, was elated at the results of Palo Alto.

Overruling the recommendation of some of his senior subordinates, who were afraid that superior skill and discipline would be neutralized in the thick woods ahead, Taylor determined to press after the defeated foe.

Preceded by a line of skirmishers, the column advanced steadily along the road until halted by heavy fire from Mexican artillery and infantry concealed by the heavy growth of trees and bushes in the ravine as well as along its banks. Arista had chosen well, and with good reason he considered his position to be "impregnable."

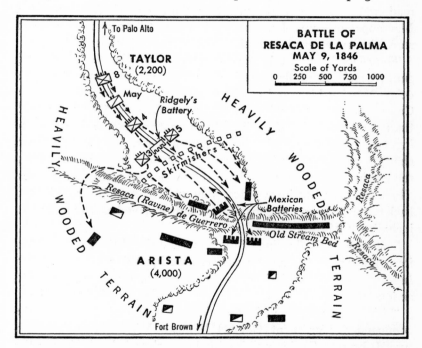

Taylor hesitated not a moment. He assumed personal command in the center, where the road approached the enemy position, while the remainder of his army deployed on both sides in compliance with the plan of action he had directed previously. He ordered up the leading artillery battery—Randolph Ridgely's—to engage the enemy artillery emplaced in a clearing in front of the ravine and beside the road. Once more accurate American artillery fire dominated the enemy, and the Mexican gunners quickly withdrew across the ravine, leaving some of their guns. Ridgely pressed forward, but now heavy musket fire from enemy infantry at the edge of the clearing forced him to stop, and the enemy cannon emplaced in the woods and ravine began exacting a heavy toll.

Taylor saw that the American skirmish line could not make headway to give the guns the protection they needed, and so he turned to order the nearest unit, a cavalry squadron commanded by Captain Charles A. May, to capture the enemy artillery at the bend of the road, where it crossed the ravine. Making a quick reconnaissance, May apparently was doubtful of his ability to cross the clearing to reach the enemy guns, and asked Taylor for further instructions.

The general, alarmed by the casualties being taken by his exposed gunners, still manfully engaging the enemy, was annoyed at this delay. Waving his sword at the enemy guns, he shouted, "Charge, Captain, *nolens volens!*" Whether or not Captain May understood the Latin version of "willy-nilly," he promptly obeyed orders. Galloping past Ridgely and his cheering cannoneers, May and his men charged across the clearing and past the ravine, temporarily silencing the enemy guns as they cut down the cannoneers with their swords. Then, more or less in disorder, May and his men turned, charged back through the enemy guns, killing many men and capturing several, including a Mexican general.

The temporary silencing of the guns, and the shaking of the Mexican position by the cavalry charge, gave breathing space. The 8th Infantry, last of Taylor's units on the road, came swinging into action.

"Take those guns, and by God keep them!" roared Taylor to its commander, Lieutenant Colonel William W. Belknap. The 8th surged forward, Taylor walking his horse close behind. Enemy fire from the banks of the ravine increased. With balls "falling like hailstones" around the general, a staff officer urged Taylor to withdraw to safer ground. But Taylor had his own remedy for that.

"Let's ride a little nearer. The balls will fall behind," he remarked.

Meanwhile the American infantry on both flanks had pressed forward through the thick underbrush, forcing their way into and beyond the ravine, despite fierce Mexican resistance. This was accomplished without artillery support, for only in the narrow strip along the road, and the clearing where it crossed the ravine, was there room enough for cannon to be employed. But the superior discipline, energy, and leadership of the Americans, outnumbered three to one, carried all before them.

American bayonets were twinkling amidst the trees. A unit of the 3rd Infantry actually reached Arista's tent, behind the enemy position. The Mexican army began to disintegrate. Arista tried to lead a last-ditch cavalry charge down the road at the American center but saw his infantry streaming away and instead turned his lancers to the Rio Grande and safety. His army had ceased to exist as a fighting force.

Ulysses S. Grant, then a second lieutenant, who was there, summed it all up later in his *Memoirs*: "General Taylor had a small army, but it was composed exclusively of regular troops, under the best of drill and discipline. Every officer from the highest to the lowest, was educated in his profession, not at West Point necessarily, but in the camp, in garrison and many of them in Indian wars. . . . A better army, man for man, probably never faced an enemy than the one commanded by General Taylor in the earliest two engagements of the Mexican War."

American casualties at Resaca de la Palma were 122 men killed, wounded, and missing; Arista lost at least 700. The remainder of the completely disorganized mass, perhaps 5,000 strong, got across the Rio Grande during that night and the following day. Taylor did not pursue. For that he has been criticized severely, and perhaps rightly. However, it must be remembered that his orders from Washington were "to take more than ordinary care." His remark in a letter to his son-in-law perhaps reveals his point of view.

"The war," he wrote, "I have no doubt is completely brought to a close on this side the Rio Grande."

Taylor's interminable drilling and marching of the past seven months had paid off. His professional army was a smoothly working machine. Palo Alto demonstrated the ascendancy of American artillery. At Resaca de la Palma the American infantry and cavalry established a moral superiority over the enemy which was to endure throughout the war.

In these two battles, as well as in his later cautious, deliberate preparations for crossing the Rio Grande, "Old Zach" clearly revealed his limitations as well as his capabilities as a leader. His was no flair for brilliant strategic movements, and the success of his tactics was due, in large measure, to the spirit and reliability of his officers and men. He had displayed a cool, calm courage which enhanced the already excellent spirit of confident, well-trained troops. In both battles his plan was simple, straightforward, and sound, relying upon the efficiency and firepower of his artillery in combination with the maneuverability and fighting capabilities of his infantry and cavalry, to drive numerically superior enemy forces from the field.

Two days after Resaca de la Palma, Taylor went to Point Isabel for a conference with Commodore Conner, commanding the naval squadron of the mouth of the Rio Grande, for the purpose of co-ordinating naval support for the coming crossing of the river. Knowing Conner to be a very formal, punctilious observer of protocol, Taylor attired himself—for the first and last time during the campaign—in his full-dress uniform as a brigadier general. Conner, out of deference for the known simplicity and informality of the Army man, came ashore in his oldest civilian clothes. Both officers were annoyed and embarrassed; their staffs were undoubtedly amused.

On May 18, Taylor seized Matamoros, on the south of the Rio Grande, and stayed there for two months waiting for reinforcements and for wagons which the Quartermaster Department was supposed to send him to enable him to move inland to Monterey. Reinforcements arrived in embarrassing profusion— but no wagons. "Old Zach" collected what he could from the nearby countryside and began his movement inland, leaving most of the newly arrived volunteers at the mouth of the Rio Grande, for further training. After a delay at Camargo, the American army reached the vicinity of Monterey on September 19. Taylor now had six thousand men, almost equally divided between regulars and volunteers. His opponent, General Pedro de Ampudia, held the city of Monterey with seven thousand Mexican regulars and about three thousand militia. Taylor promptly attacked, and a bitter three-day battle ensued. The Americans, their attacks not too well co-ordinated, stormed fort after fort, house after house, fighting their way to the central part of the old stone city, which Ampudia had converted into a veritable citadel. Early on the 24th the Mexican commander requested surrender terms. Taylor, realizing that it would take a major effort to complete the conquest of the inner defenses of the town, agreed. His volunteers were by now largely demoralized, and the regulars, who had borne the brunt of the street fighting, badly needed a rest. Further, he was running short of supplies, particularly ammunition.

Consequently his ultimatum to Ampudia, when the Mexican tried to prolong the negotiations, was largely a bluff—which Ampudia did not call. Taylor allowed the Mexicans to march out of the surrendered city with the honors of war, and agreed to an armistice of eight weeks, "or until the orders or instructions of the respective governments can be received." Taylor wanted to give his army a rest, but he also wanted to retain his freedom of action if the U.S. Government demanded further advance.

So, when Democratic President Polk disapproved the armistice terms which had been made by a Whig general—by now being suggested as a Presidential candidate—Taylor notified the enemy, and resumed his advance on November 13. On the 16th he entered without opposition the city of Saltillo, capital of the Mexican state of Coahuila.

The Administration now wished him to push on into the heart of Mexico, but Taylor pointed out that a three-hundred-mile desert lay between Saltillo and the next large town to the south, San Luis Potosí, and that Mexico City was another three hundred miles further south. Simple though an advance might appear on the maps of Washington amateur strategists, Taylor realized that with his line of communications already strained to the breaking point, it was doubtful if his army could actually complete a march across the desert. Certainly the survivors of any such ordeal would be totally incapable of battle at the far end, and he knew that a Mexican army of twenty thousand men was already gathered in the vicinity of San Luis Potosí. He recommended to Washington, therefore, that if it were necessary to capture Mexico City in order to assure victory, such an operation be carried out by way of Vera Cruz. Interestingly enough, the Army's general in chief, Winfield Scott, had already proposed a similar plan.

So, hoping that the military—and thus political—laurels gained by Whig Taylor would be canceled by Whig Scott, President Polk reluctantly appointed Scott to command of forces in Mexico, and authorized the proposed invasion by way of Vera Cruz.

In order to have sufficient trained forces for such an operation, Scott knew that he would need most of Taylor's veterans—particularly the regulars. He also knew that taking these men away from Taylor would leave "Old Rough and Ready" in a dangerously exposed position at Saltillo, at least until his own invading force had captured Vera Cruz and was approaching the capital city of Mexico. But the risk was unavoidable. Realizing that the Mexican army concentrated at San Luis Potosí was now commanded by the newly installed President, General Antonio L. Santa Anna, a man of considerable vigor and ability, Scott advised Taylor to withdraw to Monterey and, if necessary, back to the Rio Grande, should any substantial Mexican threat develop north of the desert.

Taylor understood and approved Scott's strategy, but he would have been less than human if he had not resented the necessity of giving up his veterans to another man to lead to victory. Although he was left with only 5,000 men—all untried volunteers except for 517 regular artillerymen and cavalrymen—he rejected the idea of withdrawal, and in fact pushed almost 20 miles south of Saltillo to the very edge of the desert.

It was now January, 1847, and General Santa Anna, having received trustworthy information regarding Scott's plans, realized that it would be almost two months before the Americans could move a fleet and army to Vera Cruz. He therefore determined to adopt the very plan Scott had feared: the concentration of his entire army of twenty thousand men against Taylor's exposed recruits. On January 28 he began his advance, hoping to surprise "Old Zach" south of Saltillo.

If Taylor had been foolhardy—some say "pigheaded"—in his decision to stay where he was, he was too good a soldier to let himself be surprised. On February 21, as Santa Anna's army came in sight, Taylor withdrew to a previously reconnoitered defensive

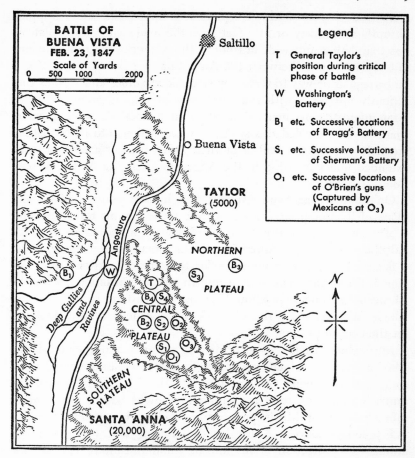

BATTLE OF
BUENA VISTA
FEB. 23, 1847
Scale of Yards
0   500   1000   2000

Saltillo

Legend

T General Taylor's
position during critical
phase of battle

W Washington's
Battery

B₁ etc. Successive locations
of Bragg's Battery

S₁ etc. Successive locations
of Sherman's Battery

O₁ etc. Successive locations
of O'Brien's guns
(Captured by
Mexicans at O₃)

Buena Vista

TAYLOR
(5000)

NORTHERN

PLATEAU

CENTRAL
PLATEAU

SOUTHERN
PLATEAU

SANTA ANNA
(20,000)

position near the hacienda of Buena Vista, less than eight miles
south of Saltillo, where the road traversed a narrow valley, about a
mile wide.

The key to the American position was a place called the Angostura, or narrows, where the rugged spurs stretching down from the
mountains forced the road to pass through a defile only forty feet
wide. Just west of the road was a network of gullies, twenty feet or
more deep, carved out of the foot of the steep western slope by a
mountain torrent. East of the road the mountain spurs took on an
unusual, plateaulike formation—extending westward like flat fingers

from the slopes of the steep eastern mountain, and dropping abruptly some forty or fifty feet near the road's edge. This plateau, less than half a mile wide in front of the American position, widened out to over a mile between the Angostura and Buena Vista. Rocky and irregular, it was traversed by steep-sided gullies and ravines that seriously interfered with the passage of horses and guns and made even infantry movements difficult. Two ravines, deeper and wider than the rest, divided this stony, elevated region into three distinct areas. It was on the central of these three plateau areas, with one extended finger reaching to the Angostura, that the American position was based.

On February 22 Santa Anna found himself confronted by this "Pass of Thermopylae." To gain time to deploy his forces, and for a wide-sweeping cavalry force of fifteen hundred men to reach Saltillo, in rear of the Americans, Santa Anna sent a message, under a flag of truce, calling upon Taylor to surrender. After Taylor declined, there was some skirmishing in the late afternoon, with the Mexicans gaining a position high on the eastern mountain from which they overlooked the left flank of the American army deployed on the central plateau.

Meanwhile Taylor learned of the turning movement of the Mexican cavalry, which was marching through passes several miles to the east. Leaving General John E. Wool in command of the army, Taylor rode back to Saltillo that night with a regiment of infantry (the 1st Mississippi, commanded by his son-in-law, Colonel Jefferson Davis), a cavalry detachment and three guns, to arrange for protection of his line of communications. Leaving the guns and two companies of infantry at Saltillo, "Old Zach" returned to the army early the next morning. But even before he could leave the city, the sound of guns told him the battle had begun.

The Battle of Buena Vista was undoubtedly the most confused and most complicated engagement in which American troops have participated. It is impossible to understand the battle, or Taylor's part in it, without following it on the map, phase by phase.

The initial Mexican attack was in two columns. One, marching down the road toward the Angostura was smashed and repulsed in disorder by Major John M. Washington's artillery battery, supported by Captain Braxton Bragg's battery positioned on the far right flank of the American army. The right-hand column, however, was more successful, sweeping from the southern plateau, driving the volunteer regiments of the American left flank off the field across the northern plateau. Their advance in the center was slowed, however, by an American artillery detachment of three guns under Lieutenant John Paul Jones O'Brien, allowing time for artillery and infantry units on the right flank to move over and establish a new position near the Angostura on the central plateau.

At this moment Taylor arrived on the field. Having observed the Mexican right-hand column pressing after the demoralized left flank of his army, he had left Jefferson Davis' 1st Mississippi to delay the enemy on the northern plateau. He then sent an Indiana regiment to join the Mississippians. The attackers were repulsed and Taylor was now satisfied that the initial setbacks had been retrieved.

But Santa Anna, sensing an opportunity to destroy Taylor's entire army if he could turn the left flank, poured reinforcements of infantry and cavalry onto the northern plateau. "Old Rough and Ready" immediately dispatched two batteries of artillery (Bragg's and Thomas W. Sherman's) to reinforce the two regiments he had holding that flank. Arriving in the nick of time, these batteries joined the outnumbered infantrymen in smashing a massed charge of Mexican cavalry. The Americans, tricked by a feigned surrender parley under a flag of truce, allowed the bulk of these demoralized Mexicans to join Santa Anna's main body near the juncture of the central and southern plateaus.

Seeing that the Mexicans were continuing the battle elsewhere on the field, Taylor now ordered a general advance of his troops on the central plateau. Fortunately for Taylor, Santa Anna had allowed his right wing to be smashed without co-ordinated attacks but he still had a three-to-one superiority in force, and at least a quarter of his army had not yet been engaged at all. And the Mexican commander had taken advantage of the lull to emplace a great body of troops, supported by several artillery batteries, out of sight of the Americans in the ravine between the central and southern plateaus. As the Americans advanced along the central plateau, the Mexican artillery and infantry suddenly struck them by surprise and with overwhelming force from the flank.

Despite the efforts of their officers, most units of the three volunteer infantry regiments broke and ran. As the Mexicans charged, the rest of the American infantry fled, leaving only O'Brien and his three guns—and General Taylor with his staff—in front of six thousand or more advancing Mexicans. Slowed for a moment by O'Brien's valiant stand, the enemy engulfed the gallant artillerymen and swept down the plateau toward the imperturbable American general. Taylor sat there on his horse, in a characteristic pose, half sideways on his saddle, left boot hooked over the pommel, his right hand—holding his drawn sword—resting on the cantle.

Fire from Washington's guns slowed down the left flank of the onrushing Mexicans, but most of them were out of range of the American guns situated below the plateau at the Angostura. With the enemy not more than three hundred yards away, there occurred one of the most dramatic scenes in the history of war. Responding to Taylor's urgent orders, the batteries of Bragg and Sherman galloped from the north plateau, past the infantry milling in confusion in the rear, and with guns and limbers careening madly as they jounced across the rocky ground, swept into position right beside the American general. As the Mexicans came within musket range —less than a hundred yards—Taylor turned and spoke quietly to Captain Bragg, who was standing a few feet away as his men prepared to fire. There was no recorder present to take down the general's words, but according to tradition he said: "A little more grape [grapeshot], Captain Bragg." The best recollection of others present however, has "Old Zach" snapping "Double-shot your guns and give 'em hell!"

And that they did. The Mexican line faltered and shivered under the impact of the rapid and accurate fire of the thirteen artillery pieces, now all that was left of the center of the American line— less than two hundred men against six thousand. As the enemy wavered, their officers urging them forward, suddenly they were struck in the flank and rear by the two regiments—perhaps a thousand men—that Taylor had placed on the northern plateau. The Mexicans fled southward, and the exhausted Americans held the field. The battle was over.

Buena Vista was the last battle of Zachary Taylor. One of the most remarkable conflicts in all the annals of war, the victory was due entirely to the inspiring courage and coolness of the American commander, and his ability to make the most of the materials available to him—and particularly his superb, omnipresent artillerymen. It is not easy to assess the leadership of Taylor. Universally idolized by his men, he was respected by most officers who served under him, but despised by some. It seemed impossible to these few—and to many subsequent historians who have read their comments—that a man who looked, acted and talked like a farmer could be at the same time keen, intelligent, literate, and a soundly indoctrinated professional. Some of the men who served under him went on to even greater pinnacles of military fame and glory. One of these has written perhaps the best evaluation of Zachary Taylor.

General Taylor was not an officer to trouble the administration much with his demands, but was inclined to do the best he could with the means given him. . . . No soldier could face either danger or responsibility more calmly than he. These are qualities more rarely found than genius or physical courage. General Taylor never made any great show or parade, either of uniform or retinue. In dress he was probably too plain, rarely wearing anything in the field to indicate his rank, or even that he was an officer; but he was known to every soldier in the army, and was respected by all. . . .

He moved about the field in which he was operating to see through his own eyes the situation. Often he would be without staff officers, and when he was accompanied by them there was no prescribed order in which they followed. He was very much given to sit his horse side-ways—with both feet on one side—particularly on the battlefield. . . . Taylor was not a conversationalist, but on paper he put his meaning so plainly that there could be no mistaking it. . . . [He was a] great and successful soldier . . . true, patriotic and upright in all . . . dealings. . . . Pleasant to serve under . . . pleasant to serve with. Taylor saw for himself and gave orders to meet the emergency without reference to how they would read in history.

How better could Ulysses S. Grant acknowledge his obvious debt to a great teacher?

CHAPTER VII ☆ ☆ ☆ *Without the Loss of a Battle or Skirmish*

It is doubtful if any American in public life has been involved in more disputes than was Winfield Scott. During the forty-eight years that he was a general officer in the U.S. Army he seems almost to have gone out of his way to cultivate enemies. Half-affectionately called "Old Fuss and Feathers" by his troops, he was described by others, with good reason, as cantankerous, obstinate, pompous, foolhardy, and hotheaded.

But this controversial man had other qualities as well. We have already noted his courage under fire, determination, boldness, and great organizational ability in the performance of duty in the War of 1812, when, at the age of twenty-seven, he was the youngest general officer in the Army. In 1832 he would earn new repute for dauntless heroism under far different conditions.

Ordered by President Jackson to assume command over the operations against the Sac Indians, Scott embarked at Buffalo, Chicagobound, with a force of a thousand regulars. Cholera broke out on his lake steamer. Fearlessly exposing himself, Scott labored day and night with his sick men crowded in the stinking 'tween decks of the pest ship. His one medical officer had taken to his bunk in craven despair. Scott, all thought of military spit and polish momentarily forsaken, pitched in personally to nurse the sick and dying, dispense medicine, and above all, dispel panic.

The epidemic successfully controlled and quarantine lifted, Scott hurried to the scene of action with his command, to find the campaign ended; Black Hawk had been already defeated at the Battle of the Bad Axe by Brigadier General Henry Atkinson and Colonel Zachary Taylor.

The next eight years brought evidence of other hitherto unsuspected skills which he would be called on to use during the remainder of his active career. Twice he averted serious trouble with the Indians, through tact and firmness; with the Sacs on the northwestern frontier and with the Cherokees in the South. In 1832, President Jackson sent him to play the leading role in delicate political maneuvers which aborted South Carolina's secessionist urge during the Nullification crisis.

Following his campaigns in the Seminole and Creek Wars in 1836, when controversies with two fellow generals resulted in a court of inquiry and vindication of Scott's conduct of both campaigns, he was again called to diplomatic duties. President Van Buren in 1838 and again in 1839 sent him as special envoy to the Canadian frontier, where passions were flaring between the two countries. Scott's outstanding diplomacy brought peaceable conclusion to what might otherwise have meant another war between the United States and England.

It is interesting to note that during this very period in which he was displaying qualities of conciliation, courtesy, and diplomacy to limit or prevent internal violence, as well as to avert serious threats of foreign wars, Scott's personal affairs were in continual turmoil, marked by almost incessant, violent, and acrimonious disputes with fellow officers and prominent civilians.

In 1841 Scott became commanding general of the Army, but when war came with Mexico in 1846, five years later, it appeared that his ambition to lead the armies of his country in battle was to be cruelly denied by political chicanery—abetted somewhat, it must be added, by his own inept dabbling in politics and his penchant for getting into controversies with Presidents. President Polk was annoyed at Scott's outspoken disagreements with the Administration's initial war policies, and afraid the general—a staunch Whig —might displace him as President after a successful military campaign. Polk proposed, therefore, to appoint Senator Thomas Hart Benton of Missouri—the suggestion was Benton's—to the rank of lieutenant general, over Scott, and to entrust to the bombastic Senator—who had never seen a battle—the command of an invasion

of Mexico which had been carefully and meticulously planned by
the general in chief. This scheme failed because of the understandable failure of Congress to pass the necessary legislation.

Polk now determined to give the command of the expedition to
Robert Patterson, a volunteer general with no military experience,
but who had the undeniable quality of being a staunch Democrat who
could supply votes in the crucial state of Pennsylvania. But Polk's
cabinet dissuaded him from this harebrained scheme, and insisted
that Scott, the nation's first soldier, was the only man to whom
the government could dare entrust the bulk of its armed strength
in one of the most hazardous military operations ever conceived.

For Scott's plan assumed two things: the availability of the cream
of a highly professional army, and the leadership of a military genius.

It was simple, sound, and bold. With the largest possible force he
intended to strike straight at the heart of the enemy country, landing at Vera Cruz and following the shortest land line to the capital.
Taylor, with reduced forces—since the bulk of his veterans would
have to go to the main effort—would remain as the pivot of maneuver in the north of Mexico. Scott was sure that an invading force
threatening the capital from Vera Cruz would attract the main Mexican forces, whose defeat was his military objective. In the light of
the unsettled state of Mexican politics he reasoned—quite correctly—that all organized resistance would collapse once Mexico
City was captured. With boldness and skill, this invasion should
bring the war to a quick and successful conclusion. Hesitation or
mismanagement would mean the loss of the entire army in the heart
of the enemy country with results so disastrous as to be incalculable.

Scott knew the Army. He had been directly responsible for its
training and preparation for more than five years, and for more than
a quarter of century earlier he had done more than any other man
to contribute to its development and improvement. He had written
and rewritten the drill regulations. He had instituted the practice of
summer maneuvers. He had inculcated in the whole Army a fierce
pride in itself and its standards. His untiring efforts had been
demonstrated by the success of the forces under Taylor in the opening campaigns of the Mexican War; success which would have been
impossible without the highest standards of training, discipline, and
professional competence throughout the Army.

And Scott knew himself and had confidence in his abilities. He knew what he had done in the War of 1812, and he properly evaluated his military and diplomatic services to the government in the years that followed. Above all, he had studied incessantly— reading, digesting, evaluating every book on military theory and history on which he could lay his hands, preparing himself for the day when he would again be called to command American troops against a foreign foe.

Early in February of 1847, after delays caused by difficulties in collecting supplies, troops and transport, Scott sailed from Brazos, near the mouth of the Rio Grande. En route his flotilla stopped near Tampico to pick up some of Taylor's troops, who had come overland from Monterey, bringing his total strength up to about ten thousand men. This was a dangerously small army, in the light of his original estimate that twenty-five thousand men were required for the expedition. But the Mexicans were aware of his plans, having captured a message he had sent to Taylor. Scott therefore felt he must press on before they could make adequate preparations to meet his invasion.

On March 9 he boldly landed his little army near Vera Cruz and quickly invested the city, which surrendered to him on the 29th, after an intensive bombardment. In another two months the yellow-fever season would settle on the coastal lowlands, so Scott hastily organized the port under a strict but benevolent military government, and leaving the smallest possible garrison, headed for the healthful highlands of the interior.

The Mexican dictator, Santa Anna, smarting from his defeat up at Buena Vista five weeks previously, had rushed southward to block Scott's advance. With twelve thousand men he organized a strong defensive position in the defiles of the Sierra Madre Mountains, near the village of Cerro Gordo. Scott sent his trustworthy engineer officers—including Captains Robert E. Lee, George B. McClellan, and Joseph E. Johnston, plus Lieutenant Pierre G. T. Beauregard— to reconnoiter the enemy's flanks, while he made a personal reconnaissance of their main positions. He decided that a frontal assault would be too costly, but Lee had discovered a rough mountain trail which passed completely around the enemy's left flank, rejoining the main road behind the Mexican positions.

Promptly advancing the bulk of his army through a region which Santa Anna had insisted was impassable, Scott struck the Mexican left flank a crushing blow early on the morning of April 18. The Mexicans were routed, losing approximately 1,000 men in killed and wounded, while the Americans captured 3,000 prisoners. Scott lost only 64 killed and 353 wounded. The enemy's losses would undoubtedly have been greater, and his own less, but for the ineptness of political General Gideon J. Pillow. Pillow's brigade failed to follow its prescribed route, and then attacked the most powerful of the enemy defenses instead of the less formidable outpost which had been its assigned objective.

Scott, seizing the mountain passes in his rapid pursuit, halted momentarily, to face a problem plaguing all American commanders since George Washington. The short-term enlistments of nearly half his army—some four thousand men—would expire in June, a short six weeks away. They would have to be sent home. Until reinforcements arrived, he would have to mark time in the heart of enemy country with what was left.

He decided to send his short-timers home at once, lest they be caught at Vera Cruz in the height of the yellow-fever season. Boldly, he then pushed on to Puebla, less than seventy-five miles from the enemy capital, where he could live off the country in a healthy climate. Deliberately he abandoned his line of communications, for to guard it would mean squandering all his remaining strength.

For nearly three months he waited warily, making his plans for the future. By the beginning of August reinforcements brought his strength to fourteen thousand—three thousand of them sick—and Scott reorganized his army.

On August 7, leaving his invalids at Puebla with a small garrison, he struck west across the final mountain range protecting Mexico City, with 10,738 officers and men, once again refusing to establish a line of communications. When word of this daring advance reached England, the venerable Duke of Wellington was aghast. "Scott is lost," he exclaimed. "He cannot capture the city and he cannot fall back on his base."

But not until he arrived at Ayotla, within fifteen miles of Mexico City, did Scott meet any resistance. Santa Anna, bitter experience having proven he could not maneuver in open battle against the

American regulars, had been content to concentrate his thirty-five thousand men close to the powerful defenses of the capital.

Reconnoitering all possible approaches, Scott's faithful engineers discovered that the main approach road passed for several miles through a well-defended defile between Lake Texcuco and a vast marsh. To the south, however, firm ground for cross-country maneuver seemed to exist. So Scott, sideslipping, concentrated on August 17 at the little village of San Augustín, less than seven miles from his goal.

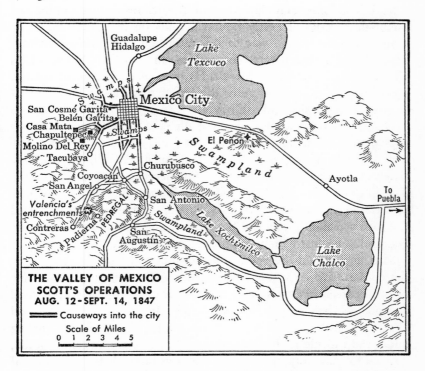

THE VALLEY OF MEXICO
SCOTT'S OPERATIONS
AUG. 12 - SEPT. 14, 1847

▬▬▬ Causeways into the city

Scale of Miles
0   1   2   3   4   5

The Mexicans shifted to meet the threat, fortifying the three towns north of San Augustín—San Antonio, Coyoacán, and Churubusco. At the same time Scott found that the alleged open, maneuverable terrain was in fact a mirage. The only road north was another causeway, flanked on the right by swamps and on the left by a rugged lava bed called the Pedregal, "which looked as if a raging sea of molten rock had instantly congealed, had then been filled by storms of centuries with fissures, caves, jagged points and lurking pitfalls, and finally had been decorated with occasional stunted trees and clumps of bushes."

Scott and his army were in a cul-de-sac.

But the alert engineers discovered one trail leading west across the Pedregal to the haciendas of Padierna and Contreras. It would be passable, with difficulty, by infantry, they reported, but not by artillery or cavalry. Furthermore, the exit of the trail was guarded by a fortified hill above it.

Scott had only four days of rations left. Immediate action was essential. A series of costly frontal assaults on San Antonio, Coyoacán, and Churubusco was to be considered only as a last resort. The lives of his men were too precious, and his force too small, to risk the carnage that would result. He ordered his engineers to make every possible effort to improve the trail across the Pedregal so that it could take cavalry and artillery.

General Worth's 1st Division was directed to keep the enemy occupied in front of San Antonio, and Quitman's 4th Division protected the army's supply trains at San Augustín. Pillow's 3rd Division was ordered to work with the engineers to open a road, while Twiggs's 2nd Division was to follow and, once the trail was open, to pass through and protect Pillow's working parties as they improved the road sufficiently to allow the artillery and the trains to cross the Pedregal. The instructions were clear and explicit.

Starting early on the 19th, the work progressed more rapidly than the conservative engineers had estimated. Emerging on the far side of the Pedregal, Pillow's advanced parties found the Mexicans hard at work on their entrenchments on the hill between Padierna and Contreras. General Pillow, foolhardy and inept, and still chafing under the ridicule he had received for his mistakes at Cerro Gordo, decided to gain glory by attacking. He gave not a thought to General Scott's clearly stated intention of avoiding battle until he had his army concentrated. First his division, then Twiggs's—over which Pillow assumed command without authority by virtue of his seniority—found themselves struggling through broken and difficult terrain, over which Pillow had attempted no reconnaissance. Frontal attack proving impossible under these circumstances, Pillow next detached two brigades to try to go around the north of the Mexican position to attack it from the rear. Again he made no reconnaissance, and gave no thought to the consequences of his orders.

At this point, late in the afternoon, Scott arrived on the scene, to find his army placed in dire jeopardy by the actions of his foolhardy subordinate. Quickly he scanned the field, and estimated the situation. The enemy on the hill near Padierna were numerous and strongly entrenched. In fact, there were some fifty-five hundred of the Mexicans' best men and twenty-two artillery pieces there, as Scott later learned. A frontal attack here would be just as costly as the one he had been working so hard to avoid. Furthermore, with the approaches through such difficult terrain, and his army so scattered, any attempt to continue Pillow's ill-conceived attack would be bound to fail. Even worse, the two brigades that Pillow had sent north of Padierna were now in danger of being cut off by the approach of an additional force of three thousand men, under Santa Anna himself. Fearful lest these troops should be overrun by Santa Anna's cavalry if withdrawn now, Scott quickly made his decision. To reinforce this threatened outpost, he sent two more brigades—all he had left near Padierna. These four brigades, fairly well concentrated, would protect his right flank and provide a base of maneuver beyond the Pedregal for further operations for the next day —provided the remaining scattered elements of Pillow's and Twiggs's divisions could be collected during the night. The exhausted engineers were called upon to reconnoiter, as well as they could in the dark, possible routes for concentration and advance the next day.

Again the engineers responded magnificently. In the late afternoon and early evening they discovered a ravine leading from the vicinity of the four brigades on the right, directly into the enemy's position near Padierna. General Persifor F. Smith, senior of the brigade commanders, planned a dawn attack on the entrenched enemy from the south, near the little hacienda of Contreras—the last direction from which the Mexicans would expect danger. But realizing that the present plight of the army had been the result of independent action by a subordinate, without consideration of the plans of the commander, Smith wanted Scott's approval. Captain Lee was sent back across the Pedregal, through a torrential rainstorm, reaching the general's command post near midnight. Scott gave his immediate approval, and he and his staff redoubled their efforts to collect the scattered units in the Pedregal. By morning he was ready to support Smith's bold venture.

By six o'clock Smith with three brigades—the fourth being left to hold off Santa Anna if he attempted to interfere—had reached a point directly behind the enemy's entrenchments. He gave the signal; the charge began. Seventeen minutes later the Battle of Contreras was over. The surprised enemy left 700 dead on the field; 813 were captured, and there is no record of how many wounded there were among the 4,000 refugees who ran the gauntlet of the American troops waiting for them to the north and east. Among the 22 guns captured were two that had been lost by the gallant O'Brien at Buena Vista. Promptly Scott pursued. Santa Anna, who had assembled 7,000 men near San Angel, withdrew rapidly to Churubusco.

The pursuers were joined by Worth's division, which had found a way across the northeastern corner of the Pedregal behind San Antonio, and so the united army fell upon the Mexican defenses at Churubusco. After a short, sharp fight the enemy was driven from the town in disorder, fleeing back into the capital city.

Scott, though tempted to continue right into the city, now halted the pursuit. His men had been through two days of violent action, and most of them had had no sleep during the intervening night. The city's defenses were formidable, and he feared disaster if his exhausted troops, disorganized by the two battles they had fought since daybreak, should be repulsed. Furthermore, he hoped that the defeats he had inflicted on the enemy would impel the Mexican government to sue for peace. For all of his bold generalship and personal bravery, Scott wished to avoid any unnecessary shedding of blood.

Early the next morning, therefore, he demanded the surrender of the city. Santa Anna—who had lost a third of his army in the previous day's fighting—requested an armistice for the purpose of negotiating peace. Scott agreed, and for two weeks negotiations were attempted. But when it became obvious that Santa Anna was playing for time, meanwhile strengthening the defenses of the capital, Scott terminated the armistice on September 6, informing the Mexicans that operations would begin on the 8th. His army, now concentrated at Tacubaya, less than three miles from the city, comprised about eight thousand men, rested, confident, and eager to end the war.

Santa Anna had perhaps twenty thousand men left, dispirited, but rendered desperate by the situation, and protected by some of the most powerful fortifications in the Western Hemisphere.

The Mexicans retained three strong positions outside the city walls, extending roughly in a line about a mile long, just southwest of the city, and covering the approaches from either the south or west. The closest of these, hardly a thousand yards from General Worth's leading division at Tacubaya, was a fortified mass of heavy stone buildings which housed a flour mill and a cannon foundry, called El Molino del Rey. Half a mile to the west was an old fort called the Casa Mata. Half a mile to the east, and just outside the city, was the most important of these fortifications, the old castle of Chapultepec, which housed the Mexican Military Academy. Situated on a high, rocky hill, Chapultepec overlooked the plain where the American army was encamped south of the city, and at the same time covered the two main causeways into the city from the west. Santa Anna had garrisoned these formidable fortresses with four thousand of his best troops, and had stationed four thousand cavalry to cover the west flank, just beyond the Casa Mata.

Scott had been informed that cannon were still being made in El Molino del Rey. Furthermore, he felt that the enemy should be driven from these nearby buildings and the Casa Mata before he made his next move against the City of Mexico. He believed that this could be accomplished by a large-scale raid, which he ordered Worth to make at dawn on the 8th. Although he did not expect a serious fight here, in his typically thorough manner he ordered General Twiggs's division to make a diversion by threatening the southern approaches to the city at the same time that Worth's division carried out the raid.

Early on the 8th the raid began. When the first storming parties were unexpectedly repulsed from El Molino and the Casa Mata by a vigorous and well-conducted Mexican counterattack, Worth called up reserves to make a deliberate assault. Not until dusk, however, were the two fortresses securely held by the Americans, after the most bitter hand-to-hand fighting of the war. The Mexicans had lost about 2,000 men in killed and wounded, 700 prisoners, and approximately 2,000 dispersed. Offsetting this, however, were Worth's casualties: 116 killed, 665 wounded, and 18 missing—proportionately a heavy loss for this small army isolated in the center of Mexico. General Worth, smarting under the loss of 23 per cent of his command, did not think the advantages gained had been worth the cost, and so believed that Scott should have planned a different approach to the capital. Scott, though realizing he had underestimated the enemy strength, nonetheless felt that Worth could have captured the two fortresses more quickly, and with fewer losses, had he pressed the initial assault with more vigor. The resulting strained relations between these two old friends were to develop into one of the most bitter enmities amongst the many in Scott's long career.

But whether justified or not, the Battle of Molino del Rey had set the stage for the final act. With the foe now cooped up in the city and in the nearby fortress of Chapultepec, Scott carefully reconnoitered the enemy defenses. He had the choice of attacking the city from the south or the west, and his army was so deployed as to permit either. He came to the conclusion that elimination of the outpost on Chapultepec was the first essential, and this objective attained, the city could best be taken by an immediate assault from the west. Three divisions—Worth, Quitman, and Pillow—were to make the main effort, while Twiggs's division was directed to conduct a secondary and diversionary attack against the defenses on the causeways leading to the city from the south. Scott's strength was now little more than seven thousand men, while Santa Anna had more than twice that number for the defense of the capital. Since the general was well aware that a three-to-one superiority is generally considered essential for success of an assault against strong defenses, he must have consciously or unconsciously evaluated the combat efficiency of his troops as being at least six times that of the Mexicans; an evaluation justified by the event.

Shortly after dawn on September 13, 1847, General Twiggs began his demonstration against the southern approaches to the city. As Scott had expected, Santa Anna rushed his reserves to repel this threat. Then, at 8 A.M. a carefully planned and co-ordinated attack was launched against Chapultepec, which had been pounded by heavy artillery for more than twenty-four hours. By 9:30 the towering hill and its fort had been seized, despite the heroic gallantry of the youthful Mexican cadets who were among the defenders.

Without a pause the pursuit continued according to plan. Quitman's division pressed down the causeway leading to the southeast gate of the city, the Belén *garita*. Simultaneously Worth's men drove north, then east along the causeway leading to the San Cosmé *garita*. With the assaults thus canalized along the narrow causeways, the Mexicans on the walls, in the houses built along the causeways, and behind a series of barricades, were able to concentrate the fire of all their weapons against the two advancing columns. With no room to maneuver, the Americans had the choice of withdrawing to initiate deliberate siege operations, or of dashing into the murderous fire. Without the slightest hesitation they pressed forward along the fire-swept defiles. By nightfall they were at the walls.

Scott and his staff labored during the night, preparing for an assault through the city streets in the morning. At dawn, however, just before the pre-attack artillery bombardment was scheduled to begin, the city surrendered, Santa Anna and most of his troops having fled during the night.

Thus, for all practical purposes, ended the Mexican War.

Scott's Mexican campaign was well-nigh faultless in concept and execution; bold, audacious even, yet calmly calculated in every respect and instance. No commander has ever asked more of his men or led troops in a more dangerous operation; yet no general has ever been more solicitous of the lives, comfort, and health of his troops.

A little-known incident of the conquest of Mexico illustrates Scott's solicitude for the soldier. On entering Mexico City he levied a contribution of $150,000 upon its inhabitants, in lieu of turning it over to the troops for pillage—a recognized custom of war at that period. Only too gladly the sum was immediately turned over to him. After spending part of it for much-needed clothing and medical stores for his troops, Scott rushed to Washington a draft for $100,000, personally endorsed by him: "The Bank of America, New York City, will place the within amount to the credit of the Army Asylum, subject to the order of Congress."

An "Army Asylum," a retreat, as he put it, "for the worn out or decayed rank and file of the Army," had been one of Scott's pet projects since he attained command of the Army in 1841. Congress thus far had refused to consider the scheme. Now, Scott felt, with this sum as a backlog, the price of the American blood so gallantly shed in Mexico, something could be done for the American soldier.

Not for years, however, did the dream become reality. The War Department at first impounded Scott's draft on the argument that the money was by law and regulations property of the United States, having been captured. But the fiery Scott, always ready to break a lance for his principles, raised such a fuss, and so vehemently argued that it was a contribution and not public property, that at long last he gained his way.

The Act of Congress of March 3, 1851, establishing what is now the Soldiers' Home in Washington (with the stipulation, still operative, that no government funds would be spent on it), released to it Scott's contribution, by then grown to $118,791.19.

It is not pertinent to a study of Scott's military leadership to retell the story of the insubordination and political machinations of Generals Pillow and Worth, and of Scott's resultant shameful treatment at the hands of President Polk, who summarily relieved him of command in the moment of his triumph. But there is one aspect of this otherwise sordid episode worth mentioning, as further indication of Scott's character.

A group of the most influential citizens of Mexico, hoping to take advantage of this situation, at once invited Scott to become the president-dictator of their country. They guaranteed him immediate payment of $1,250,000, to which would be added the presidential salary.

Scott politely but firmly rejected the offer. "If I failed to return home & face my enemies—the Executive & executive branches of the government," he later wrote a close friend, "I should have been condemned as guilty of all their foul charges, &c. . . ."

He came home instead, to be received as a conquering hero. Congress bestowed on him its official thanks, together with a gold medal, which, by fate's irony, President Polk had to deliver personally. Shortly afterward, the intrigue against Scott fizzled and he was restored to duty as General in Chief of the Army.

Scott remained the General in Chief of the Army for thirteen more years. He continued to be a stormy petrel of national and War Department politics, making new and bitter enemies, as well as new and lasting friends, right up to the close of his active career. A staunch Virginian, he sadly but unhesitatingly spurned the blandishments of his native state when it seceded from the Union just before the Civil War. "I have served my country, under the flag of the Union, for more than fifty years," said the general sorrowfully to an old friend, "and so long as God permits me to live, I will defend the flag with my sword, even if my own native State assails it." And so, unflinching under the most violent abuse and vituperation which now came from Virginians, he protected the capital and the new President during the tense days following Lincoln's inauguration, and loyally prepared the little army for war, when this could no longer be avoided. Ever conscious of the importance of sea-power, Scott was the man who recommended the eventually decisive naval blockade of the South, and it was his "Anaconda Plan" which finally crushed his native Virginia and the Confederacy. But though still impressive in his tall, soldierly magnificence, he was an old, frail, and ill man when the war came. For several months he endeavored to carry on, but he soon realized he would have to turn over his arduous duties to younger men. From the sidelines he watched with a heavy heart as some of his most promising protégés suffered defeat after defeat at the hands of the man who had been his right hand in Mexico—Lee. But before he died in 1866 he was to see his plan and his concept for winning the war carried out and vindicated by another of his Mexican War subordinates—Grant.

For half a century Scott was a leading actor in the civil and military affairs of the United States—longer than any other man of comparable prominence in American history. Never during those years did he hesitate to voice his opinion on any matter of national importance. Nor was he loath to make clear—publicly if this seemed to him appropriate—his frequent personal disagreements with his civilian superiors, whether Secretaries of War or Presidents. Yet no man, in or out of uniform, has ever been more solicitous of the Constitutional safeguards of American liberty, including the subservience of the military to civilian authority. He jealously, pugnaciously maintained the rights and honor of Winfield Scott, United States citizen, even if this meant—as it once did—denouncing a Secretary of War as a scoundrel and worse. But General Scott, the soldier, was unswerving in meticulous and loyal obedience to the official directives of his civilian superiors, regardless of his personal opinion of them as individuals.

Perhaps Scott's greatest over-all contribution to the United States and its Army was in the influence he exerted over the younger officers. Not a West Pointer, he had ever been a zealous protector of that institution from its detractors, and had gone out of his way to guide, advise, and assist the fine young officers who served under his command. His expenditure of effort and his confidence were generously rewarded during the Mexican War. And so Scott was being unnecessarily modest when he failed to mention his own role in his famous statement about the importance of West Pointers:

"I give it as my fixed opinion that but for our graduated cadets the war between the United States and Mexico might, and probably would have lasted some four or five years, with, in its first half, more defeats than victories falling to our share; whereas in less than two campaigns we conquered a great country and a peace without the loss of a single battle or skirmish."

It is time we looked into this matter of West Point.

CHAPTER VIII ☆ ☆ ☆ *The Seed and the Ground*

Captain Sylvanus Thayer of the Corps of Engineers had no idea he was about to touch off a stupendous chain reaction when on March 23, 1815, he sat himself down to write his chief, Brigadier General Joseph G. Swift. Massachusetts-born Thayer was thirty years old, a graduate of Dartmouth College, and the thirty-third graduate of a still new and little-appreciated primary school for Army officers—the United States Military Academy. He was also possessed of a long-standing obsession which two years of recent campaigning in the War of 1812 had whetted; he wanted to know what made Napoleon a great general. The nation was at peace, now, and maybe he would be permitted to gratify his ambition.

He wanted, he wrote Swift, "to obtain your consent and aid in bringing about a scheme which I have long cherished in my mind and for the accomplishment of which I deem the present a most favorable moment . . . a furlough visit to France for my professional improvement.

"I need not dwell on the advantages which the Corps or the Government would derive by sending abroad, in time of peace, a portion of its officers. I know that you view the subject in its proper light and it only remains to select those individuals who by their endowments, nature and acquisition are the best calculated to collect . . . useful information and afterwards to apply their acquisitions most carefully in the services of the Government. . . ."

It so happened that "professional improvement" of Army officers was at the moment occupying the attention of President James Madison and his Secretary of State (and, ad interim, Secretary of War) James Monroe. Engaged in the problem of cutting back the wartime Army, they were also exercised about the necessity for providing the vital element of trained leadership in what remained of the permanent establishment.

The sad results of mismanagement, poor leadership, and poor training during the War of 1812 still hung heavy on the President's mind. Only seven months had passed since with his own eyes he had seen shocking bungling culminate in disaster at Bladensburg. Mentally he could finger the sad rosary of misfits—from Hull to Winder —responsible for defeats. Perhaps he reddened as he did. Hadn't he himself appointed them?

He could also name, of course, the very few outstanding leaders who had emerged through expensive trial-and-error methods in which the fate of the nation was staked against the hope and chance that men in uniform might also be soldiers. True, the country now had three good men at the top—Jacob Brown, Andrew Jackson, and Winfield Scott. But how long would they last, and who would replace them? Above all, where would the junior troop commanders come from to provide both backbone and a leaven of continuity?

James Monroe felt the same way about it. He, also, had witnessed Bladensburg with his own eyes. Furthermore, his had been soldier's eyes, for he had commanded a regiment in the Revolution, and he knew the reason behind the recommendations of Washington, reiterated by Knox, Steuben, and Hamilton, for an institution "for instructing a certain number of young gentlemen in the theory of the art of war."

That dream he had seen come true in 1802, when Thomas Jefferson had pushed through an indifferent Congress the Act of March 16, 1802, providing for a Corps of Engineers to include ten cadets: "The said Corps, when so organized, shall be stationed at West Point, in the State of New York, and shall constitute a Military Academy. . . ."

And in the War of 1812 its few graduates had proved their worth, as well as their stamina, too. There had been men like George Ronan, killed in hand-to-hand conflict at Fort Dearborn; a heartbroken William Partridge, snapping his sword rather than yielding when Hull surrendered, at Detroit. Men like Eleazar Wood and James Gibson, killed at the head of their charging columns in an amazing sortie from Fort Erie. (At his own expense Jacob Brown had erected a monument to Wood at West Point.)

And, as Monroe pointed out to Madison, there had been graduates too, like artilleryman William McRee, who combined, as Scott had said, "more genius and military science with high courage than any other officer"; there was Swift himself, the first graduate; and there was that young fellow Sylvanus Thayer who had organized the defenses at Craney Island on Hampton Roads, which had stopped a British invasion of Norfolk.

But even that first attempt at promoting professional leadership was beginning to unravel now, if reports from West Point could be believed. Things were not going well these days at the Military Academy, it seemed. Yet that institution was the only means at hand. Somehow, some way, West Point should be preserved and bettered. Madison agreed with him.

It was in that atmosphere that General Swift presented Sylvanus Thayer's letter to the President. The spark had dropped in the powder barrel.

Three months later Thayer and McRee were bound overseas on board the *Congress* frigate, not on leave, but on duty, with instructions to "prosecute inquiries and examination calculated for your improvement in the military art. . . . You will be provided with funds for the collection of such books, maps and instruments for the Military Academy as may . . . be directed by the War Department or the Commander of the Corps of Engineers."

For more than a year Thayer and his companion would be abroad, most of the time in France, where they were given opportunity to see and absorb not only the past but the present. Monroe's letters of introduction—he had been Minister to France—opened all doors to them. They lived in a milieu of science, meeting a number of distinguished graduates and teachers of the École Polytechnique —then the most advanced scientific school in Europe—and they absorbed its methodology.

While, through the irony of fate, Thayer did not reach France until the sun of Austerlitz had set at Waterloo, nevertheless he had opportunity to relive at first hand some of Napoleon's campaigns and to meet several of his more talented staff officers. He visited at length the School of Application at Metz. And he collected an immense quantity of books, maps, and instruments to be shipped to West Point. Thayer, his lifetime ambition satisfied, absorbed this military and scientific knowledge like a sponge absorbs water.

Thus when, upon his return in 1817, he was suddenly ordered to West Point, to assume the superintendency and, as a letter from Swift exhorted him, "to take charge of everything there," he was ready. Monroe, newly elected to the Presidency, had become completely dissatisfied with the way the Academy was being run. In 1816 not one single cadet had graduated. Thayer's task was to be one of complete reorganization. He was, in effect, given carte blanche.

Thayer saw clearly the distinction between military training and military education; between the skillful artisan and the leader with intellectual background. His goal was to combine both objectives; his graduates should be men of principle, prepared to cope with novel situations.

For this purpose he devised—and put into immediate effect—what amounted to a novitiate, in which military training and education went hand in hand and only the fit would survive. All should work individually but toward a common goal.

An impartial discipline, impersonally applied, governed. And, while students, rich or poor, were on the same basis, no cadet being permitted possession of spending money, men were rewarded in professional standing in accordance with their performance.

A remarkable thing about the Thayer system was that it apparently emerged full-blown from his mind, for within a year of his taking command the Military Academy was being run, in principle, as it operates today.

His system has been compared to a triangle, with a base of probity and equilaterals of education and discipline. Honesty, then, was the keynote; an honesty that would operate without supervision, scornful of devious means whereby a man might gain for himself either something he did not deserve or an unfair advantage over his fellows.

Thayer, himself a graduate of a liberal-arts college, sought a curriculum which would provide sufficient knowledge of the arts, sciences, and languages to provide not only for the immediate military needs of the professional officer, but also to stimulate further study and research. The École Polytechnique provided such instruction, and on it and on its methodology he based his educational program.

We are not interested here in details of Thayer's pedagogical system other than to note that he was more than a century ahead of other American educators. What does interest us is the fact that he had grasped the essential factor of character building. Through example and also through discipline, both intertwined in the formal educational program, the cadet was impressed by the fact that honesty, with himself and with his fellows, paid off.

Once that premise was established, the keystone of leadership training, embracing loyalty to subordinates as well as to superiors, fell into place. Self-reliance—another quality of leadership—became second nature to men given instruction by application: the examination of a demonstrative problem followed by the student's solving —unaided—of a problem similar in principle.

From these things, as well as from the close daily contact with his fellows enduring the same hardships, confidence came to the cadet in his purely military training; a reliance upon the man on his right and on his left, the man in front and the man behind, each to assume his own share of the common task.

A stern novitiate was this one of Sylvanus Thayer's. The cadet found himself enmeshed in a rule of iron rigidity. For those already at the Academy, where a lax and almost "Dotheboys Hall" atmosphere had been in vogue, it was particularly difficult.

The new West Point began to take tangible form; a school for professional soldiers, where precision and discipline engendered mass co-operation, where Thayer's wise small sectional groupings and daily gradings gave scope to the talented to attain learning beyond that of the merely adequate. A code was coalescing—the honor system based upon Thayer's basic premise that a cadet does not lie, cheat, or steal; and a way of life which would in time permeate the entire Army.

Thayer the while was molding his faculty much as he was molding his cadets, selecting not only the best academic and tactical talent he could lay hands on, but also grooming personally selected graduates for later faculty posts to ensure continuity.

That was how a frail, intense youngster—the son of an Irish immigrant—began a career which would affect not only military thought and theory but also the technological growth of the United States. Dennis Hart Mahan, born in New York City and transplanted to Virginia, was appointed to the Military Academy in 1820. Graduating at the head of his class four years later, young Mahan was retained by Thayer as an assistant professor of engineering.

Mahan was a serious-minded individual. Aside from his flair for mathematics he had another interest; military history. Mahan's search for information about the great captains of the past naturally intrigued the superintendent, with his own deep interest in leadership.

The inquisitive Mahan wanted to know the answer to a number of questions about war. Great captains of the past, he found out, had done certain things that brought success. What were they? Was there a common denominator for military success? Were great soldiers simply born that way, or could they be made? Coming right down to then current personalities, what differentiated Winfield Scott, Jacob Brown, and Andrew Jackson from William Hull, Henry Dearborn, and James Wilkinson? If an answer could be found, Mahan felt, then a digest of leadership might be passed on to posterity, from which American officers, by study and research of their own, could profit.

So when Lieutenant Mahan in 1825 broached to his chief his hope that he might be permitted to take leave in Europe not only to recoup his health but also to pursue further studies in military history, he struck a spark of interest. Thayer had another problem on his mind; perhaps both could be solved by the same man.

President John Quincy Adams earlier that year had announced in his inauguration speech his intention "to provide and sustain a school for military science," and also to "proceed with the great system of internal improvements within the limits of the constitutional power of the Union."

Adams was answering a national demand. The Industrial Revolution, with its ever-growing need for technology, was turning to the Army and particularly to the Corps of Engineers and West Point to satisfy its almost insatiable urge. West Point, the sole reservoir of engineering skill in the United States, must not only provide the experts in increasing quantity, Thayer perceived, but must broaden and freshen its engineering curriculum. In young Mahan he had, he felt, the man to do the job.

So Mahan's desire was granted in 1826. His instructions from the War Department urgently stressed the policy. He was to obtain, while in Europe, "any information concerning roads, canals, bridges, the improvement of rivers and harbors, construction, labor-saving machinery, etc., . . . new to this country and of sufficient importance to render its acquisition desirable. . . ."

Abroad for four years—one of them spent as a student at the French Army School of Application at Metz—Mahan delved, in his dual role of engineer and student of war. When Mahan returned to West Point in 1830, Thayer, satisfied he had found his man, had him appointed Professor of Engineering and of the Art of War.

Mahan the engineer wrote a book—*Civil Engineering*—which would become the basic text for every technological school later springing up in the United States. His West Point pupils would become not only nation builders but some of them also faculty members of those schools.

But it is Mahan the expounder of the art of war who interests us here. As result of his studies abroad and his continued research, he had found, he considered, the key to leadership in battle. In imparting it to his students (he would be doing this until his death in 1871), Mahan not only became the apostle of fire and movement, but also the founder of a truly American concept of battle leadership—the spirit of the offensive, the positive approach.

What Mahan was preaching by 1847 was a doctrine which a century later would come to be known as lightning war.

Mahan was not setting himself up as a discoverer of some great new formula; far from it. He was an analyst, basing his theories upon his studies of the great captains of the past.

"In this power of analysis, sharpened by critical study and laborious research," writes one of his former pupils, "he was an accomplished master. Especially did he possess it in the consideration of a siege, a battle or a campaign, which, in his hands, from what appeared to be a complex jumble of chance events, became a striking illustration of the true principles of tactics and strategy."

What Mahan was trying to impress upon generations of cadets was study of the past for principles which might be utilized in the present and in the future. He warned against what he called "servile imitation" of tactical dispositions which, he pointed out, must change with the inventions of new weapons. The commander must keep an open mind.

True leadership, according to him, would also necessitate treating the soldier as a being "whose true strength lies in his volition"; there was more than a hint of von Steuben, there.

The necessity for training and discipline he stressed. But while primarily interested in the military education of the cadet and of the regular officer, he also, interestingly enough, specifically dedicated his published military works to the "Officers of the Militia and Volunteers." He saw the militia, if "efficiently organized," as he qualified it, as a firm bulwark of the nation. Irregular and partly trained forces could not hope to cope in equal terms with disciplined troops, however, in mobile combat.

"But place the militia soldier on his natural field of battle, behind a breastwork and . . . he will do his duty."

Colonel Blimp and the political general had no place in Mahan's pantheon of leadership.

"Let no man be so rash as to suppose that, in donning a general's uniform, he is forthwith competent to perform a general's functions; as reasonably might he assume that in putting on the robes of a judge he was ready to decide any point of law. . . ."

An agile professional brain, using imagination, was necessary, he stressed, to take advantage of the occasion of the moment. Mahan's fetish was speed. "Celerity is the secret of success" and "To do the greatest damage to our enemy with the least exposure to ourselves" were his axioms.

He was proposing a leadership which, through flexibility of mind, could seize upon new weapons and techniques and use them with the versatility of an Alexander, the mobility of a Caesar, and the strategic genius of Hannibal, to strike at the nerve centers of an enemy structure.

There it was: blitzkrieg, geared in Mahan's time to the speed of the horse-and-buggy age, but flexible in principle for application to the future. To Thayer's West Point, Mahan was adding an elixir whose flavor would become apparent in that great world case history of modern war—our Civil War.

The seed was good. Where it fell on good ground, came success in battle. Sometimes, of course, as we shall see later, it fell on ground either barren or choked with the nettles of human obtuseness.

In 1847, when the graduates of Thayer's great institution earned Scott's encomiums, many whose names would become household words by 1865 had not yet entered West Point. Those who sparked the Mexican drive were only captains and lieutenants, some of them troop leaders, others in staff jobs. But they were coming over the horizon of war; some to future fame, others to be less successful— Lee and Grant and Jackson; Beauregard, McClellan, and Bragg; Sherman and the two Johnstons, to name but a few.

None of them knew, of course, their future niches in the Valhalla of war. Nor did they know that a decade and a half later they would be testing and proving, graduate against graduate, the validity of Mahan's theories.

Even Lee, who, like Joe Johnston, had ended his cadet days before Mahan's return to West Point from France, would feel that influence. For Lee, as superintendent of the Military Academy in later days, prior to the Civil War, would be in close association with the little professor, and interested equally with him in Mahan's Napoleon Club discussions of military history up at West Point.

Lee would certainly take with him in his two invasions of the North the subconscious impression of Mahan's maxim:

"Carrying the war into the heart of the assailant's country, or that of his allies, is the surest plan for making him share its burdens and foiling his plans."

Jackson with his "foot cavalry" in the Shenandoah Valley, and pounding up the road to Second Bull Run, would be responding to Mahan's exordium to speed, and to his terse admonition always "to attack the enemy suddenly when he is not prepared to resist."

Grant, on the road to Vicksburg, deliberately cutting himself off from his communications and slipping between Johnston and Pemberton to defeat them successively in detail, would well remember the little man at West Point who had blazed the trail so clearly: "An army that throws itself by a strategic movement between several fractions of an enemy's army beyond supporting distance of each other, may, by superior activity, defeat them all in succession. . . ."

McClellan, on the other hand, was one of those who would not remember, would pay no heed to the prophecy that "no great success in war can be hoped for in which rapid movements do not enter as an element. Even the very elements of Nature seem to array themselves against the slow and over-prudent general."

When the storm clouds broke over the nation in 1861 the vehicle of leadership that Sylvanus Thayer had erected—perhaps better than he knew—and which Dennis Hart Mahan had pointed on the road to war, was ready.

The pity was that for a time neither the people of the United States nor their Administration realized what they had or how best to use it.

CHAPTER IX ☆ ☆ ☆ *Bumblers in Blue*

So long as the United States remains a nation the vast canvas of our Civil War will provide an epic panorama of combat leadership for its citizens to admire. Studded through it, however, are also outstanding examples of bumbling; failures which stand as signposts warning of the pitfalls which beset the commander in the field.

We don't find these necessarily in the box scores of battles won and lost, for the winning of a batle may not always denote the best in leadership, nor its loss the worst. As Dennis Hart Mahan once wryly commented, more than a hundred years ago: "How many great men have been struck down by the hand of adverse fortune; and how much of mediocrity has, by happy chance, been lifted far above its true level!"

Leaders were many, both great and small. The mediocre—to use the word in its true sense: average—were run-of-the-mill soldiers, who did their duty as they saw it, to the best of their ability. Some were graduates of West Point, others came from civil life. We will not concern ourselves overmuch with these hewers of wood and drawers of water.

Nor will we go into the drab tales of the manifestly unfit; the little bumblers thrust upon the armies by "political necessity," to squander the lives of their men, frustrate the plans of their superiors, and jeopardize the fortunes of their cause. There were many of them, too —men such as Butler, Frémont, Patterson, and their ilk on the Union side; Floyd and Pillow conspicuous in the Confederate forces.

Here we will confine ourselves to the really big bumblers in the armies of the United States. They were four in number. They all crossed swords with the same master in leadership; and three of them, in succession, commanded one of the most magnificent and long-suffering armies the world has ever seen—the Army of the Potomac.

All four were graduates of West Point. Unless qualified, that statement might indicate an indictment of Sylvanus Thayer, his objectives, and his "graduated cadets" of whom Winfield Scott was so proud. The Civil War record of the West Pointer group, of course, negates any such conclusion. The facts in these cases simply demonstrate the inept fashion in which the Administration and the Congress picked the leaders of the armies which they, for lack of any military policy, were forced to improvise on the spur of the moment.

Furthermore, the facts serve to prove that in last resort, as Ralph Ingersoll once wrote, "the battle is the payoff." The best that training, education, and indoctrination can do is to provide a forcing-bed for leadership. In the vital moment, the individual must provide the spark from within his own heart. Our first bumbler well illustrates this point.

He Took Counsel of His Fears

Fortune's favors rarely fall to one man in such abundance as they did to personable, brilliant George Brinton McClellan. Opportunity knocked at his door not once, but thrice; opportunity to enshrine himself in the hearts of the nation as its savior in its hour of greatest need. Thrice he peeked out, and thrice he slammed the door shut again.

Philadelphia-born McClellan apparently had done with soldiering before the Civil War broke out. A brilliant graduate of West Point, he had done well in the Mexican War. Sent to Europe as a member of a military commission to study the Crimean War of 1853–1856, he was tremendously impressed by the horrible examples of mismanagement it furnished and wrote an excellent report (later published in book form). He had by this time developed a flair for logistics and there can be no doubt that his Crimean War research affected his entire military career. Cautious by nature, he would become overcautious.

He resigned from the Army in 1857 to enter, like many other regular officers of that era, the railroad business; first as chief engineer and vice-president of the Illinois Central, and later, president of the Mississippi and Ohio, in Cincinnati, where the war found him.

Ohio's governor appointed him a major general of militia; Winfield Scott's influence, exerted on behalf of the brilliant young engineer officer he had known in Mexico, brought him a major generalcy in the army and command of the Department of Ohio.

Early in June, 1861, McClellan moved his forces across the Ohio River into what is now West Virginia, and dispersed all Confederate forces in the area. His operations, together with those of Nathaniel Lyon in Missouri, were the only bright spots in that dismal midsummer.

It was quite natural that President Lincoln, with the shock and chagrin of the Union defeat at Bull Run upon his shoulders and fearing for the safety of the nation's capital, should reach for the young man who had proven his energy and ability in West Virginia, to command all the forces in and about Washington. The press, the public, and the Army itself hailed the move.

What the new broom had fallen heir to was a disgruntled, dazed aggregation of pseudo-soldiers demoralized by defeat. Magnificent in organization, McClellan performed a remarkable job of army building.

It was the irony of fate that the Army of the Potomac, with its hallmark—"made by McClellan"—would achieve final victory only when led by better men in battle.

Even before he could start on his task, the "young Napoleon," as he was hailed, found himself quaffing the heady wine of popular favor. And something happened to him; best explained, perhaps, in his own words in letters to his wife: "I find myself in a new and strange position here; President, cabinet, Gen. Scott and all deferring to me. By some strange operation of magic I seem to have become the power in the land."

A few days later he would add: "They give me my way in everything . . . tell me that I am held responsible for the fate of the nation, and that all its resources shall be placed at my disposal. It is an immense task that I have on my hands, but I believe I can accomplish it."

And, lastly, this: "Who would have thought, when we were married, that I should so soon be called upon to save my country?"

Self-intoxicated, McClellan soon began to feel that old General Scott, his superior, was in the way. He snubbed him in shockingly insubordinate fashion. Scott requested retirement, and on November 1 McClellan became General in Chief of all U.S. land forces.

The Army of the Potomac was now an entity; discipline and training prevailed. Furthermore the men of this army had found an idol, despite—or because of—his rigid discipline and incessant training schedule. The young general—he was only thirty-five—on his great black charger, always seen at full gallop on parade, was constantly cheered as he dashed past, by men who had begun to feel themselves as soldiers.

It was his army and he knew it, just as, through mass psychology, the officers and men of this army felt then, and never would forget it, that "little Mac" was *their* general. Perhaps, in those days of early 1862, McClellan was about as near to being the legendary "man on horseback" dreaded by our forefathers as any American officer ever has been.

Meanwhile, as both army and people regained their spirit, the public clamor for action rose again—the "On to Richmond!" slogan. And as yet, the Army of the Potomac was rapidly going nowhere.

McClellan was quite right in refusing to make any move until he had organized, trained, and developed his army into a fighting machine. But then he became obsessed with the idea that his opponents were stronger than he was.

It was an obsession which would last as long as he commanded the Army of the Potomac. It is all the more remarkable as we look back at it now, for it completely violated all common sense. McClellan had picked for his chief of intelligence a fantastic character—Allen Pinkerton, renowned as a private detective. Pinkerton set up an elaborate network of agents, operating all the way into Richmond, and, according to Pinkerton, had its tentacles deep-bedded in the Confederate high command.

From this organization Pinkerton dredged up an appalling mass of misinformation, which McClellan accepted as gospel. Johnston, his principal opponent, who threatened Washington, had more than 100,000 men (actually he had 62,000). More than 200 enemy regiments were being "identified" by Pinkerton agents, with a menacing, shadowy background of additional forces, still unidentified. One report told of the issuance of 119,000 rations daily to Johnston's troops alone. So McClellan, whose well-equipped Army of the Potomac was swelling above the 170,000 mark, instead of falling on Johnston and thereby relieving any threat to Washington, proposed a move on Richmond by land and water, via Urbanna on the Rappahannock.

Not until early spring was anything done. By this time public hero worship of McClellan had turned to clamoring resentment of his delay. President Lincoln, forebearing, finally acted, ordering an advance against Johnston on or before February 22. McClellan was not ready until March 8. Johnston, informed by the really efficient Confederate spy system, simply shifted his troops from Manassas down to the Rappahannock line, where he would be as near Richmond as would be any Union advance from Urbanna.

McClellan then decided to transfer his army to Fort Monroe as a base of operations for an advance on Richmond up the Peninsula —the narrow finger of land separating the York and James Rivers. A new base would be established at White House on the Pamunkey River, as springboard for the final assault on the Confederate capital twenty miles west.

In effect, McClellan was throwing aside all opportunity to wage war on the vast maneuver ground of northern and central Virginia, to dump his troops instead on a flat, swampy, constricted area canalized by two unfordable rivers.

To make matters worse, this area was poorly mapped, and was completely unfamiliar either to the Union general or any of his subordinates. One of the many unexplained questions about McClellan was why this gifted engineer should have shown such complete disregard for terrain. His West Point training and his experience in Mexico under Robert E. Lee, where careful reconnaissance had been one of the principal factors in victory on the battlefield, should have taught him better.

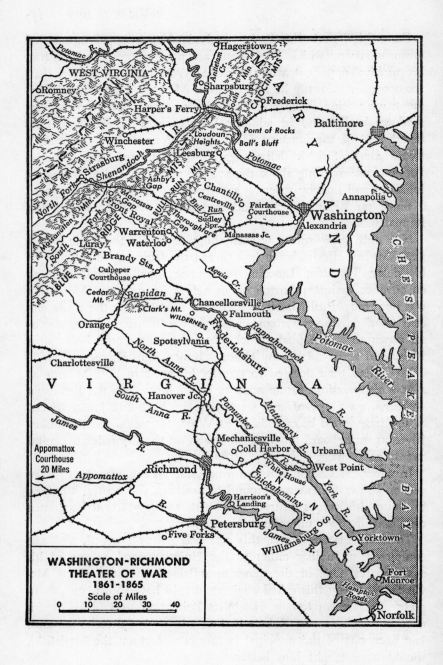

WASHINGTON-RICHMOND
THEATER OF WAR
1861-1865

Scale of Miles

0   10   20   30   40

By this time the "young Napoleon" of mid-1861 had become inwardly an irascible hypochondriac, warring with the President and the Administration, hagridden by the delusion that he—a savior—was being thwarted by traitors in Washington. Great gobs of troops had been taken from him to protect the capital, in fact interfering with his calculated dream of strategic maneuver. Even his over-all command—as General in Chief—had been stripped from him; he had in his hand only the Army of the Potomac.

Outwardly, he was still the peerless leader on the galloping black horse, eliciting huzzas from young soldiers filled with the valor of ignorance; flipping his cap to their cheers, drinking in their adulation.

This was the general who on April 4, 1862, moved out from Fort Monroe with ninety-two thousand well-equipped troops. Richmond-bound at last. Less than twenty miles he went, to run up against an entrenched line barring the way from Yorktown over to the James, some ten miles of earthworks bristling with cannon.

Behind that screen was Confederate General "Prince John" Magruder, putting up a colossal bluff. He had in all between fifteen thousand and seventeen thousand men and some real cannon, but most of the ugly black snouts McClellan's binoculars could see poking from the earthworks were merely painted logs of wood—so-called "Quaker" guns. Now and again, behind the embrasures, Union observers could see the glinting bayonets of bodies of troops continuously moving into position; actually, two Confederate regiments were passing and repassing the same spot—one of the hoariest bits of military deception.

One quick punch—a reconnaissance in force—and the deception would have been revealed. Magruder's cordon defense, punctured, would have crumbled. But that was not McClellan's way. He took one glimpse, then decided that the enemy position could be taken only by siege. Who could tell how many Confederates were waiting for him there?

So the great Army of the Potomac settled down to a month of toil in the mud. Trenches were dug, traverses cut, a vast quantity of heavy ordnance shipped down from Washington.

To the enemy it was almost inconceivable. Joe Johnston, ordered down to protect Richmond, came dashing into Magruder's defenses to see for himself, before putting his reinforcements in.

"No one," he reported, "no one but McClellan could have hesitated to attack."

Had Johnston had his way, there would have been no attempt to stop McClellan in that position. He knew all too well the tremendous superiority of the U.S. forces in men and guns. But he was overruled. So he took over the defense, with some 50,000 men. By this time McClellan's army had been increased to 105,000.

However, Johnston had not the slightest intention of attempting to stand and slug it out. Meticulous McClellan at long last finished his immense engineering labors. For May 6 a full-dress bombardment was slated; a bombardment that "would have compelled the enemy to surrender or abandon his works in less than twelve hours."

D day never came. Three days before, Johnston slipped away in the night. Slowly, dubiously, the Army of the Potomac penetrated the empty entrenchments; even more slowly took up a floundering pursuit in the ever-present mud.

The first strike had been called on George B. McClellan.

By May 31 McClellan, with his new base established at White House, was closing in on Richmond, which Johnston was protecting in an arc extending roughly from Mechanicsville above to the James below.

Opportunity was knocking on McClellan's door for the second time. McDowell was coming down from Fredericksburg with 40,000 men, and with that combination McClellan felt he might risk a battle with the mythical 200,000 Confederates that Pinkerton now told him were lurking around Richmond.

So he had lined up three of his corps along the north bank of an apparently insignificant little river named the Chickahominy, where they could link with McDowell when he arrived, and pushed another corps—Keyes's—south across the river to a point five miles from Richmond, between Fair Oaks Station on the railroad, and a crossroads called Seven Pines. No armed United States soldier, as it turned out, would be as close to Richmond again for nearly three years.

But Johnston had his own ideas about the situation. The Chickahominy was wide over its banks with the rainy season; the rickety bridges water-washed. He struck Keyes, so invitingly placed. Yet, despite initial setback, the Union line held. Sumner's corps with much difficulty crossed to reinforce Keyes and from lower down the river two fighting division commanders of Heintzelman's corps—

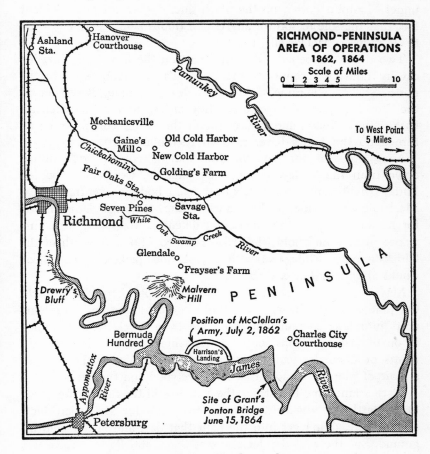

one-armed Phil Kearny and Joe Hooker—also came up in support.

It was an indecisive battle, except for one thing. Johnston, wounded by a shell fragment, was replaced by Robert E. Lee. The Army of Northern Virginia had been born.

McClellan, still astride the Chickahominy, now received stunning news. McDowell wasn't coming, after all. Far up in the Shenandoah Valley a man named Jackson was running amuck and Washington had recalled McDowell to shield itself. McClellan, still determined to take Richmond, dreamed of siege operations as he massed four of his corps south of the Chickahominy, but he left his V Corps, under Fitz-John Porter, on the north side, despite the quite evident fact that the sole reason for any Union troops being there had been to link with McDowell.

Two things happened. Lee sent Stuart on the first of his dazzling cavalry raids to reconnoiter the peninsula. Swinging wide to the north, Stuart then came slicing down the Pamunkey River line to the York, destroyed large quantities of supplies at McClellan's base, White House, and riding around the entire Union Army, returned up the James River road to Richmond.

Also, Lee sent for Jackson. Stonewall's "foot cavalry," rushed down from the Valley by rail and marching, were to hit behind Porter's right flank while Lee's own main body, concentrated near Mechanicsville, came crushing against him. It was a daring move, for he was stripping the Richmond defenses. Magruder, with only 25,000 men, would hold McClellan's 60,000 who were south of the Chickahominy, while Lee with 47,000 and Jackson with 18,000 would attend to Porter's 30,000.

Magruder, cast again in the role of deception, outdid himself. On June 26 bugles blew, voices could be heard constantly, ordering units into line; sporadic bursts of fire from rebel batteries rained in on the Union troops south of the Chickahominy, little detachments of Confederate infantry assailed the Union picket line in a score of pinprick attacks that kept everybody on their toes.

At the same time Lee struck the V Corps in the first of the Seven Days' Battles. It was a near thing. Fortunately for McClellan, Jackson was late, didn't get into the fight that day, and Porter held his ground. But the next day Jackson was there, and Porter's corps was bent back in narrowed arc around Gaines's Mill, with Sykes's division of regulars in last-ditch defense, while the remainder of the Army of the Potomac fidgeted.

Back in his headquarters, McClellan—who never visited the front—pondered over this exasperating situation. The Confederates, with their 200,000—hadn't Pinkerton, the infallible Pinkerton, told him?—could well be mounting a powerful assault against Porter and at the same time be about to crush the rest of his army.

That night McClellan decided to retreat. Already he had wired Washington he was being attacked by superior forces. He would fall back to the James, abandoning his White House base. And so he ordered, at a corps commanders' meeting.

Two men took this pretty hard—Kearny and Hooker, who, it seems, had not been entirely fooled by Magruder's deceptive tactics in front of their divisions. When they learned of the decision, from their corps commander, Heintzelman, they forced their way into McClellan's headquarters tent. The fiery Kearny demanded permission to attack at once; Richmond was only five miles away. He and Hooker could march straight in. Hooker agreed (he thought one division could do the job), and Heintzelman approved.

McClellan was unmoved. Perhaps Kearny's language berating him made him all the more stubborn. A staff officer present later stated he expected Kearny to be thrown into immediate arrest; but he wasn't.

The battles of Golding's Farm, Savage Station, White Oak Swamp-Glendale, and Malvern Hill followed, as the Army of the Potomac sullenly fell back.

In none of the actions was the Army of the Potomac defeated. Each in fact could be considered a tactical success for the men in blue, as each Union army corps fought individual battles, with little or no guidance from McClellan. In the last day of the battles, at Malvern Hill, all Confederate assaults were decisively repulsed. But McClellan made no move to counterattack; rather he ordered another withdrawal. Grimly the Union troops fell back to Harrison's Landing on the James, where a new base was established, too strong for Lee to assault.

Nor did McClellan shine even in retreat. To those who incline to the opinion, as some historians have it, that the Seven Days' actions constituted "a masterly change of base" one remarks on the shocking loss of supplies, and the abandonment of the wounded and of great quantities of equipment. One notes the haphazard withdrawal—unsupervised and unco-ordinated by the leader—which at Savage Station "forgot" two batteries of artillery and three regiments and a battalion of infantry.

Batteries A and C, 4th U.S. Artillery, slept by their guns that night, to awake to reveille blown by Confederate bugles, and find rebels bivouacked all about them. Captain George W. Hazzard got his men on their feet, hitched up and, at a walk, lest attention be attracted, led them to safety—which was a bit of leadership in itself. He also gathered in on the way a "lost" battalion of infantry. And the 104th Pennsylvania and the 56th and 100th New York regiments, also forgotten, rejoined the army only after a three-day wandering.

Whatever one makes of all this, the fact remains that a second strike had been called on George B. McClellan. But the tired, bewildered men of the Army of the Potomac—saving only those regiments he had "forgotten"—would still cheer him to the echo on his every appearance in their dreary Harrison's Landing encampment.

Three fateful months would pass before opportunity's third knock struck at McClellan's portal. Meanwhile he sulked in his new headquarters at Aquia Creek (the Army of the Potomac had been moved by water from the James), and watched his troops drain away under his eyes to build up another army—the short-lived unfortunate Army of Virginia, soon to come to disaster under another bumbler; a story we will come to shortly.

The Army of the Potomac remained a paper army now; little more than a headquarters and camp detachments, until an urgent flash from President Lincoln sent the "Young Napoleon" rushing northward.

Through the dusk of September 2, 1862, men were marching on the Fairfax road leading to Washington; great masses of disgusted, beaten men in blue, reeling up from Manassas and Centreville and the bloody heartbreak of Second Bull Run. The Army of Virginia—most of whose components were the men of the Army of the Potomac—was coming home from a drubbing.

And as they shuffled, silent, through the dust, an odd soughing sound came whispering down the lines, from head to tail of that long column. Cheers, it sounded like to the men in the rear; what idiots would be cheering now?

But it *was* the sound of cheers, coming louder; cheers rippling in tempo with the progress of a little knot of galloping horsemen coming through. A man on a great black charger was in the lead. A man wearing a wide gold sash; a man flicking his cap in an odd little salute that only one man could give.

"McClellan! McClellan! General McClellan is back!"

He was. The Army of Virginia was dead; long live the Army of the Potomac!

A transformed army, a jubilant, confident army, continued its march into the Washington defenses; singing, cheering, its cares and sufferings forgotten now that its leader had returned. It was one of the most remarkable demonstrations in our military history; a complete illustration of everything embraced in our frame of leadership. Exactly fifteen days later this spendthrift of leadership would squander it all, by the banks of a little Maryland creek they called Antietam.

Following the Second Battle of Bull Run, Lee had invaded the North, with 55,000 men and 284 guns. By September 9 the Army of Northern Virginia was spread wide in three segments incapable of immediately supporting one another. Jackson's corps had re-crossed the Potomac to swing in wide arc to attack from the north the Federal garrison at Harpers Ferry; part of Longstreet's corps was on the heights overlooking that place from the north and east banks of the Potomac and Shenandoah; and the remainder—less than 20,000 strong, under Lee's own command—was probing north towards Hagerstown.

Up from Washington in pursuit, McClellan's revamped Army of the Potomac was marching through Maryland on the chord of Lee's arc—97,000 men and 300 guns, with all the *élan* of a devoted, fighting force, confident in itself and its commander. By September 12 McClellan reached Frederick, Maryland, to receive a gift rarely accorded a general in the field; a crumpled piece of paper wrapped around two cigars and hurried by its finders to his headquarters. It was a copy of Lee's order detailing the wide separation of his forces.

"Seldom in war," remarks Steele, the military historian, "has a commanding general been so favored by luck."

McClellan disdained the gift. Instead of an immediate eruption through the South Mountain passes to destroy Lee's scattered forces in detail, he probed timorously at the small Confederate flanking force guarding the mountain gateway, took two precious days to carry it, and then two more to concentrate for his main effort.

Lee, with some twenty-five thousand men in hand and the unfordable Potomac at his back, elected to stand at Sharpsburg, calling in his far-flung elements. By the time McClellan was ready, on September 17, his opponent had his full force assembled—less one division still coming up the road from Harpers Ferry.

McClellan's plan was to hit Lee's left with three of his army corps, followed by another corps to hit the enemy right. The only natural obstacle in the path was Antietam Creek, fordable at any point. But McClellan didn't know that; he had made no reconnaissance.

So his assaulting columns sought only the known bridges and fords. His main effort broke down into a series of disjointed attacks; his left hook—Burnside's corps—spent itself in the costly storming of a bridge since bearing Burnside's name (his men could have marched across the creek at any point, but literal-minded Burnside had been told to "carry" the bridge). By nightfall more than twelve thousand Confederates and ten thousand U.S. soldiers were sprawling on the bloodiest one-day battlefield of the war, Lee had expended all his reserves in a magnificent defense, and McClellan still had Porter's V Corps, fresh and spoiling for battle, on the field in reserve.

Fortune's finger was beckoning but McClellan couldn't see. Some twenty thousand Union men, never engaged in the battle, stood idle. For another full day Lee impudently faced the threat that never came, then slowly and unharassed the Army of Northern Virginia retraced its steps, recrossed the Potomac, and retired into its homeland to lick its wounds.

George Brinton McClellan, who could have ended the Civil War at Antietam Creek, had struck out.

He Couldn't Be Wrong

John Pope of Kentucky was an obstinate man; a cocksure individual brooking no opposition to his fixed opinion. He was physically brave, as he had proved in the Mexican War at Monterey and Buena Vista, and later in heading a detachment of engineers plotting transcontinental railway routes from the Mississippi to the Pacific.

As a brigadier general of Volunteers in charge of the district of Missouri in 1861 his rough handling of Confederate guerrillas brought quick results. In early 1862 his short, sharp, successful campaign along the Mississippi to capture New Madrid and Island No. 10 brought him to the attention of President Lincoln, who sorely needed a general who would fight.

So Pope came east as a major general, to command a new army—the Army of Virginia. He came with all the din of the popular clamor against dilatory McClellan ringing in his ears, and he charged into his command with the stupidity of a snorting bull in a china shop. He enraged his own soldiers by a bombastic address casting aspersions on their bravery as compared with the men he had commanded out West, where as he said, he was used to looking at the backs of his enemies. He began issuing orders dated "Headquarters in the Saddle," which drew ridicule not only in his own command but among his enemies.

"Pope appears to have his headquarters where his hindquarters ought to be," was Robert E. Lee's dry comment.

But Pope was itching for a fight. Based on the great Union supply depot established at Manassas, he moved south down the railroad line toward Richmond. Jackson, sent by Lee to check him, met Pope's leading corps—Banks's—at Cedar Mountain, August 9, 1862. For once in his life Banks was in a fighting mood, and with but 8,000 men in hand—more or less—he fell on Jackson with such ferocity as to check him. Both sides recoiled for a bit.

Lee knew Pope had some 45,000 men. He knew also that McClellan's Army of the Potomac was being moved north from its Harrison's Landing cantonment. Were this force to combine with Pope, 130,000 U.S. troops would be available for an overland push against the Southern capital. Pope would have to be slapped down before that happened. So Lee, master strategist, with 55,000 men in all, made a plan.

This is how the land lay: Northern Virginia's Piedmont, where the armies stood, reaches east from the Blue Ridge to tidewater, in mainly flattish, slightly rolling country. But from the Potomac up by Point of Rocks and the Loudoun Heights there juts southward into its expanse the spine of the southern Catoctins; a row of little hills locally called the Bull Run Mountains. This parallels the Blue Ridge for some fifty miles, down to Waterloo, to form a sheltered valley.

Pope's Army of Virginia was concentrated in the flatland area east of the Bull Run Mountains, just north of the Rappahannock and Brandy Station; Lee was facing him just to the south. Lee made the land work for him.

Out into the dusk of August 24 Jackson's corps went foot-slogging west, turned into that sheltered valley between the Blue Ridge and the Bull Run Mountains screening him from Pope, and hustled north. At Thoroughfare Gap in the latter range, he turned east to fall like a thunderbolt on Pope's Manassas base. He had made a fifty-four-mile march in forty-eight hours, to plant himself squarely between Pope's rear and Washington.

The capital went into panic; Pope into frothing rage. As a bull whirls to the sting of the banderillas, he turned and plunged north.

The Union commander was not worried about his own strength, for, marching down from Washington, Heintzelman's corps was already at Warrenton, while east from Aquia Creek, the debarkation point for the Army of the Potomac, Porter's corps was on the way. Pope was just plain mad. He would overwhelm the Rebels who were so conveniently and impudently putting themselves in a trap. He ordered a concentric advance on Manassas.

Pope himself reached Manassas, to find his depot gutted and deserted. Jumping to the conclusion that Jackson—he knew now it was Jackson's corps—was in full retreat, Pope kept his widely scattered troops in a fruitless succession of marches and countermarches to find him. Actually Jackson had ensconced himself along an unfinished railway embankment and cut, hidden in woods slightly northwest of the old battlefield of Bull Run.

What Pope didn't know, and never would realize until too late, was that Lee, with Longstreet's corps, had followed Jackson's route twenty-four hours behind him and was now coming through Thoroughfare Gap. A ruse and a division of forces—one of the most daring in all Lee's daring brilliance—was nearing its culmination.

On the morning of August 29 Jackson sprang the trap. Again one must use the simile of the bullring. With the grace of the matador waving his cloak, Jackson disclosed his position by opening fire on a part of Pope's troops, and his enemy charged in. Concentrating everything in hand, Pope's attack closed on the railway cut; his left on the Warrenton Pike, his right reaching to Sudley Springs.

A vainglorious message to Washington announcing impending victory, and orders to Porter, far over on the left, to attack Jackson's right and rear, went out simultaneously.

But Porter didn't come. He had discovered Longstreet's advance—straight down the Warrenton Pike—to hit Pope's left, and had deployed to stop it. He so informed Pope, but Pope knew better.

Peremptorily, that night, Porter was ordered to delay no longer. Victory, felt Pope, was within his grasp. He even ordered McDowell's corps to prepare for a pursuit of the enemy he considered he had cornered. So Porter moved; moved from his position facing west against Longstreet, to attack north against Jackson.

Pope's attack on August 30 pounded vainly against Jackson's ready-made rampart. Longstreet, his path cleared by Pope's stupidity, came crashing in on the open left of the Union army, rolled it up, sent it reeling back over the old Bull Run battlefield of July 21, 1861, and across Bull Run itself.

As in the first battle, the Henry House hill became the center of resistance. Here Porter's V Corps, with Sykes's division of regulars as its snarling rear guard, held the field, enabling the rest of the Army of Virginia to execute an orderly retreat.

And that was Second Bull Run. There was an appendix to the saga next day; the sharp, stinging fight at Chantilly, where dashing, one-armed Phil Kearny, repulsing Jackson's drive at the Union right flank, rode headlong to his death, into a line of advancing Confederates.

Then the Army of Virginia went marching back to Washington to its dissolution; defeated by its own commander's mistakes.

Not that Pope admitted failure; the faults of other men, he

clamored, had deprived him of victory. And the hot lava of his recriminations seared, above all his subordinates, Fitz-John Porter. Through Pope's accusations Porter was later court-martialed and convicted (much of the testimony against him was perjured) for his alleged failures in a battle which in fact he helped save from becoming a disaster. Not until 1879 would he be cleared; but that's another story.

So we leave John Pope; a man lacking in almost every quality of leadership save that of pugnacity.

Too Little and Too Late

Major General Ambrose Everett Burnside, commanding the IX Corps of the Army of the Potomac, received the surprise of his life on November 7, 1862. To him came an aide of President Lincoln, announcing that General McClellan had been relieved from command and that he, Burnside, would replace him. Burnside, the man with the formidable mutton-chop whiskers that would give, back-handedly, to that mode of coiffure the nickname of "sideburns," held no delusions of grandeur, had no dreams of supreme command.

Why Burnside had been picked is somewhat of a mystery. A West Pointer who had graduated too late to take part in the Mexican War, he had resigned in 1853, engaged unsuccessfully in arms manufacture in Rhode Island for a few years, shifted to railroading with the Illinois Central. When war broke out his Rhode Island connections brought him a colonel's commission in the militia. At First Bull Run he commanded—without any special distinction —a brigade. In 1862 his successful handling of an expedition along the North Carolina coast brought him a major generalcy. But his actions at Antietam had been less than brilliant. Certainly as a combat corps commander he did not compare with Hooker, Sumner, or Franklin.

But Hooker was cantankerous, Sumner was old, and Franklin had been a protégé of McClellan. Burnside, on the other hand was close to Halleck—newly appointed General in Chief—and his modesty, patriotic spirit, and amiable manners sat well with President Lincoln.

Being a friend of McClellan, Burnside didn't want to take his place. Doubting his own competence—a matter in which his subordinates in the Army of the Potomac were in full agreement—he had no stomach for the job. But orders were orders; so Burnside went to work. And the first thing he did was to draw up a new plan of campaign.

At that time the Army of the Potomac was bivouacked in the Manassas–Warrenton–Culpeper Court House area.

Theoretically, it was most strategically placed, for it sat between the two main concentrations of the Army of Northern Virginia— Jackson up in the Shenandoah Valley and Longstreet below the Rappahannock. McClellan had been dallying with the idea that he might fall on one or the other and defeat Lee in detail. But, in usual McClellan fashion, he hadn't quite sold it to himself, which was why Lincoln decided to make a change.

Burnside appears to have been that most dangerous type of army officer—both stupid and industrious. Being stupid, the geographic objective of Richmond enticed him from the obvious military necessity of destroying the enemy forces in the field. Being industrious, he felt he must do something, anything! He proposed moving down opposite Fredericksburg, to cross the Rappahannock and strike for Richmond. The President approved.

Speed was essential for success. Winter was coming on, and the Rappahannock would soon be unfordable. Burnside moved down into the plain across the river from Fredericksburg on November 17–19. Actually, he could then have pushed two army corps across the still fordable river and seized the heights above; only a small force of screening Confederate cavalry opposed him. But Burnside feared to divide his army, so he waited for the ponton bridges he had ordered.

Meanwhile Lee, who until the very last minute had not believed that the Union commander would have attempted an assault at such an unfavorable point, merely sent Longstreet's corps down to Fredericksburg to occupy the heights. Not until November 22 did he bring Jackson down, and then to a position on Longstreet's right, to bar what he rightly considered would be the logical solution—a Union crossing further down-river to turn his flank and get between Richmond and himself.

The weather was stormy, the river rose; still the pontons didn't come, and Burnside waited. He waited until December 9, when the bridging material did arrive, and, incidentally, until Lee, sure now of his opponent's intention, had established himself firmly on the ridge of the natural amphitheater ringing Fredericksburg.

Standing today along that ridge and looking down into the plain and town below, and the river running fast beyond, it is almost impossible to believe that any sane soldier would have deliberately chosen to make a river crossing and a frontal attack against such position.

But that is what Burnside did, and this is how he did it: He had reorganized his army into four so-called Grand Divisions, three of which were present; the fourth, scattered all the way back to Harpers Ferry, was not in the picture. Covered by Union artillery which pulverized the town itself, Sumner's Grand Division, Burnside's right, assaulted Fredericksburg across ponton bridges hastily laid under fire.

Sumner gained the town, then debouched in mass formation to charge up to Marye's Heights beyond. Caught under the crossfire of Confederate artillery and small-arms fire and unprotected by the Union artillery, now outranged, his columns melted. Hooker's Grand Division, ordered in to retrieve the situation, met the same fate. As Longstreet's chief of artillery said, "a chicken could not live" on that ground when the Confederate batteries opened.

At the same time Franklin's Grand Division, crossing the river below the town on additional ponton bridges, gained the flatland. The spray of its assault actually reached the Confederate position on the ridge, to fight a bitter hand-to-hand engagement before Jackson's all-out counterattack prevailed.

When night fell the Army of the Potomac was clinging only to the blackened fragments of Fredericksburg and the railroad line paralleling the river. Between them and Lee's impregnable ramparts on the heights its dead and wounded lay in frightful windrows.

Still bumbling Burnside was not satisfied. That night he ordered the assault resumed next day; was finally dissuaded only by the pleas and recriminations of his shocked and indignant subordinates. Forty-eight hours later the United States troops retired across the river unmolested; Jackson's first thought of a counteroffensive on his portion of the front was reversed in consideration of the heavy Union artillery fire he would have to undergo near the river.

Huddled in their drab cantonments by Aquia Creek, lashed by torrential rains, the men of the Army of the Potomac gritted their teeth. Their generals did more; in almost open mutiny against Burnside, they seethed and grumbled, with "Fighting Joe" Hooker's voice the loudest. Two of them went to Washington to complain.

Burnside, badgered, himself went to Washington, demanding the dismissal of Hooker and six other generals; were this not done he would resign.

Abraham Lincoln took him at his word. The complaining generals stayed. Burnside was permitted to resume his old command, the Ninth Corps—and Hooker took the army.

He Usually Liked to Fight

"Fighting Joe" Hooker was proud of his nickname. He had reason to be; it had been hung on him by his division, and American soldiers and sailors are not prone to bestow a nickname without reason. Above all, they can't be dragooned into adopting such a thing. There was a general once—not a bad general, either, as run-of-the-mill division commanders go—who let word be gently dropped through his command that "Fighting John" would be a nice thing to call him. Unfortunately for him, he was addicted to wearing a nice clean white collar in the field, under his old-fashioned hook-up blouse. Within a week and forever after he was known as "Celluloid Jack."

So, coming back to Joseph Hooker from Massachusetts, one gathers from his nickname and from his record that he was a fiery division and corps commander in combat.

His one chance to lead an army in battle was a complete washout.

Hooker was another of those West Pointers who, after showing promise in the Mexican War, resigned. He took up farming in California for several years, then was appointed superintendent of military roads in Oregon. Commissioned a brigadier general of Volunteers at the outbreak of the Civil War, he added to his combat fame in every engagement from Williamsburg to Antietam.

It was quite natural that Lincoln should have appointed him to command, for outside of Phil Kearny there had been no bolder combat commander in the East than Hooker; and Kearny was dead. Nor is there any doubt that Lincoln chose him for his fighting ability despite his insubordinate actions and criticism in the case of General Burnside.

The President stressed this in the letter appointing him, January 26, 1863, relating his faults.

"I have heard," Lincoln went on, ". . . of your recently saying that both the Army and the Government needed a dictator. Of course, it was not for this, but in spite of it, that I have given you the command. Only those generals who gain success can set up dictators. What I now ask of you is military success, and I will risk the dictatorship. . . . I much fear that the spirit which you have aided to infuse into the army, of criticizing their commander and withholding confidence from him, will now turn upon you. I shall assist you as far as I can to put it down. Neither you nor Napoleon, if he were alive again, could get any good out of an army while such a spirit prevails in it. . . ."

By the end of April, Hooker had revitalized the Army of the Potomac into the best-equipped, best-organized, and largest army ever to be assembled to that time on the North American continent. He did a good job. His 122,000 infantry, 400 guns, and 12,000 cavalry were grouped into 7 army corps of infantry and 1 of cavalry.

Against him Lee, who had sent Longstreet away with two divisions to gather provisions down along the lower James, had some 54,000 infantry, 6,500 cavalry, and 228 guns. But what his troops lacked in numbers, equipment and rations they made up for in morale. He had a "hot" team.

Hooker, still in the Aquia Creek area, proposed to send his cavalry on a wide sweep around the northwestern flank of Lee, who was concentrated in the vicinity of Fredericksburg. Once that was well on its way, he proposed to make a turning movement of this same flank with the greater part of his force, at the same time demonstrating before Fredericksburg with a holding attack.

Supremely self-confident, vainglorious even, he took up his new job now with a swagger. "My plans are perfect," he stated a short

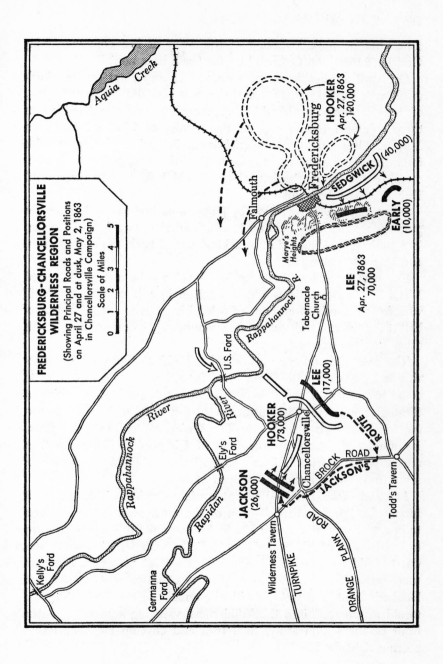

FREDERICKSBURG-CHANCELLORSVILLE
WILDERNESS REGION

(Showing Principal Roads and Positions
on April 27 and at dusk, May 2, 1863
in Chancellorsville Campaign)

Scale of Miles

0 1 2 3 4 5

HOOKER
Apr. 27, 1863
120,000

SEDGWICK (40,000)

EARLY
(10,000)

LEE
Apr. 27, 1863
70,000

Marye's
Heights

Tabernacle
Church

Fredericksburg

Falmouth

U.S. Ford

LEE
(17,000)

JACKSON'S ROUTE

HOOKER
(73,000)

Chancellorsville

BROCK ROAD

Todd's Tavern

JACKSON
(26,000)

Wilderness Tavern

TURNPIKE

ORANGE PLANK ROAD

Rappahannock River

Rapidan

Ely's Ford

Germanna Ford

Kelly's Ford

Rappahannock R.

Aquia Creek

time after he took command of the Army of the Potomac. "May God have mercy on General Lee, for I will have none."

On April 27 the Union cavalry streamed away, not to come back until, as it turned out, the campaign was over. Behind it the Army of the Potomac forded the Rappahannock and the Rapidan in three columns, to converge at the hamlet of Chancellorsville on May 1. Over opposite Fredericksburg, Sedgwick, left there with forty thousand men, moved across the river too, below the town, to make the demonstration which should hold Lee in place until Hooker's main body hit him.

But a quick delaying action by Jackson, pushed out by Lee for the purpose, momentarily held up Hooker's advance guard. And Hooker, in a funk, halted instead of attacking, pulled back his leading units, and began to entrench!

For once in his life "Fighting Joe" Hooker—the man who berated McClellan because he wouldn't let him assault at Gaines's Mill, who forced South Mountain, who led his corps in sanguinary combat at Antietam (and was severely wounded), to say nothing of his other battles—was dodging a fight.

The spectacle of a great army, imbued with the spirit of the offensive and launched with the avowed intention of its commander to come to grips with and destroy his opponent, suddenly recoiling at the first contact with its outnumbered foe, entrenching and preparing for defense, is a sorry one. The Union earthworks today yawning amidst the trees on the field of Chancellorsville, more than ninety years afterward, bear silent witness to Hooker's change of mind, more potent than thousands of words.

Lee and Jackson held pregnant conference that night. Out of it sprang the "perfect battle"—one of the most audacious plans ever to be attempted in war. For Lee had determined to encircle an army twice the size of his own. General Early, with ten thousand men, was to hold the Fredericksburg Heights against Sedgwick, Lee with some seventeen thousand more in hasty entrenchments would hold Hooker's front, and Jackson with the remaining twenty-six thousand would march west into the Wilderness, swinging around the entire front of the Union army, then turn and envelop Hooker's unsuspecting right flank.

While the Army of the Potomac, reined back on its haunches, dug frantically, Jackson's corps was moving fast, as only Jackson could move, westward into the tangled scrub of the Wilderness. By sunset he turned north and then east, just short of Wilderness Tavern, to deploy in the thickets on a front that would hit the southward-facing Union entrenchments at a right angle.

Launched at six o'clock in the evening, his co-ordinated attack thundered straight down those gaping ditches to roll up a dazed, bewildered foe.

Howard's corps crumpled; Sickles, next in line and with his right flank jutting out into the Confederate path, was rolled back. A disorganized mass of fugitives streamed eastward. And Jackson, riding into the night to reconnoiter for himself how best to complete the destruction, fell, mortally wounded by a shot from his own men.

Sporadic fighting continued during the night. At dawn, Stuart, who had taken Jackson's place, pressed the Confederate attack. By this time the Army of the Potomac was huddled in a sort of arrowhead shape, its right and left on the Rappahannock; its center—where Sickles, Slocum, and Burnside were fighting almost back to back—was being attacked both by Stuart from the west and Lee's holding force on the south and east. The Union artillery, well served, did much to stem the enemy advance.

Even now Hooker—still twice as strong as the battle-weary enemy—might have retrieved the situation. Two of his corps—Reynolds' and Meade's—which had not been engaged at all, composed his right wing. They could easily have encircled Stuart's left and rolled Lee's army back again. Sedgwick, over at Fredericksburg, had crossed the river and was driving Early in; Lee had to send back part of his own force to Early's assistance. But Hooker was finished; no thought of counterattack was in his mind. To add to his previous indecision, the shock of a shell striking beside him at his headquarters partly stunned him. But he wouldn't completely relinquish command; he ordered a general retirement.

For the fourth and last time, the Army of the Potomac retired to its cantonments, misused through a commander's lack of combat leadership.

In justice to Hooker, one must add that of the four who failed against Robert E. Lee, he was the only one who would make a comeback. McClellan never received another active command; Pope was relegated to Indian fighting in the West; Burnside went on to make another ghastly bumble as a corps commander at Petersburg. But "Fighting Joe" Hooker, summarily relieved from the Army of the Potomac while leading it north into Maryland after Lee's second invasion of the Union, would redeem himself in battle. He would fight and win—under Grant's command—the "Battle of the Clouds" on Lookout Mountain, and under Sherman he took prominent and efficient part in the Atlanta campaign of 1864. He had found his level of leadership—the combat command of an army corps. Some men are like that.

None of this explains why trial and error, a slow process at best, was the solution of command in the Army of the United States in the Civil War.

To understand what had happened, one must remember that President Lincoln, faced in 1861 by the fact that only by force of arms could the eleven states seceding from the Union be brought to bay, also found he had no force to employ.

In early 1861 the Army consisted of five regiments of cavalry, ten of infantry, the Corps of Engineers, and the various staff and administrative departments. Its actual strength was 16,367 officers and men, scattered in little packets along the Western frontier, the Canadian border, and the Atlantic coast. Against this were gathering in the Southland 100,000 volunteers enlisted for a year's service, 35,000 of them—more than twice the United States strength—already under arms when Fort Sumter fell.

The hordes which thereafter gathered from the militia and volunteers to make up the Army of the United States, were officered by men appointed by the various state governors, mainly without regard for any other quality than political preferment. It having been decided that the regulars would remain encadred in their units, their officers—except for a few whom some governors wangled with much difficulty from the War Department to lead "hometown" troops—remained with them.

Of the 1,036 professional U.S. Army officers in uniform in 1861, 286 forsook their allegiance and took commissions in the Confederate forces. Only 248 of the remainder became colonels, and of these but 142 ever donned general's stars.

Yet, oddly enough, we can say that this war was a West Pointer's war. In 55 of the 60 important battles both sides were commanded by Military Academy graduates; a graduate commanded one or other of the opponents in the remaining 5.

That is worth consideration. There were 684 graduates in active service in the beginning; 168 became Confederates. When the war ended 308 West Pointers, including 161 captains, were still majors or lower.

But—102 graduates in civil life came back to the colors (32 per cent of those who had earlier resigned), and of them 53 became general officers, and 82 in all reached the grade of colonel and higher.

Most in this last category came back in the militia or volunteers, thanks to governors who included their names among the crowds of patronage seekers. For this, at least, the nation would have cause for gratitude.

What it all amounted to was that President Lincoln and the Congress, instead of splitting up the little Regular Army and distributing its members amongst the mass of state-raised volunteer greenhorns as a leaven, ignored it. Consequently Lincoln was compelled to pick his leaders hit-or-miss, to prove their competence by the slow and costly method of trial and error on the battlefield.

Jefferson Davis, on the other hand—himself a onetime professional Army man—at once utilized the small group of regulars who joined his cause, and 92 additional West Pointers who came in from civil life, seeding them through his new-raised forces. Militarily, the Union had acted as a confederacy; the Confederacy as a nation.*

As the dreadful mill of war ground on, two giants emerged from the grist.

* Figures assembled from data in *Register of Graduates and Former Cadets of the United States Military* (New York: West Point Alumni Foundation, 1947–1951); Emory Upton, *Military Policy of the United States* (Washington: U.S. Government Printing Office, 1904), pp. 236–238; and Francis B. Heitman, *Historical Register of the Officers of the United States Army* (Washington: U.S. Government Printing Office, 1903), Vol. II, pp. 180–184.

CHAPTER X ☆ ☆ ☆ *The Giants of the Civil War*

Ulysses S. Grant and Robert E. Lee, so different in origin and appearance, shared several characteristics in common; things pertinent to any examination of the men as leaders. In the first place, each was a graduate of the U.S. Military Academy. Next, both epitomized the essential characteristic of the American leader who would rise to the heights; subservience to the civil power. Finally—and this is important particularly in the case of Grant, who has been accused of squandering the lives of his men—while cherishing the lives and well-being of those they commanded, neither man hesitated, when the chips were down, to expend those pawns in furtherance of the objective.

We might as well set this last matter straight in the beginning. Grant, with 107,000 men in round numbers at the opening of the Wilderness–Spotsylvania–Cold Harbor campaign, lost 55,000 in killed, wounded, and missing in 38 days of battle; 52 per cent of his initial strength. Lee, with 61,000, lost about 39,000, or 59 per cent. The heaviest day's loss for the Union army in this campaign was at Spotsylvania, June 10, 1864: 7,133. But Lee, at Gettysburg, on July 3, 1863, had in an hour expended 7,644 of the 15,000 men who took part in Pickett's gallant, ill-fated charge.

They did such things because they were soldiers, with the singleness of purpose of the leader fixed in the attainment of his objective. Kindhearted, simple gentlemen, they abhorred war in itself. But

166

Lee, at Fredericksburg, was voicing the sentiments of both when he observed:

"It is well that war is so terrible—we should grow too fond of it."

Let's look first at Grant, the shabby little thirty-nine-year-old ex-army officer whom war caught up with in 1861, while he was clerking in his father's leather store in Galena, Illinois.

"A First-Section Man"

There is something of predestination in the career of this man Grant, for his feet were set on the road to glory through the very vagaries of the stupid, ill-advised system of political appointment of army officers hampering the United States in Civil War days.

It was Governor Richard Yates, of Illinois, who gave Grant back to the Army, commissioning him a colonel of Volunteers. It was Representative Elihu B. Washburne of Illinois, craving his share of patronage in the appointment of brigadier generals, who shortly afterwards tossed stars to the only colonel coming from his district.

Neither of these things might have happened had not the officers of a rowdy Illinois regiment rebelled against their incompetent colonel. When they demanded a replacement, Governor Yates grasped for the first straw at hand—the former army captain whom he had appointed as State mustering officer.

Grant had graduated from the Military Academy in 1843. He fought in Mexico under Winfield Scott and was twice brevetted for gallantry in action—at Molino del Rey and in the storming of the San Cosmé gate of Mexico City. Peacetime soldiering was not to his liking and it was said that he drank too much. He resigned in 1854 and from that time until the guns spoke at Sumter he was just one more little civilian to whom the fates had been unkind.

When war fever struck Galena, the home-town company of volunteers needed a drillmaster and Grant took the chore. He followed them to Springfield while waiting for an answer to his letter to the War Department proffering his services again. But the answer didn't come (it never would come, in fact), and meanwhile his persistency got him his job in the state capital.

Then it was that the officers of the 21st Illinois Infantry came storming in to Yates seeking a new colonel, and about that time

Washburne, down in Washington, began clamoring for a political
plum in the shape of a brigadier generalcy.

But if Lady Luck or fortune or fate, whatever you wish to call it,
saw to it that Grant was the man underfoot when these things
happened, for the rest of the way he walked alone.

A long road and a hard one this man would travel. At times it was
a broad highway; at frequent spots it came to a dead end. How his
task was accomplished, how the obstacles were overcome or by-
passed, are oft-told tales.

The Henry-Donelson campaign was succeeded by Shiloh's shock.
Vicksburg took months to solve. There was the Chattanooga campaign, where he picked up the pieces of Rosecrans' Chickamauga
disaster to get a nasty situation under control. The succeeding victories of Lookout Mountain and Missionary Ridge swept Tennessee
clear of Confederate troops and paved the way for Sherman's later
advance into Georgia.

The highway opened wide on March 9, 1864. In Grant, Lincoln
had found his general and the United States Army a leader. Once
more the Army of the Potomac would go to war, guided this time
by a man who knew the business.

It would be total war, with unity of command and a single ultimate objective: the destruction of the two principal enemy forces.

"It is my design," wrote Grant to Sherman then, ". . . to work all
parts of the army together and somewhat towards a common end.
. . . I will stay with the Army of the Potomac and operate against
Lee's army wherever it may be found. . . . You I propose to move
against Johnston's army, to break it up and get into the interior of
the enemy's country as far as you can, inflicting all the damage you
can against their war resources. . . ."

There would be the Wilderness–Spotsylvania–Cold Harbor campaign; a succession of checks and blocks to Grant's passage. The
road would open wide again with his magnificent by-pass across the
James, rightly ranked by Steele "among the very finest achievements
of strategy to be found in our military history." He was halted then
at Petersburg's dead end until he forced Lee out into the open at
long last, and Appomattox spelled the end.

The point is that Grant's resilient persistence got him there—

the infectious persistence that Sherman characterized as "simple faith in success."

From beginning to end his operations demonstrate the simple aggressiveness of an honest man, applied with lucidity and an elastic mind to the solution of the problem. Therein lay Grant's greatness as a leader. No great captain has ever better understood the fact that, once in contact with the enemy, the leader is no longer at liberty to do what he wishes, but must do what best he can.

Take the Vicksburg campaign: a masterpiece of combat leadership.

"I Could Not Be Interfered With"

Two hundred and fifty feet above the wide, swirling Mississippi, the fortress city sat the bluffs at the crossroads of the Southern Confederacy. So long as it stood, there would be no trade between the Northwestern states and the outside world. When and if it fell, the Southland would be split from end to end. Until that time, however, the fact that Union troops had taken Memphis and Corinth above it, and held the lower reaches of the river from New Orleans up to Baton Rouge, mattered little. For now, in early April, 1863, Vicksburg seemed inpregnable.

Across the way from Vicksburg, in the mud of Young's Point, the stubby little man whose classmates at West Point had affectionately called "Sam," and who smoked innumerable big black cigars, was pondering these things. He had an army seventy-five thousand strong, scattered from Milliken's Bend above Vicksburg to New Carthage below, and he had already made several unsuccessful attempts to get at Vicksburg from the north and root it out.

Now, as Grant saw it, there remained but three plans to try: a direct assault across the river to escalade the bluffs; a return to Memphis to make a long, laborious swing eastward which would avoid the swampland, bayous, and rivers immediately protecting Vicksburg on its northerly face; or go down the west bank, cross below the city and, with no base of supplies, move from the south against the rear of the fortress.

The first would be suicidal; the second would look like a retreat and the United States was getting sick and tired of retreats. Al-

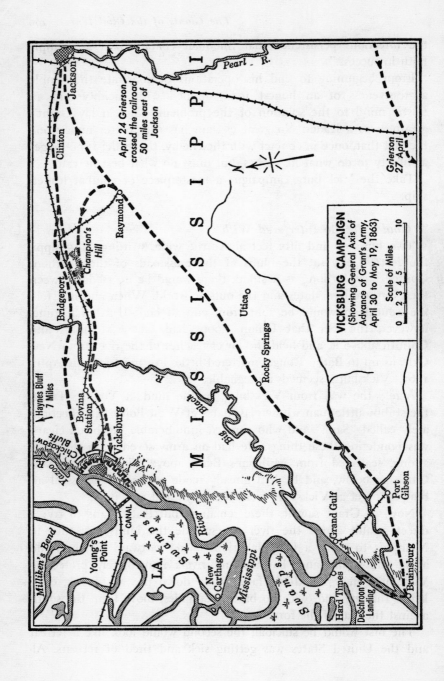

VICKSBURG CAMPAIGN
(Showing General Axis of
Advance of Grant's Army,
April 30 to May 19, 1863)

Scale of Miles
0 1 2 3 4 5   10

April 24 Grierson
crossed the railroad
50 miles east of
Jackson

Grierson
27 April

Pearl - R.

Jackson

Clinton

Raymond

Champion's
Hill

Bridgeport

Utica

Rocky Springs

Haynes Bluff
7 Miles

Bovina
Station

Vicksburg

Chickasaw
Bluffs

Yazoo R.

Big Black R.

Milliken's
Point

Young's
Point

CANAL

New
Carthage

L A.   S w a m p s

Mississippi   River

S w a m p s

Port
Gibson

Grand Gulf

Hard
Times

DeSchroon's
Landing

Bruinsburg

M I S S I S S I P P I

ready the impatient press was clamoring, as the American press always clamors in its wartime amateur masterminding fashion, for Grant's removal. The third possibility involved a risk seldom justified in war, for in and about Vicksburg, Confederate General John C. Pemberton had some thirty-two thousand effectives, and inland General Joe Johnston had additional forces. Actually, as Grant at this time estimated, his enemies could have put more than sixty thousand men against him if they concentrated them.

Grant took the third choice. He would cross the river below Vicksburg. Commodore David P. Porter, USN, commanding the river fleet co-operating with him, ran the Vicksburg batteries cleverly, with gunboats and a fleet of empty transports, and Grant took his troops overland, with much difficulty, down to New Carthage.

The plan was simple, broad, and, because it worked, magnificent. The same day that Porter ran the batteries, Sherman moved by water from Milliken's Bend up the Yazoo as if to attempt a frontal assault on Chickasaw Bluffs, north of Vicksburg (he'd tried this once before and had been repulsed). That same day, too, from up at Grand Junction, Tennessee, fifty miles east of Memphis, Grant launched the most strategically important cavalry raid of the Civil War.

Colonel Benjamin H. Grierson, with a force of Illinois cavalry a thousand sabers strong, lashed down through Mississippi on a twenty-five day rampage across Confederate territory until then untouched by war. He wouldn't stop until he had cut the east-west railway line linking Vicksburg with the enemy heartland and the north-south line crossing it at Jackson. He would end up May 2 at Baton Rouge to join Federal General Banks's inchworm progress up from New Orleans.

Grierson's exploit set the Confederate hierarchy in the West atwitter. Pemberton at Vicksburg, already worried about Sherman's demonstration north of him, learned that "strong Union forces" were scouring the interior. Bragg, up Shelbyville way in Tennessee, fencing with Rosecrans, began to worry about his rear, and Joseph E. Johnston, commanding the entire Confederate Department of the West, tried to reappraise the general situation.

Then, as Grierson's rovers approached the last lap in their five-hundred-mile ride, with the countryside behind them rocking, Grant began ferrying his troops across the Mississippi, on board Porter's transports, to the little town of Bruinsburg, forty miles below Vicksburg. That was April 28. Pemberton began concentrating all the forces he could lay hands on, and called on Jefferson Davis back in Richmond for reinforcements. The Confederate President, torn between his obsession that Vicksburg must be held at all costs, and his solicitude for Bragg's army, ordered Johnston to take personal command to retrieve the Vicksburg situation.

Grant's initial moves constituted a brilliant seizure of the initiative. Now his fertility of mind, which had produced such turmoil among his opponents while adhering to the principle of the objective—clearing the Mississippi River—would have another test; this time of flexibility.

Thus far in his operation, the general plan was that, once across the river, his progress would be assisted by a junction with General Banks coming up from Baton Rouge. Between them, they could clear the east bank of the Mississippi from Port Hudson just above Baton Rouge up to Vicksburg.

Two days later McClernand's corps, the leading element of Grant's Army of the Tennessee, moved inland. It clashed with the first of Pemberton's troops rushed down to stop him. By morning of May 1 a sharp fight near Port Gibson cleared the Confederates away and Grant halted on the southern bank of the Big Black River, which comes wandering down behind Vicksburg to empty into the Mississippi at Grand Gulf. There Sherman's corps, hustled down the west bank of the river from its demonstration at Chickasaw Bluffs, began to join him on May 6. Pemberton began concentrating on the north side of the Big Black River.

Then came word from Banks. Nathaniel P. ("Nothing Positive") Banks was positive for once. It would be some time before he could reduce Port Hudson, and even after that he could send but twelve thousand men to co-operate with Grant. In other words, he was still more than sixty miles away and wasn't going to be much nearer.

Grant faced a new decision. He could surrender the initiative, consolidate his forces about Grand Gulf as a base and defer further operations until Banks came; a matter perhaps of a month or longer, during which time his enemies could concentrate all they had to oppose him. Or—he could plunge into the midst of the still scattered Confederates and defeat them in detail. He knew that Pemberton was on his north and that another force was assembling at Jackson, the vital railway junction on which Vicksburg must depend for supply and reinforcement.

Grant's own estimate tells the story:

"To wait for his [Banks's] cooperation would have detained me for at least a month. . . . I therefore determined to move independently of Banks, cut loose from my base, destroy the Rebel force in rear of Vicksburg and invest or capture the city.

"Grand Gulf was accordingly given up as a base, and the authorities at Washington were notified. I knew well that [General] Halleck's caution would lead him to disapprove of this course; *but . . . the time it would take to communicate with Washington and get a reply would be so great that I could not be interfered with.*" (Italics supplied.)

Maybe there was a twinkle in those blue eyes when Grant toyed with that thought.

"As I hoped in the end to besiege Vicksburg, I must first destroy all possibility of aid. I therefore determined to move swiftly toward Jackson, destroy or drive any force in that direction and then turn upon Pemberton."

That is what he did. With 40,000 men, 120 wagons, and less than 5 days' rations, he moved east. So far as Washington was concerned, he might have been in Africa.

It was springtime in Mississippi. The strawberries were ripe, the ground was firm, the farms rich in cattle, poultry, and hogs. The Army of the Tennessee lived well and marched fast. It also fought well. By May 14 Grant had pushed General Johnston out of Jackson, locking Vicksburg's back door. While Sherman mopped up, Grant reversed his march, moving directly westward toward Vicksburg.

Pemberton, meanwhile had unintentionally done his best to assist Grant. Mesmerized by Jefferson Davis' injunction to hold Vicksburg at all costs, Pemberton ignored until too late the pleas and orders from General Johnston to strike at Grant's rear. For several days he fumbled about seeking to cut the Union army's communications—an impossible feat, since Grant had none. When Pemberton moved at last, crossing the Big Black River in an effort to unite with Johnston, he met Grant's advance in force at Champion's Hill on May 16.

For a while it was quite a fight; Pemberton's men battled stoutly. Grant watched, imperturbably, at the critical point of the battle line, directing operations.

". . . leaning complacently against his favorite steed," was the way one corporal saw him, "smoking—as seemed habitual with him —the stump of a cigar. His was the only horse near the line and must, naturally, have attracted some of the enemy's fire. . . . I am sure everyone who recognized him wished him away; but there he stood—clear, calm, and immovable. . . ."

Actually, had Grant's directive for an envelopment been followed, Pemberton, with the river behind him, would have been cut off. But McClernand, a political general in uniform only because of his influence, mishandled his corps. So Pemberton got away. Next day, after a sharp brush with McPherson's corps, he withdrew across the Big Black to retire into the defenses of his doomed citadel.

It was in this last fight, at the bridge near Bovina Station, that Washington reopened communication with Grant. A mud-spattered officer from Banks's staff galloped up to present a message from General Halleck, routed via New Orleans.

It was a peremptory order, dated May 11, to desist his campaign, and take the army down to Port Hudson to help Banks. Joint operations against Vicksburg could come later.

Grant pointed to Lawler's brigade, at that moment charging over the enemy's last breastworks east of the river. With a dry remark that it was now too late to abandon his operation, Grant swung into the saddle.

"I immediately rode in the direction of the charge," writes Grant, "and saw no more of the officer who had delivered the message."

In eighteen days Grant had marched his army some two hundred miles to defeat enemy detachments in five engagements—four in a six-day span. He had inflicted losses of eight thousand men and eighty-eight guns and had locked his principal opponent up in his fortress. The Big Black River operation evidences for all time the vision, audacity, and strategical genius of Grant.

It was the most daring American feat of arms since Winfield Scott cut loose from his communications to plunge into the heart of Mexico in 1847.

By May 19 Vicksburg was invested. On July 4, 1863, Pemberton surrendered the starving city. "The Father of Waters," commented President Lincoln, "again goes unvexed to the sea."

Ulysses S. Grant, unvexed also, went on. And up at West Point his old preceptor, Dennis Hart Mahan, drew a pen picture of his pupil:

". . . Always a first-section man. . . . His mental machine was of the powerful low-pressure class, which condenses its own steam and consumes its own smoke, and which pushes steadily forward and drives all obstacles before it."

King of Spades

Back in 1847 Dennis Hart Mahan had written an estimate and a prophecy: "There probably has existed no great engineer who, when called upon, has not shown himself a superior general; nor a great general who did not fully acknowledge and appreciate the art of fortification. . . . Military history is full of examples where the scale of great and decisive battles has turned on the taking or holding of a mere field-work that had occupied but a few hours time to throw it up."

The best exemplar of that estimate would be Robert E. Lee, Virginia patrician and son of another great soldier—"Light-Horse Harry" Lee.

Assessment of the combat leadership of Robert E. Lee is impossible without taking into consideration the basic premise that to be successful the Confederate States of America needed only to maintain themselves as a nation. They had seceded from the United States, which proposed to invade the rebellious area and reduce it by force of arms; the Union's strategy must be offensive to be successful.

The South would be successful so long as its armed forces remained intact within its borders, preserving its government. Its military strategy, then, was defensive. The genius of Lee lies in his immediate acceptance of this fact and in the methods by which he sought success in arms; a continual grasp for what chess players call the "move" and soldiers the "initiative." Lee, aware that the best defense is the offense, used tactical offensive measures on the battle-field to maintain the strategic defense demanded by the political situation.

Audacity, vision, and canny use of the terrain to aid his opera-tions characterized nearly all of Lee's operations. To him the spade was equal in value to the musket; his quick-dug entrenchments were *points d'appui* from which to launch the stabbing ripostes which would time and again halt an opponent superior in man-power. Grumbling, as American soldiers always grumble when forced to dig, Lee's men soon gave him the nickname of "King of Spades." But they dug, and learned, if not to like it, that at least it brought beneficial results.

Aside from his enemies, Lee had other obstacles to hurdle. One of these was the geographical obsession of his government with the safety of its capital. That, of course, was even more true of the United States. The mutual proximity of both Washington and Richmond to the principal seat of war hampered the military lead-ers of both sides.

More serious to Lee was the fact that the Southern Confederacy, by its very nature, contained within its states' rights structure the seeds of its own dissolution. Time and time again he was deprived of vital munitions, food, and manpower through the refusal of indi-vidual state governors to co-operate in the national defense.

He did have the benefit of a hard core of professional officers to lead his troops—386 Regulars and ex-Regulars who joined the Con-federate forces. But among those were such diverse and difficult spirits as grandiose Pierre Gustave Toutant Beauregard, stubborn James Longstreet, and touchy Joseph E. Johnston.

So, of necessity, all through the Civil War Lee was forced to compromise in the general good; to cajole as well as to order; to make the best of the material on hand—never in profusion at best; to piece, patch, and shift, and at the same time to command the respect and devotion of his men. That he was able to do these things, to win victory after victory, and that even in the moment of dissolu-tion at Appomattox, starving, exhausted soldiers would crowd around him shouting through their tears, "General, say the word and we'll go in and fight 'em yet!"—is indeed best evidence of his leadership.

Lee came to the Confederacy as an active, fifty-four-year-old professional soldier stepping to command at the height of a successful career. He had made a name for himself as an engineer on two counts—accomplishment of public works in peacetime and analysis of terrain in war.

His ingenious salvage of St. Louis as a river port, in 1838, by harnessing the Mississippi River to self-scour a channel through the silt choking access to the waterfront, was one of the major accomplishments of the Corps of Engineers.

As Scott's engineer officer in the campaign from Vera Cruz to Mexico City in 1847, he contributed mightily to success. At Cerro Gordo it was Lee who found the mountain trail by which Scott turned his enemy out of an apparently impregnable position. Later, at El Peñon, on the road to Mexico City; and at the lava bed of Pedregal, near Contreras, it was Lee whose indefatigable reconnaissance found the way through seemingly impassable obstacles leading to the victories of Contreras and Churubusco. At Chapultepec, where he was wounded slightly, he shared in the common glory of Scott's "graduated cadets."

From 1852 to 1855 Lee was superintendent of the U.S. Military Academy; from that time until he resigned to offer his sword to Virginia, he served with a cavalry regiment. Through this wide variety of service his personal acquaintance with the officer corps of the old Regular Army, their personalities, temperaments, and idiosyncrasies, was wide and intimate. Thanks to his own logical, dispassionate thought processes, Lee made tremendous use of this gift of knowledge when he met his former comrades on the battlefield.

McClellan's meticulous hesitancy, in particular, he appears to have catalogued (as did Joseph E. Johnston, too) from the beginning. This was most dramatically proven in the Antietam campaign, as we have already noted. Lee, with his forces spread from Harpers Ferry to Hagerstown, made no bones about concentrating and standing in front of Sharpsburg, with the Potomac at his back and tremendous odds in front of him. And when the day's bloody fight was over and all Lee's reserves expended, he remained in position for another twenty-four hours before leaving the field, seemingly contemptuous of McClellan's latent power to crush him.

So, too, with John Pope's bullheaded obstinacy. Lee's daring division of his forces before Second Bull Run was made in the confidence that Pope's tendency to jump at conclusions would lead him to blunder.

The tortuous timidity of "Old Brains" Halleck, his fellow engineer, was not unknown to Lee, nor was Hooker's troublemaking tendency. But there was one man Lee didn't know well, except by hearsay, until he clashed with him. And against that man Lee took none of the audacious chances characterizing his previous campaigns. That was Ulysses S. Grant.

Against Grant, Lee waged a campaign of aggressive defense outstanding in tactical brillance and most remarkable because of his inspired leadership which kept a lost cause going far longer than could be expected. Not only was Lee's generalship exceptional; exceptional too, were the qualities of personal leadership which kept the Army of Northern Virginia intact as a fighting team long after its physical resources had drained away.

But there was no more division of force in the open field. Certainly there was nothing comparable to his previous floutings of McClellan, Pope, Burnside and Hooker.

Lee's record in the Civil War, from the time that he took over the command of the Army of Northern Virginia when Johnston had been wounded at Seven Pines, is a magnificent page of our military heritage. Much of the story has already been told here in relating the misfortunes of those pitted against him.

The Seven Days, Second Bull Run, Fredericksburg, and Chancellorsville belong to Lee. His two invasions of the North were both audacious and brilliant in strategical concept. Each caused the Army of the Potomac to make hurried parry. They fell squarely into the category set twenty years previous by Dennis Hart Mahan; operations where "the entire movable army strikes at the enemy in the heart of his own country. Such resolutions by great generals are stamped with the mark of true genius."

It was fate rather than counterstrategy that caused Lee to fail both times; nevertheless, each time he brought back an army still able and willing to fight. Antietam, tactically, we must award to Lee, who held the battlefield, although it is listed frequently as a Union victory and strategically—since Lee had to withdraw to Virginia— it was. But certainly it was of his own volition and in his own good time that Lee broke contact there; McClellan didn't drive him off.

Of Gettysburg—a meeting engagement on ground which neither leader would have chosen—one can say that it was the irony of fate that reconnaissance and judgment of terrain, Lee's forte, failed him there. And when Gettysburg was lost Lee the man rose to his greatest personal height in his moment of defeat.

"It is I that have lost this fight," he told a division commander reeling back from the last assault. "And you must help me out of it the best way you can."

But all that was over and done, in early May of 1864, when Lee first clashed with Grant. The Army of the Potomac had started south once more across the Rapidan to move onto the old battle-field of Chancellorsville. Lee, with the bulk of his forces further west, learned from observers on Clark's Mountain that the move was on, divined his enemy's intention to turn his right flank, and moved to hit him before he could get out of the tangled scrub of the Wilderness.

From their widespread cantonments to the west of the area his three corps came pounding eastward May 4—Ewell, A. P. Hill, and (following Hill) Longstreet, while in wide loop from Fredericksburg, Stuart's cavalry moved south and west.

Lee had some 61,000 men and 274 guns; Grant about 105,000 and 316 guns. Their advance elements clashed in the second-growth thickets, little streams, and marshes all crisscrossed by winding trails and wood roads. They piled up in that mess, an area 14 miles long and 10 miles wide, in a series of piecemeal engagements, where observation was nil, artillery almost useless, and control impossible.

For two long days they fought, then as if by common consent drew away from one another for a day of bewildered rest, while be-tween them the undergrowth smoldered in innumerable brush fires in which screaming, wounded men were roasting.

The two armies were facing along an east-west line, now. Once more the Army of the Potomac had been stopped. Judged by past

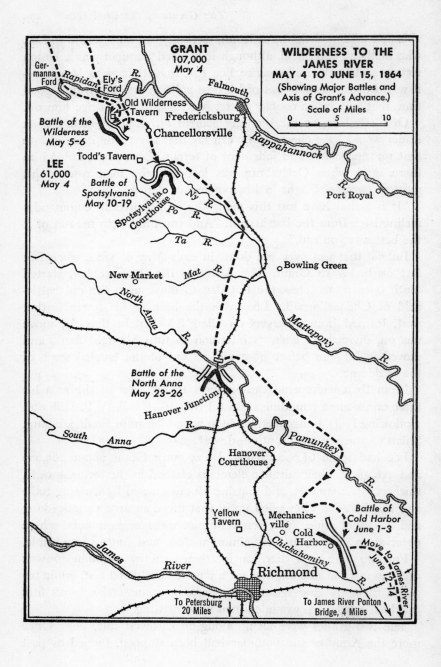

GRANT
107,000
May 4

WILDERNESS TO THE
JAMES RIVER
MAY 4 TO JUNE 15, 1864
(Showing Major Battles and
Axis of Grant's Advance.)
Scale of Miles
0   5   10

Germanna Ford
Rapidan R.
Ely's Ford
R.
Falmouth

Old Wilderness Tavern
Fredericksburg

Battle of the Wilderness
May 5-6
Chancellorsville

Rappahannock

LEE
61,000
May 4

Todd's Tavern

Battle of Spotsylvania
May 10-19

Spotsylvania Courthouse
Ny R.
Po R.
Ta R.

Port Royal
R.

New Market

Mat R.

Bowling Green

North Anna R.

Mattapony

Battle of the North Anna
May 23-26

Hanover Junction

South Anna R.

Pamunkey

Hanover Courthouse

R.

Yellow Tavern

Mechanicsville

Cold Harbor

Battle of Cold Harbor
June 1-3

James River

Chickahominy R.

Richmond

Move to James River
June 12-14

To Petersburg
20 Miles

To James River Ponton
Bridge, 4 Miles

performances, it should admit defeat and backtrack across the river. That was how things had gone before. That, perhaps, was how a man of genius less than Lee's might have figured it. Lee didn't; he would take no chances against a man of Grant's reputation.

He started sideslipping in the night, down toward Spotsylvania Court House, with Fitz Lee's division of Stuart's cavalry out ahead on the Brock Road, along which any Union offensive move must come.

It came, all right; Grant's irrevocable persistence to turn the enemy's sensitive right flank. But it stumbled slowly through a succession of roadblocks, felled trees defended by detachments of Lee's cavalry. When it debouched next morning near Spotsylvania Court House it was met by a sleet of musketry and artillery. For Longstreet's corps (Anderson commanding, Longstreet having been wounded) was already entrenched across the road. The "King of Spades" was at it again, a splendid demonstration of the strategic defense.

Before Spotsylvania's quick-dug fieldworks Grant hammered, while Lee—in the forefront of battle always—controlled the defense in person.

When Hancock's corps stormed over the "Bloody Angle" in the predawn of May 12, threatening the collapse of the entire Confederate line, Lee was there. He personally organized the counterattack and would have led it, but his officers and men forcibly prevented him.

"Lee to the rear! General Lee to the rear!" came the roars; his charger's reins were jerked from Lee's hand, the horse turned back.

It was a repetition of the scene six days earlier in the Wilderness, when Hood's Texans of Longstreet's corps had forcibly prevented Lee from joining them as they counterattacked down the Orange Plank Road.

The defense was adamant, but so was the offense. Again Grant slipped southward; again Lee as swiftly paralleled the move and the armies clashed at Hanover Junction. Lee actually beat Grant to that position—another potential "Bloody Angle" with its nose resting on the North Anna. Grant would have none of that, however, and the Army of the Potomac went easing down toward the old

Seven Days' battlefields, seeking always a way around Lee's right flank; to lever him away from Richmond, now but nine miles away.

Once more Lee's intuitive genius blocked the way, as he raced for Old Cold Harbor, a stone's throw from the 1862 battlefield. He won the race, began throwing up a network of entrenchments as springboard for an attack; it was the "King of Spades" at his best. But Grant, "King of Iron," was pushing in and Cold Harbor instead became a defensive action for the Confederates. It was a magnificent defense, against which the Army of the Potomac pounded vainly.

It ended when Grant, breaking off action, made the amazing James River crossing under Lee's very nose, forcing him to shift down to Petersburg. There would be no more maneuvering for the Army of Northern Virginia until April 3, 1865, and the last reeling, gallant attempt to keep the field, ending at Appomattox.

In Grant and Lee one finds all the essential characteristics of leadership in high command. Both will stand always as great captains. The interesting thing to the student of war is that since these twain opposed one another on the battlefield, the record is there. No speculative "if" is needed to weight the balance in comparison.

But why compare them?

From the Wilderness to Appomattox there were two Hannibals; no Terentius Varro was present. And that's a very nice tribute to the military heritage of America.

In comparing the sum total of all the campaigns of both men, of course, there is room for respectful criticism. Both were human; both made errors; and both, incidentally, were assisted by strong right-hand men, major lieutenants in whom they put their trust.

Let's look now at some of these right-hand men.

CHAPTER XI ☆ ☆ ☆ *Strong Right Hands*

Ability to delegate authority is one of the attributes of leadership. The quality of this delegation and its scope depend both upon the leader and those whom he commands.

Occasionally, a leader is blessed with a subordinate who not only grasps what is desired but is able, on his own initiative, to elaborate the plan in such fashion as to attain results even beyond the original concept. Men of this category are in effect virtuosos, improvising to expand a simple tune into a rippling symphony. Parenthetically, history's record shows that subordinates of this sort usually differ radically from their commanders in temperament and personality.

Both Robert E. Lee and Ulysses S. Grant were so blessed; the first with Thomas Jonathan Jackson, the second with William Tecumseh Sherman.

One point in common these stalwart lieutenants had: inflexibility of purpose. Each, from his own viewpoint, saw the cause he supported outlined in broad, bold strokes of black and white; there were no grays of compromise.

Both men, from time to time, within their own respective nations (the word is used advisedly; the Civil War was in fact the collision of two hostile nations), were accused of mental unbalance. But whereas those who called Sherman crazy were civilians and jealous political appointees in uniform, Jackson's reputation dated from his V.M.I. instructor days. Also, Sherman's calumniators acted out of viciousness and ignorance; Jackson's critics, conversely, in more or less amused admiration and awe.

The disciplinary methods of their respective leaderships were in violent opposition. Jackson ruled his troops with rod of iron. Sherman's control was flexible; he guided his command as the perfect horseman guides a spirited animal—the curb was there, but the hands on the reins were easy. Sherman took his subordinate commanders into his confidence; Jackson's close-lipped reticence hid his intentions until the moment combat was joined.

Yet each produced, and led victoriously, a combat team fanatical in its devotion and fearless in battle; a "hot" team, imbued with the will to win.

Let's look at these two warriors, in turn.

Like a Stone Wall

It is fate's irony that Thomas Jonathan Jackson, embodiment of fluidity of action—the lightning stroke, blitzkrieg, or any other synonym—should be immortalized by reference to one of the few times in his violent war making that he was involuntarily brought to bay.

But there it is. Like a stone wall he stood on the crest of the Henry House hill in the first Battle of Bull Run, and not all the brilliancy of his later fantastic Shenandoah Valley campaign, his lightning stroke that set up the Second Battle of Bull Run, nor the genius with which he elaborated in action Lee's planning of the battle of Chancellorsville, can ever wipe the "Stonewall" from his name.

Perhaps it is because of the monolithic character of the man himself; the granite façade presented in all his relations, not only to his commander and to his own men, but also to his enemies.

Only in the heat of combat were his dour features transformed by the radiant glow of the happy warrior; only in the privacy of his own home, apparently, could the unbending spirit melt into the adoring husband and loving father.

Jackson, born at Clarksburg, now West Virginia, graduated from the Military Academy in 1846; a gangling, big-framed youth whose awkwardness could never after be quite concealed by uniform. From his lawyer father he evidently inherited the keen inquisitiveness of mind that set him on the way to study war.

"You can be whatever you want to be," the young Jackson wrote as his personal maxim. What he wanted to be was a soldier. As result, years later, he would make another remark—a perfect paraphrasing of Dennis Hart Mahan—which is the clue to all his tactical and strategical genius:

"Always mystify, mislead and surprise the enemy . . . and when . . . you overcome him, never give up the pursuit as long as your men have strength to follow. . . . To move swiftly, strike vigorously, and secure all the fruits of victory, is the secret of successful war."

His own personal bravery, as well as his tenacity of purpose, he demonstrated as a young lieutenant of artillery during the assault on Chapultepec in the Mexican War. His three-gun section, supporting the infantry along a narrow causeway, was raked by Mexican fire from a breastwork on the hillside, and its animals all either killed or injured.

Jackson, with a handful of his men, manhandled one of his guns off the road into firing position, and with one sergeant—the rest of the crew had huddled in a nearby ditch—then began returning the Mexican fire.

Ordered by General Worth to withdraw from his exposed position, Jackson replied that it was more dangerous to withdraw than to stand fast and if they would give him fifty veterans he'd take the breastwork. Later, when victory had been won, General Scott singled out Jackson for praise before a group of officers, and the lieutenant writhed in an agony of shy embarrassment.

This shyness, covered by brusqueness and austerity, he carried with him to Virginia Military Institute when he resigned from the Army in 1852 to become professor of natural and experimental philosophy, and instructor in artillery.

As result he was far from popular among the cadets. This attitude, plus his Presbyterian piety, his fetish for punctuality, and his studied shabbiness of dress, earned him the nicknames of "Old Tom" and "Crazy Tom." None of this worried Jackson; he was interested in proficiency, not popularity.

Parenthetically, such personal idiosyncrasies of great leaders are very interesting. For instance, there would later be a man named Pershing, all spit and polish, but who, from the time he left West Point, was never punctual at a formation. He didn't do so badly in war, either.

Jackson, after Bull Run, for several months in the first year of the Civil War earned a reputation for squabbling both with his subordinates and with those above him. He could hardly be blamed for this, as a matter of fact. There were no giants of the military art in northwest Virginia, where he operated at the time.

And then he found his man. Robert E. Lee's reputation was known in the "old" Army—both as soldier and as student of war. Like Jackson he was an ardent student and admirer of Napoleon. To the grim ex-professor and ex-artilleryman, Lee was someone to admire and respect. Between them there was none of the warm camaraderie existing between Grant and Sherman; that was not their way. Nor could the difference of years of age and of seniority in the "old" Army be easily bridged. Jackson's rigidity, too, was in sharp contrast to the deep spirit of conciliation, compromise, and "makedo" which characterized Lee's actions and were, in his case, part and parcel of the leadership chore being thrust upon him.

But there was mutual confidence. So Jackson got his chance.

Fire in the Valley

It was early spring, 1862. Northward the Shenandoah Valley yawned invitingly, as did the vital Baltimore & Ohio Railroad and Chesapeake & Ohio Canal crossing its mouth. Guarding that Potomac River line was Federal General Banks, his 15,000 men scattered from Frederick up through Harpers Ferry to Cumberland. Over beyond the Allegheny Mountains on the western shoulder of the Valley was General Frémont with 15,000 more. East of the Blue Ridge in the main theater of war Washington city bristled with a garrison of 20,000 men; General McDowell, with 40,000 additional, hovering in its Virginian vicinity. McClellan's Army of the Potomac, more than 100,000 strong, investing Yorktown, threatened Richmond, almost 100 miles below Washington. And at Fortress Monroe, sea gate to the Confederate capital, another Federal garrison stood.

Inside this bristling arc the Confederates lay. General Joseph

E. Johnston with some 60,000 men was poised to thwart any move by McClellan, while across the Blue Ridge, Jackson at Woodstock, with 10,000, glowered north down the Valley. About Yorktown, down on the Peninsula, "Prince John" Magruder, with 13,000 more, was entrenching to oppose any threat from Fortress Monroe. Other smaller packets of troops garrisoned Richmond and Norfolk.

From the Confederate point of view the Federal threat to Richmond was the vital danger. Anything that delayed or prevented concentration of force in McClellan's hands furthered the Rebel mission; so thought Robert E. Lee, then military advisor to Jefferson Davis.

When Banks crossed the Potomac, moving to Winchester to cork up the Valley, Jackson met him in a series of feints and parries, carefully avoiding any pitched battle. Banks, finally convinced that he had driven his opponent out, moved most of his troops eastward to co-operate with McClellan.

Jackson immediately pounced. At Kernstown, March 23, he fell on General Shields and was repulsed. But Shields, sure that his opponent would not have attacked unless he had been reinforced, called on his chief, Banks, for help. "Nothing Positive" Banks came bumbling back, therefore, and Washington was alarmed by the apparent threat—just what Jackson wanted to accomplish.

Meanwhile Frémont was preparing to move across the mountains and southward up the Valley, with Staunton and finally Knoxville his grandiose goal.

While Jackson, his cavalry an impenetrable screen to Banks, was slowly withdrawing, he received Lee's directive. McDowell was moving overland toward Richmond to join McClellan, now launched on his Peninsula campaign. Jackson's job was to create a diversion which would cause the federal government to hold McDowell in northern Virginia.

Ewell's brigade of eight thousand men was sent as reinforcement. But how the mission was to be accomplished was up to Jackson. Thus rose the curtain on one of the most brilliant diversionary operations in the history of war.

Jackson was at Swift Run Gap. Banks was coming south up the Valley, Frémont moving in from the west. Screening his movements with his cavalry, Jackson left Ewell to contain Banks. With the

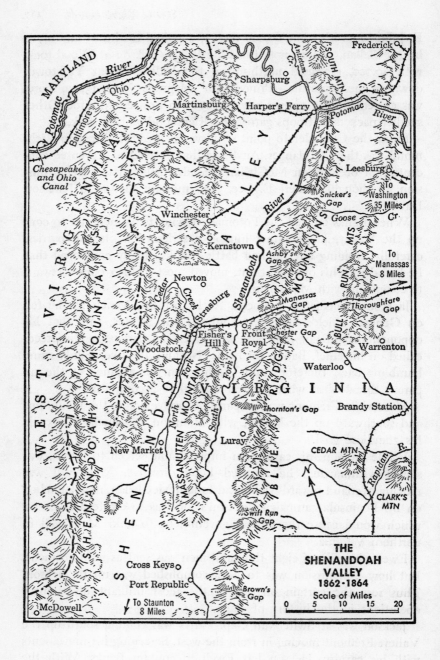

THE
SHENANDOAH
VALLEY
1862-1864

Scale of Miles

0   5   10   15   20

rest of his force he entrained, seemingly to move east toward Richmond. But the trains moved west, instead, and on May 8 he came crashing into the unsuspecting Frémont at the hamlet of McDowell.

Frémont was defeated and pursued for a few miles. Then Jackson whirled back into the Valley to take care of Banks, now halted at Front Royal, with his advance brigade at Strasburg.

From Port Republic almost to Front Royal the Massanutten Mountains, a narrow hill mass with but one main crossing—New Market Gap—split the Shenandoah Valley; a perfect mask for hide-and-go-seek before the days of aerial observation.

So Jackson, coming down the Valley turnpike west of the Massanuttens, swung through the gap in a rapid right hook that knocked the unsuspecting Banks out of Front Royal. Then he drove him back to Winchester, defeated him decisively, and pushed him back right across the Potomac at Harpers Ferry.

Washington went into panic. Up from Manassas, McDowell was ordered to march on Front Royal, his proposed junction with McClellan canceled. From the west Frémont, smarting from his previous defeat, was converging on the same point. By May 30, fifty thousand Federal troops, lashed by the rage of Secretary of War Stanton, were closing in on Jackson's sixteen thousand, now concentrated at Winchester. Shields's division of McDowell's army had stormed into Front Royal, twenty miles to his right rear. Frémont was only fifteen miles away to the left.

The trap was set, but its springs were weak; the Federal commanders too cautious. Jackson sent Ashby's cavalry to delay Frémont, supporting him later by Ewell. At the same time a detachment began demonstrating against Shields. And all the while Jackson's seven-mile-long double train of booty and the rest of his troops were pouring south up the Valley through the Strasburg bottleneck. It was touch-and-go. The last of the fast-marching "foot cavalry" slipped away practically in sight of Frémont's advance guard.

Then came the master stroke—a double counteroffensive; two simultaneous battles against two opponents. Sending Ewell to Cross Keys to defeat Frémont on June 8, Jackson himself, next day, with his Stonewall Brigade, assaulted Shields's advance elements at Port Republic, five miles away. Then Ewell, his job finished, hurried up in support, and the united force quickly threw the enemy from the field.

One week later Jackson was on his way to join Lee in the Peninsula. From April 30 to June 9 his men had marched some four hundred miles to fight five battles on terrain of his own choice and defeat four different Union commanders. Immense quantities of stores had been seized at Front Royal, Winchester, and Martinsburg. Above all, Washington had been terrified, and McDowell would now never be released to swell the Army of the Potomac.

With an effective strength of sixteen thousand men Jackson had disrupted the entire Union offensive plan and had tied up more than seventy-five thousand troops in the Valley and in the vicinity of Washington. Yet, in each battle but Cross Keys, Jackson, although seriously outnumbered by his local enemies, by maneuver put into action superior battle strength at the vital time and place. (Cross Keys was something else; Jackson gambled Ewell's eight thousand there against Frémont's thirteen thousand; the "Pathfinder's" vacillation on the battlefield was notorious.)

It was indeed a job well done; the masterly elaboration of a comparatively simple task of counterirritation. Had Jackson never fought another battle, his laurels would still rest in the Shenandoah Valley, where he turned a brush backfire into a roaring conflagration.

He did it by an amazing demonstration of iron discipline, relentless drive, and masterly military mentality, exhausting both leader and led. When it was over Jackson was burned out; his men dazed on their feet. Nothing else can explain his failures, at Mechanicsville and again at Gaines's Mill, to co-operate in Lee's well-planned opening operations of the Seven Days' Battles, June 26 and 27; nor his torpor at Malvern Hill on July 1.

But Lee had not lost faith in Jackson, as he proved two months later when—as we have seen—he crushed John Pope in the Second Battle of Bull Run. And Jackson's execution of his part of the plan was faultless from the time he started his corps on the fifty-four-mile hike (they did it in two days) till he plumped it deep in Pope's rear after capturing and sacking his supply dumps at Manassas Junction.

But in what followed Jackson was on his own. His was the sagacity making use of half-built railway cut and fill just west of Bull

Run; the best and perhaps the only terrain in which he could conceal his corps, and then successfully maintain himself against Pope's superiority of force. His was the decision when to reveal his position and lure Pope to battle, and his was the leadership which held that line until Lee came pounding in with Longstreet's corps for the kill.

There was foretaste of the future in this operation; of daring armored blitzkrieg or airborne drop deep into enemy territory, long years after these gaunt, gray soldiers should have passed from the scene. Celerity, it seems, is the secret of success, by whatever yardstick measured.

There was punch, there was direction, there was precision; all applied intelligently and loyally in furtherance of the given basic objective. No wonder, then, that from that time on, Jackson was indeed Lee's right arm in crises.

There would be three of these before the misdirected bullet of one of his own men cut Jackson down at Chancellorsville in the moment of victory. There would be Lee's first invasion of the North; with Jackson selected to capture Harpers Ferry (and still come back in the nick of time to Antietam). There would be the uncertain period, prior to Fredericksburg, when Lee pondered on Burnside's next move and kept Jackson as safety man far up the field in the Valley.

Finally, there would be that night of May 1, 1863, on the eve of Chancellorsville; Jackson huddled beside Lee, tracing diagrams on the ground in the flickering campfire light before stalking out to take his II Corps on the long swing around Hooker's right flank that ended in the thunderbolt.

A simple envelopment was what Lee had asked; a full-scale assault in perfect surprise, buckling up the enemy's entire right wing, was what Jackson gave him. But when it was done, Lee had lost his "right arm," and the grim spirit of his warrior lieutenant would "cross over the river and rest under the shade of the trees."

He Marched to the Sea

No man of his generation—with the exception of Grant—better grasped the meaning and the objectives of total war than did William Tecumseh Sherman. His sweep through Georgia from Atlanta to the sea—a swath more than two hundred miles long and eighty miles wide—destroyed most of the agriculture and industry on which the Southern Confederacy depended for war making.

Turning north then to drive four hundred more miles from Savannah to the Carolinas, he completed his march of destruction. He had ravished the heretofore untouched heart of the Southland and in the doing destroyed almost the last vestiges of its will to win. It was the culmination of Grant's grand strategy to dismember the Southern Confederacy while destroying her forces on the battlefield.

Sherman's was the second most important role in the grim tragedy; a part which, if properly played, would be equal to that of Meade's Army of the Potomac, which was under Grant's personal direction. It was, in fact, the essential complement.

There was fertile soil in this operation for any and all the differences, jealousies, and selfish aspirations to which any commander on an important mission may succumb.

A grandstand player might well have attempted to capitalize on such an opportunity. But Sherman's operations, from the moment that Grant first unleashed him against Johnston until the job was completed, furnish an outstanding example of enthusiastic and intelligent subordination.

When, at the end, Lincoln's assassination changed the complexion of the situation and a rabid War Secretary accused Sherman of treason because of his magnanimity to a defeated foe, Grant, in his own quiet, efficient way, hurried to calm the waters and protect Sherman.

Here was two-way loyalty indeed; fulfillment of Sherman's own words to Grant, already expressed a year earlier: "I knew wherever I was that you thought of me, and if I got in a tight place you would come—if alive."

Sherman, sensitive, tense as a coiled watch spring, met war at the First Battle of Bull Run, where, as he remarked, "For the first time in my life I saw cannon-balls strike men and crash through the trees and saplings above and around us, and realized the always sickening confusion as one approaches a fight from the rear."

Born in Lancaster, Ohio, Sherman graduated from West Point in 1840, but saw no real combat service in the Mexican War, having been stationed on the Pacific Coast. Resigning in 1853, he came

back to the colors in 1861 after an uneventful and not too successful dabbling in banking, the law, and schoolteaching. He was the
first superintendent of the then Louisiana Military Academy—now
Louisiana State University—at Baton Rouge in 1860, resigning later
when secession spirit flared with the seizure of the U.S. arsenal there.
Through his brother, Senator John Sherman, he was recommissioned
in the Regular Army as colonel, 13th U.S. Infantry.

Shifted west after Bull Run, where he had commanded a brigade
of New York and Wisconsin militia, Sherman for a short time was
in charge of all U.S. troops in Kentucky. His association with Grant
began shortly before the battle of Shiloh, the preliminaries to which
reflect little credit on either man. Faulty reconnaissance and neglect
in fortifying Pittsburg Landing resulted in near-defeat.

But both Grant and Sherman, who commanded one of his divisions, plunged into the fighting, exposing themselves with the utmost personal courage to snatch victory from the chaos.

It was during this early period that a closer bond united the pair.
Asked, in confidence, by Secretary of War Simon Cameron to give
his estimate of the war situation, Sherman had declared that 200,000
men would be needed to clear the Mississippi Valley. Cameron
publicized the statement and Sherman was publicly branded as a
"crazy man."

Grant, too, was under fire of both the high command and of
public opinion after Shiloh; his career saved only by Mr. Lincoln's
terse "I can't spare that man; he fights." Both men, then, were for
the moment partners in adversity. But whereas the imperturbable
Grant simply shrugged the brickbats from his shoulders and pursued
his own way, Sherman's reactions were electric and explosive.

But Grant stayed and Sherman stayed, their personal relationship
blossoming into an intimacy rarely to be found between two soldiers under similar circumstances.

In the swampy bayous of the Yazoo, in the Big Black River thrust,
in the Chattanooga operations, in the rescue of Burnside from Longstreet, at Knoxville; wherever there was a special job to be done
for Grant, dependable Sherman was there to do it. From a reliable
corps commander at Vicksburg he blossomed to a reliable army
commander at Chattanooga; Grant's mainstay.

Small wonder, then, that when Mr. Lincoln found his general and

Grant went East in March, 1864, to assume supreme command, his Western mantle fell on Sherman.

There was something inspiring about this thin, erect soldier with the intense eyes and jutting red beard; with his fixed hatreds and equally fixed loyalties. It was the spirit of leadership. It was demonstrated in many ways from the expressed threat to shoot on the spot an officer who should have known better than to absent himself without leave, to the sneaking of a hungry soldier into his mess tent to gorge himself on thick sandwiches.

And, of course, the concomitant of battle leadership was his everlasting ability—shown a thousand times—to be on the spot where the fighting was thickest. With it in his restless mind was always the axiom of his old West Point instructor in the art of war, Dennis Hart Mahan: to do the greatest damage to the enemy with minimum loss to his own troops.

As a result, his men, who respected him, also loved him. "Uncle Billy" could do no wrong. They were of different mold than the Easterners of the Army of the Potomac, these long-legged, rangy Western men. In them the rowdy spirit of the frontier still raged strong. Sherman understood them and they understood him.

They stood now, south of Chattanooga, some 100,000 strong. There was Sherman's old Army of the Tennessee, commanded by McPherson; Thomas' Army of the Cumberland, and Schofield's Army of the Ohio, their commanders picked by Sherman and Grant between them. Before them lay the Georgia border and Joseph E. Johnston, entrenched at Dalton, with some 60,000 men (including unreliable Georgia militia).

The time was ripe; Grant's instrument ready. So to Sherman came the famous directive of April 14, 1864, as confirmation of a project already blocked out in principle: ". . . You I propose to move against Johnston's army, break it up, and to get into the interior of the enemy's country as far as you can, inflicting all the damage you can against their war resources."

On May 7, Sherman made his first move. On that same day, five hundred miles to the northeast, the Army of the Potomac was clawing its way out of the bloody mess of the Virginia Wilderness, bound south. The big two-horned push was on; a massive double envelopment on a continental scale.

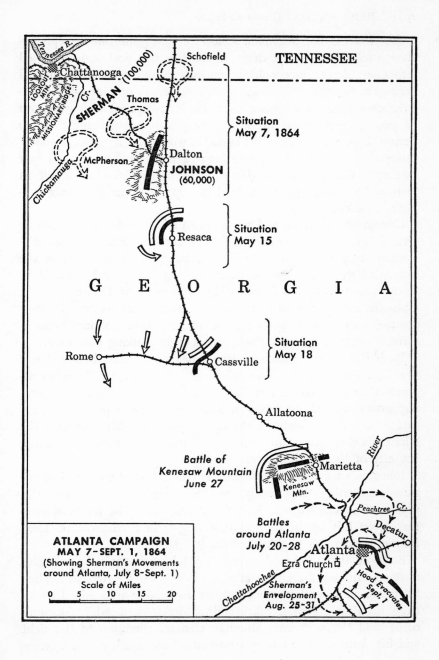

TENNESSEE

Tennessee R.

Chattanooga

Schofield

SHERMAN (100,000)

LOOKOUT MTN.

MISSIONARY RIDGE

Thomas

Cr.

Chickamauga

McPherson

Dalton

JOHNSON
(60,000)

Situation
May 7, 1864

Resaca

Situation
May 15

G E O R G I A

Rome

Cassville

Situation
May 18

Allatoona

Battle of
Kenesaw Mountain
June 27

Marietta

Kenesaw
Mtn.

River

Peachtree Cr.

Decatur

Battles
around Atlanta
July 20-28

Atlanta

Ezra Church

Chattahoochee

Hood Evacuates
Sept. 1

Sherman's
Envelopment
Aug. 25-31

ATLANTA CAMPAIGN
MAY 7–SEPT. 1, 1864
(Showing Sherman's Movements
around Atlanta, July 8–Sept. 1)
Scale of Miles

0   5   10   15   20

But if Grant had Sherman, so too Lee had Johnston—Joseph Eggleston Johnston; gunner, dragoon, and topographical engineer rolled into one; fifty-seven-year-old professional and the canniest tactical defensive fighter—bar none, in the authors' opinion—the Confederacy possessed. Johnston knew the odds against him were two to one in manpower; he knew Sherman's mission must be to destroy him, and he was determined it would not happen. A master of terrain, he used it now. And for two and a half months, in four successive delaying operations, with minimum loss to himself in men and matériel, Johnston held his opponent to an average advance of a mile a day.

Conversely, Sherman had no desire to fritter away his strength by frontal attacks over ground of his enemy's choice. He knew the country, too; he'd been over it years before as a subaltern in the 3rd Artillery, settling militia claims arising from the Florida War. So he strove to uproot Johnston by maneuver. At Dalton, Resaca, Cassville, and Allatoona in turn, he winkled Johnston out of strong positions, each time by the same maneuver—a holding force in front, to prevent counterattack, and a wide flanking movement.

Each time the Confederate leader deftly withdrew before it was too late. At Kenesaw Mountain only, on June 27, Sherman attempted frontal assault. But that failed and once again a wide turning movement did the business. Skillfully Johnston pulled back before he could be caught in the open and destroyed; back over the Chattahoochee River and into the outskirts of fortified Atlanta, key city of the South.

Johnston's army was still intact, the Union line of communications was lengthening dangerously, and Sherman's objective was still unwon. The Confederate leader's reward was to be removed summarily, on July 17, by the parlor strategists in Richmond, rendered frantic by Atlanta's plight. That did it.

Bellicose John B. Hood, succeeding Johnston, took the offensive at once, bringing the Union advance to momentary standstill. Then Sherman, in long left wheel, threw him back into his defenses from his Peach Tree Creek assault. Shifting then, while Slocum's corps held the river line, Sherman changed direction to the right and bit deep into the enemy communications south of the city.

The jig was up; even impetuous Hood realized it and he cut and ran, leaving Atlanta to his opponent. A gaping split had been made in the Southern heartland.

Sherman had gained the focal point of the South's industry. But it was a hot potato, still inhabited by a good half of its normal thirteen thousand population, and frothing with the spirit of secession. To garrison and control Atlanta would absorb at least a division of much-needed troops. Remembering the past frustrating experiences of Union commanders at Vicksburg, Memphis, Natchez, and New Orleans, Sherman would have none of it. Peremptorily, he ordered the evacuation of the civil population, "in the interest of the United States." Those desirous of going South would receive safe-conduct and transportation for themselves, their servants, and their effects, into Hood's lines. Those going North would be furnished rail transportation and food to destinations of their choice. Atlanta would become a military depot.

Loud was the protest, shrill the vituperation, as Sherman had expected.

The mayor of Atlanta and his councilmen made piteous plea. Hood, acquiescing in the proposed truce and transfer because, as he wrote, "I do not consider I have any alternative," bitterly denounced, "in the name of God and humanity," what he declared "transcends, in studied and ingenious cruelty, all acts ever before brought to my attention in the dark history of war!"

Sherman, adamant, summed up his whole philosophy of war in his answer to the mayor. ". . . My orders were not designed to meet the humanities of the case," he told him. ". . . We must stop the war that now desolates our once happy and favored country. . . . War is cruelty . . . and those who brought war into our country deserve all the . . . maledictions a people can pour out. . . . Now that war comes home to you . . . you deprecate its horrors. . . . I want peace and believe it can only be reached through union. . . . I will ever conduct war with a view to perfect and early success."

"Perfect and early success" was indeed a pressing question now. Even though, as Grant put it at the time, Sherman had "accomplished the most gigantic undertaking given to any general in the war," he had not destroyed his adversary's army. Already the resilient

Hood was rallying his troops along the western flank of that five-hundred-mile-long communcations line back to Nashville. Already will-o'-the-wisp Forrest and his whirling horsemen were nibbling at it.

The whole campaign might still end, Sherman felt, in going on the defensive, which would not help Grant at all. It would mean the failure of the entire strategic plan and an indefinite extension of the war. His proposed alternative made even Grant gasp.

Leaving Hood out of the play, with Thomas and his Army of the Cumberland to take care of him, Sherman proposed to drive east to the sea with the rest of his command, living off the country. Linking then with Union seapower, he would from a new base strike north to join Grant and crush Lee. In the drive he would so sear the enemy homeland as to remove once and for all any hope of further resistance. As he expressed it, he would "make Georgia howl."

Grant, momentarily demurring—he felt that Hood's army should first be eliminated—finally was convinced. "Go on as you propose," he wired Sherman on November 4, 1864.

So it was that on November 12, having stripped his forces of all impedimenta and of all his sick, Sherman ripped the last strand of telegraph wire connecting him with the world. Three days later, chanting, "John Brown's body lies a-mouldering in the ground," sixty thousand lean, husky veterans followed "Uncle Billy" out of gutted Atlanta's ruins toward the sea. A nation that had just re-elected Abraham Lincoln to the Presidency waited and worried. Foreign strategists and armchair "military experts" shook their heads and predicted—perhaps hopefully—what they had predicted sixteen years before, when Winfield Scott disappeared into Mexico: disaster. The Southern Confederacy angrily shrieked impotent objurgations soon to be turned into anguish. Ulysses S. Grant, for the time being stymied in front of Petersburg, waited and perhaps pondered on Sherman's words written him back in September: ". . . I admire your dogged perseverance and pluck more than ever. If you can whip Lee and I can march to the Atlantic, I think Uncle Abe will give us a twenty days' leave of absence to see the young folks."

On December 10 Sherman had reached the sea and linked—

through the U.S. Navy—with Washington and the world again. Eleven days later Savannah was in his hands. Grant's strategical plan, which started with the Henry-Donelson campaign, had been consummated; the Southern Confederacy was cut in two from west to east.

There had been a minimum of fighting on the march; for there was no real opposition available. The short-range purpose of the move—destruction—had been accomplished, just as it was accomplished up in the Shenandoah Valley by Sheridan during the same period. The breadbasket of the South, with its just-stored harvests, was scuttled; Sherman's army looted or destroyed everything in sight. It had been the destruction of property rather than human lives, an impersonal destruction. Sherman, believing that war was hell, did his best to make it so for the enemies of the United States.

Behind him, back at Nashville, slow-moving, dependable, precise George Thomas, the "Rock of Chickamauga"—a general who would not fight until he was ready but who then exploded—demolished Hood's army on December 15–16. Thomas, seen in retrospect, has many of the same qualities as the man who seventy-eight years later fought his own fight in his own good time at El Alamein; like Britain's Montgomery, America's Thomas "tidied things up" before he struck.

On February 1, 1865, Sherman started north on the final stage of his dog-leg belt of devastation. The operation differed from the march through Georgia on several counts: the weather was abominable, the country was not so prolific to his foragers, and the opposition, while not serious to his veteran units, was nevertheless almost incessant.

Finally, if the systematic ravaging of the enemy's country had been more or less impersonal during the Georgia campaign, every man jack of the invaders, from granite-faced general to the last private in the rear ranks, felt that South Carolina had started the Civil War, and saw no reason to soften the scourge of invasion.

Columbia, South Carolina, first fired by Wade Hampton's retreating defenders, was mostly ashes and rubble when Sherman's people left it. All the way to Fayetteville, North Carolina, where link was made with General Alfred H. Terry, who had taken Wilmington, the path of ruin lay behind. At Goldsboro, in mid-March, they were challenged again by Joe Johnston, called back to command what was left of his old army dissipated by Hood. Johnston was easily brushed aside. The end was near.

It came on April 9, at Appomattox, when Grant dragged Lee's reeling fragments down. Johnston capitulated to Sherman five days later, at Durham, North Carolina.

Thanks to Sherman, the great pincers controlled by Grant had engulfed the Southern Confederacy in their eighty-mile-wide maw.

A magnificent partner, this man Sherman; terrible in war, fiercely loyal to country and commander. It is nice to know that his qualities of leadership were appreciated by that commander. Perhaps the best evidence lies in Grant's words to him February 7, 1865, when the North was loudly singing Sherman's praises and predawn darkness still lowered over the mud and frustrations about Petersburg:

". . . I have received your very kind letters, in which you say you would decline, or are opposed to, promotion. No one would be more pleased at your advancement than I, and if you should be placed in my position, and I put subordinate, it would not change our personal relations in the least. I would make the same exertions to support you that you have ever done to support me, and would do all in my power to make our cause win."

CHAPTER XII ☆ ☆ ☆ *There Were Others*

Twenty Miles Away

On October 19, 1864, Virginia's Shenandoah Valley was the scene of one of the most remarkable demonstrations of personal leadership in the annals of war; a stunned, defeated army turned in its tracks by the magnetism of one man, who carried it back to victory. Such things do not happen often; for a parallel one might hark back to George Washington at Monmouth in 1778.

The man was swarthy, tempestuous, bullet-headed Philip H. Sheridan; the battle Cedar Creek. What the world best remembers today of that occasion is the refrain of a ballad, "And Sheridan twenty miles away."

The sun had gone down the day before on Sheridan's Army of the Shenandoah, comfortably bivouacked along the east bank of Cedar Creek, a Shenandoah tributary. The creek joins the river where the northeastern tip of the Massanutten Mountains splits the Valley—the craggy, wooded obstacle about which Stonewall Jackson, more than two years before, had played the deadly game of hide-and-seek which won him immortal fame.

Less than a month previously, Sheridan, at Fisher's Hill, had smashed his only opponent in the area, Jubal Early. No serious danger was now expected from the fragments of the enemy, despite an intercepted message indicating that Lee was sending Longstreet up to reinforce Early (a canard, by the way, whose origin has never been explained).

Sheridan had left his army under the command of Major General Horatio G. Wright, of the VI Corps, to confer in Washington with President Lincoln on the most practicable method of moving out of the Valley to join Grant before Petersburg to help eliminate the Army of Northern Virginia.

So, that night, Sheridan, on the way back, bedded down comfortably at Winchester, twenty miles down the Valley. And that night Jubal Early's rallied men were threading the Massanutten trails, concentrating for a daring blow which intended to destroy their much more numerous enemies. John B. Gordon, the brilliant and uxorious Confederate general whose wife, much to Early's disgust, accompanied him on all his campaigns, had conceived the plan after careful reconnaissance, and rasp-tongued Early found it good.

Encircling the left of the Union army, his main effort would roll it back. Another spearhead would at the same time drive straight down the Valley pike. One of his two little cavalry divisions would provide a diversion by attacking the Union right, while the other, pushing for Front Royal, would get in the rear of Sheridan's army.

It was a good plan, a bold plan. And it worked. With the dawn, and in complete surprise, the gray tempest fell on Crook's VIII Corps, the Union left, and stampeded it.

In succession the XIX and VI Corps began to crumble. The latter, the best troops in Sheridan's army, made three successive stands, to no avail. By noon Crook's corps was but a mob of fugitives, the XIX Corps was breaking up and the VI, badly split, was retiring sullenly. The cavalry, over on the far right flank, was confused. More than a score of guns had been captured and turned on their former owners. General Wright, slightly wounded, was trying, without too much success, to establish a delaying position with the VI Corps, some four miles back of the original positions.

The Army of the Shenandoah was licked; its main concern now was how to get away. It was not yet in complete rout, although Crook's corps, as it turned out, would not be rallied for more than twenty-four hours. But everyone was moving to the rear; some more rapidly than others. The Valley and the fields on both sides were crowded with men and wagons and horses, surging slowly north toward Winchester.

Units were mixed and men would not obey the orders of officers strangers to them. A paralysis of leadership had closed down. One more sharp thrust would have completed the stampede.

But Early's troops, flushed with initial victory, were also hungry and ragged. They fell like locusts on the Union camps, to eat and loot. And Early did not stay them; did not, or could not, keep the control essential for a *coup de grâce*. Two precious hours would elapse before he reorganized and struck again.

In Winchester that morning, Sheridan, after a leisurely breakfast, trotted out of town with a handful of aides, to join his waiting escort, the 17th Pennsylvania Volunteer Cavalry. There was a rumble of distant gunfire to the south; probably, the general concluded, a reconnaissance in force which he knew General Wright had in mind.

But the cannon growls grew heavier as they proceeded; then a stalled wagon train, and a trickle of northbound fugitives spelled something wrong. Radically wrong, it developed, as one officer shouted that the army had been surprised and was retreating.

Sheridan was off like a shot, his aides and three sets of fours from the escort hammering behind; the remainder he left to form a straggler line and corral all fugitives.

Up the pike and through a swelling stream of retreating men the little clump of horsemen ploughed. At times they had to take to the fields in steeplechase over walls and ditches, so crowded was the road. And as they galloped, Sheridan's bull voice was roaring: "Turn back, men! Turn back!"

It was Sheridan at his best; the thickset little man on the big black charger, "Rienzi," waving the flat hat crushed in his right hand, as all these men had seen him time and time before in battle. And turn they did; turned and cheered and started back, warriors once more, following the leader they knew.

Leadership, as we have seen before, sparks response as fast and as far-spread as does the chill flame of panic. Behind that fast-moving group churning the dusty pike, not only were the men who had seen and heard him moving back, but their shouts and gestures were picked up by others out in the fields. They, too, began to call and point at the dust cloud eddying southward, and the chant reverberated:

"Sheridan! Sheridan! Sheridan!"

It wasn't all hell-for-leather, for every once in a while Sheridan would pull up to call to some particularly large group. And always the response was the same.

At Newtown, halfway, the road was entirely blocked, and Sheridan swung wide around the village. But a young man who would one day be President of the United States saw him, and out of the ruck Major William McKinley went pelting up the pike too, to spread the good news.

The men in Wright's thin-spread delaying line; the men of the VI Corps who had stayed and thus far staved off disaster, didn't know at first what was happening. Behind them rose the roar of voices, full-mouthed; the voices of the men who had broken and run. They were cheering, it seemed.

Then out of the highway blur a horseman rocketed up on the ridge—the man on the big black horse. And as Sheridan stormed from brigade to brigade the booming cheers rang down the line. Sullen, snarling men caught their second wind and began to smile and joke. When Early at last gathered enough strength to hit the line his assaults rebounded.

That was but the beginning. Sheridan—everywhere at once, it seemed—was going to counterattack.

"Jubal Early drive me out of the Valley?" he snorted to a pessimistic subordinate. "I'll lick him like blazes before night!"

But he was in no hurry. The stragglers were pouring back in their thousands; hunting up their outfits, shaking down into discipline again. These men would fight all the harder now, to clear themselves of the shame of having broken. So it was almost four o'clock before Sheridan gave the signal.

The rejuvenated VI and XIX Corps heaved forward all along their line. Merritt's cavalry division covered the left, and Custer's the right. Early's command crumpled like a pasteboard box under a road roller. The lost cannon were retaken, and twenty-four more in addition. By nightfall the Confederates were driven back across

Cedar Creek to Fisher's Hill; next day had retired to New Market. The last real Confederate resistance in the Shenandoah Valley had been crushed.

A firebrand had been this man Sheridan, from the time he first donned cadet gray at West Point to the end of his long career. As a cadet his pugnaciousness cost him a year of seniority—something not to be sneezed at in those days of slow promotion—for he drew his bayonet on an upperclassman who gave him what he considered to be an unjust order. His punishment was to be turned back one class, the justice of which he later frankly acknowledged.

But with his hair-triggered temper, Sheridan combined something else: sagacity. And part of the latter attribute was the ability to learn, both from his own and from other men's experience and mistakes.

He was not a tactful man; he spoke his mind, whether talking to President or private soldier. In council he frequently disputed proposed operations, and nearly always was able to win his own way by forthright exposition.

On the other hand, Sheridan never dodged responsibility, never hesitated to take the initiative, and flung his vibrant personality into the thick of every engagement.

A captain of infantry when the war broke out, Sheridan was given a colonel's commission, commanding the 2nd Michigan Cavalry. His rise in the Western campaigns was rapid—from Perryville through Stones River, Chickamauga, and Chattanooga. When Grant assumed the supreme command and sought for the command of his cavalry "a thorough leader . . . the best man in the army," Major General Sheridan was picked.

In the final campaign of the war in the East his handling of his cavalry corps at Five Forks and in the pinning down of the Army of Northern Virginia at Appomattox were perfect demonstrations of fire and mobility, combining as they did both shock action mounted, and fighting on foot. They were, in fact, the forerunners of armored cavalry maneuver of today.

But Sheridan's fame as a combat leader will always rest upon his amazing achievement at Cedar Creek.

Jine the Cavalry

The aura of romance clings to the devil-may-care cavalryman down through the ages. It shines through the grime and misery and agony of war, sometimes glossing mistakes, sometimes illuminating good generalship. This aura was never more apparent than in the Civil War. And yet, cold analysis of cavalry operations from 1861 to 1865 is for the most part disappointing from the viewpoint of real leadership.

One might well agree with Steele's generalization that most of the cavalry raids of the war were "perilous and useless expenditures of horseflesh."

Most of the cavalry commanders were *beaux sabreurs*, personally brave to the point of folly. They were gallant soldiers, followed with ardor and with acclaim by men who loved them, and they were capable of arousing their followers to a frenzy of combatativeness. But all too frequently they were knights-errant who contributed little to the successful prosecution of the war by their respective sides.

We must, then, regretfully strike from our list of great leaders the brilliant and gifted cavalryman, J. E. B. Stuart, with a penchant for riding around Union armies.

They call Stuart "the last of the Cavaliers." The nickname is, alas! all too true. The parallel between the Confederacy's dashing leader of horse and equally dashing Prince Rupert is remarkable. Rupert, commanding the Royalist horse at Naseby, in 1645, scattered the Cromwellian cavalry by his impetuous onset and headlong pursuit. But he returned from his foray only to find the main battle lost, and with it the crown of Charles I of England.

Stuart, once unleashed, also assigned his own goal, which was not his prerogative. As a subordinate commander in the Army of Northern Virginia, the goal assigned by its commander should have been his. So it was that his most famous exploit, taking his command entirely around the Army of the Potomac during the period June 25–July 2, 1863, was a colossal blunder.

Lee, after Chancellorsville, had decided on his second invasion of the North. The Army of Northern Virginia crossed the Potomac and plunged northward. Behind it the Army of the Potomac traipsed, well to the eastward, with its primary mission the protection of Washington. Lee, anticipating that his opponents would follow him, called on Stuart.

"If you find he [the enemy] is moving northward . . . you can move . . . into Maryland, and take position on General Ewell's right, place yourself in communication with him, guard his flank, keep him informed of the enemy's movements and collect all the supplies you can for the use of the army. . . ."

So over from the Blue Ridge came Stuart and his jangling horse. He found the enemy all right. But then he chose to break all communication with his commander, slice eastward between the enemy rear and Washington, then circle wide and turn westward again across its advance. In consequence, Lee was left in the dark both as to the whereabouts of his enemy and of his own cavalry.

To compound the error, Stuart early in his daring move captured a large Union wagon train—"125 best United States model wagons and splendid teams with gay caparisons." And this he dragged after him, like a small boy with a shining new toy, to impede his mobility on the rest of the long 180-mile ride.

Not until July 1, when he was attempting to storm Union-garrisoned Carlisle, Pennsylvania, with his exhausted troopers, did Stuart find Lee. The Army of Northern Virginia, a galloping courier told him, was engaged with the enemy at a town called Gettysburg, thirty miles to the south.

It was late afternoon of the next day that Stuart rejoined; the fateful battle, which never would have been fought had he carried out his assigned mission, was moving to its inevitable end.

It was a high price to pay for 125 wagons.

There are at least three exceptions, however, to any sweeping criticism of the cavalrymen. Sheridan's leadership at Five Forks and Appomattox has already been mentioned. The remaining two exceptions concern respectively a professional and an amateur soldier; men poles apart in background and education, but who both deserve more than passing mention within the frame of our analysis.

We look first at the amateur.

Fustest With the Mostest

Tennessee-born Nathan Bedford Forrest had had no time for formal schooling as a boy; he had to get out and support himself, his widowed mother and the rest of her brood. When the Civil War broke out he was a prosperous, forty-year-old Mississippi planter, who had parlayed his gains as a horse, cattle and slave trader into cotton. This full-chested, husky graduate of the school of hard knocks, standing just over six feet one, as handy with a knife in a brawl as he was at whooping it up in a religious camp meeting, was a far cry from the Virginia patrician of the "Jeb" Stuart mold.

Yet in four years of war Forrest rose from private soldier to lieutenant general, had sorely bedeviled both Grant and Sherman, and was safety man for Bragg, Beauregard, Joseph E. Johnston and Hood in turn. Furthermore, he had evolved and practiced his own axiomatic theory of war—"git thar fustest with the mostest." There is some question whether self-educated Forrest would have expressed himself so ungrammatically as this; yet even if apocryphal, the succinct, colorful statement was typical of the homespun but sound concepts of a man characterized by General Grant as a "brave and intrepid cavalry general."

There is more than a hint of parallel in the careers and characters of Forrest and Daniel Morgan of Revolutionary War fame—both untutored insofar as formal education was concerned, yet equipped with exceptional innate genius and drive which led them to success in military as well as civil life.

Having volunteered as a private, Forrest at his own expense then raised a battalion of cavalry, obtaining for himself, as was the custom, a lieutenant colonelcy. His first claim to fame was at Fort Donelson in 1862, when he refused to join in the surrender and led his command safely through the swamps to rejoin Albert Sidney Johnston. For this, the one bright spot of that Southern defeat, he was promptly made a colonel.

At Shiloh, when Beauregard, after Johnston's death, finally retired, it was Forrest who covered the retreat, breaking up pursuit by a mounted charge that shivered the Union advance. This won him his brigadier generalcy. During the opening phases of the Vicksburg campaign, Forrest's brigade, raiding the railroad north of Jackson, Tennessee, in December, 1862, was one of the contributing factors to the failure of Grant's initial move to invest Vicksburg from the north.

Later, Forrest's command formed part of Bragg's Army of Tennessee during the Tullahoma and Chickamauga campaigns. During the former he played hob with Union communications. In the latter, augumented to a division of four brigades, Forrest's command became the right flank element of Bragg's army, combining both mounted action and fighting on foot in the battle of Chickamauga itself.

One notes that Forrest and his troopers relied more on fire action than the thundering charge of the old-fashioned saber-brandishing cavalrymen. As a matter of fact, few, if any of them, carried sabers; they were armed with revolvers, shotguns, and captured Federal small arms.

Quite capable of taking their places on the firing line as infantry, they used their horses for transportation mainly. Forrest, ignorant of and therefore unhampered by preconceived notions of military tactics, in all his many combats—either acting independently or as part of an army—demonstrated the principles of fire and movement. He got where he wanted to at the fastest rate, usually obtaining surprise. Then, dismounting a portion of his command to hold and fix his opponent, he would come whirling in on a flank with his main effort, mounted or dismounted as best suited his purpose.

What stands out in Forrest's career is the versatility with which he handled his mounted force, as well as the resiliency he imparted to it. Twice—on the Cumberland River at the opening of the Henry-Donelson campaign in early 1862, and again on the Tennessee in October, 1864—he actually attacked Union gunboats from the riverbanks. In the latter fight he captured a gunboat and a transport, and for a few days manned both vessels with his cavalrymen.

When one considers the undisciplined character of such a force as Forrest led, his versatility gives evidence of a high quality of leadership; evidence strengthened by the rapidity with which, until the very end, he regrouped again and again after defeat to resume the offensive. To him fell the task of covering other men's mistakes on stricken fields; plucking chestnuts out of the fire. And to accomplish that successfully necessitated exceptional leadership ability.

After the Union defeat at Chickamauga, as Rosecrans' troops retired into Chattanooga under cover of Thomas' rocklike defense, Bragg's dilatory follow-up so incensed Forrest that he openly criticized his superior's conduct. As a result he and his command were transferred to the Mississippi theatre where, until October, 1864, he was once more scourging Federal communications. On one raid he penetrated northward as far as Paducah, Kentucky. During this period occurred an incident which has beclouded Forrest's reputation: the so-called "Massacre of Fort Pillow."

Fort Pillow lay on the Mississippi, forty miles north of Memphis. An earthwork of moderate strength, it mounted six guns and its garrison consisted preponderantly of Negro units. Dismounting his troopers, Forrest stormed the ramparts April 12, 1864. Overwhelming the defenders, the Confederate cavalrymen shot many of the colored Union soldiers after they had laid down their arms. Or so the official records seem to indicate. Forrest's Southern admirers point out, however, that this was a most confused action, and insist that no Federal troops—white or black—were slaughtered after the survivors formally surrendered.

When Hood, after evacuating Atlanta, moved north in his tempestuous but rash attempt to cut Sherman's communications, Forrest's cavalry corps rejoined the Confederate army, and throughout the Franklin and Nashville campaign Forrest, now a lieutenant general, played a vital part in the operations.

Then, in the Confederacy's twilight, he met his nemesis; a professional soldier who had elaborated on Forrest's crude but capable concept of fire and movement to make his cavalry corps the horse-and-buggy-day prototype of armored blitzkrieg.

Shadow of Things To Come

When twenty-seven-year-old James Harrison Wilson of the Corps of Topographical Engineers, whose heavy moustache and imposing imperial somewhat disguised his youthful, handsomely aquiline features, found himself in charge of the Cavalry Bureau of the War

Department in February, 1864, he had already learned much a...
war. Having graduated from West Point in 1860, he had earn...
a brevet for gallantry in action at Fort Pulaski at Savannah, Georgia;
he had been a staff officer of McClellan at Antietam; and he had
been on the staff of the Army of the Tennessee during the Vicksburg
and Chattanooga campaigns. Now he wore the stars of a brigadier
general of volunteers, and he had the chore of reorganizing the U.S.
Cavalry—up to this time in the war a much misunderstood and
much abused arm.

The technological-minded Wilson concluded that cavalry's value
depended on firepower and movement; that the day of the hell-for-
leather saber-brandisher, galloping haphazardly across country,
had closed. The horseman must also be capable of fighting on foot.

This brought up the very practical point that whenever this were
done, any cavalry force immediately lost a quarter of its firepower;
one man in every four became a horseholder. It was at this moment
that Wilson's attention was drawn to a newly invented repeating
carbine on which President Lincoln looked with favor. The Spencer
carbine was a seven-shooter, feeding its cartridges up through the
butt of the piece. Its then newfangled brass-cased cartridges were
put up in packeted rows of seven, each ready to be stuffed in the
magazine in one movement. Best of all, the weapon was available
in quantity. Here indeed was the answer to the cavalryman's dilemma,
and Wilson acted. The U.S. Cavalry was at once issued the Spencer.

Shortly afterwards, Grant's reshuffling of the cavalry in the East
brought Wilson into the field to command a division of Sheridan's
corps; a spot he filled well from the Wilderness to Petersburg, earn-
ing another brevet for personal gallantry. Then in November, 1864,
the curtain rose on his bid for greater combat leadership laurels.

Sherman cut loose from Atlanta and his communications, on his
march to the sea, leaving Thomas behind at Nashville with a scratch
army of odds and ends to take care of Hood. Grant sent his most
promising cavalry division commander down to Thomas, to organize
a badly needed cavalry corps; that man was Wilson.

At Nashville, November 6, Wilson found a double job on his
hands. Not only was he to train fifteen thousand alleged cavalrymen—mostly recruits—and provide their mounts (there were less

than seven thousand animals on hand), but he would have to use them in battle at the same time, for Hood was moving on Nashville.

Less than three weeks after his arrival, Wilson was able to take the field in the delaying actions south of Nashville in the Franklin area, and when forty days had elapsed his corps was fighting as Thomas' right flank element in the battle of Nashville, which ended with the collapse of Hood's army.

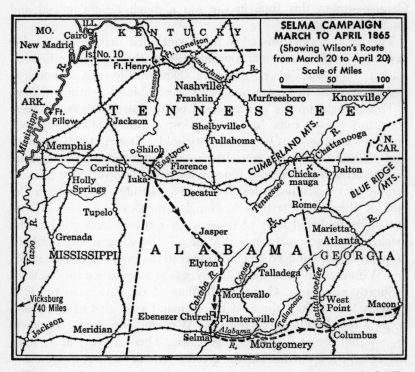

Forrest, who had been sent away by Hood to raid the Nashville & Chattanooga Railroad, was absent from the field that grim day of December 15, 1864. But he got back in time to cover the retreat of Hood's remnants to the Tennessee River.

Time was running out now for the Confederate cause. But deep in the heart of Alabama still lay the city of Selma, a fortified stronghold and the last arsenal of the Southland. In front of it was Forrest, his cavalry corps still intact. Thomas decided to clear the matter up;

Grant approved. So on March 22, 1865, Wilson's corps crossed the Tennessee River up in the northwest corner of Alabama.

Since Nashville, Wilson had worked night and day to further train his men. He had made meticulous preparation for his expedition, which was, in effect, an independent command. He had 12,000 mounted men in 3 small divisions, commanded by Emory Upton, Edward M. McCook, and Eli Long respectively; 1,500 additional dismounted troopers hiked or rode the small train—300 wagons—including a light ponton train of 30 boats. Each mounted man carried 5 days' light rations, 4 pounds of grain, 100 rounds of ammunition, and 2 spare horseshoes. Five days' extra light rations were on pack horses, 45 days more were in the wagons, as well as some 100,000 rounds of ammunition. Actually Wilson was prepared to live off the country. Two light batteries of horse artillery—8 guns in all—rolled with the corps.

Moving in three columns, the corps covered seventy miles in three days, concentrating at Jasper, where the first brush with Forrest's outposts occurred on March 25. At Elyton, sleepy hamlet in the cotton fields, where Birmingham's bustling metropolis now stands, Wilson turned directly south toward Selma. He skirmished with Forrest's detachments at Montevallo and again at Six Mile Creek. Determined resistance developed at Ebenezer Church, six miles north of Plantersville.

Here Forrest, entrenched, made a stand. Badly outnumbered, the Confederate cavalrymen at first put up their usual vicious opposition, opposing Wilson with a strength of less than two thousand men and six guns.

Long's division, leading Wilson's advance, deployed one regiment on foot in frontal attack supported by his artillery, through which came a mounted charge by another regiment, penetrating the initial Confederate position. Forrest's attempt to rally failed, as Upton's division, on Wilson's left, moving at a fast trot, dismounted and came in on foot on Forrest's right. The Confederates, in some disorder, retreated south through Plantersville, where Wilson bivouacked that night.

At dawn next morning Wilson pushed on to Selma, nineteen miles away. The city lay on the north bank of the Alabama River.

A bastioned line of entrenchments ringed it, protected on the river at both flanks by unfordable streams. The curtain wall, from six to eight feet in height, with a ditch in front five feet deep and about fifteen feet wide, was surmounted by a battery of more than thirty guns, mostly fieldpieces.

In front of this formidable obstacle lay some six hundred yards of open ground. Behind its walls was resilient Forrest, always as dangerous as a coiled rattlesnake at bay, with some four thousand men. Wilson's problem, it seemed, was very similar to that of British General Pakenham at New Orleans in 1815, facing Andrew Jackson's bastions. There was, however, this exception: Pakenham's troops were seasoned veterans of the Peninsular War, while but 150 action-packed days had elapsed since Wilson first started organizing his corps.

Wilson's solution, like that of Pakenham, was to make immediate frontal assault. There the comparison ends, for Wilson took advantage of the momentum, both spiritual and physical, of his command, in the hot pursuit; and of his confidence—shared by every one of his troopers—in the tremendous superiority of fire-power, man for man, granted by their repeating carbines. It was not for nothing that one Confederate said of Union cavalry about this time, "they load up in the morning and shoot all day." So his decision, far from being the bravado of a Pakenham, was that of a confident, competent leader.

By four o'clock in the afternoon, Wilson's troops were in position, dismounted to fight on foot, with Long's division leading—five regiments in line. Covered by the fire of their eight light guns, the cavalrymen swept over the fire-swept open space and up to the ditch. They reached it, they tumbled into it, and then, scrambling and climbing upon one another's shoulders, they overflowed the parapet. Upton's division came charging behind in the same fashion.

Forrest's bolt was shot. Once across the curtain wall, the Union troopers regrouped and pressed towards the city, into which the main body of the defenders fled. Forrest himself, with a handful of men, galloped to safety out of the eastern side of the fortification and up the Burnsville road.

Wilson had bagged the last arsenal of the Confederacy, together with thirty-two guns, and nearly three thousand prisoners. The foundries, ammunition depots, and stores all went up in smoke. Then Wilson flung a ponton bridge across the Alabama—870 feet wide at this point—and on April 10 moved east. He had captured sufficient horses to mount all his men, so now he destroyed his surplus wagons before he plunged on the two-hundred-mile long dash, which dissipated the last vestiges of the South's industrial resources. Montgomery, Columbus, and West Point in turn were taken. By April 20 he was in Macon, Georgia, where word was received of Lee's surrender.

To cap the climax, learning of Jefferson Davis' attempt to escape, Wilson captured him on May 11.

Only leadership of the highest degree could have transformed, in this short space of time, and during the midst of an active campaign, an agglomeration of recruits, replacements, and green horses into the pliant, smooth-running, confident outfit that steam-rollered its way from Muscle Shoals to Macon. Brooking no opposition, it functioned in a series of both mounted and dismounted actions, ranging from outpost skirmishes to the assault of a fortified city.

It is small wonder that George T. Denison, the British military historian of premechanized cavalry days, terms, Wilson's Selma campaign "one of the most extraordinary affairs in the history of cavalry."

Now, having compared Forrest and Wilson—men so dissimilar in background and training—let's go back to note one more flaming example of leadership; this time in a lower echelon. It concerns a theological student from Maine and his transformation into a battle-wise regimental commander.

"One Hell of a Regiment!"

That's what young West Pointer Adelbert Ames, erstwhile 1st lieutenant in the 5th Artillery, groaned when he donned eagles to command the 20th Maine Volunteer Infantry. Ames, a Regular's regular, at First Bull Run, when a subaltern in Griffin's battery, had refused to leave the field when wounded, but made his men prop him up on one of his caissons.

Now—it was August, 1862—he found himself commanding a

rabble in arms; undisciplined, un-uniformed, tobacco-chewing Maine farmer boys as different from his redlegs in Griffin's battery as daylight is from darkness. Nor were their officers much better, even the lieutenant colonel, one Joshua Lawrence Chamberlain, whose military knowledge consisted of his scholarly recollection of the Jericho campaign of his Biblical namesake.

Chamberlain knew that much, for he had studied theology at Bowdoin, in preparation for the ministry, and had been an instructor there when he received a more immediate and urgent call.

This is not Adelbert Ames's story, but rather the story of his cachet. For by the time Gettysburg was fought, although Ames had long left it, he had produced a polished fighting regiment. And Joshua Chamberlain, under his tutelage, had blossomed—for gallantry in action—into a brevet brigadier general and was commanding it.

It was afternoon, July 2, 1863. Longstreet's attack, with Hood's division on its right, was overlapping Sickles' rashly advanced "peach orchard" position. Meade's engineer officer, Brigadier General Gouverneur K. Warren, had discovered the Union failure to occupy Little Round Top—to the left and rear of Sickles—and with great presence of mind had diverted two brigades and an artillery battery of Sykes's corps to seize that key point before Hood's Texans could get there.

Chamberlain's 20th Maine, on the left of this reinforcement, came panting to the crest of Little Round Top to look down on the Texans, ramping and shouting and shooting their way up the hill out of the Devil's Den below. The Maine men met and held them down the slope, just as Chamberlain found he was being outflanked by another Texan column pressing from further up the draw between Little and Big Round Top.

So Chamberlain refused his left flank. On the drill ground this was not difficult; one just marched a part of the command to the rear until the straight line was bent back sufficiently to form a V, then faced the marching men about again.

Under fire, with an assaulting enemy closing in, it is a different thing. Men once ordered to the rear are not inclined to stop again, nor are soldiers who see their comrades falling back themselves inclined to stand. Yet that is just what Chamberlain accomplished, by sheer personal energy. When he was through, half the companies of the 20th Maine were facing south, the other half westward, shooting it out in that jumble of rocks and trees and shrub, and they had stopped the first enemy rush.

That southern leg of the V was thin: Chamberlain started into this fight with but 350 men, and he now had to space them out to prevent being outflanked. Hardly 30 yards away the Confederate line was building up again. Sheer weight of numbers, it seemed, would crush the Maine men next time.

At that moment, through the roar of the close-in fire fight, came a new burst of shouting and yelling from the north—a threat that perhaps the other flank of the entire Little Round Top position was being outflanked.

Just what does one do when ammunition is running low and half one's men are down? When outnumbered in front by an attacker, and worried about the rear?

Chamberlain ordered his men to fix bayonets, and charged.

Following their leader and the color guard with its fluttering flags, the thin line of men in blue smashed through the first line of astounded Texans, struck the second, swept the saddle between the Round Tops and never stopped until it rested victoriously on the crest of Big Round Top across the way.

And night came down with the Round Tops—the shank of Meade's "fishhook"—irrevocably in the possession of the Army of the Potomac; for the rest of Sykes's V Corps was by now deployed in full strength along the crests won by a regimental commander's leadership.

CHAPTER XIII ☆ ☆ ☆ *From Plains to Tropics*

The period from the close of the Civil War in 1865 until the outbreak of the Spanish-American War in 1898 is considered by some to have marked the nadir of the United States Army—its Dark Ages. In one way it was, for, beginning in 1866, our regulars underwent a succession of prunings which emasculated their strength. At the same time the antiquated bureaucratic organization of the War Department stultified what little professional progress a succession of economy-minded Congresses might have permitted. Insofar as theory and practice in the higher branches of the science of war were concerned, our Army stagnated.

Yet, paradoxically, this was an era where personal leadership in combat was not only essential but usually present. For during that time the Army fought no less than 943 engagements against the Indians—running the gamut from skirmish to pitched battle in 12 separate and distinct campaigns and a host of other disconnected incidents.

Most of these engagements were fought under conditions adverse to the regulars. Inferiority in numbers and in weapons, political wire-pulling, land-grabbing, corruption in the Indian Bureau, and an almost complete misunderstanding on the part of the general public, produced a situation in which only personal leadership could produce results.

General Sheridan summed the matter up in his annual report for 1868 as commander of the Department of the Missouri:

"The present system of dealing with the Indians, I think, is an error. There are too many fingers in the pie, too many ends to be subserved, and too much money to be made. . . . The Army has nothing to gain by war with the Indians; on the contrary it has everything to lose. . . . It suffers all the hardships and privations, exposed as it is to the charge of assassination if the Indians are killed, to the charge of inefficiency if they are not; to misrepresentation by the agents who fatten on the plunder of the Indians, and misunderstood by worthy people at home who are deceived by these agents."

Nevertheless, for thirty years more the Army would be fighting the Indians, generally west of the Missouri-Mississippi River line. From the Canadian border to the Rio Grande it protected the construction of the transcontinental railroad system, the cattle industry, the mineral richnesses of Colorado, Nevada, Idaho, and Montana, and the entire tide of westbound settlement spreading from thin lines of railroad iron and the singing telegraph lines above them.

It fought by platoon or company, by battalion or detachment; rarely was a single full regiment gathered under one command. In every one of these engagements, so far as the Army was concerned, defeat could mean death; death on the field or later death by torture as a prisoner, for—with one exception—the Indian neither knew nor recognized the rules of civilized warfare. So in each fight the difference between the quick and the dead depended on the leader. He might be a tough enlisted man, a shavetail just out of the Point, or a grizzled veteran of the Civil War. But he had to be willing to fight, and he had to lead, else his scalp and those of his men would drape lodgepoles or jiggle on warriors' belts about some flaming war dance.

This little Regular Army—it never averaged over thirty thousand until 1898 and for most of the period it was less than twenty-five thousand strong—was a far cry from the huge citizen armies of the Civil War. Its enlisted strength consisted of a tough aggregation of volunteers who for reasons of their own preferred thirteen dollars a month and found—with fighting thrown in—to a peaceful existence on better pay. Its officers, except for the new classes produced each year from West Point, were men with Civil War experience—either regulars or erstwhile volunteers who had been lucky enough to satisfy their desire to stay in the service. And, of course, with the exception of a few of the more prominent leaders of that war, by 1866 all the veterans were serving in grades far below their Civil War standings.

Sherman and Sheridan held their rank. A few others, including blustering John Pope, clung to brigadier's stars. But, as a sampling of the cutback, take Major General John Gibbon, who had led the Iron Brigade and later a division in the Army of the Potomac; he was now a colonel, commanding the 7th Infantry. Major General George Crook thought himself lucky to trade his stars and his division for a majority in the 3rd Infantry. And Wisconsin Volunteer Colonel Arthur MacArthur—great father of an illustrious son—to stay in the regulars had exchanged his eagles for the bare shoulder straps of a second lieutenant, 17th Infantry.

Other men there were, too, who followed the Indian wars in the ranks; such, for instance, as William H. H. McCall, honorably mustered out a brevet brigadier general. Two years later he was riding in Forsyth's Scouts with the three big white V's and diamond of a first sergeant splashing his sleeve.

Thus the pattern ran. Men who had commanded thousands on stricken fields were now commanding companies in whose ranks marched former comrades, former enemies, Irish and German immigrants, ne'er-do-wells, and adventurers. They would be welded in the fires of battle, tradition, and discipline into what Field Marshall Lord Wolseley, England's great field commander of the nineteenth century, in 1882 called, man for man, the best army in the world.

This little Army, pitted against the Plains Indian, found to its cost it had to unlearn the tactical lessons of 1861–1865. For this was guerrilla warfare against an enemy who fought when he felt like it and melted away at will. What he lacked in organization and discipline he made up for by mobility and savage personal courage. The Sioux, Cheyennes, and Comanches were the finest light cavalry in the world. The Apache, using his pony for transportation, preferred to do his fighting on foot. But all these hostiles could cover ground at amazing speed in comparison with the movements of regular troops.

The saga of the Indian-fighting Army is not for this book. But out of its operations the stories of two men epitomize American leadership in the seemingly endless drama of battle, murder, and sudden death on the Western Plains from 1866 to 1898.

One of these men was a professional soldier, the other an Indian chieftain. They never met on the battlefield.

The Gray Fox

That was what his Indian foes called George Crook, Indian-fighter *par excellence*. Crook outthought them, outmarched them, and out-fought them. More than that; he made them respect him.

Red Cloud, Oglala Sioux chieftain, summed up his former ene-my's impact on the Indian, when Crook died in 1890: "General Crook came; he, at least, had never lied to us. His words gave the people hope. He died. Their hope died again. Despair came again."

An interesting character, this man Crook; a fighter, and a thinker too, combining the wary intelligence of a combat soldier and the reasoned logic of an administrator with bulldog determination. To him the Indian was not just a mad dog to be shot down; he was a human being—primitive in existence and objective—to be controlled and led to better things. The control might begin with an iron hand, but it should end in a new outlook balanced with justice.

That was why Crook was able to outfight the Apache in Arizona in the early seventies and turn him into a peaceful farmer. Later, in 1882, when his work had been undone by lesser men, he would ride into Arizona again and subdue the Chiricahua Apaches. Ac-tually, with the consent of the Mexican government, he would lead a single troop of cavalry and some Indian scouts two hundred miles into the Sierra Madre Mountains of Mexico to control them. It would be his reward to see unjust treatment and broken promises later send Geronimo off on his last wild fling, and another man sub-due him. But it was Crook's plan, and Crook's influence that in the end turned the Apache—cruelest cutthroat of all the Western In-dians—into a self-respecting, law-abiding farmer.

These things alone would set him squarely within our framework of leadership. But it was the Big Horn and Yellowstone expedition of 1876–1877, against the Sioux and Cheyennes, that marked the real combat leadership of George Crook. That was the time that Crazy Horse, Sitting Bull, Dull Knife, American Horse, and all their host of Plains hostiles set the government by the ears and terrorized the Western settlements in the greatest of their uprisings.

The Plains Indian, one must remember, made his forays in the summer, when the lush prairie grass afforded grazing for his ponies. In the winter he holed up. If he didn't return to the reservation, his tepees and lodges were pitched in some sheltered cranny among the mountain buttes, a wise decision in country where the mercury dropped sometimes to 30° below zero.

Thus far, the Army had been conforming to the same general plan—campaigning in the summer, going into winter quarters when the snows came. That made it easy for the thin-clad savages, who could outmarch any body of regular troops when the marching was good, and had nothing to fear from them in the winter.

Crazy Horse's hostiles had not come back from their rampages of 1875; they had gone to earth somewhere in the Powder River country, in what is now southeastern Montana. When the spring thaws and sun set the prairies green they would emerge again and the whole vicious circle would be renewed, for the Army had as its mission sweeping them up and putting them back on their reservations.

Crook was determined to change this. He was a brigadier general again, commanding now at Fort Fetterman on the North Platte, some thirty miles east of Casper. He was tired of fighting a war when and where the enemy wished; he would carry the war to him, instead. If the Indian didn't like fighting in winter he had better become a good Indian and go back to his reservation.

This, of course, meant that his own troops must be able to stand the cold. Crook saw to that; he was, in fact, the first American commander to adapt the uniform to weather conditions. It was an experimentation, rather than an adaptation. For Crook's men donned layer after layer of clothing—of any sort, so long as it was warm. Two suits of woolen underwear were a "must." Over them shirt, blouse,

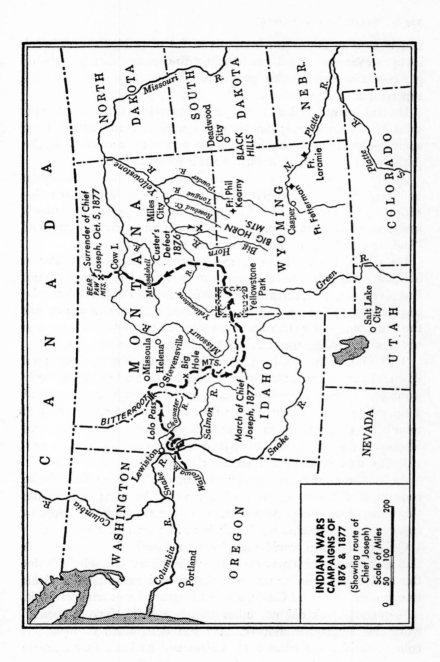

**INDIAN WARS
CAMPAIGNS OF
1876 & 1877**
(Showing route of
Chief Joseph)

Scale of Miles

0 50 100 200

and trousers of any color; overcoats of fur or padded canvas; wool socks and moccasins under hide boots; fur caps and double layers of gloves—such was Crook's provision, adhered to under his keen supervision.

He had learned in his early Apache campaigns the necessity and value of the pack mule. So his mules were carefully picked, their aparejos—packsaddles—fitted under his personal supervision, and the packers chosen for their knowledge and reliability.

All this was part and parcel of the lessons in fire and mobility he had learned as a cavalry division commander under Wilson in 1864–1865. His plan was to flush the enemy, hit him, pursue him mercilessly, and finally wear him down. It would be an endless round of "find 'em, fix 'em, and fight 'em" until the Indian gave up.

He started north March 1, 1876, with ten troops of cavalry, a bobbing pack train, two companies of infantry, and a wagon train. But five days later, in a snowy bend of the Powder River, the wagon train peeled off, the infantry stayed with it as a guard, and the mounted men went splashing through the cracking ice for one of the most grueling marches U.S. troops had ever made.

They rode with saddles practically stripped. From the general down, officer and man alike were limited to the clothes they actually wore, plus blanket or buffalo robe. Individual mess gear consisted of a tin cup. But each man packed four days' rations and a hundred rounds of ammunition on his person, and the pack train carried fifteen days more of half rations and sufficient ammunition to provide fifty rounds per man. That was all.

As for the animals, no grain was carried; they must live off the country as did the Indian ponies, pawing the grass from under the snow, if necessary. And there would be no grooming, either—currycombs and brushes were back in the wagon train.

Officers and men would mess together; Crook and his staff with the pack train, which was one of his obsessions. His solicitude for the mules, incidentally, was one that would pay off, even if his troopers, who all loved Crook, also made great play of lampooning it.

"General Crook did not allow us either knife, fork or spoon," writes his biographer, Bourke. "He had determined to make his column mobile as a column of Indians and he knew that example was more potent than a score of general orders."

For eleven days the expedition, traveling as light as ever regular soldiery moved since the days of Genghis Khan, combed the country between the Big Horn Mountains and the Black Hills. Frequently ice holes had to be cut in frozen streams to obtain water. Men and animals had to be kept moving through the nights, lest they freeze to death. Through it all Crook, riding sometimes with his scouts, sometimes through the column, kept spirits up in the icy chill.

Six feet tall, long-legged, clad as unconventionally as his men, Crook rode always with rifle across his pommel, a fur-clad dynamo with bristling brown beard. He was, in fact, pitting his brains against the red man's, wagering his command's stamina against the law of diminishing returns, for this sort of grueling march could go only so long.

Luck was with him, for the moment. Crazy Horse's camp was located, tucked in a cliff cleft up on the Little Powder. Six troops went riding into the night, Colonel Joseph J. Reynolds at their head, to pin the redskins down. Crook would close the trap behind. But Reynolds, jumping the encampment at dawn, failed to send word back of his action, and after scattering the warriors and bagging the pony herd, suddenly ordered withdrawal.

The Indians rallied, someone panicked, and the cavalrymen went reeling back on the main body in disorder, the fruits of victory lost. Infuriated Crook, all his well-planned scheme gone for naught, returned to his base and Crazy Horse had scored the first round.

They would meet again, three months later on the Rosebud, in the heat of a sunny June 17. Once more Crook had pushed on a stripped-saddle march, following Indian traces that led into a canyon amphitheater in the northern spurs of the Big Horns. At least a thousand braves were visible—an inviting target for a charge. But Crook, wisely wary of a trap, first felt them out with five troops, while the rest of the command, including two companies of mounted infantry, riding his wagon mules, deployed in support.

It *was* a trap. The advance became involved in stiff action and Indian countercharges. On the slopes, and in the right and rear of the main command, more braves popped up. But Crazy Horse, perhaps overeager, had tipped his hand too soon. Crook's infantry stopped the flanking threat, and the cavalry action in the amphitheater built up as additional troops went charging in.

Before the fighting ended the command found itself engaged with Indians outnumbering them five to one, only Crook's clever troop-leading preventing possible disaster. At last Crazy Horse withdrew, but it was really a drawn battle, for Crook, too, had to return to his wagon train, and parked on the Tongue River to reorganize.

Meanwhile, up along the Yellowstone, miles to the north, Briga-dier General Alfred T. Terry was moving westward, his command including Lieutenant Colonel George A. Custer and the 7th Cavalry. Terry knew nothing of the Rosebud fight. But his scouts discovered a broad Indian trail and he sent Custer up the Rosebud to locate the hostiles and get south of them. Meanwhile Terry planned to join with Gibbon's command, down from Helena, Montana, which he had ordered to halt at the mouth of the Big Horn, and then would push southward with his united force toward the vicinity in which he knew Crook was operating. By such concentric movement, Terry felt, they could bag the whole outfit between them.

But impetuous Custer spoiled it all. Instead of circling, he fol-lowed the trail, which was actually that of Crazy Horse's entire horde, retiring from the Rosebud fight. When he flushed them, en-camped on the Little Big Horn, Custer in his flamboyant way de-cided to go it alone instead of alerting Terry.

A grandstand player to the end, Custer compounded his error by dividing his own force. With five little companies—as they called cavalry troops in those days—he led less than two hundred men into the midst of five thousand Indian warriors, to be annihilated. The rest of the command, then surrounded, was saved only by the ar-rival of Terry and Gibbon, after a two-day desperate fight.

The Indians, of course, decamped before the avenging troops could attack. Crook's command, reinforced and marching light, as usual, followed them grimly northeastward into the Dakotas.

All through August into early September Crook tracked his enemy, never quite catching up. Again it was a stripped-saddle march for the cavalry, a one-blanket-and-poncho hike for the infantrymen, who covered the ground at a rate Stonewall Jackson's "foot-cavalry" could appreciate, sometimes thirty miles a day. First, it was hot. The fleeing hostiles had done their best to aggravate that by burning the prairie behind them. Then it rained. Rations grew short and game was hard to find on the scorched areas. Horses began to give in; their flesh eked out the last of the bacon and hardtack in the mule train.

Even as Crook realized that both men and beasts were approaching the limit of endurance, the chill bite of a prairie autumn made matters worse. Deadwood City, nearest point where food might be had, lay a good five-day march to the south. Bitterly, Crook gave up the chase and turned south. Ahead he sent a detachment of 150 men, all he could mount, together with the remaining animals of the pack train, to buy supplies. The rest of the command would stagger along as best it could.

So began what became known as the "horse-meat" march, for broken-down animals were now their only food. And as they plodded, a fringe of hostiles, like vultures after a crippled animal, clung just beyond gunshot. Major Anson Mills, commanding the detachment on whose success now hung the future of the entire command, pressed on ahead.

Mills's scouts fell upon an Indian trail; pursuing cautiously, they discovered a pony herd and quick reconnaissance disclosed an Indian village, its lodges and tepees clustered beneath a ridge called the Slim Buttes, near the South Fork of the Grand River.

It was American Horse's tribe, part of Crazy Horse's Sioux. The Indians were feeling the pressure of Crook's hounding and had begun to separate. Mills rushed a courier to Crook, one day's march behind, as fast as a jaded horse could push, and attacked the camp at dawn September 9, to pin the enemy down. Twenty-five men, mounted on the best of his horses, charged, stampeding the pony herd through the tepees and scattering braves and squaws, while the remainder of the detachment, on foot, in two columns, closed in.

Part of the Indians were driven off; another part took shelter in a ravine and had to be harried out. In the midst of the fracas Crazy Horse himself, with six hundred braves, came dashing to the rescue.

But Crook had gotten the word. Urging his men to superhuman effort, he brought his half-starved command up in the nick of time. Their stomachs were empty but their cartridge belts full. Crazy

Horse was repulsed, and the last of the cornered Indians surrendered, including American Horse, who was mortally wounded.

It was a rich find. There was plenty of food in the lodges for the hungry men. There were sadder things, too; 7th Cavalry guidons and equipment and 7th Cavalry horses in the captured pony herd. But a body blow had been inflicted on the enemy. Crook marched to Deadwood, then returned to Fort Fetterman for an immediate refitting.

In less than a month he had his cavalry in the field again, prepared for another winter campaign. This time a four-hundred-mule pack train went with them. The trail led into the Big Horn Mountains, where they began to buck another winter while the mercury hovered about the zero mark.

Crook had received word of a huge Cheyenne village somewhere up in the headwaters of the Powder River. His plan was his usual one—a powerful striking force to find and fix the hostiles; the remainder of the command to smash in for the kill. Col. Ranald S. Mackenzie rode into the area with eleven troops of cavalry and a detachment of Shoshone Indian scouts. True enough, the Indian encampment lay in an ice-bound gorge, Crazy Woman Fork of the Powder River. In the dead of a freezing moonlight night, Mackenzie surrounded the place, which the Cheyennes, considering it impregnable, had guarded but poorly.

At dawn, November 25, in complete surprise, Mackenzie charged in column of troops. Nude warriors, rifles in hand, rolled and darted into the open through hurried slashes in their skin tepees. Some actually swam the icy stream to gather on the cliff above it.

Meanwhile Crook, alerted to the attack, was hot-footing it in with his infantry—a twenty-six-mile march, accomplished in twelve hours. He was not needed; Mackenzie's men, in a fight that ran through most of the day—some of it hand-to-hand—had broken the back of Cheyenne resistance; the survivors evaporated.

Two hundred and five lodges, with all kinds of supplies and ammunition, went up in smoke that night. Seven hundred ponies were gathered in, and additional sad relics of Custer's fight were retrieved. Dull Knife, chief of the Cheyennes, was rebuffed by Crazy Horse when he brought news of defeat. Turning in rage, Dull Knife surrendered his tribe to Crook; many Cheyenne braves then enlisted to fight the Sioux.

A month later, Colonel Nelson A. Miles with seven companies of his 5th Infantry, and two guns concealed in wagons, found Crazy Horse himself, his encampment pitched on a bluff. Miles stormed it, his two guns suddenly disclosed, their shells screaming overhead. Crazy Horse's band broke and fled, abandoning their camp.

Crazy Horse had had enough. Through his uncle Red Cloud, he sent word to Crook and on May 6, 1877, came riding into Red Cloud Agency to surrender to the Gray Fox. The Big Horn and Yellowstone Expedition had completed its work.

But over on the other side of the Rocky Mountains another campaign was in the making.

Fight No More Forever

He was a chief of the Nez Percés. Thunder-Rolling-Over-the Mountain was his name; Young Joseph or, more simply, Joseph, was what the white man called him. He was about thirty-seven years old in 1877; tall, handsome, intelligent, and intense. And for 106 days in that year he would match the best the Army could gather against him in 1,500-odd miles of marching and fighting; of ambush, rearguard actions, pitched battles, trench warfare, and clever maneuver. His anabasis trailed from Oregon, through Idaho, Wyoming, and Montana, to within thirty miles of the Canadian border and the safety he sought for his peace-loving, agricultural tribe. There, in his eleventh clash with regular troops, he was at last brought to bay.

Joseph was chief of the southern branch of the Nez Percés, some seven hundred people in all, of whom three hundred were well-armed, well-mounted, sharpshooting warriors. Since 1804, when they had welcomed Lewis and Clark, it had been the Nez Percé boast that they had never killed a white man nor broken a promise.

It was different now. The government, breaking its treaty pledge, was trying to oust them from their fertile Wallowa Valley homeland in northeastern Oregon. Some hotheaded young braves, gone berserk in the face of this injustice, had raided a neighboring settlement to murder and scalp white men, women, and children. In June, 1877, Brigadier General Oliver O. Howard, who already had received orders to move the Nez Percés, sent three troops of cavalry pounding down from Fort Lapwai, near Lewiston, to straighten matters out.

But Joseph had not waited. The tribe, with its flocks of ponies, sheep, and goats, had drifted east. In hot pursuit the cavalry plunged rashly into White Bird Canyon on the Clearwater. Joseph, who had sent his women and flocks into hiding along the Salmon River bluffs, was lying in clever ambush. The regulars were routed with the loss of more than one-third of their ninety-odd officers and men.

The die was cast. General Howard, now hurrying up with all the troops he could gather—227 officers and men, detachments of infantry, cavalry, and artillery, with a howitzer and two Gatling guns —found Joseph entrenched on the far bluffs of the Salmon River. Howard plunged across, got his men with difficulty up the steep slopes, to find the Indians gone. Joseph had pulled out, crossed the river himself, and cornered a detachment of Howard's cavalry. Howard plodded back to relieve his detachment, and Joseph retired to the south fork of the Clearwater, where Howard found him on July 11.

Again the Indians were entrenched, something previously unheard of in redskin combat, and Howard, who had traded an arm for a Medal of Honor at Fair Oaks in 1861, realized he was in for a battle. His first assault was repulsed; he, too, was forced to dig in and —crowning indignity—a mounted charge led by Joseph actually captured the three guns. Fortunately for the troops the Indians didn't know how to use them. Only after forty-eight hours' fighting was Howard able to dislodge his opponent and recapture the guns. Joseph, covering his retreat in professional manner by a smart delaying action, moved back across the river and started northeast, easily keeping a three-day lead over his pursuers.

Across Idaho and up through the Lolo Pass in the Bitterroot Mountains the Nez Percés went, to break into the valley where William Clark had passed sixty years before them. North, now, would be the shortest route to the Canadian border, but Missoula and its surrounding settlements barred the way. So Joseph turned south up the Bitterroot and through the Great Divide of the Rockies at Gibbons Pass, to the solitude of the Big Hole Basin, where he hoped to rest his horses and his people. Howard, to whom the breakneck Lolo Pass had been a major obstacle, was left far behind.

But Joseph had not reckoned on the Singing Wires, the telegraph. News of the Nez Percé flight had reached Omaha, headquarters of the Department of the Platte, and from Helena, Montana, stout John Gibbon, with urgent orders, was already hiking southwest with six companies of infantry—about two hundred men—and a howitzer in his light wagon train.

Gibbon reached the Big Hole Basin on August 8, reconnoitered, found the Indians had posted no guards. Next dawn he assaulted, in complete surprise, breaking into the encampment from three sides. In twenty minutes he held the camp. But Joseph rallied his warriors in amazing discipline. Sharpshooters picked off the soldiers and a mounted charge hurled Gibbon's men back to a knoll where they dug in in two lines, back to back.

The wagon train, parked five miles away, was also attacked. At dawn next day a squad tried to bring up the howitzer and pack mules with two thousand rounds of ammunition from the train to Gibbon's position, but the move was discovered and thirty Nez Percé braves charged and took them. Had they been able to serve the howitzer, Gibbon might have shared Custer's fate.

For two days it was touch and go. Gibbon, handling a rifle himself, was severely wounded by a sharpshooter, but had himself propped up against a tree and continued to direct the defense. Joseph, with the wind blowing toward the defenders' knoll, set fire to the tall prairie grass. But at the last desperate moment the wind shifted and Gibbon's gasping men were spared.

Far down the Bitterroot, to Howard's advancing column, a galloper had spurred for help that first morning. With his two leading troops of cavalry Howard pressed to the rescue, arriving the third day of battle. And as he came the firing died away. Canny Joseph, warned by his scouts, broke off the action and disappeared. He left eighty-nine dead behind him, including some women and children, while Gibbon's loss was twenty-nine killed and forty wounded.

Howard, sensing that the Indians would make for the Yellowstone National Park, sent a cavalry detachment to block Tacher's Pass while he himself stood fast. It was a smart plan, but Joseph's scouts were watching. The Nez Percés halted, too. The detachment, having waited fruitlessly at the pass for two days, started back. That night at Howard's bivouac a sentinel watched a cavalry column plodding sedately in, thought they were the returning detachment and let them pass unchallenged.

It was Joseph, leading forty-five of his warriors in disciplined column of fours. Once inside the lines, they whooped and charged, with rifles blazing; stampeded all the pack mules and some of the cavalry horses, decoyed a hastily gathered detachment of troopers into ambush. By the time Howard's command had shaken down from its surprise, Joseph was gone; this time through the pass, now unguarded, into the Yellowstone, with his entire tribe.

There was no pursuit for the moment; the exasperated Howard had to wait for more pack mules. And meanwhile the Nez Percés were moving northeast through the National Park, on the way attacking two parties of tourists. One of these civilians was killed, another wounded; but on Joseph's strict orders the two women accompanying them were left unharmed.

But the telegraph was clicking again. Up from the Powder River country came Colonel Samuel D. Sturgis with eight troops of cavalry and a mountain gun, racing northwestward to cut off the Indians. Joseph reached the Yellowstone ahead of them, crossed and halted to rest. Sturgis in surprise attack in Canyon Creek, September 13, stampeded the pony herd and captured four hundred animals—a bitter blow. Once again Joseph proved his leadership, holding his braves together, and in skillful delaying action beat off the troopers long enough to let the tribe escape along the Musselshell River to its confluence with the Missouri.

There, at Cow Island, the embattled fugitives crossed the Missouri after a skirmish and struck northwest for the Canadian border. Ahead of his flock Joseph sent couriers up into Canada, seeking help from Sitting Bull and his Sioux warriors, who had taken refuge there after Crook's campaign of the year previous.

Keeping well ahead of Howard and Sturgis, the Nez Percés reached the Bear Paw Mountains. On Eagle Creek—sometimes called Snake Creek—Joseph halted for a much-needed respite. Nearly half the warriors were dead or wounded, the pony herd depleted, food and ammunition running short. But the Canadian border was only thirty miles away and he still hoped for help from Sitting Bull.

That help never came. Instead, from Fort Keogh on the Yellowstone (now Miles City), Indian-fighter Colonel Nelson A. Miles, with six troops of cavalry, five companies of infantry, and an artillery detachment, some 350 strong, unexpectedly arrived. The telegraph for the third time had foiled Joseph's plan.

Miles immediately attacked, swept through the camp, but could not dislodge the Indians from a deep ravine in which they at once entrenched themselves.

For four days the fighting continued, hand-to-hand at times, while the shells from Miles's howitzer kept pounding through the ravine.

Both sides suffered from the cold of the Montana autumn. By that time the Indians' food was finished, the ponies gone, the last cartridges were being expended and the squaws, children, and wounded men whom Joseph would not desert were huddling in cracks and crannies for shelter from small-arms fire and artillery shells. To cap the climax, on the fourth day General Howard and his pursuing column came up to join Miles.

Next day, October 5, a white flag waved from the creek bed; the firing ceased. And out into the open came Chief Joseph alone, his rifle across his pony's withers. Up to and into the Army lines he rode. He tried to hand his rifle to Howard, who waved him to Miles. Miles took the gun; then both officers shook hands respectfully with the sad, proud chief.

Then Thunder-Over-the-Mountain, superb in defeat as he had been in battle, raising his right hand to the sky, spoke eloquently to the white men and to those of his chiefs still alive, telling why he had had to surrender: to save his people from extinction. He concluded:

"From where the sun now stands, I fight no more forever!"

There were but 70 warriors left to follow him into captivity, together with 320 women and children—all half-starved, and some of them sick or wounded.

It would be nice to be able to state that Miles's immediate soldier-promise to return the tribe to its reservation was honored. But the government didn't see it that way. The Indians were shipped south to a particularly unhealthy portion of what was then the Indian Territory, where they began to die like flies. Miles, who felt his honor had been impugned by such betrayal, kept up a one-man fight for justice. In 1884 the Congress finally heeded his plea and Joseph and the remnant of his tribe were returned to the vicinity of their old homes in the Northwest.

Some critics have argued that Joseph was not the real military leader of his band; they speak of Looking Glass, and of Lean Elk, both of them hard fighters, who did indeed carry their share in combat leadership. Joseph's brother, Ollokot, has also been given credit. Against this argument one must place the fact that the Nez Percés moved under command of Joseph; hence to him must go the credit of holding them together under combat conditions quite contrary to the usual Indian's character. And certainly only the leadership and authority of Joseph could have restrained the Nez Percés from looting and burning such small settlements as they passed on their *via dolorosa* through the Bitterroot Valley. Instead, the Indians actually paid for coffee, flour, sugar, and tobacco they obtained at Stevensville.

There was no doubt in the minds of the regulars against whom the Nez Percés fought—Gibbon, Howard, Sturgis, and Miles. And that, after all, should be the criterion.

Chief Joseph well deserves a place on the long honor roll of American leadership in battle.

Chart for the Future

This thirty-year war against the Indians, of which the foregoing consists of but two meager samplings, solidified the basic pattern of U.S. Army leadership. Three essentials predominated: the men must be cared for, they must be trained to fight, and they must be led into battle by a man ready and willing to fight. The thesis embraced the basic examples set by Washington, von Steuben, and their successors.

But, perforce, the concept focused on little wars, omitting all consideration of the broader aspects of leadership. The lessons of the Civil War and its high command had not yet been digested. Dennis

Hart Mahan's theories were fading since his death in 1871, and there was but little incentive for scholastic research in our semi-cloistered Army busy chasing Indians.

One man did something about it.

Emory Upton, West Pointer and apt pupil of Mahan, had risen from battery commander of artillery to the leadership of a cavalry division in the Civil War. Within that bracket he had also commanded in turn a regiment, a brigade, and a division of infantry. At Spotsylvania, May 9, 1864, commanding a provisional division of twelve infantry regiments, Upton assaulted the Confederate works in a tactical formation embodying all the elements of what would in later years be termed a breakthrough: penetration, exploitation of the gap shoulders, and reinforcement of the advance. It was not his fault that the operation failed after initial success. For his feat he received from Ulysses S. Grant the unusual distinction of a battlefield commission as brigadier general of Volunteers.

Upton thus combined tactical genius, thirst for strategic education, and a practical knowledge of battlefield leadership in all three combat arms.

He was Commandant of Cadets at the Military Academy when General Sherman in 1875 ordered him on a two-year tour of Europe and Asia, to investigate and report upon the armies and the military trends of the rest of the world. No better man could have been chosen. So, in passing, one must credit Sherman with an assist in what would turn out to be a far-reaching step in developing leadership.

For Upton, returning, made use of all the knowledge gained abroad in an exhaustive analysis of our own military efforts from the days of the American Revolution through the Civil War. His manuscript, entitled *The Military Policy of the United States*, was endorsed by Sherman with the following penciled words:

"I doubt that you will convince the powers that be, but the facts stated, the references from authority, and the military conclusions are most valuable and should be printed and made accessible. The time may not be now, but will come when these will be appreciated and may bear fruit even in our day."

Sherman was right. Upton's work, promptly pigeonholed in a War Department file, slumbered in its dust. It took the wrath of a nation infuriated by the bunglings of the war with Spain to bring it to view, twenty years after its author had died.

Elihu Root, dynamic lawyer appointed Secretary of War in 1900, surveying the Augean stable he had inherited, found in Upton's manuscript what he was looking for, and from its recommendations grew a War College, a Command and General Staff School, and a General Staff. Upton's dream of higher education in leadership became fact.

The devotees of small-unit combat leadership on the Plains, in Cuba, in the Philippines, and China found their horizons broadening. The payoff came in 1917.

CHAPTER XIV ☆ ☆ ☆ *Iron Men*

During the autumn of 1918 an American army attacked the most vital sector of German-held France. In forty-seven days of continuous battle, across a highly organized area which the enemy was defending tooth and nail, it crunched through to victory. It consumed German divisions one after the other—all that could be scraped up to oppose it—in one of the world's greatest demonstrations of massed, relentless, aggressive combat power. When the sound of the cannon died away on that Meuse-Argonne front, General Erich von Ludendorff, Germany's master of both offensive and defensive warfare, had lost the game, and World War I was over.

The U.S. First Army, which before the end of the offensive had swelled to an army group—First and Second Armies—had been in existence only two months before the offensive opened on September 25–26. Its command and staff had functioned in but one previous operation. Of the six army corps headquarters involved, but one could be really termed battle-wise. As for the troops, only fourteen of the twenty-five infantry divisions had seen prior combat—a few of them seriously. Less than that proportion of veterans existed in the nondivisional army and corps units engaged, as well as in the air squadrons. Approximately nineteen out of each twenty of its 1,200,000 men had been in uniform for less than a year. Compared to the German troops and command opposing them, war-hardened by nearly four years of combat, the American Expeditionary Force entered the Meuse-Argonne offensive an amateur aggregation.

It is apparent, then, that only leadership of the highest order could have accomplished such a result. It was furnished by one fifty-seven-year-old cold-eyed, granite-faced soldier: John J. Pershing, who demanded the impossible and attained it.

His was the vision and elasticity of mind which grasped what was needful for victory, and his was the dynamic obstinacy and single-purposed initiative which transformed an American gesture, made in the valor of ignorance, into a ruthless battle competence.

Some two million Americans in France feared him; many of them hated him. But all of them respected him. Comparatively few of the men he commanded in battle ever saw him, but every man knew his name. He was harsh to the point of despotism; inexorable and unforgiving in his treatment of officer and man alike. No one ever made more than one mistake under Pershing's command; he wasn't there to make a second. Yet no American commander had greater concern for the physical welfare of his soldiers.

For Pershing there would be no plaudits from the ranks; none of the response which personal magnetism generates. Yet individuals accomplished prodigies of valor in carrying out the demands of his impersonal, inflexible will.

Offhand, here would appear to be a contradiction to some of the attributes of leadership, in particular the personal touch. Yet personal relationships formed the core of Pershing's leadership.

"These personal relationships played such a dominating part . . . that the student of the military art who seeks to deduce principles from the story of the A.E.F. must constantly take them into account. . . ."

So stated General James G. Harbord, Pershing's own chief of staff and right-hand man; himself a leader of dynamic character.

The fact of the matter is that through a peculiarly broad and varied service, John J. Pershing, when picked by President Woodrow Wilson in early 1917 to command a nebulous thing to be called the American Expeditionary Force in France, knew either personally or by reputation practically every officer of the little Regular Army and many of the National Guardsmen who had served on the Mexican border from 1915 until we declared war on Germany. That he was empowered to pick his own commanders and staff gave him opportunity to utilize that knowledge.

As result his demands fell upon subordinates who knew what he wanted. They, in turn, demanded of the soldiers they controlled, and in this manner the personal touch was transmitted down to the last man in ranks. The soldier might not like it; in fact he didn't. But he knew that somewhere up above was a slave driver named "Black Jack" Pershing, and one either did what he wanted, or else. It was as simple as that.

Born in Laclede, Missouri, the son of a railway section hand, Pershing battled his way into West Point through competitive examination, graduating in 1886. As a subaltern of cavalry he fought Apaches, did a tour of duty as tactical officer at West Point, served in the Santiago campaign of the Spanish-American War and in the Philippine Insurrection.

During all this time Pershing was garnering a reputation for pugnacity and efficiency. In 1903 his masterly leadership of a small punitive cavalry column against the Moros in the Lake Lanao country of Mindanao attracted the attention of President Theodore Roosevelt. Upon the inauguration of the War Department General Staff, also in 1903, he became a member of the original group. While on this duty he was detailed as an observer of the Russo-Japanese War in Manchuria, in 1904-1905. His reports attracted further Presidential notice, and on September 20, 1906, Captain Pershing found himself promoted to brigadier general; much to the momentary chagrin of most of his seniors in the Army. Some of them, perhaps unjustly, attributed his rise to the fact he was married to a Senator's daughter.

The hand of fate touched Pershing in 1916. When our growing difficulties with Mexico came to a head with Pancho Villa's raid on Columbus, New Mexico, Pershing was ordered to the border to command a punitive expedition into Mexico against the bandit. Hardly had he arrived in El Paso when his wife and three small daughters were tragically burned to death by fire in their quarters at the Presidio of San Francisco.

Under such harrowing shadow, it was a grim and aloof man who led the expedition into Mexico. Pershing's orders were to "pursue and disperse" Villa's band. They assumed the existence of peace between the United States and Mexico; no towns were to be entered, and neither railway nor telegraph used without Mexican permission. That the Mexican government, on the other hand, considered the expedition to be an act of war, never entered into the plans of the cautious State Department and visionary President who had committed fifteen thousand U.S. troops and their commander to a footless, ten-month will-o'-the-wisp campaign under almost impossible conditions.

Loyally, unswervingly, Pershing carried out his orders. He never caught Villa, but he pursued and dispersed his band. His force clashed—always on the defensive—with Mexican government troops impeding its movement, and brushed them aside when necessary. From the commander down, the troops learned an unforgettable lesson: where there's a will, there's a way. The entire operation was one of improvisation of supply and evacuation, over almost impassable desert trails through hostile country, as Pershing's cavalry probed southward, its deepest sweep taking it four hundred miles below the border.

In early February, 1917, the force was withdrawn, and Pershing, made a major general during the campaign, settled down at Fort Sam Houston, Texas, commanding the Southern Department. He had satisfied that most finicky of Presidents, Woodrow Wilson. Three months later he was in France, with a hand-picked thirty-one man staff, commanding an as yet nonexistent expeditionary force.

He carried with him a broad and flexible directive:

In military operations against the Imperial German Government you are directed to cooperate with the forces of the other countries employed against that enemy; but in so doing the underlying idea must be kept in view that the forces of the United States are a separate and distinct component of the combined forces, the identity of which must be preserved. This fundamental rule is subject to such minor exceptions in particular circumstances as your judgment may approve. The action is confided in you, and you will exercise full discretion in determining the manner of cooperation. But until the forces of the United States are in your judgment sufficiently strong to warrant operations as an independent command, it is understood that you will cooperate as component of whatever army you may be assigned by the French government.

The directive, in addition, gave Pershing carte blanche in the organization of the A.E.F. In fact, Pershing had drafted this himself, with the approval of the Secretary of War, Newton D. Baker, to whom must go the credit first for appreciating that our commander in the field must be unhampered by "absentee landlordism," and later for upholding his hand.

"If you succeed," Baker in effect told his general, "all will be well; if you fail, the public will probably hang us both at the first lamppost."

Pershing was at the height of physical and professional vigor, with thirty-one years of service behind him. His well-proportioned stature and poise belied his six-foot height until posed beside Allied leaders in France. Then one could realize that here stood the most soldierly figure in Europe, a warrior, impeccably turned out.

It might be well to ponder on the fact that had the present personnel-management procedures of the Defense Department, with its machine-record-*cum*-career management classifications, been in force, John J. Pershing, as well as the majority of the army, corps, and division commanders selected by him, would probably never have been in France at all; they would have been retired, long rated as tired old war horses, fit only for the knacker's yard. Fortunately for the United States, things were not run that way in 1917.

Delving immediately into the existing situation, Pershing and his hard-worked staff found out two basic facts at once. First, the Allies did not want an American army; they wanted American manpower in the shape of cannon fodder to fill their own depleted ranks. Secondly, combat on the Western front, as waged by the Allies, had degenerated to the stubborn defensive of trench warfare; a negation of every principle of fire and movement to which American professional soldiers were accustomed. The spirit of the offensive had died on the Allied side.

These things Pershing would not buy. He wanted an American Expeditionary Force in France a million men strong by May, 1918, with future plans for thrice that strength. He wanted infantry divisions built, tailored, and trained to his own ideas; divisions twenty-seven thousand strong, with a thousand officers each; divisions intended to hit and keep on hitting. He wanted his own theater of war (he picked the Lorraine front), supplied through ports on the western coast of France, so his lines of communication would not conflict with the Allies'. He wanted port equipment and an efficient service of supply.

He wanted a disciplined A.E.F., its infantrymen trained in combat marksmanship, its artillery sharpshooting, prepared to wage offensive warfare.

Thanks to his own superhuman personal efforts and those of the men with whom he surrounded himself, and thanks also to the support of Newton D. Baker, Pershing got those things. All the while he was fighting a personal battle on two fronts.

His general staff he revamped; based on the existing American concept, but also embodying many French principles. And as the troops came over—slowly at first and later with a rush—he officered them by commanders he knew and who knew him; men who as lieutenants and captains had proven their aggressiveness and leadership ability on the Plains, in Cuba, the Philippines, China, and Mexico. Friendship had nothing to do with it; efficiency was the yardstick.

Concurrently with training and administrative and logistic build-up went war plans. Sticking thumblike into the Lorraine front where Pershing wanted to fight was the St.-Mihiel salient, held and organized by the Germans since 1914; a flanking threat to the entire western front. Plans for its reduction by a full-scale American assault were perfected by Pershing's staff and approved by him within two months of his arrival in France.

The only doubtful thing about it was the date. For the enemy—the wily Ludendorff—combined with the Allied leaders to delay the formation of an American army. Five successive German offensives in early 1918 slashed and tore at the Allied front, almost—but not quite—split the French and British, and sent cold shivers of fear down Allied spines.

These things increased tension and friction on Pershing's second front—his violent personal clashes with Allied commanders and Allied heads of government, which had started almost from the moment of his arrival. To their reiterated coaxings and demands for American reinforcements to their respective armies he turned deaf ear. His A.E.F. was not a replacement depot for Allied armies. American divisions he would loan, that they might gain combat experience, but they were to be returned to him upon demand. An independent American army must be formed.

He could—and did—go so far as to smash his fist on the conference table in front of England's Lloyd George, France's Clemenceau, and Italy's Orlando when they tried to pry his command away.

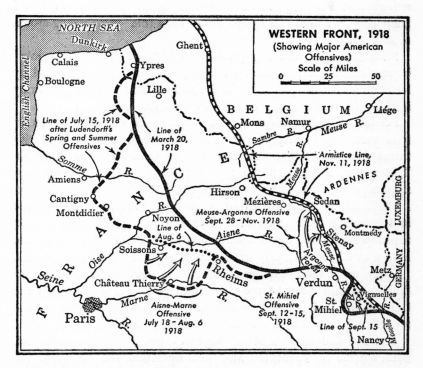

"Gentlemen, I have thought this program over very deliberately and will not be coerced!"

No wonder, then, that these men running the war through a debating society they called the Supreme War Council hated Pershing. "Tiger" Clemenceau bristled at what he termed the "development of General Pershing's exactions," and his "invincible obstinacy." Lloyd George snorted at mention of his name, and Orlando wrung his hands. No wonder they made continued efforts through diplomatic channels to obtain his removal—efforts thwarted by War Secretary Baker's unremitting championship of Pershing's cause before President Wilson.

Nor is it any wonder that foreign military critics inherited that viewpoint and whispered of Pershing's narrow views. General Sir Frederick Maurice writes that Pershing's comments "seem singularly naïve and lacking in understanding." Brash pundit Liddell Hart's remark that Pershing "revealed strange limitations of outlook and knowledge in a man cast by fate for so big a role" bears strong aroma of sour grapes.

Such things are now but spindrift on history's waves. What must be remembered is that there stood an American soldier charged by his commander in chief to maintain an independent American army in the field, fulfilling that charge in both letter and spirit.

Pershing could—and did—come to Marshal Ferdinand Foch in spontaneous generosity to offer reinforcements when Ludendorff's threats became really serious. Our 2nd and 3rd Divisions at Château-Thierry and Belleau Wood met the enemy on the Marne and stopped him. Then came Cantigny, the first all-American offensive; a small, one-regiment affair, but eye-opening to both friend and foe in the savage impetuosity and co-ordination displayed in the successful assault. Shortly afterward, another German stab across the Marne at Château-Thierry was stopped by three American divisions.

Later, when the French used two American divisions to spearhead their successful Aisne-Marne counteroffensive, and it was plain the German bid had failed, Pershing announced it was now high time for the A.E.F. to become a tactical entity, and made his point.

The new-fledged First Army began concentrating in mid-August, 1918, for the big event; the St.-Mihiel operation, the first all-American large-scale offensive, so long desired. An attempt by Foch to obtain French control—the suggestion that French Generals Degoutte and Malcor head the army's general staff—was refused by canny Pershing, more or less diplomatically. Then Foch, who by this time was exercising a supreme command of sorts over both Allied and U.S. operations, sprang a bombshell.

On August 30 Foch came to Pershing's headquarters. His plans, he stated, had changed. The Americans were needed elsewhere, and the operation must be called off.

That was just too much.

"You have no authority as an Allied Commander in Chief," stormed Pershing, "to call upon me to yield up my command of the American Army and have it scattered among the Allied forces where it will not be an American Army!"

"I insist!"

"You may insist all you please, but I decline absolutely to agree to your plan. While our Army will fight wherever you may decide, it will not fight except as an independent American Army!"

Foch, pale and shaking with rage, left. Next day the pair met at the headquarters of General Henri P. Pétain, who was now commanding the French armies. Pétain, as blunt a fighting man as Pershing, understood. He patched up the quarrel. The St.-Mihiel operation, conceded Foch, could go on. But there was a proviso. A general Allied offensive would start September 25; the full American strength must be shifted in time to take part. Its zone, as he pointed out on the map, would lie along a northerly axis through the Argonne Forest and the Meuse valley.

And that was, perhaps, John J. Pershing's greatest moment, for he instantly agreed, pledging his strength of will and the temper of his troops to fight and win one offensive, then launch another sixty miles away, all within two short weeks.

It would necessitate immediate planning, imposed upon the initial operation; an almost split-second shifting and concentration of 600,000 men and 2,700 guns, most of them already committed to one major operation, over to the second front. They must win at St.-Mihiel, in time to be juggled over a slim three-road network, during hours of darkness, to their jump-off line for the Meuse-Argonne operation. It is doubtful if military history can furnish a parallel to an undertaking of such magnitude.

That was what Pershing promised; that was what he did.

On September 12 the First Army launched a double envelopment of the St.-Mihiel salient; an American army corps closing in on each side while French troops attached to Pershing's command held the nose. Despite excellent planning and skillful use of fire and movement, surprise was lacking, and a large part of the enemy retreated safely before the pincers closed. But when the U.S. 1st and 26th Divisions joined hands at Vigneulles at the end of forty-eight hours of fast fighting, a significant success had been gained. The St.-Mihiel salient which had threatened the Allied flank for four years was eliminated; 16,000 prisoners and 443 guns were in American hands.

Best of all, no doubt longer remained as to the caliber and skill of American arms.

On September 25–26, thirteen days after it had jumped off at St.-Mihiel, the First Army assaulted in the Meuse-Argonne area, plunging on a twenty-four-mile front, into a grim area of rugged hills and woods carefully fortified by three highly organized German defensive zones and a fourth partly completed. This terrain was held by an enemy who, knowing that American success here meant disintegration of his entire front, defended it tooth and nail.

For forty-seven days of continuous combat one of the world's decisive battles raged. Roughly it divided into three phases. From the jump-off until October 3 the Americans moved, rapidly at first, then slowed down as the outnumbered battle-wise Germans skillfully tripped some of the green American divisions involved.

On October 4, with veteran divisions replacing the exhausted starters, the second phase commenced; a phase which embraced the toughest fighting of the offensive, for our troops were up against the most highly organized German zone; the backbone of the defense. It became a succession of foot-by-foot advances as Pershing's battering ram crunched through.

The third and final phase began November 1. By this time Pershing had enlarged his zone. The Second Army had blossomed on the right, attacking across the Meuse to attain the commanding heights beyond. Exhausted divisions once more had been replaced, and First Army this time burst its bonds; out into the open beyond the enemy defenses, and into real warfare of movement. By November 8 the outskirts of Sedan had been reached and the Hirson-Mézières-Montmédy-Metz railway line, carotid artery of German supply on the western front, was cut. Germany's military men realized that further resistance would be useless. On November 11 came the armistice and the end.

From beginning to end the Meuse-Argonne operation was one of incessant pressure down through the chain of command; the impulsion of Pershing's will, which accepted no excuse and terminated each local slowdown with a new attack order. How his lieutenants —the men Pershing had chosen to lead his armies, army corps, and divisions—translated their commander's will into action is something else again. This, too, was a flamboyant demonstration of combat leadership, as we shall see.

Save the Infantry

Stern indeed was the breed of American leaders spawned in World War I; the men who under Pershing successfully bridged the gap between leadership of a platoon into battle with the stirring "Follow me!" of our little wars, and manipulating to victory great masses of men whose strength was measured in tens of thousands. It was a tough breed; some few would later become known and feared in our Army as arrogant bullies, but these were exceptions. The leadership of the "Pershing men" would leave its mark on the U.S. Army for a score of years. And, all things considered, theirs was a beneficial influence, laying the foundation for another, greater effort.

These were men of direct action; action based on the necessarily elementary tactics of the A.E.F., which had but two aggressive plays. The 1st Division went into battle with brigades abreast and regiments abreast in each brigade. The 2nd Division hit the line with its two brigades in column. One or other of these formations was used by other divisions.

The divisional artillery supported the attack, opening the way with its firepower; the efficiency of the whole dependent upon the mutual confidence of infantry and artillery. The greater the battle experience of a division, the greater was this interdependence.

Personal reconnaissance by the leader was a *sine qua non*; so, too, was his presence—if not in the immediate front lines, at least in areas most sensitive. Once the operation was launched, the division commander floated; the minutiae of direction was left to his chief of staff, the executive at the command post.

Such at least was the theory; the leader violating it in practice did so to his own personal peril.

There was little room for display of the milk of human kindness in this leadership. All down the line the authority was relentless, brooking no excuse. And yet we can find one of these leaders at least, who, possessing something of the stern, uncompromising way of Stonewall Jackson—which was how keen reporter Frederick Palmer saw him—could also blend with it some of the *noblesse oblige* of Robert E. Lee. This man, who rose from command of a field-artillery brigade to that of an infantry division and finally to that of an army corps in four months of war, was Charles Pelot Summerall. His combat fame is woven into the history of the 1st Infantry Division.

The quality of Summerall's leadership consisted of the essence of loyalty, up and down. The cold lash of his tongue shriveled, indeed, the delinquent whose fault had been discovered by this perfectionist. But, on the other hand, his equally dispassionate but openly declared praise, on the spot, for duty well performed left a warm glow in the heart of the recipient. Therein he differed from Pershing. The turnout of a guard, the appearance of a platoon, or even a squad on inspection or the routine operation of a company kitchen; any of these efficiently performed, could elicit a word of commendation from the tall, severe Summerall, whose language and appearance smacked more of the pulpit than the battlefield, and who roamed his command incessantly.

Like most of Pershing's lieutenants, Summerall, Florida-born son of a clergyman, graduated from West Point in 1892, had learned his trade in little wars. An artilleryman, he had pushed his guns up to support the infantrymen in a score of hot spots in Luzon and Mindanao in the Philippines before his first highlight flashed in the rubble and din of a reeking close-in street fight in China during the Boxer Rebellion.

First Lieutenant Summerall, commanding a two-gun platoon of Riley's Light Battery F, 5th Artillery, was supporting the advance of the 14th Infantry as the China Relief Expedition battered its way through the sprawling rabbit warren of Peking, August 15, 1900.

Summoned to break the massive, ironbound gate of the Imperial City wall confronting the advance, Summerall's platoon unlimbered hub to hub in the narrow street and the tall young lieutenant stalked up to the portal, unconcerned by the hot fire pouring down from its Chinese defenders above him. Deliberately he chalked a great white X on the timbers, upon which his gunners trained their pieces point-blank, to blast an opening with their first volley.

So much for background. Let's go now to France, where Summerall's conviction that the artillery existed only to support and preserve the infantry brought about in World War I a revolution in the battlefield tactics and technique of field artillery.

"Whenever there is sufficient artillery," wrote Summerall once, "it can neutralize the enemy, if properly employed, and save the infantry while ensuring success."

"Saving" the infantry is in this case a relative term, as it always has been and always must be on the battlefield. The 1st Division in World War I sustained 21,612 casualties, 4,411 of them battle deaths; most of them occurring under Summerall's command. The point is that Summerall, while never hesitating to hurl men into battle to attain his objective, devised a method by which casualties would be held to a minimum, and no man's life would be squandered fruitlessly.

He used his method first at Soissons, when his division was spearheading the attack of the Tenth French Army in the Aisne-Marne offensive. The division, as usual, was attacking with brigades abreast; Summerall, who had been commanding the artillery brigade, had just been promoted to division commander. Reconnoitering in advance, he realized that he did not have sufficient artillery to sustain an assault on so broad a front. He solved the problem by hurling his infantry brigades into action alternately.

In front of each attacking brigade, in turn, Summerall poured the fire of every divisional gun, utilizing the flexibility and range of modern artillery to mass the shellbursts on the vital spot of the moment, much as one would switch the hose stream from side to side in watering the lawn.

As the doughboys of the attacking brigade clawed their way

through the wheat fields, assisted by the guns, the other brigade, momentarily motionless, maintained intense small-arms fire, keeping the Germans on its front too busy to worry about what was happening on their flank. This was a bit of Summerall psychology, past experience having proved to him that men will fire back, instinctively, at what is firing at them.

What Summerall invented was a modern application of the Napoleonic concept of the *grande batterie*. Where Napoleon of necessity physically massed his short-range cannon in one big group to support his main effort and to blast the enemy out of the way, Summerall's modern guns, regardless of their positions, were swung to accomplish similar massing of shellbursts in one area. It was simple. But, as they said of Columbus and the egg, no one had ever thought of it before.

It wasn't all beer and skittles at Soissons. Tenacious and skillful German resistance at one point brought the division to a grinding halt. Summerall, in the front lines to see for himself, rallied the troops in his immediate vicinity, inspiring them to renew the attack and finally storm the enemy strong point. He got the Distinguished Service Cross for this.

Summerall next put his artillery concept into practice during the second phase of the Meuse-Argonne offensive, when the 1st Division, taking over from the 35th, bucked its way into the Hindenburg Line. First one brigade, then two regiments in succession, smashed through, in a series of power punches; each individual effort assisted by the fire of all the divisional guns blasting into its zone.

Again the scheme succeeded, where, as Summerall himself later commented, "otherwise we would have failed."

In the midst of that effort, Summerall went on to the command of V Corps, next-door neighbor on the right, to the 1st Division. And through his plea, to army headquarters, his corps zone was extended to the left, so the 1st Division would remain under his command.

But the offensive slowed, all along the line, until Pershing relieved the battle-worn units on the front and ran in a fresh team. Even that new setup made but slow progress, and on November 1 the third and final phase began, with the veteran 2nd Division and the 89th this time making up Summerall's assault elements. Once more

he invoked the power of the artillery, this time in a rolling barrage
—a carpet of fire twelve hundred yards deep—in front of his doughboys. The heavy guns of army and corps artillery joined the lighter
divisional guns, supporting the effort, in close co-ordination with
the advance of the foot troops.

Behind this Niagara of fire the infantry plunged through the last
fringe of German defenses and into open country beyond. The
back of enemy resistance was broken and the slugging match became
a pursuit.

What Summerall had accomplished, in command of a corps as
well as a division, was to weld the artillery and infantry of his
command into an articulated and integrated team. The artillery was
imbued with the belief that it existed only to help the infantry over
the hard spots. The infantry expected artillery help. This theory of
the infantry-artillery team was already inherent in American tactics
at the time. To give Summerall sole credit for the concept would
be both incorrect and unjust to the little group of pre-World War
I regular officers—including Summerall—who had evolved it.

But Summerall's employment of the members of his team, the
alternating right- and left-hand punches of his infantry, each one in
turn supported by the flexible nozzles of his entire artillery strength,
were refinements of personal leadership which inspired both confidence and pride in the men he commanded. The result was an
irresistible team spirit, responding to his every demand.

This was particularly true of the 1st Division, with which he was
most intimately connected. This was the spirit which evoked from
Pershing this unique citation:

"The Commander-in-Chief has noted in this division a special
pride of service and a high state of morale, never broken by hard-
ship or battle."

It is not too much to say that Summerall *was* the spirit of the
"Big Red One." And so deeply rooted was this spirit that its tradition would reach out to inspire a new generation of soldiers in this
same unit a quarter-century later in an even greater war.

More than that, Charles P. Summerall had established the basis
for the modern artillery fire direction which would make American
guns supreme on all the fronts of World War II.

On all counts, then, this soldier, who, following in the footsteps of Pershing, would later become Chief of Staff of the Army, falls squarely within our frame of leadership.

To sum up, this conflict of World War I, our initial adventure overseas against a first-class military power, within the space of one hectic year and seven months and two hundred days of actual battle, forged a concept of successful leadership substantiating every one of our past experiences in war. Its lessons were analyzed in our growing service schools and permeated our military thought.

It was a shocking thing that our entry into World War II, twenty-three years after the drumfire ceased on the western front of France, should have been marked by a momentary denial of all this; a stunning illustration of what Toynbee calls the nemesis of warfare: a chain of which "each link has been a cycle of invention, triumph, lethargy and disaster."

CHAPTER XV ☆ ☆ ☆ *A Fumble and Its Consequences*

Precisely at 7:55 A.M. on Sunday, December 7, 1941, the full force of a Japanese aerial attack struck the island of Oahu, Hawaii, in complete and devastating surprise. When it was over, the battleships of our Pacific Fleet, moored helplessly by pairs in their Pearl Harbor base, had received a mortal blow. Our Hawaiian Army air strength—its planes ranged neatly wing to wing, like sitting ducks, on airfield ramps—was a tangled mass of smoking wreckage.

No disaster of the magnitude of Pearl Harbor could have occurred without the failure—somewhere and somehow—of leadership. A total of eight official investigations searched for scapegoats and found them. However, as the spate of impassioned special pleadings shows, confusion and argument still exists on the matter, including its use as a political football.

Here we are concerned with Army leadership. It makes no difference, in assessing responsibility, whether one believes or disbelieves that the President and his Secretary of State goaded the Japanese into war as a measure of desperation. It makes no difference, either, if these two men, like the civilian Secretaries of War and Navy, had their eyes fixed on the Japanese threat in Southeast Asia. They had repeatedly given warning to the military men who had the professional responsibility to be ready, within the limits of the means available to them, for any contingency.

It makes no difference that Japanese exceptional military skill, shrouded by perfidy and assisted by almost incredible luck, accomplished its mission. Nor, indeed, does it matter that, as adjudicated in the always brilliant light of afterthought, Japan might well have inflicted defeat upon our Pacific Fleet and our Army forces in Hawaii regardless of how well alerted they might have been on December 7, 1941.

The point is that we were surprised, both strategically and tac-

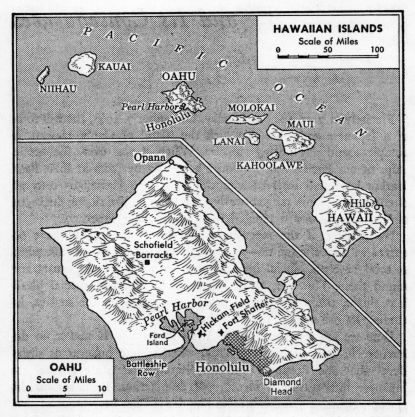

tically. The responsibility for our failure lay in two places—Washington and Hawaii. The guardians of a nation's security never have the right to excuse failure by attributing it to chance or to the cunning of any enemy. It is their responsibility to leave nothing to chance, their duty not to be outwitted by any foe.

At the moment of the attack two infantrymen, professional

soldiers both, filled posts of vital importance. In Washington was General George C. Marshall, Chief of Staff, responsible for the entire United States Army and all its installations. On Oahu was Lieutenant General Walter C. Short, commanding the Hawaiian Department, the most vital overseas outpost of that Army.

Marshall, product of V.M.I., had earned a well-deserved reputation for brilliant staff work in Pershing's A.E.F. Later, he had taken prominent part in developing the Infantry School at Fort Benning, Georgia. Short, graduate of the University of Illinois, had entered the Army from civil life in 1901. He had been chosen personally by Marshall early in 1941 to command the Hawaiian Department.

Two other men there were, in respectively parallel positions of command that day; in Washington, Admiral Harold H. Stark, Chief of Naval Operations, was Marshall's counterpart; in Hawaii, Admiral Husband E. Kimmel, Short's opposite file, commanded the Pacific Fleet.

On these four leaders lies, in varying degree, the responsibility.

The story of Pearl Harbor is common knowledge. A recapitulation of some of the major events leading to the disaster is essential, however, to provide a basis for evaluating the extent to which leadership failed.

Official Washington was under no illusions as to the warlike intentions of Japan in late November and early December, 1941. On November 27 General Marshall and Admiral Stark sent similar warning messages to Army and Navy commanders in the Philippines, Hawaii, Panama, and the West Coast of the United States and Alaska. Marshall's message read, in part: "Negotiations with Japan appear to be terminated to all practical purposes. . . ." The message then reiterated President Roosevelt's desire that Japan commit the first overt act. But this, it was pointed out, "should not be construed as restricting you to a course of action that might jeopardize your defense. *Prior to hostile Japanese action you are directed to undertake such reconnaissance and other measures as you deem necessary* [italics supplied]. . . . Report measures taken. . . ."

Admiral Stark's message, which was also sent to General Short and the other Army commanders in the Pacific area, bluntly opened with the words: "This is a war warning."

But if Washington was almost certain that war with Japan was about to break out, it was equally convinced that the first Japanese blow would be struck in Southeast Asia, and this thought was communicated to the overseas commanders. The concentration of a large proportion of Japan's naval and military might in this region seemed to indicate that the garrison in the Philippines was more gravely threatened than any other American outpost in the Pacific. The War Department apparently did not give much attention to General Short's reply to the warning message he had received, reporting the measures he had taken in Hawaii as follows:

"Report department alerted to prevent sabotage. Liaison with the Navy."

And so, with his report apparently satisfactory, General Short felt that he had done all that was necessary to prepare for war. He was pleased that there should not be any serious interruption of the much-needed training of his rapidly growing command. His radar stations were operating from 4 A.M. to 7 A.M.; all antiaircraft ammunition was safeguarded at a central ammunition depot in accordance with his provisions for antisabotage alerts. If he thought at all about the reconnaissance he had been directed to initiate, he assumed that this was a Navy responsibility. Although his relations with Admiral Kimmel were cordial (despite later malicious reports to the contrary), he gave no thought to inquiring what alert measures the Navy was taking; he would have considered any similar request from Admiral Kimmel as unwarranted interference in Army affairs. When reports of a peculiar long-distance call from Honolulu to Tokyo, apparently regarding the number of Navy vessels in Pearl Harbor, was brought to his attention Saturday evening, December 6, he saw no reason why this couldn't be investigated the next Monday morning.

By December 6 official nerves in Washington were as taut as bowstrings. We had broken Japan's secret code, and we knew that the negotiators in Washington had been instructed by Tokyo to stall for time, obviously while the military got ready to strike. Except for four aircraft carriers, Naval Intelligence had pinpointed the major elements of the Japanese fleet; Army and Navy concentrations and ship movements in the East Asian area meant that war was only a matter of hours. Japanese diplomatic representatives had been instructed to burn documents and destroy coding machines, save for one to be kept operating in the embassy in Washington until further notice.

During the night, and early on the morning of the 7th, we intercepted several more revealing messages from Tokyo. General Marshall's assistants placed these on his desk, but no one thought of interrupting the Chief of Staff's regular Sunday morning horseback ride. So it was not until he arrived at his War Department office at 11:15 A.M. that Marshall was presented with the latest intercepts. One of these ordered the Japanese envoys in Washington to submit "our reply to the United States at 1 P.M. of the 7th, your time." Another directed the destruction of the last coding machine when the messages had been decoded.

"Something is going to happen at one o'clock," said Marshall to his aides, and rapidly wrote a message for immediate transmission to all major commands in the Pacific area, including, of course, Hawaii:

"The Japanese are presenting at 1 P.M. EST today, what amounts to an ultimatum. . . . Just what significance the hour may have we do not know, but be on alert accordingly."

It was now almost noon (6:30 A.M. in Honolulu). Marshall pondered a moment. Should he pick up the telephone and call the overseas commanders? This was feasible, but if the conversations were picked up by the Japanese they would learn one of our greatest secrets: that we had broken their code. He inquired how long it would take for his coded radio message to be delivered. He was assured that it would be in the hands of the recipients, decoded, within thirty minutes. He let it go at that.

Swiftly the official radio flashed to Panama, to the Philippines, to our West Coast. But there was trouble, it seemed, in getting through to Hawaii. The message-center officer sent it to Honolulu by commercial radio, which was usually just as fast. But it was delayed slightly that morning and finally reached Short twelve hours after the Japanese attack had been launched.

Out of the mountains of recorded testimony, all available, the following conclusions regarding responsibility for Pearl Harbor emerge:

In Washington the War Department staff over which General Marshall presided was at the time a complicated but still a "one-man" shop, where delegation of responsibility was the exception rather than the rule. When Marshall was absent, the operational wheels tended to freeze. This situation was to some extent due to cumbersome organization, and to some extent due to the personality of the Chief of Staff.

General Marshall, in a letter to General Short on February 7, 1941, had stressed that "the risk of sabotage and the *risk involved in a surprise raid by air and submarine* [italics supplied] constitute the real perils of the [Hawaiian] situation." Yet, although definitely warning Short on November 27 of the threat of war, and ordering him to report the measures he would take in response, Marshall did not check up on those measures; was unaware of Short's "sabotage" interpretation in his reply of the same date. And General Leonard T. Gerow, heading the War Plans Division of General Marshall's General Staff—as he later testified in taking full responsibility for the slip—had made no provision for following up operational orders. The net result was that both Marshall and Short remained in blissful ignorance of a vital misinterpretation of orders.

Marshall, like Stark and indeed like all of the members of their respective staffs who knew the situation, permitted himself to be hypnotized by the concrete evidence of a Japanese aggressive build-up in Southeast Asia; a threat to our Philippines outpost. This theme, it will be remembered, ran as background to nearly all the warnings sent Hawaii. Thus succumbing to the illusive diagnosis of "enemy probable intentions," Marshall—again like Stark—ignored the danger warning provided by our inability to locate at least four Japanese aircraft carriers; a significant factor in "enemy capabilities."

Finally, on December 7, having indicated his full realization of the significance of the "one o'clock" intercept—that less than two hours separated peace and war—and having decided not to use the telephone, Marshall failed to require surveillance and report on the delivery of his final warning.

These, certainly, were lapses in leadership. Among other things, they evidenced also that General Marshall had forgotten an old military axiom: issuance of orders is futile if their implementation be not followed up.

In all fairness, it should be noted that these leadership lapses would have been inconsequential had the subordinates on the spot taken adequate security measures on the basis of instructions and information received by them. Perhaps equally serious lapses on the part of other commanders in the past have been overlooked in these pages when the consequences have not been grave and the over-all efforts of leadership have been successful. But when a mistake, no matter how trivial, contributes to disaster, the circumstances cannot be glossed over.

So much for Washington. As soldiers we do not feel qualified to judge the exact nature and degree of the shortcomings of Admirals Stark and Kimmel—with one significant exception in the latter's case, which we shall point out.

On Oahu, the situation is clear-cut; military leadership at the top failed utterly.

As to General Short, it is painful to list the failures of an officer we have known personally, one who was respected, trusted, and loved by many of our contemporaries. But a study of leadership in the United States Army would not be complete without some analysis of its failure at Pearl Harbor. Perhaps General Short should not have been in the position he held; if that is the case, then the man who selected and appointed him—General Marshall—should perhaps be blamed. Possibly other officers of like rank and experience would have failed as completely—though Army commanders on the West Coast, in Panama, and in the Philippines did take adequate security measures on the basis of identical warnings. Whatever may be offered in extenuation, the nation, his superiors, the men under him, and those relying on his protection, all had a right to expect from a professional military man—*who had received a warning that hostilities were "possible at any moment"*—that:

He would carry out his instructions to "undertake . . . reconnaissance." Full use of his available radar facilities would have been a minimum measure commensurate with the warning.

He would realize, particularly in the light of specific instructions to this effect, that his first responsibility was to provide for the security of the Pacific Fleet; training requirements were secondary to this overriding mission.

He would endeavor to find out the security measures being undertaken by Admiral Kimmel, so that both commands could make the most effective and economic employment of the limited means available.

He would heed intelligence information brought specifically to his attention, implying that hostile actions against Oahu and the Pacific Fleet were a possibility.

In carrying out even the most limited alert of his command, he would make sure that the antiaircraft defenses protecting the island and the fleet would have at least a few rounds of ammunition at the guns, rather than keep all ammunition at a central point some hours' distance from most guns.

Above all, as an outpost commander, alerted to the danger of war, he—and equally Admiral Kimmel—would take every possible measure to prevent surprise. Like sentinels on post, they were responsible for keeping "always on the alert, and observing everything that takes place within sight or hearing." As stated by the joint Congressional committee which made the final investigation of the disaster, "the field commander . . . is not privileged to think or contemplate that he will not be attacked. On the contrary, he is to assume and expect that his particular post will be attacked."

To General Marshall's credit one must chalk up his ability to profit by his mistakes. In less than three months after Pearl Harbor, he had completely reorganized the War Department, decentralizing the mass of relatively minor administrative and executive matters that had choked major strategical and tactical decisions. His newly created Operations Division of the General Staff—which Marshall well termed his "command post"—ensured co-ordinated action and direction of Army activities in theaters of war which would soon stud the globe.

Three years and nine months after that Pearl Harbor heartbreak, V-J Day dawned September 2, 1945, in Tokyo Bay. The transformation of the United States Army—which Winston Churchill would later term "a prodigy of organization, of improvisation . . . a mystery as yet unexplained . . . to find the leaders and vast staffs capable of handling enormous masses and of moving them faster and further than masses have ever been moved in war before. . . ."—must be noted.

It was in effect a wedding of professional military leadership and of technology. For logistics—the procurement, equipment, supply, maintenance, and transportation of men and matériel—had become one of the major aspects of war. Without logistical power properly applied the most grandiose schemes of strategy would die a-borning.

This fact the awakened Marshall had recognized when he reorganized his War Department after Pearl Harbor. Ground Forces, Air Force, and coequal Service of Supply became the major operating elements of the United States Army.

The Service of Supply, commanded by General Brehon B. Somervell, became the biggest business in history. It employed more people, spent more money, and handled more commodities than any other organization in the world before it. It landed from five to twelve tons of equipment with every soldier sent overseas, and followed with another ton per man per month in food, clothing, and ammunition. It built the Army's roads and camps and hospitals, and it operated the largest radio network in the world.

This—and Marshall's over-all responsibility—must be remembered as we scan field leadership around the globe in World War II.

CHAPTER XVI ☆ ☆ ☆ *Two Promises and Their Fulfillment*

"The President of the United States ordered me to break through the Japanese lines and proceed from Corregidor to Australia for the purpose, as I understand it, of organizing the American offensive against Japan. A primary purpose of this is the relief of the Philippines. I came through and I shall return!"

"We got a hell of a beating. . . . We got run out of Burma and it is humiliating as hell. I think we ought to find out what caused it, go back and retake it."

Stout words of determination spoken by two American generals when each was hardly better than a refugee. Douglas MacArthur voiced his defiant promise on March 17, 1942, at lonely Batchellor Field, near Darwin, in northeastern Australia. Joseph W. Stilwell's grim resolution to recoup frankly admitted defeat was announced two months later, May 22, at an impromptu news conference at obscure Dinjan, northeastern India.

The history of American leadership offers no more dramatic situations than the parallel tales of how these two men came to be at the Godforsaken spots where they spoke these words, and of the manner in which they set about redeeming their pledges. Few American soldiers since Washington had experienced such depths of adversity, and yet had nevertheless been able to persevere to ultimate victory. In defeat and in triumph both had displayed the highest professional military competence, had shown their deep and sympathetic understanding of their men—their human tools—and had

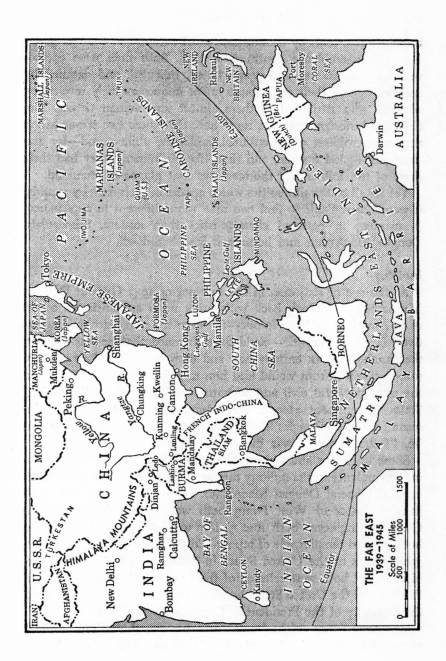

THE FAR EAST
1939–1945

Scale of Miles
0   500   1000   1500

inspired these tools by demonstrations of exceptional courage under fire. The resemblance continues further. Both men were controversial figures in war and peace, hated, ridiculed, and damned by enemies among their own countrymen; unquestioningly revered by admirers who attributed to them almost superhuman virtues. The objective historian, however, must note that these two strong-willed men were soldiers of exceptional brilliance, ability, and—for the most part—good fortune; and that, like all humans, they had their share of the foibles and shortcomings that plague all mankind.

Yet for all of the similarities which appear in their military records, it would be difficult to find two men more different in appearance, in manner, in personal characteristics than austere, immaculate Douglas MacArthur and homespun Joseph Stilwell.

Invictus

At the age of sixty-one, in the summer of 1941 General Douglas MacArthur could look back with pride upon an illustrious career as an American soldier. No one—not even the romantically imaginative MacArthur himself—could have dreamed that he was only on the threshold of an entirely new and even more illustrious military career, which in turn would lead him to a third and separate role as the most powerful civil administrator ever to represent the United States Government abroad. Our concern here is to evaluate the second career of Douglas MacArthur, the soldier, in which his promise, "I shall return," was the central theme.

Some historians and commentators have professed to find a striking resemblance in the military careers of General George B. McClellan and General Douglas MacArthur. Both were exceptionally brilliant graduates of West Point; both were officers in the Army's Corps of Engineers; both rose rapidly to high rank as young men; both reached the pinnacle of top rank in the Army; both commanded great armies of the United States in battle; both had political ambitions; and both were relieved of their commands in wartime by a President of the United States because they had implicitly challenged the authority of the President as Commander in Chief.

The comparison might be apt save for one thing. The military career of a soldier can be judged only on one basis—leadership in battle. McClellan failed as a leader even when fortune smiled upon him; even when the opportunity to succeed was clearly within his grasp. MacArthur enjoyed more military successes, probably, than any other soldier in American history; he proved his combat leadership in defeat as in victory; he sought and seized every possible opportunity to win success in battle, opportunities frequently discernible to, and exploitable by Douglas MacArthur alone.

This ability to seize promptly the most fleeting opportunity, was perhaps his most outstanding characteristic as a soldier. It had been amply demonstrated in World War I, when MacArthur had made a brilliant record as the youngest division commander in Pershing's A.E.F. In that war he had proven his physical courage, frequently exposing himself to enemy fire—once even personally leading a dangerous patrol into no man's land—and getting wounded in the process. His moral courage was demonstrated later in 1932, when as Chief of Staff of the United States Army, he carried out President Hoover's orders by personally assuming command of the troops which evicted the "Bonus Marchers" from Washington, rather than turning this distasteful task over to any of his subordinates.

But he had retired as chief of staff of the Army in 1935, and had gone to the Philippines where he, like his father before him, had previously served with distinction for many years. At the request of his old friend Manuel Quezon, he became military adviser to the government of the Philippine Commonwealth, with the honorary title of field marshal. An old war horse, gone to pasture, was determined to spend his declining years in helping the new country to prepare itself for the independence promised by the United States for 1945.

By midsummer of 1941 MacArthur was just reaching the halfway mark of a ten-year program to produce a cohesive Philippine Army, which, upon independence, would be the armed land force of the Commonwealth. Proud though he might be of what he had accomplished to date, the General had no illusions that this embryo army was ready for war.

On July 26, in the face of mounting Japanese threats of aggression, President Roosevelt ordered the reincorporation of the Philippine Army into the United States armed forces. At the same time he recalled General MacArthur to active duty to command all U.S. and the Commonwealth forces in the Philippines. Calmly, efficiently, MacArthur prepared for war, though he realized that it would be many months before he could hope to defend the Philippines successfully against a Japanese attack. He called up the reserves of the Philippine Army and began an intensive training program, despite the handicaps imposed by lack of weapons, equipment, and experienced leaders. But, as the end of the year approached, and in the light of promised reinforcements of American ground troops and air units, and of equipment for his Philippine Army, he began to feel that his efforts might be successful. In just a few more months, he believed, he would have the capability to oppose and defeat the anticipated Japanese invasion.

But he was to be denied this time for further preparation. On December 8, as Japanese bombs were smashing the U.S. Pacific Fleet at Pearl Harbor, MacArthur had on Luzon some 11,000 American ground troops, about 12,000 Philippine Scouts—Regular Army units composed of Filipino soldiers—and about 50,000 men of the Philippine Army (another 50,000 were scattered elsewhere in the archipelago), comprising one regular army division and four sketchily trained, inadequately equipped reserve divisions. In addition he had a U.S. Army Air Force contingent of about 8,000 Americans, equipped with some 250 aircraft, of which 35 were Flying Fortresses and 107 were P-40 fighters.

These air units, however, were to be of little use in the defense of the Philippines. Large-scale Japanese air attacks from bases in Formosa quickly overwhelmed the American Air Force, destroying most of the planes on the ground. Unquestionably this disaster was due largely to the lack of battle experience of the American airmen, and to the largely inadequate facilities on the ground for the support, maintenance, and protection of heavy-bombardment aircraft. But there is also little doubt that the Japanese task was made easier by inadequate security of the airfields, and allowing the Japanese to find most of the large planes unprotected on the ground at lunch time on December 8. Both General MacArthur and his Air Force commander, Lieutenant General Lewis H. Brereton, have been blamed for this disaster. Certainly a commander must assume the responsibility for failures by his subordinates; but there was even less excuse for inadequate local security at American air bases in the Philippines than there had been earlier that day at Oahu. Not only had the local Air Force been warned of the danger of attack by MacArthur's headquarters, but American aircraft had actually been involved in combat operations against the Japanese before the disastrous attacks. We leave this controversial matter without further comment.

Few military plans are perfect. Enemy probable intentions and capabilities must be at best an educated guess; the enemy's mental reactions to a given situation and the thought processes of the enemy commander himself are enigmatic. The imponderables of morale of the moment, in both friend and foe, as well as the vagaries of the weather, further complicate the battlefield situation to the point where anything may, and usually does, happen.

It is therefore rare indeed when the pattern of a military operation follows closely the concept of the leader's initial plan. This can occur only when the plan was conceived by a leadership which combines sound military judgment with vivid imagination, and which then executes the plan with skill, courage, will power, and daring. In the annals of war only a handful of men—the so-called "Great Captains" of history—have had the genius to accomplish such rare feats repeatedly.

It is therefore all the more remarkable that the first battle in which Douglas MacArthur exercised over-all command went according to plan. The plan was not original with him; its major aspects had been worked out by American staff officers (including MacArthur) twenty and more years before, since the possibility of Japanese aggression against the Philippines had long been recognized, and the likelihood of major hostile landings on Luzon, north and south of Manila, correctly anticipated. The plan contemplated major defensive actions north of Manila against invaders landing at inviting Lingayen Gulf, while other troops conducted a delaying action against an enemy push from the south of Manila. If, as likely, enemy strength proved too great, both defending forces would withdraw slowly to join near Manila, then retire into the easily defensible Bataan Peninsula.

Withdrawals and delaying actions are tricky affairs, even with well-trained, well-led soldiers. In the first place, withdrawing troops, harassed and punished by an aggressive and numerically superior foe, are not easily halted and reformed into an effective defense. Secondly, the attacker, by virtue of his greater strength and the momentum of his initial drive, retains the initiative, and thus may force the defender to abandon his plan at the very outset.

The American plan could succeed only if the two delaying actions were carefully co-ordinated and timed, from beginning to end. Were the northern force—Major General Jonathan Wainwright's I Corps—driven back too quickly, the southern force would be cut off and destroyed in the vicinity of Manila. This latter command— Brigadier General Albert M. Jones's II Corps—had to retreat from Manila by a single road across the thirty-mile-wide swamp delta of the Pampanga River. If Jones began too early his withdrawal across this defile, then Wainwright would be struck from the rear, and in all probability only a few survivors of I Corps would be able to get back into Bataan.

MacArthur, then, was faced with a difficult choice when the main Japanese landings came, as expected, north and south of Manila on December 22 and 23, 1941. He could abandon most of Luzon—plus a good portion of his army and many supplies—without a fight, by withdrawing his unreliable Filipinos, and the leaven of regular American and Philippine Scout troops, back to prepared positions on Bataan. Or, in hopes of gathering the bulk of his forces into the Bataan fortress, he could risk total disaster by attempting the intricately co-ordinated delaying action. Typically, he chose the latter course. He was relying upon the coolness, courage, and discipline of his small group of trained officers and men—American and Philippine Scout regulars.

He was not disappointed. At first the Filipino militia, like militiamen everywhere, ran away more than they fought. But as the regulars, white and brown alike, fought back, counterattacked, withdrew, and struck again, the new soldiers gained confidence with experience. And on December 30, forced back to within twenty miles of the lone escape road for the southern force, Wainwright's I Corps —the northern force—was still intact. But the II Corps was still south of Manila, carrying out its part of the plan, and the Japanese were threatening to push around Wainwright's right flank to cut off its escape route. MacArthur directed Jones to withdraw northward through the defile by forced marches, and at the same time ordered Wainwright to counterattack, and to hold at all costs until the II Corps had passed.

Wainwright carried out MacArthur's orders by an unexpected counterattack with a mixed force of Philippine Army, Philippine Scouts, and American regulars. The onrushing Japs, surprised and

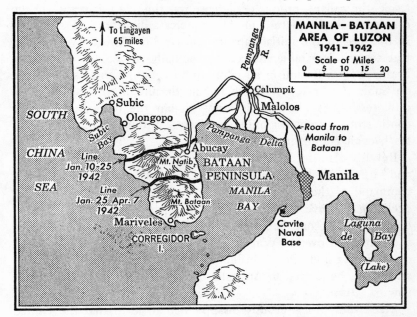

hurt, were halted in their tracks, and the last elements of the II Corps crossed the Pampanga River bridge to safety. Then, with little pressure from the now cautious foe, Wainwright withdrew into Bataan.

All according to plan.

Speaking of his decision to try to execute this plan, MacArthur later wrote:

"This decision, and its brilliant implementation by the field commanders involved, made possible the months of delay to the

Japanese advance caused by the sieges of Bataan and Corregidor. I have always regarded it as the not only most vital decision of the Philippine campaign, but in its corollary consequences one of the most decisive of the war."

No one has ever accused General MacArthur of hiding his light under a bushel; but few would disagree with his evaluation of the significance and brilliance of the "sideslip to Bataan."

There is no need here to recount the sad, glorious tale of these two sieges to which MacArthur referred. Though the end was tragic, the gallant, protracted defense was the one bright spot in the otherwise dismal picture of Allied defeat, disaster, and surrender in the face of the initial Japanese onslaught. Though eventual defeat seemed inevitable, MacArthur actually prepared a plan for a breakout from Bataan in an effort to seize the Japanese supply base on Subic Bay, a few miles to the north, and if this should prove unsuccessful, to disperse his army to join the numerous guerrilla contingents already beginning to operate throughout Luzon under his over-all command.

But his plan for this attack was not approved in Washington, and in February he was instructed to proceed to Australia to assume command of the newly designated Southwest Pacific Area. At first declining to leave the Philippines, he departed only after repeated orders, the last one being from the President personally. Turning the command over to Wainwright, MacArthur departed Corregidor on March 11 and after a thrilling and dangerous voyage by PT boat and plane, he arrived in Australia on the 17th, to voice his defiant vow to return.

MacArthur was grievously disappointed to learn that the United States and Great Britain had decided to concentrate the bulk of their combined efforts to defeat Germany before turning to overwhelm Japan. He bitterly resented this decision, because he still had hopes of rescuing Wainwright's troops on Bataan, if all available American forces could be assembled for the purpose. Or, if this failed, then at least he would be able to redeem his promise quickly, and gain prompt revenge for his fallen comrades. But the American Government, for sound military reasons in which these authors concur, had agreed with the British, even before we got into the war, that the more deadly menace of Hitler's Germany must be destroyed before we could turn to deal finally with Japan.

MacArthur, whose command also included Australian troops, was therefore given initially only sufficient American resources to permit him a reasonable chance of holding his own against any further Japanese advances in the Southwest Pacific Area. At this time, when German troops were pounding at the gates of Moscow, Stalingrad, and Alexandria, the Combined Chiefs of Staff simply did not have sufficient resources to allow MacArthur to undertake any major offensive operations against the Japanese.

MacArthur, however, did not allow such limitations to inhibit his imagination. After throwing back a Japanese attempt to take Port Morseby in New Guinea, he planned to take the offensive. He did not think just in terms of the limited, local offensive which the Combined Chiefs of Staff contemplated for him at the Casablanca Conference early in 1943. Less than a year after his departure from Corregidor, and with forces considered adequate only to contain further Japanese advances, MacArthur was already starting on the long road back to the Philippines, more than seventeen hundred miles beyond his outposts in eastern New Guinea, and in the face of enemy forces perhaps four times as strong as his own.

During 1943 MacArthur conducted two simultaneous converging operations in his theater. In the Solomons, Admiral William F. Halsey, commanding MacArthur's right wing, a mixed Army-Navy-Marine force, drove westward toward the island of New Britain, where the major Japanese base of Rabaul was located. At the same time, on the left, Lieutenant General Walter Krueger commanded the Sixth Army, almost equally divided between American and Australian army troops, also advancing toward New Britain along the east coast of New Guinea. By February 1944 Halsey's forces had seized bases in the Solomons less than a hundred air miles east of Rabaul, while Krueger's troops had cleared all of eastern New Guinea, and had established themselves securely on the southern tip of New Britain itself.

The Admiralty Islands, lying west of New Britain, were strategically important because of their airfields and harbors, and because, once in American hands, they would seal the ring around Rabaul,

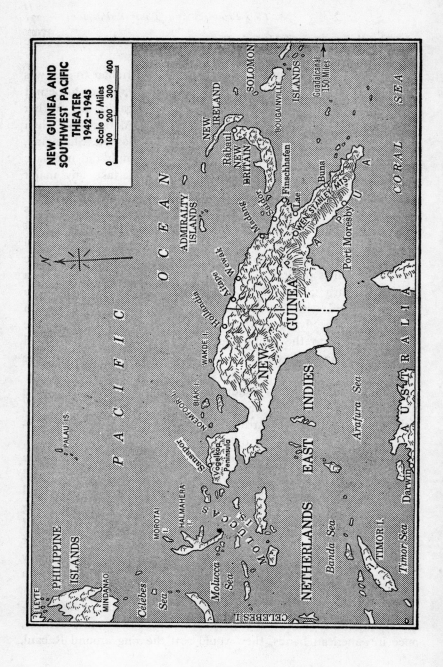

thus completely isolating the main Japanese base in the Southwest Pacific. The Japanese realized this, and had strong forces, well supplied, holding the islands. An operation was scheduled for April, 1944, but MacArthur in late February thought a bold attack might catch the enemy by surprise and, if successful, this would advance his timetable by two months. When his staff almost unanimously recommended against such a daring operation until more forces were available, MacArthur nonetheless decided upon a reconnaissance in force on Los Negros Island, to be carried out by elements of one division. Since his staff considered the operation so hazardous, MacArthur announced that he would accompany the leading units ashore, and then decide personally whether to continue the assault or to withdraw from the Admiralties until more resources were available.

The initial surprise assault was successful, and a vital airfield seized before the enemy realized what had happened. MacArthur, turning to the division commander, ordered him to bring the rest of his troops ashore. "Hold what you have taken," he is reported to have said, "no matter against what odds. You have your teeth in him now—don't let go."

Despite later fanatical counterattacks the division held, and then with reinforcements, forged ahead. The Admiralty group was secured by early April. Rabaul with about 125,000 Japanese troops was isolated and impotent, and MacArthur's schedule was advanced two months. His advance was gaining speed and momentum.

His next move was one of the most brilliant operations in the annals of war. So perfect were the planning and execution that a Japanese army was encircled and virtually destroyed as the result of apparently routine actions in which only relatively small enemy forces were engaged and defeated. In strategic concept and in the speed and apparent effortlessness of execution, therefore, MacArthur's Hollandia campaign can well be compared with Napoleon's brilliant Ulm campaign.

Opposed to American-Australian forces in the Finschhafen-Saidor area of northeastern New Guinea was the Japanese Eighteenth Army, some sixty-five thousand strong. Anticipating further moves along the northern New Guinea coast, the Japanese high command had built up a large supply and maintenance base at Hollandia, beyond the reach of MacArthur's fighter aircraft based in the Finsch-hafen area. Hollandia was also being readied by the Japanese as a center for future offensive and defensive air operations, and three large airfields were already operational. Realizing that MacArthur had made no major advances beyond the range of his land-based fighter aircraft, the Japanese had only a few security troops in the vicinity of the Hollandia base itself. The bulk of the Eighteenth Army, about fifty thousand men, was concentrated in the Madang-Wewak area, where MacArthur's next blow was expected. This time the enemy was confident that the Australian-American attackers could be repulsed.

Outguessing the enemy, MacArthur determined to make a five-hundred-mile jump along the New Guinea coast to seize Hollandia itself. His daring plan was approved by the Joint Chiefs of Staff, and Admiral Nimitz furnished him with Admiral Marc Mitscher's fast carrier task force to provide the air support and air cover essential to the success of a large-scale amphibious operation. Because of the danger of operating carriers in the vicinity of the numerous Japanese air bases in New Guinea and the Caroline Islands, however, the Navy refused to allow these carriers to remain in the coastal waters of New Guinea for more than four days.

The departure of Mitscher's task force would leave the beaches and their approaches open to air attack, thus permitting the enemy to isolate the assault forces from reinforcements and supplies. It was essential, then, that a secure base for land-based fighters be operational before the withdrawal of the carriers. There was no assurance that any of the three enemy Hollandia airfields—situated well inland behind a coastal mountain range—could be seized and made operational in time.

So, while Mitscher's carriers were supporting the landing of two divisions in the Hollandia area, MacArthur planned to have a reinforced combat team land simultaneously at Aitape, about 125 miles further east, to seize and enlarge the enemy airstrip there. Aitape, west of the main concentration of the Japanese Eighteenth Army, was within extreme range of the American airfields three hundred miles to the east. This operation, then, could be covered by air from existing bases and it was expected that the airfield there could be made operational before the carriers off Hollandia were withdrawn. Thus it would be possible to provide continuous fighter protection over the troops fighting at Hollandia. Meanwhile, Australian troops would maintain pressure on the main Japanese army near Madang.

It went like clockwork. Allied cover and deception plans had caused the Japanese to further weaken the Hollandia garrison by transferring some of its troops to Wewak and Madang to meet the anticipated assault there.

On April 22 two American divisions landed, one on each side of the enemy Hollandia supply–air base complex—on beaches twenty-five miles apart—and initiated a well-conceived double envelopment. In five days the entire region was in our hands, at a cost of less than one hundred men killed and about one thousand wounded. The Japanese, leaving some five thousand dead behind them, were dispersed into the jungle.

At Aitape the landing was equally successful, and an airstrip was ready by April 24, after stiff resistance had been encountered. Some 9,000 Japanese were killed, to our losses of 450 killed and 2,500 wounded.

Cut off by this brilliant double stroke, the main body of the Eighteenth Japanese Army, 50,000 strong, was left impotent in its Madang-Wewak positions, far to the east, unable further to influence MacArthur's advances.

This Hollandia-Aitape operation, in which once more meticulous planning was matched by faultless execution, is a typical example of the tactics and strategy of MacArthur's campaigns. By-passing the major centers of enemy strength in sweeping envelopments, his amphibious landings rarely encountered serious resistance at the beaches. Thus, by rapid maneuver, the strategic concept of "hitting 'em where they ain't" became the tactical pattern of leadership at all levels.

The leapfrog advance up the coast continued unabated, as MacArthur kept the confused and reeling foe off balance by a series of blows. On May 17 Wakde Island was seized; on the 27th a division landed on the formidable Japanese fortress of Biak Island, which was captured only after a bitter battle. Little over a month later, on July 2, landings were made on neighboring Noemfoor Island, and on July 30 Sansapor, on the Vogelkop Peninsula of New Guinea's western tip, was seized, with almost no opposition.

By the end of July, therefore, New Guinea had, for all practical purposes, been conquered, although more than a hundred thousand Japanese troops still languished in isolated areas along its thousand-mile-long northern coast, with a like number cut off around Rabaul on New Britain. Sporadic violent but useless fighting would continue for several months as the enemy flopped about like fish in a net.

In this campaign thirty-five thousand Japanese had been killed, with a total loss to MacArthur's troops of less than twenty-five hundred killed and about sixteen thousand wounded. In all military history there is no instance of comparable results in territory gained and losses inflicted at such insignificant cost.

In late July, just as the struggle for New Guinea was coming to its close, General MacArthur received a summons to report to Admiral Nimitz' headquarters at Honolulu for a conference with the President. He was not told the purpose of the conference, and was instructed not to bring any of his general staff with him. Arriving at Pearl Harbor on July 26 with only two personal staff officers, MacArthur next day discovered that the purpose of the conference was to determine the future strategy against Japan.

MacArthur's recommendation to the Joint Chiefs of Staff that the main United States effort should continue from his New Guinea position up to the Philippines, and thence to a final assault against Japan, was being hotly contested by a Navy plan to assume the main effort in the Central Pacific. Now that MacArthur had seized New Guinea, and Admiral Nimitz was in the process of securing the Mariana Islands, a decision had to be made as to which of these strategic concepts should be followed.

On the 27th and 28th of July, Admiral Nimitz' staff—all available at their home headquarters—put on an impressive and meticulously organized presentation of the Navy concept for the President and his chief of staff, Admiral Leahy. What was proposed, and what MacArthur felt had already received tentative sanction by the

Joint Chiefs of Staff and the President, was to by-pass the Philippines, attack Formosa, land in China, and from that springboard make a final attack upon an isolated Japan. MacArthur's part in all this would be a subordinate follow-up campaign; he would land on Mindanao and thence "work up north" with a skeleton force of approximately two divisions. The remainder of his Sixth and Eighth Armies would, of course, be employed under Admiral Nimitz' command in the proposed main effort through Formosa and China.

Not until this complete exposition of several hours had terminated was MacArthur asked to comment. He had no documents, and he had with him no staff officers to put on a presentation comparable to that which Nimitz' officers had just made. But for three years he had been thinking of nothing but Pacific strategy, and his prodigious memory retained all significant details of operational and logistical factors affecting that strategy. He spoke for forty-five minutes. First he appraised the entire enemy situation, including the disposition of Japanese forces and their capabilities. Then he related the disposition of his own forces, now poised for the final assault to liberate the Philippines, and outlined his own concept for future operations. In his own inimitable, resonant, logical language he compared the two plans, pointing out what he considered the serious strategic and tactical fallacies underlying the plan espoused by Admiral Nimitz. Most important, he demonstrated that the Navy plan would require a prohibitive expenditure of American lives in an assault on Formosa, and in major operations on the continent of Asia.

It is a tribute to the objective, unbiased perception of Admiral Leahy that, having previously been on the point of endorsing the plan of his fellow admiral, he now was convinced by the logic of soldier MacArthur. He so informed the President, who was also beginning to waver.

Roosevelt made up his mind, it would seem, during a later short interview with MacArthur alone. The General threw his career in the scales. Apparently he told the President that the Navy plan would mean abandoning not only the Filipino people, but also the thousands of American prisoners there in Japanese hands. No President, he suggested, could face the American people after having thus rejected solemn covenants to faithful allies and gallant fellow countrymen. Roosevelt, far from taking offense at such plain talk, was convinced. The Philippines would be the next objective.

When general and President parted the next day, July 29, MacArthur gave Roosevelt this final assurance: "Mr. President, with all the problems you have to worry about, I hope you will dismiss from your mind any concern that Nimitz and I may not work together in complete harmony. We see eye to eye and I promise you that we will work as an harmonious team."

And so, with former differences forgotten, the staffs of the General and the Admiral completed joint plans for the invasion of the Philippines; the first major assault to be in the central Philippines on the island of Leyte on December 20, following a preliminary landing on Mindanao in November. The Joint Chiefs of Staff approved, and the parallel drives of the Southwest Pacific and Central Pacific Theaters began to converge. On September 15 MacArthur's Army-Navy team landed on Morotai in the Halmahera Islands between New Guinea and the southern Philippines. That same day, Nimitz' Navy-Army team landed on the Palaus further north. An unobstructed route to the Philippines was thus secured.

Meanwhile, to cover these two preliminary operations, and to prevent interference from nearby Japanese bases, Admiral Halsey's Third Fleet had successively struck powerful carrier blows at Yap, the Palaus, Mindanao, and the central Philippines. By September 13 Halsey reached a momentous conclusion. He sent a message to Admiral Nimitz reporting that Japanese strength in these regions had declined to a remarkable extent. He recommended that planned intermediate operations on the enemy base at Yap, against the coast of Mindanao, and on other nearby islands, be abandoned, and that our forces strike the main blow at the central Philippines as soon as possible.

Nimitz immediately reported this recommendation to the Joint Chiefs of Staff, then meeting with their British opposite numbers at Quebec. He offered to place at the immediate disposal of MacArthur the amphibious force, including a corps of Army troops, then loading at Hawaii to attack Yap. The Joint Chiefs requested

MacArthur's views. The General and his staff made a hasty estimate of the situation, including recalculation of all of the complex factors which govern amphibious operations. Within twenty-four hours MacArthur informed the Joint Chiefs that he could mount the assault on Leyte on October 20 instead of December 20. The new target date, a two months speed-up in plans, was only thirty-five days away; scarcely time to load the necessary supplies and to get the assault troops to the ports, on board ship, and out to sea.

On October 19 two assault forces approached the east coast of Leyte. The Third, commanded by Admiral Wilkinson, brought a corps from Hawaii as promised by Nimitz, and Admiral Barbey's Seventh—which had landed MacArthur's men all up the coast of New Guinea and the nearby islands—carried another corps from the Southwest Pacific Area. These two corps composed the Sixth Army, commanded by General Walter Krueger. This force was loaded on some 350 transports, cargo ships, LST's, and 400 other assorted amphibious craft.

Covering the landing and already pounding the beaches, was the Seventh Fleet, under Admiral Kinkaid, which included six renovated battleships that had been put out of action by the Japs at Pearl Harbor, less than three years before. Air cover for the vast armada was provided by planes from the Seventh Fleet's eighteen escort carriers.

Out to sea Admiral Halsey's mighty carrier task force, which helped prepare the way for the landings by air bombardment, stood watch for possible Japanese naval opposition to the landing.

At 10 A.M. on the 20th the main assault landings began, as the two corps—X on the north, XXIV on the south—swept over Leyte's beaches on an eighteen-mile front. While the leading elements were still fighting to secure the beaches, MacArthur, accompanied by President Sergio Osmeña of the Philippine Commonwealth, splashed ashore from a landing craft. Seizing the microphone of a portable radio transmitter, he made his famous broadcast to the seventeen million loyal people of the Philippines, who had been waiting two and a half years for this moment,

"I have returned. By the grace of Almighty God, our forces stand again on Philippine soil. . . . Rally to me. . . . . Rise and strike."

The war would last another ten months, and in those months there would be bitter struggles and many more lives would be lost. But the end was now clear; it was only a matter of time. The determination of the United States had been eloquently proclaimed in words, and proven in deeds, by her best-known spokesman in the Far East.

A promise had been redeemed.

Illegitimati Non Carborundum

That was Joseph W. Stilwell's personal motto. "Don't let the bastards grind you down!" was his free translation of this bit of outrageous dog Latin. It fitted the man to a *T*.

Saturnine Stilwell, with his sharp tongue and keen wit, had been dubbed "Vinegar Joe" by his associates early in his Army career. He graduated from West Point as number 32 out of 123 members of the Class of 1904—one year behind Douglas MacArthur. Unlike most of his classmates near the top of the class, Stilwell chose the lowly infantry, rather than the more popular engineers, cavalry, and artillery. No man has better epitomized his branch of service.

He saw combat service in the Philippines during the closing phases of the Philippine Insurrection. In France in World War I, an exploding ammunition dump came near to ending his military career; his left eye was seriously and permanently injured, but he was able to persuade his superiors that he should not be retired for physical disability. During the years following World War I he served in China on three different occasions—first as a language student, twice later as a military attaché. During those years he came to know the Chinese people, and particularly the Chinese soldier, as have few other Occidentals.

When World War II broke out, Stilwell was a major general commanding the U.S. III Corps on the West Coast. He was soon called to Washington to take charge of planning an early operation against Casablanca in French Morocco. But hardly had he undertaken this task when, in February, 1942, he was called in to see Secretary of War Stimson. Stilwell's China experience had caught up with him.

The United States Government had decided to send a senior

American general to China to establish an enlarged military mission in that country, and take over the functions of the air-training mission and military Lend-Lease mission already there. Since it was now realized that the proposed Casablanca operation was premature, and since Stilwell, a major general with thirty-seven years' service, probably knew more about China than any other man in the United States Army, he was a logical choice for the task. He was to assist in the training and supply of the Chinese Army, and to advise Generalissimo Chiang Kai-shek, and his military subordinates, on overall matters of strategy and tactics. At the same time he would become chief of staff to the Generalissimo, who had accepted the invitation of the Combined Chiefs of Staff to assume the post of Allied Commander in Chief of the China Theater.

Early in March, one month after his appointment to his new task, Stilwell arrived in Chungking, where he reported to the Generalissimo. En route he had been promoted to lieutenant general. During that month much had happened in the Far East. Singapore had surrendered to the Japanese on February 15. Allied naval forces in the Far East had been practically annihilated in the Battle of the Java Sea, February 27–28, and on March 9 the Dutch formally surrendered the Netherlands East Indies to Japan. The Malay Barrier, which had been expected to limit Japanese advances in Asia and the Pacific, had been irretrievably lost, the Allies split in twain.

Even more serious so far as Stilwell's interests were concerned, the Japanese had started a vigorous offensive in Burma and seemed to have the disorganized, outnumbered British defenders on the run. With Burma in Japanese hands, the Allies would be split once more. China, its artery for Lend-Lease supplies lost, would be cut off from all land contact with her allies. There could be no land lines of communications worthy of the name over the Himalayas from India, or across the deserts and mountains of Turkestan from Russia—even if stricken Russia could have diverted any supplies from its own death struggle with Hitler. It was doubtful, therefore, whether China could remain in the war if Burma were to fall into enemy hands.

In this desperate crisis the Generalissimo offered to send troops into Burma to help in its defense. The British, distrustful of Chinese intentions in that region, had refused an earlier offer of such assistance, but now, with the Japanese in possession of Rangoon, Burma's capital, and with enemy columns driving deeper into the country so as to threaten India itself, they were glad to accept.

So, down the Burma Road poured two Chinese armies, the Fifth and the Sixth. In actual combat strength the Fifth Army was perhaps comparable to a Western or Japanese division; the Sixth Army was little better than a rabble with practically no significant combat potential. The commander of this Chinese Expeditionary Force was Lieutenant General Joseph W. Stilwell, as he learned to his surprise when he reported to Chiang in Chungking.

Stilwell promptly left for Burma to assume his new command. At Maymyo, the beautiful summer capital, he reported to General Sir Harold Alexander, the over-all British Commander in Burma and under whom, presumably, the Chinese Expeditionary Force was operating. There had been no unified Allied command organization established, however, and command relationships were unclear, to say the least. But for the moment, the tactical situation was fairly obvious.

There was a lull in the Japanese offensive, as they reorganized themselves in the Rangoon area, in preparation for a further advance. The Allied defenders were busily organizing a defensive line across the narrow portion of south-central Burma, about a hundred miles north of Rangoon. Their task was clearly established by geography; there were only three possible avenues of advance, up three great river valleys—Irrawaddy, Sittang, and Salween—separated from each other by high, jungled mountains. On the right were the exhausted British, organized as I Burma Corps, holding the Irrawaddy Valley. They were recovering somewhat from the demoralization of defeat, under the firm leadership of a new commander, Major General William Slim. In the center the Chinese Fifth Army held the Sittang Valley and had moved a division south of Toungoo. On the left the Chinese Sixth Army was holding the most easily defensible position, athwart the deep, narrow valley of the Salween.

Having learned the situation, Stilwell moved promptly away from Maymyo to Pyabwe, headquarters of the Chinese Fifth Army,

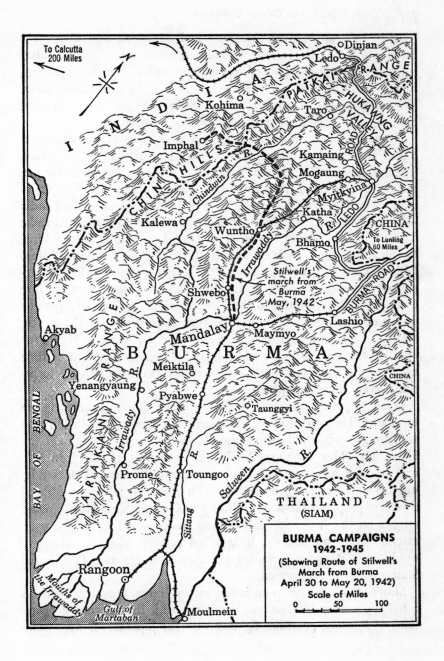

To Calcutta 200 Miles

Dinjan
Ledo
PATKAI RANGE
HUKAWING VALLEY

I N D I A

Kohima
Taro
Imphal
Kamaing
Mogaung
Myitkyina
Katha
Kalewa
Wuntho
CHINDWIN R.
CHINA
Bhamo
To Lunling 60 Miles
LEDO R.
Chindwin
CHIN HILLS
Stilwell's march from Burma May, 1942
Shwebo
BURMA ROAD
Akyab
Irrawaddy
Mandalay
Maymyo
Lashio
B U R M A
Meiktila
CHINA
Yenangyaung
Pyabwe
ARAKAN RANGE
Taunggyi
BAY OF BENGAL
Irrawady
Salween R.
Prome
Sittang R.
Toungoo
THAILAND (SIAM)
Rangoon
Mouths of the Irrawaddy
Gulf of Martaban
Moulmein

BURMA CAMPAIGNS
1942-1945
(Showing Route of Stilwell's
March from Burma
April 30 to May 20, 1942)
Scale of Miles
0   50   100

roughly halfway between Maymyo and Toungoo, and about 130 miles north of the leading Chinese division south of the latter town. He gravely disapproved this location of the army headquarters, so far to the rear of the fighting troops, but the army commander ignored his hints to move forward. Stilwell began to realize that his authority over his command was far from complete.

He was, in fact, in about as strange a position as any American officer has ever found himself. He was Chief of Staff of the China Theater; he was Commander in Chief of Chinese Armies in Burma, but with command responsibilities quite unclear; he was Commander in Chief of all American forces in China, Burma, and India —a responsibility soon to be formalized into the China-Burma-India Theater; and he was in charge of all Lend-Lease material for China. In the first of those posts he was clearly responsible to Generalissimo Chiang Kai-shek. In the second, his Burma command, he was apparently responsible both to General Alexander—and through him to General Wavell—and to the Generalissimo. In his third post he was directly responsible to the U.S. War Department. In the fourth, with its diplomatic overtones, he was apparently responsible to President Roosevelt. No one could imagine it at this time, but as time went on the command relationships of General Stilwell were to become even more complex.

Japanese pressure against the three major allied elements began to mount. Their main effort was against the Chinese 200th Division at Toungoo which, though surrounded for several days, held unflinchingly. This unexpected Chinese toughness appeared to Stilwell to offer an opportunity for counterattack. General Alexander was up in Chungking conferring with the Generalissimo. Stilwell therefore proposed the action directly to General Slim. Co-ordinated attacks on the Irrawaddy and Sittang fronts would throw the overextended Japs off balance. Slim asked Stilwell what the objective would be. "Rangoon," replied the American general. This suited Slim, and so it was agreed.

Slim's attack got off to an initial success, but was soon brought to a halt by enemy infiltrations, combined with the subversive operations of Burmese guerrillas fighting with the Japanese. It was touch-

and-go, and had the Chinese attack jumped off at the same time, Slim probably would have been able to brush these annoyances aside and continue the advance. But on the Sittang front the Chinese 22nd Division, despite Stilwell's personal front-line example, simply could not or would not get started. And so the plan, which might well have succeeded, bogged down. The British withdrew to their lines at Prome, and the Japs increased their pressure against the steadfast Chinese 200th Division. British blamed Chinese, Chinese blamed British, and crusty Joe Stilwell blamed both for the failure.

Sensing this as the psychological moment, the enemy now seized the initiative, and throwing caution to the winds made a major bid for quick victory in Burma. Initially the main Japanese effort was thrown against the tired British, and their almost precipitate retreat forced Stilwell and his Fifth Army to withdraw promptly up the Sittang to keep from unduly exposing his right flank. He sent a regiment from the newly arrived veteran Chinese 38th Division to help cover the British withdrawal through the Yenangyaung oil fields. Then, as Japanese pressure increased, he sent two divisions over to the Irrawaddy front to attempt to retrieve the desperate situation, thus dangerously weakening his own Fifth Army front. To the surprise of most of his American staff, but not to Stilwell, these outnumbered Chinese troops responded magnificently in the face of defeat and disaster. With Stilwell constantly and courageously exposing himself to enemy fire and the attacks of the enemy fighter planes that now dominated the air, the tough, disciplined Chinese *lao bing*—literally "old soldier," the equivalent of the American "GI"—smiled approvingly at this unusual Occidental commander, and carried out his orders. It looked as though the front might be stabilized below Mandalay, despite the apparent collapse of the British, of whom Stilwell was now openly, and somewhat unjustly, contemptuous.

Then, about April 21, disaster came. Quietly the Japanese had been building up strength in front of the Chinese Sixth Army in the Salween Valley. A powerful blow struck the unprepared Chinese 55th Division, which evaporated. One of Stilwell's staff officers reported that Stilwell said, in amazement: "It's the goddamndest thing I ever saw. Last night I had a division, and today there isn't any."

He didn't stop to wonder or worry about this, however. As always, he responded immediately, almost automatically. The Japanese were dashing for Lashio and they must be stopped. With Alexander's approval he moved the hard-fighting 200th Division from the British front, and rushed them to Taunggyi, a critical road junction 150 miles south of Lashio. But misunderstandings, and missing trucks, delayed the movement. The 200th reached the vicinity of Taunggyi just one day after the Japanese had seized the town. Stilwell rushed to the front, and personally took command of a company under heavy Japanese fire. When reinforcements arrived, he led a counterattack which pushed the Japs back for more than twenty miles, and for a short time the Chinese actually held Taunggyi, cutting the Japanese lines of communication.

But the Japanese commander of the flying column, displaying first-rate leadership on his own part, ignored the situation in his rear. He was living off the countryside, getting plentiful supplies from Allied depots, and he swept into Lashio without opposition.

The Burma Road was blocked; China cut off from the rest of the Free World. But of more immediate concern to Stilwell was the fact that his Chinese Expeditionary Force was isolated in Burma, with its only escape route to China cut off. Meanwhile, the continuing Japanese advance up the Irrawaddy Valley was threatening to cut the one remaining road that led from Mandalay through Kalewa across the mountains from Burma to Imphal in India. And since the retreating British were clogging this road, Stilwell had to find another route, or routes, through narrow jungle trails, further north.

Refusing to abandon his troops by flying out of Burma with the last plane to leave Shwebo on April 30, Joseph W. Stilwell gathered his official household, soon to be augmented by other refugees, and marched northwest. Or, as he reported it, "I then picked up my headquarters group and brought them out."

Thus did Stilwell dismiss, with one curt sentence, a 400-mile trek with 100-odd men and women of various nationalities and races.

The route lay up the Irrawaddy Valley, then over steep jungle hills to the Chindwin Valley, across the Chindwin, and finally up and over the 8,000-foot range of mountains disarmingly known as the Chin Hills, to Imphal and safety. The last 150 miles was all done on foot, and completed in the amazing time of 14 days. During this anabasis the irrepressible 59-year-old veteran outmarched men half his age, and by sheer personal leadership coaxed, bullied, jollied, and dragged with him his heterogeneous group through dense jungle, across wide, swift rivers, and over unmapped jungle-mountain trails. His own weight dropped from 140 pounds to 120 during those terrible two weeks.

On May 20 he arrived at Imphal. Resting only overnight, early the next morning he proceeded by automobile and train to Dinjan, the nearest airfield, whence he could fly to New Delhi. And at Dinjan, on May 22, he made his famous, honest, offhand evaluation of the first Burma campaign, voicing his grim determination to "find out what caused the loss of Burma" and to "go back and retake it."

Stilwell, in fact, already had a pretty good idea of what happened, and how. He was even at that early date planning what to do about gettting ready to "go back." He plunged at once into the task he had laid out for himself.

The first job was to reorganize the scattered elements of Chinese troops who had fled into India. The 38th Division had marched out almost intact into Imphal, having acted, to all intents and purposes, as the rear guard of the British retreat. And the 22nd, another good division, had reached Taro, on the upper Chindwin River in northern Burma, where it was maintaining itself through the monsoon. This division, as soon as the rains began to let up in the late summer, was to withdraw across the tall Patkai Mountains into the pleasant tea-growing valleys of northeastern India.

As these Chinese units were collected, Stilwell brought them to a training center which he established at Ramgarh, in the Indian province of Bihar, some two hundred miles west of Calcutta. The Ramgarh training center was staffed with a group of the best young American officers that Army Ground Forces could send in response to Stilwell's urgent request. Here the Chinese, who had already proven their worth as soldiers, were issued new American and British equipment, and put through an intensive course in the employment of modern arms. To these veterans of the Burma Campaign, Stilwell was able to add thousands more Chinese soldiers—these mostly untrained recruits—shipping them in on the supply planes which would otherwise have returned empty across the "Hump" from China.

During the latter part of 1942, and in early 1943, three Chinese divisions went through the Ramgarh training center. The first of these was the 38th, commanded by General Sun Li-jen, soldierly, scholarly graduate of Virginia Military Institute and Purdue University. This division, brought up to full strength of about eleven thousand men by recruits flown in from China, and issued brand-new weapons and equipment, as soon as it had completed its training course was shipped back to the Burma-India border, with headquarters near the town of Ledo in Assam. Next to go through this process was the 22nd Division, which had marched over the mountains into India when the monsoon rains stopped, late in 1942. In August of 1943 a rejuvenated 22nd arrived near Ledo, to join the 38th.

The next task of the Ramgarh training center, begun even before the 38th had completed its course, was to use the recruits and a few veterans from China to build up a new division, the 30th, plus a number of independent units—artillery, armor, infantry, engineer, quartermaster, and others—to round out a balanced, modern army corps. For Stilwell was determined that this new force, now called the Chinese Army in India, would be self-contained, and that it would be able to meet the best Japanese troops on even terms. He had long been reconciled to the fact that he could not expect any significant number of American combat troops—one pickup infantry regiment was all that had been promised to him. So if he was to fulfill his promise, retake Burma, and reopen a land route of communications to China, he would have to rely upon his Chinese troops, with whatever additional co-operation he could get from the British.

Stilwell was not able to spend much time at Ramgarh—though that was where his heart lay, and that was where he went whenever the heavy burden of his other duties would allow. But he now had four widely dispersed headquarters, and at each of these he exercised a different responsibility. As Chief of Staff of the China Theater—an Allied command—under the Generalissimo, his headquarters was in Chungking, China. As Commander in Chief of the American China-Burma-India Theater, his headquarters was in New Delhi, India. As Deputy Supreme Allied Commander of the Southeast Asia Command, under Lord Louis Mountbatten, he had to spend a great deal of his time at SEAC headquarters, at Kandy, Ceylon. And as the Commanding General of the Northern Combat Area Command—from which he exercised his operational control over the Chinese Army in India—his headquarters was initially in Ledo, India, and later moved to Burma behind the fighting front.

The Northern Combat Area Command (NCAC) was under the operational direction of the British Fourteenth Army, which was in charge of all Allied ground operations in Burma. As Deputy Supreme Allied Commander of SEAC, Stilwell frequently *issued* orders to his old friend, British General Slim. (Slim, incidentally, was one of the very few Britishers that Stilwell liked; the feeling was mutual between two splendid fighting men.) But as Commanding General of NCAC, Stilwell *received* his orders from Slim.

The absurd complexity of Stilwell's command relationships is demonstrated by a letter of commendation received by one of his American officers during the subsequent campaign. A glowing report about the activities of this man, who was liaison officer with a Chinese division, was sent through Chinese channels to Chinese Army headquarters in Chungking. This resulted in a letter of commendation being sent, through American channels, to the officer. The letter, signed "By Command of General Stilwell," was addressed to the Commanding General, CBI Theater—who was General Stilwell. In proper military form it was forwarded by indorsement, signed "By Command of General Stilwell," to the Commanding General, NCAC—who was General Stilwell. Finally the letter was sent, by a second indorsement, to the officer; this indorsement, of course, was signed "By Command of General Stilwell."

As he tried to wear all of these hats, and to meet the demanding and challenging requirements of his many responsibilities, Stilwell really had only one main thought in his mind: to carry out his mission by driving the Japs from Burma and reopening a land route to China. Dangling at the end of a ten-thousand-mile supply line, realizing that his command was lowest on the priority of the Combined Chiefs of Staff when they parceled out Allied resources, Stilwell found himself plunged into a maelstrom of conflicting political forces; buffeted by conflicting interests of the United States, Great Britain, China, and the seething unrest of independence-minded India. As if this were not enough, he was inevitably and inextricably involved in jealousies both within and without his command, finding himself in conflict with other American, as well as with British and Chinese, military men. Finally, vacillating policies in Washington were transmitted down that long line of communications as along a rope, with Stilwell at the end in a gigantic game of "crack the whip."

These circumstances, the like of which no American soldier had ever been faced with before, would have taxed the patience and finesse of even the most able diplomat. And Stilwell was no diplomat; he was a field soldier.

Stilwell's directive, as we have noted, was in essence to increase the fighting ability of the Chinese Army, in order that the Japanese could be defeated. China was to supply the manpower, the United States the training, equipment, subsistence, and over-all leadership. Burma now being in Japanese hands, and China isolated and threatened with strangulation, the immediate problem, as Stilwell saw it, was to reopen ground communications—the Burma Road. Burma then, must be the first main battleground. He co-ordinated the efforts of all of his diverse commands towards this objective. In addition to the Ramgarh training center, another was opened in Kunming, in Yunnan Province of southwest China; the entire Chinese army must be retrained if the job was to be completed.

Major General Claire L. Chennault, formerly commanding the "Flying Tigers," China's gallant Foreign Legion air force before the United States entered the war, was now back in U.S. service in command of the Fourteenth Air Force, which had been established in China. He disagreed violently with the concept of his commander, Stilwell. He felt that China could be freed from Japan's grip by air power alone. Since the airborne supply line coming over the "Hump" could not provide full maintenance for both an expanded air force and an expanded ground force, one or the other must take a back seat.

In May, 1943, at the Washington Conference, there was a show-down between these two tough fighters. Chennault made his arguments so strongly, with able assistance from Army Air Force staff officers, that President Roosevelt gave air-lift supply priority to Chennault. The President overruled Stilwell's objection—supported by General Marshall—that increased air activity, without ground protection, would only bring about a Japanese land campaign against these bases. This in turn would jeopardize proposed long-range air activities against Japan itself by B–29's that were to be based in China.

A year later a large-scale Japanese ground-force assault swept over Chennault's seven principal bases, driving the B–29's from China and seriously disrupting Allied plans. Stilwell's concept was proved correct. Not that it did him much good; he had been forced to carry the fight into Burma with what he had: his three American-trained Chinese divisions, plus (later) one American infantry regiment—Merrill's Marauders—and some of British General Wingate's Chindits.

The second Burma campaign began in November, 1943. And it seemed that it would stop almost as soon as it started. The spear-head of the drive was Sun Li-jen's 38th Division. The veterans of this division knew the enemy well. Many of them had been fighting the Japanese since the Battle of Shanghai in 1931. It could not be said that they feared the Japs; it was merely that in their experience, their lack of equipment and inferior mobility had always forced them to go on the defensive. And so, as they met the old enemy once more in North Burma's densely jungled Hukawng Valley, they automatically went on the defensive. It didn't matter that they had new and improved equipment; they did not care what their American instructors had taught them at Ramgarh; here were the Japs, and there was only one way to fight Japs. They dug in.

The enemy immediately took advantage of this immobility, and promptly surrounded each of the three leading battalions. This did not particularly bother the trapped Chinese, any more than it bothered their commander. General Sun had been worried at first, when there was no report from one battalion for several days. Then, when radio contact was re-established, and he learned that they had been surrounded, he breathed a sigh of relief. "Now I know where they are," he said.

Because General Sun knew, as everyone else in Burma soon learned, that the Chinese soldier on the defense, if properly armed, equipped, and supplied regularly, was the most determined defensive fighter in the world. And American planes were available on the airfields of northeastern Assam, to fly over the mountains and drop rice and ammunition to the beleaguered troops. This was far more comfortable than the fighting they had known in China.

As soon as he learned of this setback, Stilwell flew personally to the Hukawng Valley, to supervise and direct the relief of the surrounded units, and to encourage the Chinese forward. He joined the leading battalion of the Chinese relief force, and had to be almost physically restrained by his staff from leading their assault. While the battle was still in doubt, he sat in a little clearing, smoking a cigarette, receiving progress reports by radio and messenger. While members of his staff sought protection in the undulations of the ground, he was seemingly oblivious of crashing mortar and artillery shells, and of the whine of rifle and machine-gun bullets through the trees. Then a man on the other side of the clearing was hit by a rifle bullet; a moment later another. It was obvious that there was an enemy sniper nearby; one of his aides suggested that they should move to another position. Stilwell ignored the frightened young officer, and turning to the American artillery commander, who was sitting beside him, remarked calmly, "If that bastard comes much closer he'll run us out of here." A patrol was quickly formed to sweep the woods, but Stilwell had forgotten the sniper by this time; he was on his feet moving forward. The assault had broken through, and he wanted to go to congratulate the commander who had held out under a month's siege.

This, of course, was the stuff from which soldiers' legends grew. But no legend could ever exaggerate the calm courage of Stilwell under fire, his fabulous long-distance marches through enemy-infested jungles, frequently accompanied only by one or two aides, or the almost miraculous way in which he would appear at critical points to inspire his men to greater efforts. All of his American subordinates brought back a fund of anecdotes—all fantastic and mostly true—about this amazing man whom they adored. But they adored him no more than did the simple Chinese soldiers who fought under his command. This was a kind of generalship to which the Chinese had never before been exposed, and they responded to it as fighting men have from the dawn of history.

Certainly the Chinese officers did not lack courage. Their leadership, particularly company and platoon commander veterans of the first Burma campaign, was magnificent. But it was not the custom of Chinese generals to expose themselves at the front; most of them felt that they had already taken their chances at this sort of thing, and if they had been lucky enough to remain alive long enough to become generals, well, it was time for the younger men to take their turn. This may be a rather reasonable and logical attitude—but it doesn't win battles.

One can trace an interesting pattern of Chinese reaction to Stilwell—and his undiplomatic, direct, blunt, aggressive attitude—from fighting front in Burma to Chinese Army headquarters in Chungking. It ranged from adoration by the *lao bing*, through admiration by junior officers, and grudging respect by his slow-moving generals in Burma, to fear, opposition, and downright hatred by many of the most senior officers in Chungking. Stilwell, "picking up his divisions on his back," as one observer put it, was winning his battle in Burma, but he was losing a war in Chungking, where that same back was exposed to subtle Oriental knifing.

Having proven to his Chinese troops that they could fight and beat the Japanese on their own terms in the jungle, Stilwell was able to goad the division commanders into a slow but steady offensive. It was not an easy job, for him or for them, and some of the Americans who served with the Chinese in Burma tended to be critical of the apparently leisurely pace. The Japs were outnumbered, true enough, but on the narrow jungle trails two men with a machine gun could stop a regiment indefinitely. And the Japanese commander, a first-rate tactician named Tanaka, conducted a classic delaying action.

So the Chinese would press cautiously down these scattered trails, till they met opposition and were forced to halt. Then, following Stilwell's tactics, they would reach out to the flanks, frequently hacking their way through almost impenetrable undergrowth, until the enemy position was enveloped. Then, with combined rifle, mortar, and artillery fire, they would press forward to drive the enemy out. Time and again, day after day, this continued.

Sometimes Stilwell would use his American infantry, Merrill's Marauders, to spearhead an assault. Relying upon the importance of "face" to the Chinese, Stilwell was sure the *lao bing* would not allow himself to be excelled by the GI. The psychology worked, and by the spring of 1944 the advance was accelerating. As the Chinese gained confidence, and their commanders gained experience, Stilwell began more daring maneuvers, sending regiments, battalions, and finally entire divisions on sweeping envelopments. By the time the monsoon rains began in June, his troops had reached the Irrawaddy at Myitkyina, and had swept through the cities of Kamaing and Mogaung in north-central Burma.

All this time Stilwell's troops had been supplied almost entirely by air, through the magnificent efforts of Major General Howard C. Davidson's Tenth U.S. Air Force. And behind the advance, Chinese and American engineers were building a road—the Ledo Road —which was to become the new land link to China.

When the rains came, everyone—British, Chinese, Japanese, even the Americans—expected military operations to close, as they always had ceased in monsoon season in South Asia. But Stilwell had no intention of stopping. His two leading Chinese divisions, he knew, were exhausted, so he did let them slow down in the early monsoon days, but he maintained the pressure against the valiant Japanese defenders of Myitkyina, and with a fresh British division to lead the way, continued to press the astonished foe.

Stilwell did not like Britishers. He had seen them at their exhausted worst in the first Burma campaign, and he mistrusted the smooth diplomatic skill which they displayed in Allied headquarters.

But in the commander of this British 36th Division he found a bluff fighting man like himself. "Do you know what I expect from you?" he is reported to have asked General Francis Festing when the Britisher reported to him in July. "You expect us to fight, sir," was the reply. "We'll get along," growled Stilwell.

A few weeks later, when the British division had driven its way far beyond the Chinese divisions on its flanks, Stilwell sent a peremptory order to Festing to stop his advance. The British general asked permission to send out patrols, and fighting soldier Stilwell could not deny the request. Festing promptly sent out two reinforced battalions! Having cleared enemy resistance by such "patrolling" up to the next river line, Festing flew back to headquarters to respectfully ask permission to occupy the intermediate territory. Stilwell looked over his glasses, and a grin crossed his face. "Okay," he is reputed to have said. "But no more goddam battalion patrols until the Chinese are ready to keep up with you."

Then, as the monsoon ended, the order came. Two new Chinese divisions had been flown in to augment his command, as had another American regiment. Stillwell now had a real fighting force of more than six divisions. Striking swiftly, he drove the unprepared foe back to the Irrawaddy between Katha and Bhamo. Then as enemy resistance stiffened on the two main axes of his advance, he threw two divisions and an American brigade across country towards Lashio. The main Japanese force in North Burma, the Thirty-third Army, was about to be trapped in a double envelopment—the holding force at Bhamo, and Chinese divisions just across the border at Lungling, providing the anvil for this hammer swinging down from the Irawaddy—and thrown back against the impassable Salween River. A brilliantly conceived and planned maneuver, its success was inevitable.

Stilwell had kept his promise. He had come back. North Burma was in his grasp. The campaign was about to end in dramatic glory.

In the moment of victory Stilwell was relieved, on October 19, 1944.

More than six months would now elapse before Japanese resistance in Burma would finally collapse, under combined British-Chinese-American pressure. It would be vain to speculate on whether things would have been different either in Burma, or in China— where a new Japanese advance was again threatening the Chinese war effort—had Stilwell stayed on. And such speculation would be unfair to his successors, stout General Daniel I. Sultan who took over in Burma and India, and brilliant General Albert G. Wede- meyer who succeeded Stilwell as the chief of staff to the General- issimo in China. Stilwell's relief, and his departure from the scene, were accompanied by far-reaching political and military reshuffling, which caused both of these capable generals to face entirely differ- ent situations in the new theaters they had inherited.

Such speculation, too, would be unfair to the gallant British effort, under Stilwell's old friend General Slim, which in May, 1945, gained revenge for the dismal days of early 1942 by a lightning drive to Mandalay, and thence onward to Rangoon.

But to the *lao bing* and the occasional American soldier in north- ern Burma, the change in tempo, the apparent slackening of the effort, and the abandonment of Stilwell's plan to envelop the Jap- anese Thirty-third Army, meant much. These men neither knew nor cared about the political forces which had swirled about Stilwell, or the global strategic factors which had affected his roles in Chungking, New Delhi, and Kandy. They would have laughed at suggestions that Stilwell was not an adroit diplomat. So what? Like them, he was a soldier. In 1942 he had taken a beating in Burma, had taken it like a man and had promised to go back and retake it.

All they knew was that they had lost the best damned soldier they had ever known; a leader who had led them back to victory over the Japanese.

CHAPTER XVII ☆ ☆ ☆ *Decisions Big and Little*

In 1917–1918, American troops in Europe fought against Germany as an independent army in a loose confederacy of allies. A modicum of over-all control, forced by stark necessity and most reluctantly conceded after nearly four years of war, was exerted by a French general over this confederacy. But unity of command in the strict military sense was nonexistent, and the American commander jealously preserved the independence of his army with every jot and tittle of an inflexible will power.

In 1944–45 American troops in Europe—in even greater number than on the previous occasion—fought against Germany as one element of an integrated allied command, over which an American general, Dwight D. Eisenhower, exerted supreme control. Unity of command was prerequisite.

In both cases the American commander was acting in accord with the expressed directive of the President of the United States. The label "A.E.F." remained the same, but whereas in the earlier war it stood for American Expeditionary Force, in the latter case, it signified Allied Expeditionary Force.

One further and most important difference must be noted. In 1917–1918 Pershing, we remember, made his own plans and decisions; he had been given complete liberty of action by the President. Eisenhower's basic plans were made for him by the Combined Chiefs of Staff, the military high command of the United States and the United Kingdom, who in turn were expressing the will of their respective heads of state, President Franklin D. Roosevelt and Prime Minister Winston Churchill. Eisenhower's job was to enforce that will upon the enemy.

But, as Dennis Hart Mahan had expressed it a century ago, "once within the sphere of the enemy's operations, a commanding general is no longer at liberty to do what he wishes, but what he best can."

Battle is the payoff. Under Eisenhower the A.E.F., consisting of ground, sea, and air forces, assaulted German-held France across the English Channel, swept the enemy from his holdings, rolled him across the Rhine and, following, destroyed his armed forces within his own country. So stands the record.

In accomplishing this stupendous task, Eisenhower, through the fortunes of war, was compelled to make six major command decisions vitally affecting the result. Upon those decisions must rest any assessment of his combat leadership; for leadership upon the grand scale is expressed more by decisions and the ability to make subordinates carry them out, than on personal presence in the combat zone.

Let's look at this man.

Gregarious Ike Eisenhower, country boy from Denison, Texas, graduated from West Point in 1915. He saw no combat service in World War I, but later had the good fortune to serve under men who had had much to do with its winning. He was for a time under Fox Conner, who had been Pershing's chief of staff; and later under Pershing himself. He served as an aide to Douglas MacArthur, and he had a short but enlightening tour as chief of staff to Walter Krueger, that cold analyst of war who was commanding the Third Army during the Louisiana maneuvers of 1941.

In between there had been tours at the Command and General Staff School (he graduated number one man in his class) and at the Army War College. In early 1942, when General George C. Marshall revamped the War Department after the Pearl Harbor disaster, Eisenhower was picked to head the newly organized Operations Division of the General Staff. Then he went abroad.

When Eisenhower assumed command of the A.E.F. in January, 1944, he came with the background of successful campaigning be-

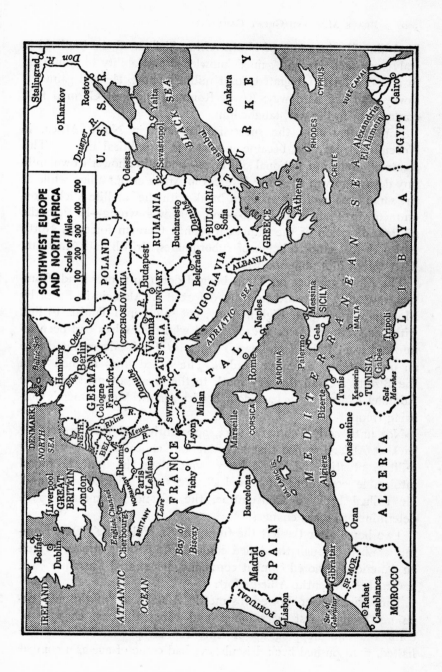

SOUTHWEST EUROPE
AND NORTH AFRICA
Scale of Miles
0   100 200 300 400 500

hind him. His invasions of North Africa, Sicily, and the foothold in Italy were fact. He had gained knowledge and ability to command in action a huge, integrated, joint military effort. He had gained it slowly, and the hard way; Erwin Rommel, the best German field commander in the war, taught him.

Immediately after the successful landings in North Africa, in November, 1942, Ike became involved in a political morass. This stemmed from our national objective—and Eisenhower's own military desire—to win the French forces in Africa as our allies, while at the same time avoiding an open break with the satellite Vichy government in France itself. So—and this was wrong—he left the military direction of the campaign against German forces in North Africa to his senior echelon of subordinates, British and American. They served him none too well.

The Allied advance on Tunis bogged down in winter mud. Rommel, retreating westward from his defeat at El Alamein in Egypt by Montgomery's British Eighth Army, got safely into Tunisia to link with the German forces already there, who themselves had been reinforced from Italy. Eisenhower's "race for Tunis" degenerated into an overstretched defensive cordon. The Allied lines reached from the Bizerte area all the way south to the great salt marshes where Rommel had set up a back-door barrier against Montgomery's pursuing troops.

Not until early February, 1943, apparently, did Eisenhower, far back at Algiers, realize that anything was radically wrong with his military situation. Making a hasty swing along the front, he found intolerable conditions of mixed elements and divided command. He rushed back to Constantine, the advanced command post, determined to make changes.

Two hours after Ike left the front, on St. Valentine's Day, Rommel crashed through the Allied cordon. His slashing strokes bagged an American armored combat command, penetrated Kasserine Pass, and rocked the entire Allied effort.

Then Eisenhower showed his mettle. A series of "off-the-cuff" decisions brought fast regroupings and concentrations, changes of command and stepping up of American air power. Rommel was halted, then pushed back. Eisenhower had come of age as a combat commander. The rest of his Mediterranean operations is history.

This, then, was the background of the man who had now been put in command of the mightiest force ever placed as an integrated unit in the hands of a single commander.

"You will enter the continent of Europe," read his directive from the Combined Chiefs of Staff, "and, in conjunction with the other United Nations, undertake operations aimed at the heart of Germany and the destruction of her armed forces. . . ."

He was heading an offensive meticulously prepared and planned over a two-year period. It contemplated frontal attack upon a mighty fortress, across a narrow but tempestuous stretch of water which had not been bridged in war since William the Conqueror invaded England. The plan called for an amphibious assault on France's northern coast, across a fifty-mile-wide stretch of beaches.

Command Decisions

Between the two American landing beaches ran the Douve, a wandering river with a marshy estuary; both unfordable. Not an ideal situation, it had to be faced, for capture of Cherbourg port to the west was essential to further operations. So the problem was two-fold: to get the Utah Beach troops inland safely on their way to Cherbourg, and to link that beachhead with its easterly neighbor, Omaha. Were both these things not accomplished, defeat in detail might follow.

The original solution was to drop the two U.S. airborne divisions, the 82nd and the 101st, well inland, south and west of the river, to accomplish both tasks. But at the last minute Ike's British air commander, Marshal Sir Trafford Leigh-Mallory, made violent protest. The air lift, he pointed out, would have to come in low from the west, across the entire Cotentin Peninsula, in moonlight. Enemy antiaircraft fire would chew it to mincemeat. In his opinion— the opinion of a competent airman and loyal staff officer—it meant catastrophe.

Eisenhower was faced with the first of his six major combat decisions in this theater. Weighing the pros and cons, he made his choice; the drop would go as planned. It did; but before results proved the leader's calculated risk to have been well taken, came another, greater decision, which only he, wrapped in the mantle of command loneliness, could make. On that decision must rest the fate of a million men and, perhaps the whole campaign.

D-day had been fixed for June 5. Expert meteorologists and hydrographers, conning weather records for a past score of years, studying the all-important Channel tide tables, graphing the hours of dawn and all the other factors on which depended both surprise

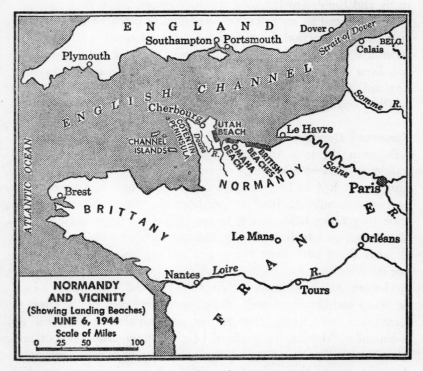

and the ability to get ashore in landing craft through the enemy's underwater obstacles hedgehogging the beaches, had fixed the period June 5–7 as most favorable.

But on June 3 the weather preposterously kicked up in the Channel. Ike, postponing the assault for twenty-four hours, weighed his problem.

Some 176,000 men and 20,000 vehicles were already on board more than 4,000 ships. The vessels, together with as many additional ship-to-shore craft, were either at sea or about to leave. Poised for take-off on British airfields were 2,000-odd planes and 900 gliders carrying 3 airborne divisions. Six battleships, 2 monitors, 22 cruisers, and 93 destroyers were marking time afloat. Vast fleets of bombing and tactical aircraft stood on runways.

The greatest triphibious operation ever seen was coiled like a spring; its manpower at mental and physical peak. One might hold it one day; but what about the future? Two weeks would pass before tide and time would again coincide. Launched against storm and high surf the assault might well be doomed. Postponed until June 19, it would become an uncoiled, flabby thing whose laxness might never be wound again to combat pitch. In addition, the Germans would almost inevitably have been warned. No one could expect to conceal much longer this enormous frothing of activity.

At 4 A.M. June 5, with the meteorologists venturing a guess that there might be a momentary slackening of the wind and rain still lashing the Channel, Ike cast the dice with fate.

"We'll go tomorrow," said he in effect.

The rest, of course, is on record, including the storm which whooped out of the northwest on June 19 to spread rack and ruin along the Normandy coast. But by that time the lodgment had been made, and U.S. troops were driving on to Cherbourg.

So much for Ike's first two vital decisions, against which no carping criticism can be raised. Now to the four which have become so controversial. We will take them in order.

By September the A.E.F. had brushed the enemy out of most of France. But Bradley's 12th Army Group was being slowed in its swift pursuit by lack of gasoline, while Montgomery's British 21st Army Group on the north flank was being maintained in fuel supply. Truth was that the A.E.F. had outrun its long supply line from the Normandy beaches and Eisenhower was favoring the British at the expense of the Americans.

There were several cogent reasons for this decision. Primarily, were the A.E.F. to continue, it was absolutely necessary that the port of Antwerp be recovered as a new base of supply, and Antwerp was on the axis of Montgomery's advance. Besides this, the original plan of invasion had visualized a later main effort by a stroke through

Germany's industrial heart, the Ruhr, also on the axis of Monty's advance. Additional was the urgent need to capture the launching sites of the V–2 missiles which were by this time seriously affecting British home morale.

So Montgomery got the breaks, and on the American side of the

picture the offensive ground almost to a halt. In Bradley's 12th Army Group resentment rose; particularly insofar as Patton's Third Army was concerned. Patton felt that if adequately supplied, he could punch all the way through Germany.

Montgomery reached Antwerp in September, but the port could not be used until transports could pass up the Scheldt estuary unimpeded, and the British troops did not root out the German river forts until November. So chauvinistic American critics chalked up both this delay and Montgomery's failure at Arnhem against Eisenhower.

On the other hand, Montgomery had proposed he get all available means and a clear field to make a sharp punch-through north of the Ruhr on his own. And when Eisenhower turned that down, British criticism flared sharply. It is indeed debatable whether either Patton's or Montgomery's plans for a "do or die" thrust into Germany could have succeeded so long as enemy forces in strength remained west of the Rhine.

Eisenhower's decision was that Monty would have first—but not exclusive—priority, and Bradley take second place. After taking Antwerp, Montgomery would be favored with all possible logistic and personal reinforcement to carry out the original planned main effort across the Rhine north of the Ruhr. But not until all enemy forces west of the river were eliminated.

The Supreme Commander had chosen between two radically different military concepts. Montgomery favored a main effort across the relatively flat terrain of the North European plain, aimed at Berlin. Bradley—and Patton—advocated a penetration into rugged Central Germany. They felt that their project offered but one main obstacle—the Rhine, as opposed to a multiplicity of broad rivers and canals on the northern front. And, of course, they also thought that a proven driver like Patton would make the affair a success. When this was over, they held, Germany would be in complete collapse; there would be no last stand in Central Europe.

If there was more than a hint of nationalistic pride and rivalry in each of these concepts, it must be remembered, too, that Eisenhower was himself subject to political strains from his bosses.

Adolf Hitler on December 16, 1944, ended for the moment all considerations on this subject. His irrational but potent Ardennes offensive sliced through between U.S. First and Third Armies on a sixty-mile front and started for the Meuse. Its objective was to split the British and American forces and eliminate the new Allied base of Antwerp, now operational.

The surprise necessitated another battlefield decision. The blow had fallen on the center of Bradley's 12th Army Group, which consisted of the Ninth, First, and Third Armies in that order from north to south.

First Army, its right flank shattered, lay on the north of the German spearhead, Third Army to the south. Bradley, at his command post in Luxembourg, was practically cut off from his two northern armies. Further north of them lay Montgomery's 21st Army Group, one of its corps already moving down to backstop the enemy flood behind the Meuse.

As Eisenhower saw the situation, two distinct battles now had to be fought; one on each side of the gap. He turned over to Montgomery all that part of the U.S. 12th Army Group on the north; Bradley on the south retaining but one army, Patton's Third. That decision still ranks as one of the world's great controversial military judgments; the pros and cons, quite naturally, obscured and warped by international jealousies and partisanships.

Calm assessment of Bradley's generalship both before and after leads to the conclusion that he could have re-established the situation had he been left to the job. Equally logical is the conclusion that the penetration did in fact create two separate fronts. But a decision was necessary and history relates that Eisenhower's choice was successful. There, it seems, one must leave it.

The Bulge healed, the A.E.F. closed in on the Rhine, to blot out all enemy forces on its western bank. Eisenhower's plan was crystallized: a full-dress Rhine crossing by Montgomery, in the Ruhr region, with the Ninth U.S. Army added to his strength, and all possible logistical weight thrown to him. While Monty made the main effort, two U.S. army groups, south of him—Bradley's and Devers'—would play secondary roles.

That situation changed almost in the twinkling of an eye, through no fault of the meticulous Montgomery. He mounted his Rhine crossing in fine style on March 23. But by the time he had consolidated his bridgehead on the far side and was prepared to advance, Bradley with two American armies was already nearly a hundred miles inside Germany. Trapped between the British and the Americans was the major portion of enemy forces in the west, in the heart of Germany's industrial center.

Thanks to a dazzling display of American initiative Eisenhower had, willy-nilly, been presented with an unexpected fistful of new trumps. In a new command decision he led from strength. The Montgomery main effort was discarded; Bradley got the nod, with the U.S. Ninth Army, on the right of the British army group, returned to his command.

The greatest double envelopment in history resulted as two steel-tipped pincers—Simpson's Ninth and part of Hodges' First Army— snapped shut on 350,000 hapless German troops. Meanwhile the rest of Bradley's command, with Devers' army group on its right, was sweeping into Germany toward the Russians advancing from the east.

To all intents and purposes the war was over, Germany prostrate. But Nazi fanaticism, fed by the terror inspired by the Allies' "unconditional surrender" fiat, was still rampant. Shrill threats of some mystic underground resistance—the renaissance of a Barbarossa legend—spread. They were believed by Allied intelligence officers; Hitler and his die-hards would retire to an already prepared "national redoubt" in the Bavarian-Austrian Tyrol, to wage a last-ditch warfare.

As it turned out, this was complete myth. But in mid-April, 1945, the danger was very real to SHAEF (Supreme Headquarters Allied Expeditionary Force). As Eisenhower himself at the time visualized the possible German attitude: "If you were given two choices—one to mount the scaffold and the other to charge twenty bayonets, you might as well charge twenty bayonets."

To Eisenhower the "destruction" of Germany's armed forces, laid down in his directive, was paramount to all else. And on that basis he made his last and again controversial command decision. Forgetting Berlin—which had already been parceled out by his masters as an island in a postwar Soviet zone of occupation—he ordered further A.E.F. advance eastward halted along the line of the Elbe and Mulde Rivers and the mountain nose of Czechoslovakia, while his right would drive south in wide arc into the Tyrol to stamp out the last vestige of Nazi armed resistance.

This, then, is the record of Eisenhower's principal command decisions. Involved, of course, in the prosecution of the campaign were scores of other lesser problems. All of these, it seemed, trod, in one way or another, upon nationalistic toes, the majority of them wearing American shoes. It is not too farfetched to say that most of his higher commanders in U.S. uniform became convinced that where Eisenhower was concerned the British could do no wrong, and that in his effort to maintain the integration essential for success he leaned backward against American interest far more than was necessary. The essential thing to remember, however, is that his mission was accomplished, and that, regardless of any resentment, these same commanders gave him unstinted loyal support.

There are also those, both in the United States and abroad, who have gone on record to assert that Eisenhower's command of the A.E.F. was that of a genial chairman of the board, concerned with making everyone happy, a figurehead divorced from the military prosecution of his mission; that better soldiers did his thinking for him.

In fact, from the record, Eisenhower's leadership was a compound of strategic and tactical judgment, and a vast capacity for compromise. The job entailed logical, quick thinking, plus a magnetic personality. These things he provided. Personable, approachable, his ability to think quickly and logically on his feet, so to speak, was a great asset. No group addressed by him, from officers of his command and staff, to war correspondents seeking a controversial battle of wits, but was impressed by this plain man. In homely, spontaneous phrases, he left no doubt in his hearer's minds that he knew what he was doing and how to do it.

This leadership was totally different from Pershing's in the previous war. In part this was due to personality. He occasioned none of the cold awe which Pershing inspired. Ike, as he was known affectionately to the millions in his command, had a homespun appeal to his soldiers.

The man in the ranks knew him, if not in person, vicariously through *Stars and Stripes,* the U.S. Army's daily newspaper. It publicized and pictorialized his frequent visits both to training camps and later, in action, during his necessary spotty front-line appearances. These ran the gamut from his first "good luck" visit to his paratroopers on the eve of the assault, up to the end of the campaign. And, wherever he went, he talked to soldiers. So his personality was established to a point of intimacy which naturally transmuted itself to his later enormous popularity at home.

On the other side of this picture we find circumstances open to criticism. The cosmopolitan character of his vast command—embracing armies, navies, and air forces of several nations—was a breeding ground for interservice and international rivalries which, despite all efforts, sharpened as they spread down the echelons of command. It became also a forcing bed for self-centered "empire builders," ambitious individuals on the make for position and promotion. Some of their operations took place right under the Supreme Commander's nose.

Compounding this were the visting firemen, the meddlers, both civilian and military, foisted on SHAEF mainly by Washington influence. They ranged from do-gooders to representatives of interests having political affiliations in the national Administration. All this fermented in Eisenhower's headquarters; it affected administration and command, and officers chafed under it, as they did also under the absurd and sometimes offensive housekeeping regulations which set aside such abnormalties as "Yankee Doodle Rooms" (private bars) and other special privileges for general officers, things heretofore unknown in either American or British regular services.

This was a far cry, indeed, from the Spartan atmosphere of the first A.E.F. Pershing would not have tolerated it for one instant.

The complex nature of Eisenhower's command status deserves some attention. Integrating the diverse services into a smooth-functioning, hard-hitting military team was in itself a colossal task. But over all, in addition, were the frequently conflicting viewpoints of men, governments, and peoples. These major elements continuously jostled both one another and Eisenhower himself.

As a U.S. Army officer he was responsible to the War Department for the operation and administration of all U.S. troops, aside from his over-all Allied command responsibility, which placed him in continuous jeopardy insofar as public opinion in both the U.S. and

Britain was concerned. This public opinion was stirred by the partisan and frequently intransigent attitude of the free press of both nations.

Later on, when the A.E.F. had freed France from the German clutch, the French people and French press would add their clamor, in stresses caused by an inferiority complex. This was directly reflected in the words and actions of the temperamental Charles de Gaulle.

Nor did Winston Churchill make things easy for the Supreme Commander. Metaphorically, the incomparable Prime Minister put his ample bulk in Ike's lap for the duration of the war in Northwest Europe, and his showers of suggestions, like sparks from a blade on the grindstone, sometimes added to Eisenhower's worry and embarrassment.

These factors were in addition to the official military fingers dipping into Eisenhower's pie. Leaning over the shoulders of the Combined Chiefs of Staff were the purveyors of its ingredients: for the United States, both War and Navy Departments; for Britain the War Office, Admiralty, and Air Ministry. Canadian military departments were also concerned. Had it not been for his immediate insistence that U.S. Army General Staff procedure govern SHAEF's operations and administration, these kibitzers would have turned the Great Armada into complete bedlam.

In retrospect, Eisenhower had been given a job seemingly impossible to perform. He did it, and made it look far easier than it was. He couldn't have accomplished the task without the loyal support of excellent troop leaders in every combat echelon of his command. In many cases the leadership displayed was superlative. Let's look more closely at two of these. One concerns a chain reaction stemming from a platoon of armored infantry all the way up to the Supreme Commander himself. The other is the story of a flamboyant soldier fully worthy of comparison with Stonewall Jackson.

Miracle at Remagen

Pfc's Charles Penrod and Ralph Munch, on the advance guard point, saw it first; a gaunt, spidery span jutting from the little town far below them, to reach across the broad, brown, fast-running Rhine to the eastern shore. It was unbelievable. Their quick shout brought Second Lieutenant Emmet J. Burroughs, the platoon commander, up on the run; with him came First Lieutenant Karl Timmermann, the company commander.

From their vantage point, crouching on the crest of the Appolinaris Kirche hill overlooking Remagen, the four stared, incredulous. Ever since it had swept over the Cologne Plain, the First Army had been collectively hoping to find a bridge intact; a vain hope thus far, for the enemy had blown each one reached, practically in their faces.

The officers put their field glasses on the scene. It was indeed a bridge. More than that, it was intact; vehicles and pedestrians were crawling across it.

Karl Timmermann did three things, simultaneously. He sent a jeep racing back with the news to his task-force commander, Lieutenant Colonel Leonard E. Engeman. He nodded to Burroughs, who began unloading his mortars from the platoon vehicles halted behind the crest. And he mentally calculated the distance from the hill down to the bridge below. Little more than a mile, it would be. Wouldn't take too long if one went helling in, covered by mortar fire. His Company A, 28th Armored Infantry Battalion, could do it.

It was high noon, now, on this cold, drizzly day of March 7, 1945. The miracle of Remagen was in the making.

Timmermann's message brought Engeman up in a whirl; behind him the remainder of the task force slowly closed up. One look was enough for Engeman. He started Timmermann's company down the hill, its scouts flitting ahead. The rest of the infantry battalion deployed in close support, and the tankers revved up their engines.

Task Force Engeman—one battalion each of armored infantry and tanks, with a company of engineers—was one of the two columns of Brigadier General William M. Hoge's Combat Command B of the 9th Armored Division, Major General John W. Leonard commanding.

Engeman's instructions that morning had been to screen toward the Rhine on CCB's left, while Hoge pushed the rest of his command south, to secure crossings of the Ahr River, a Rhine tributary. His move into Remagen started, Engeman flashed back word of his find and his action. Hoge, radioing Engeman to close on the bridge, followed fast in person. Two thoughts pressed as he looked down: Could the doughboys actually cross that bridge before it was destroyed? And if so, what was the enemy strength on the other side?

Minutes were ticking off; the only way to find out was to try. Behind the fire of the tank battalion the infantry quickly cleared the town of snipers—there had been no organized resistance—and made for the bridge itself.

A German prisoner blurted that demolition was set for four o'clock. It was now a quarter to four. Timmermann's company started across. As they did a blasting charge at the western entrance blew a crater in the road but harmed nobody. Then came a puff on the upstream side and when the roar and smoke cleared away one truss and a section of roadway had gone.

Timmermann saw the main span was still secure, and led his company on, a trickle of olive-drab ants, as Hoge saw it from above. With the initial wave ran three of the engineers, seeking and disarming dynamite demolition charges which had been skillfully placed.

Rifle and machine-gun fire from the far bank was returned by our tanks, and the infantry, scrambling across, deployed to press up the steep hill road leading to the Erpeler Ley cliff. The engineer company was already swarming over the bridge, trying to repair that roadway gap, so the tanks could follow.

Hoge, before he could report his marvel to Division, was flabbergasted to receive new instructions over the radio. Third Army, to the south, had crashed through the Siegfried Line. First Army was speeding up to link with it. Hoge, despite any previous orders, would push up the left bank of the Rhine, with unlimited objective.

And leave this prize? Not Hoge. Ordering the far bank build-up to continue, he rushed in person to his division commander, to explain the situation. General Leonard, electrified, ordered Hoge to forget the new orders; he was to go back, get his whole combat command across and establish a bridgehead. Leonard himself immediately flashed the good news back to Corps and Army.

It was about five o'clock when Lieutenant General Courtney

Hodges, at First Army Headquarters, received the word. Ordering Leonard to get his whole division over, he alerted all army corps, and new orders began to spill out. It was six o'clock when General Omar Bradley's phone rang at 12th Army Group headquarters. Bradley, engaged at the moment in hot argument with a SHAEF staff officer bringing a directive which would subtract some of his divisions from his strength, picked up the phone.

It was Hodges. He had the Remagen bridge, he said. He was already pushing everything he could up to make a secure bridgehead, including naval personnel to establish ferry service, and engineers with heavy ponton equipment.

"Shove everything you can across," ordered Bradley, and called Eisenhower.

Ike, at Rheims, was at dinner with three of his airborne commanders when Bradley called.

"Brad, that's wonderful! Sure, get across with everything you've got. . . . To hell with the planners—I'll give you everything we've got to hold that bridgehead!"

And there, in brief, is the story of a multiple play which helped change the course of a campaign, for until Bradley had that bridgehead he had been slated to play a secondary part to Montgomery in the final stage.

In all probability, there is no other example extant of such a succession of sound command decisions made in the space of less than eight hours; of a display of initiative running in rapid-fire order from GI Joe to the man on top.

That is the miracle of Remagen.

Lions Tremble

Like a comet blazing its way through the steady sparks of a constellation, the leadership of George Smith Patton, Jr., streaked across the calm, confident troop-leading which characterized the U.S. 12th and 6th Army Groups during the campaign in Western Europe.

Here was the spirit of lightning war, wrapped up in one man; a whirlwind of fire and movement, personally devoid of fear. Here, too, was an *enfant terrible*, whose simple faith and outspoken directness shone through compromise, hypocrisy, and political expediency with devastating force; sometimes to the embarrassment of his superiors and also, by the same token, to his own detriment. Not that Patton cared one tinker's damn; he wasn't built that way.

Somebody once characterized professional soldiers as cynical sentimentalists. If ever a man deserved that title it was Patton. But someone else, some omniscient scribe in the palace of the Sultan of Morocco, engrossed on Patton's citation to the Grand Cross of Ouissan Alouite, in 1942, an even more pertinent tag line:

"Lions in their dens tremble on hearing his approach."

Cavalryman Patton, of Virginian military forebears, was born in California, graduated from West Point in 1909. He learned something of war at the kness of a stern taskmaster—Pershing, whose aide he was during the Mexican Expedition of 1916. During World War I he commanded, with distinction, a tank group, and was converted into an ardent exponent of mechanized war. This was a conversion not hard for a soldier brought up in the Pershing doctrine of "find 'em, fix 'em, and fight 'em."

A many-sided individual—expert horseman, capable yachtsman, Bible student, poet, writer of many articles upon his chosen profession—Patton's basic interest in life was war. All his life he studied war and the psychology of war, with but one purpose: to lead men to victory. "It isn't the date of a battle that counts," said he once on the subject of military history. "It's what happened there."

He went to the command of the Western Task Force in the 1942 invasion of North Africa with a spectacular reputation already made. His ivory-handled pistols, impeccable uniform, and iron discipline were his trademarks. So, too, was his roaring presence. Patton, whose philosophy of leadership consisted in the fixed opinion that a commander "does what is necessary to accomplish his mission, and nearly eighty per cent of his mission is to arouse morale in his men," believed that in a lightning war the leader must electrify them. He did.

That invasion job completed, Patton was rushed by Eisenhower to restore the morale of the II Corps, demoralized after Rommel's stroke at Kasserine Pass. He came down on it like a thunderclap, shocked it to its collective feet by a combination of impassioned invective, a display of personal fearlessness under fire, and uniform regulations transforming them from an aggregation of Sloppy Joes to spick-and-span soldiers. Then he turned its command over to Bradley while he went on to command Seventh Army in the Sicilian invasion.

In Sicily the Seventh Army blazed like a whirling pinwheel around Montgomery's sedate advance up the eastern side. From the Gela beaches north to Palermo, thence eastward to the Messina tip, "Old Blood and Guts" was unstoppable. And war correspondents, for whom his spectacular mannerisms made the best of copy, spread the Patton legend back home. Straining for similes, they portrayed him as a hell-for-leather, devil-may-care, modern Custer. Lost was the fact that in combat Patton used his brains. Far better it would have been had they compared him to "Mad Anthony" Wayne, but nobody thought of that. This was unfortunate when, at the height of this fame, Patton got a nasty jolt.

He had, it seemed, committed the sin unpardonable in an officer: he had slapped a soldier. To make matters worse, the man was an inoffensive convalescent in a hospital. So ran the story, keyholed out of Africa and distorted later out of all proportion through clumsy, evasive mishandling at Eisenhower's headquarters.

Now a man who can, like Patton, unashamedly burst into tears at sight of his men killed and wounded in action, in line of duty, might well be expected to burst into rage when confronted by a man he believes to be a craven dodging military responsibility and contributing to the deaths of other men. That was the background of the "slapping" incidents (there were two of them), when Patton, overwrought at sight of his wounded in hospital, smacked the faces of two soldiers he considered malingerers.

The army he commanded expressed their own opinion at Palermo, at a mass Red Cross gathering when Patton stepped on the platform, saying: "I just thought I'd stand up here and let you soldiers see if I'm as big a s.o.b. as you think I am." They practically raised the roof with their cheers. The American public, unfortunately, received no such impression. So, for a time, Patton the hero became Patton the brute.

It was all forgotten a few months later when Patton in France, now commanding the Third Army, came whirling out of the Nor-

mandy beachhead to begin the greatest armored dash the world
had yet seen. Beside it the much-vaunted German blitzkrieg
paled.

In twelve days Patton ploughed an area roughly 250 miles wide and
100 miles deep, isolating the Brittany peninsula. His columns swept
through a dazed German Seventh Army down to the Loire, and
from the Atlantic coast to Le Mans on the east. Tanks and motorized
infantry stabbed in simultaneous spurts through bewildered enemy
units, their tempestuous advance spurred every now and then by
the sobbing bull horn of a well-known jeep and an even better-
known voice bellowing to know why they weren't going faster.
Patton called it "touring France with an army." Other soldiers call
it a classic example of relentless pursuit.

His racing columns then continued eastward for another three
hundred miles, until the gasoline supply was diverted to assist
Montgomery's advance up in the north. By that time, August 30,
Patton—joyous extrovert—was at Nancy and in the vicinity of Metz.
He took the gas stoppage as a personal insult, intended to disrupt
his avowed determination to smash all the way into and through
Germany. His roars of anger stirred the embers of dissension between
British and American elements.

His next exploit came that dark December of 1944, when the
German Ardennes offensive burst. Patton's Third Army at the time
was biting into the Saarland of Lorraine. Called upon to counterattack the southern flank of the German thrust, Patton performed
the seemingly impossible task of shifting in four days the entire
movement of Third Army from an attack in west-east direction to
another attack in south-north direction.

Six days after his riposte began, one of Patton's armored divisions
had smashed through to the relief of beleaguered Bastogne; three
weeks later to the day, he had carved his way to link with the
First Army's southerly reaction and the German threat was dissipated.

All these performances, masterly as they had been, constituted but
prelude to the final pyrotechnic five-hundred-mile arc of Patton's
sweep from the Rhenish Palatinate to Czechoslovakia's rugged
Erz Gebirge and down the Danube to Linz in Austria.

Man in a Hurry

Montgomery (the U.S. Ninth Army added to his strength) was preparing for a full-dress Rhine crossing. Bradley had Hodges' First Army already across and crowding into the Remagen bridgehead, while Patton's Third was supposedly marking time north of the Moselle. Devers, with Patch's Seventh Army and the First French, was mopping up in Alsace. Between Patton on Bradley's right and Patch on Devers' left two German armies lay embedded in the Palatinate—the last enemy forces remaining west of the Rhine.

The noses of all American leaders were out of joint, for this was March 12, 1945, and Eisenhower had not yet changed his plan. Montgomery was to cross the Rhine, and sweep into Germany north of the Ruhr; diverted American strength and supply would aid him, and American armies playing second fiddle would watch the Rhine.

Neither Bradley nor Patton had forgotten Montgomery's ill-timed public announcement, during the Battle of the Bulge, when he had been given command of the American armies on the north, implying that he had averted an American disaster. That and a following brief but unsuccessful campaign in the British press to appoint Montgomery as ground commander of the A.E.F., still rankled. Now, a rumor that ten American divisions might be taken from Bradley's army group to reinforce Montgomery after he had crossed the Rhine was growing.

Bradley loosed Patton; initial objective, to crush remaining German resistance west of the Rhine, which was part of Eisenhower's objective, too. Third Army charged across the Moselle into the Hunsruck Mountains of the Palatinate. Devers at the same time unleashed Patch's Seventh Army to strike through the Siegfried Line into the Saar. Between them they caught the enemy flat-footed.

Patton hurled four armored divisions, with infantry close behind, in thirteen separate columns, cross-stitching the hilly, forested terrain with its winding road net. The Germans, caught in this hurly-burly with the Rhine behind them, caught again in the strokes of the converging drives of Patch coming from the south, collapsed in stunned amazement.

On the ground, Patton's armored elements were coming from

every-which-way, it seemed, while overhead the planes of two tactical air forces also crisscrossed in support. Without troop-leading of the highest order on the part of all U.S. commanders, no such extemporization of lightning war would have been possible. Patton's remark on starting—"Tell Devers to get out of the way or we'll pick him up with the Krauts"—was characteristic. Actually, the two flank army corps commanders concerned worked in complete and amazing harmony.

In ten days Patton had overrun four thousand square miles of enemy territory. The MP's were still counting his sixty-three thousand German prisoners into the cages when he topped it all by popping across the Rhine.

No one was more surprised than Bradley when Patton called him up, that morning of March 23.

"Brad, don't tell anyone, but I'm across . . . sneaked a division over last night."

Opportunistic? Not a bit of it; foresighted, rather. The infantry division that crossed at Oppenheim that night, in complete surprise, rowed and paddled and motored over; in rubber assault boats, in DUKW's, and in landing craft manned by U.S. Navy personnel. None of these are normal equipment of a skirmish-line rush. Neither are the steel treadway and heavy ponton bridge equipment that within twenty-four hours spanned the Rhine to tremble under Patton's onrushing armor.

Most of this heavy equipment Patton had lugged behind him all across France. The Navy contingent he had wangled when the Moselle River crossings were being first considered, and—just how one does not know—craftily hung on to at a time when all available landing craft were being scraped up for Montgomery's river crossing.

All in all, Patton had handed Bradley a pretty fine gift—twenty-four hours before Montgomery would launch his much-touted Rhine crossing. And Bradley would have been more than human not to tell the world:

"Twelfth Army Group announces that at 2200 hours last night, without air or artillery preparation, Third Army troops crossed the Rhine River and established a bridgehead on the far shore. Since that time they have been expanding and enlarging their bridge-head."

Not expecting such action, German opposition did not materialize until Patton's armored columns were rolling to seize the Main River crossings at Frankfurt. By the time Montgomery had crossed the Rhine far above, Hodges' First Army, unleashed by Bradley from the Remagen area, was speeding eastward, too. The stage was set for Eisenhower's new decision and the great Cannae.

While Bradley picked up the leadership of the A.E.F.'s main ef-fort, in the last brilliant phase of one of the world's greatest cam-paigns, George Patton was racing eastward to Czechoslovakia and the Danube Valley, its eastern high-water mark. He had changed the course of history, and he had placed himself irrevocably, within his sphere as an army commander, among the great leaders in American history.

Follow Me!

Innumerable further instances of outstanding leadership in this global war might be cited. Within the limitations of our screen, however, we can but pay our respects to these others.

Picking at random among the sagas of the troop leaders further down the line, one might mention the affair at "Parker's Cross-roads" in the Battle of the Bulge. There Major Arthur C. Parker, with three howitzers and a handful of artillerymen and doughboys for two red days held the Second SS Panzer Division until rolled over by the sheer weight of enemy armor.

Down on the firing line itself, one selects a final tantalizing glimpse of anonymous leadership.

This, too, happened in the Battle of the Bulge, when two regi-ments of the 106th Infantry Division were being crushed in the Schnee Eifel hills. A group of infantrymen, shocked by the sudden burst of enemy fire all about them, huddled in a daze. Out of the woods behind them stalked one lone, large Negro soldier, tommy gun nonchalantly tucked under an arm laced by a corporal's chev-rons.

He approached a wounded officer.

"Colonel, sir, you-all seem to be alone here. I'm from the 333d Field [an artillery unit also smashed in the action]. Anything you want me to do?"

"Get that platoon organized, corporal. Move north, covering the flank."

"Yes, sir!"

And magically, it seemed to that watching officer, to the booming voice of a corporal who knew he was in command, and knew his trade—leadership—the demoralized platoon fanned out and moved forward, fighting men once more.

One would like to know that soldier's name. His deed epitomizes all the other countless instances where men—from division commander to squad leader—induced the will to win in American soldiers on World War II battlefields.

CHAPTER XVIII   ☆ ☆ ☆   *Leaders Unafraid*

Fighting Division Commander

Leadership and courage are not synonymous. All successful leaders have been brave men; but not all brave men are leaders. In the Korean War, for instance, 107 Congressional Medals of Honor were awarded; our highest decoration for bravery in combat. But courage alone is not enough to bring victory in battle. In honoring courage, we may exaggerate its importance.

We must examine carefully, for instance, the actions which won the first Medal of Honor awarded in Korea. No one questions the valor of Major General William F. Dean, who gained indelible renown as a modern David by singlehanded battle against Communist tanks in the Korean town of Taejon in mid-July 1950. But General Dean was a division commander. Would not General Dean have better performed his duties as division commander by remaining at his command post to control the actions of several thousand men, rather than thus giving in to his understandable, and otherwise laudable, instincts as a fighting man? More important, can there be any justification for a division commander to expose himself to serious danger in this way, and thus run the risk of leaving his command leaderless in a grave crisis?

Let us look analytically and critically, therefore, at William Frische Dean, and at his actions on the 19th and 20th of July, 1950.

Strapping Bill Dean entered the Army from civil life in October, 1923, to become a second lieutenant at the age of twenty-four.

When World War II broke out, he was a lieutenant colonel on duty as a member of the Army's General Staff in Washington. He had risen to the rank of brigadier general when he landed in Normandy in June, 1944, and in July was promoted to major general. In December of that year he was assigned to the command of the 44th Division, which he led until the collapse of Hitler's Germany five months later.

In the fall of 1947 General Dean was sent to Korea to become the military governor of American-occupied South Korea. A little more than a year later, the new Republic of Korea was established under the authority of the United Nations, and General Dean turned over the administration of the country to its newly elected officials. American forces promptly began to withdraw from the peninsula, leaving only a small Military Advisory Group (called KAMAG) to help train the small Republic of Korea (ROK) Army which we had helped the new government to establish before our withdrawal. Early in 1949, therefore, General Dean had moved to Japan, and later that year he assumed command of the 24th Infantry Division, one of four divisions in our occupation forces in Japan. This was Dean's post, then, when on June 25, 1950, he first learned of the North Korean attack across the thirty-eighth parallel. Five days later he received orders to move his understrength division immediately to Korea to assist Republic of Korea forces in repelling the invasion.

Immediately, in accordance with his instructions, he sent by air a small task force of two infantry companies and an artillery battery. Lieutenant Colonel Charles B. Smith, the task-force commander, reported to the American KAMAG commander on July 1, and his little command was immediately sent north to meet the advancing enemy, and to bolster the faltering ROK army. Dean, having prepared the remainder of his division to follow by water, flew to Korea on the 2nd, and established his headquarters at Taejon next day.

On July 5 Task Force Smith was struck by the North Koreans at Osan, some forty miles south of the capital city of Seoul. For seven hours the little American unit, though hit from front, flanks and rear, held against an entire division, supported by more than

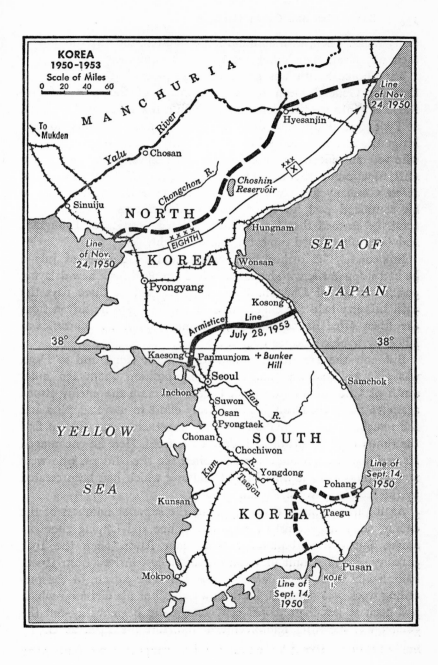

KOREA
1950-1953
Scale of Miles
0   20   40   60

MANCHURIA

To Mukden

Yalu River

Chosan

Sinuiju

Chongchon R.

Hyesanjin

Line of Nov. 24, 1950

Choshin Reservoir

XXX
X

NORTH

Hungnam

SEA OF

Line of Nov. 24, 1950

XXXX
EIGHTH

KOREA

Wonsan

JAPAN

Pyongyang

Kosong

Armistice Line
July 28, 1953

38°   38°

Kaesong   Panmunjom   + Bunker Hill

Seoul

Inchon

Suwon

Osan

Pyongtaek

Han

R.

Samchok

YELLOW

Chonan

Chochiwon

SOUTH

SEA

Kum

Taejon

R.

Yongdong

Pohang

Line of Sept. 14, 1950

Kunsan

KOREA

Taegu

Mokpo

Pusan

KOJE I.

Line of Sept. 14, 1950

thirty tanks. Then, with ammunition exhausted, the survivors fought their way clear, abandoning most of their equipment.

Task Force Smith was gone. But its splendid resistance gained time for General Dean to move elements of the 34th Infantry Regiment into another defensive position a few miles further south, at Pyongtaek. Dean now discovered that it wasn't possible to take his green, inexperienced soldiers—with only a scattering of combat-wise veteran officers and noncommissioned officers—and have them start functioning the way his seasoned 44th Division had fought across Germany five years before. By the time he had returned to his command post, to speed more reinforcements to the fighting front, he learned that his carefully selected position at Pyongtaek had been abandoned almost without a fight.

Immediately he rushed north again, and by evening of July 6 he had stopped the withdrawal, and had arranged for a new delaying position north of Chonan. For the better part of three days the 34th Infantry held the enemy at Chonan, finally being driven from the town after its commander, Colonel Robert B. Martin, was killed by a North Korean tank.

But now the 21st Infantry had reached the front, and so Dean was able to establish another delaying position about ten miles south of Chonan, in front of Chochiwon. Here the enemy struck again on the 10th. Dean, bending every effort to move supplies and the remainder of his division forward, nonetheless was able to find the time to spend part of each day at the front. Here he encouraged his regimental commanders and inspired the tired troops, who were now getting over the initial fright and awe which had been created by the ferocious North Korean assaults.

Again, after a bitter three-day fight, the superior numbers of the enemy, smashing against the thinly held line and lapping about its flanks, forced a withdrawal to the Kum River. Here the 19th Infantry, the final unit of Dean's division, just arrived from Japan, had already taken up a defensive position. The pattern of the preceding week was repeated. Dean now had all of his division—which had been at less than 70 per cent strength to begin with—but the enemy was receiving reinforcements too. On the 14th, as enemy columns threatened to envelop his left flank, Dean pulled back from the Kum to establish a new position, in front of the city of Taejon.

He knew that General Walton H. Walker and the Eighth Army Headquarters were now arriving at Pusan, where the 25th Division was also unloading and that the 1st Cavalry Division was also landing across open beaches at Pohang. If he could hold the enemy long enough for these two fresh divisions to establish themselves, then there seemed to be a good chance of holding southern Korea. But if his weakened and exhausted division were to collapse now, the enemy would be able to rush southward, seize Pusan, and push the fresh divisions into the sea before they could get organized. A week, even two or three days, might make the difference.

Dean sent the 21st Infantry back about fifteen miles to the southeastward along the road to Taegu and Pusan to establish a new delaying position, and at the same time sent his division command post back to Yongdong. He remained in Taejon, however, and assumed personal direction of the fight that was raging along the defensive perimeter. Enemy pressure steadily mounted, and by the 19th of July it was evident that Taejon could not be held much longer.

What should Dean have done? In the over-all interests of his division, and even more important, in the interests of the entire American expeditionary force now so desperately trying to establish a precarious toe hold in southeastern Korea, where should the commanding general of the 24th Division have stationed himself? Was it with one exposed element of his division, where he could influence only a handful of men at any single instant? Or should he have been with his division headquarters, where he could keep at least some sort of tenuous touch with his entire command, so long as radio and telephone held out, and from whence he could integrate his division into the efforts of the entire army under General Walker?

Let's see what Dean has written about this, some three and a half years after the event:

My reasons for staying in the town were simple, although of course there can be much argument about them. . . . But these reasons were compounded of poor communications, which had cost me one valuable position up at Pyongtaek, and the old feeling that I could do the job better—that is, make the hour-to-hour decisions necessary—if I stayed in close contact with what was happening. My staff was quite capable of operating the headquarters at Yongdong, under the direction of Brigadier General Pearson Menoher; and frankly, it was easier to get a message through toward the rear (or so it seemed) than toward the front.

None of which changes certain facts: I was forward of my own head-quarters on the night of July 19; the situation was so confused that I could not even be certain we still held a solid line northwest of the city; and very few important command decisions were made at that time. Very few of the things I did in the next twenty-four hours could not have been done by any competent sergeant—and such a sergeant would have done some of them better. I have no intention of alibiing my presence in Taejon. At the time I thought it was the place to be. Three and a half years later I still do not know any other place I could have been to accomplish more. The accomplishments, I think, would have been virtually zero in any case.

General Dean, no matter how hard he may try, cannot be wholly objective in this analysis of his decision to stay in Taejon. Let's see what a respected analyst of combat operations, Brigadier General S. L. A. Marshall, USAR, noted for complete objectivity, has said about this matter:

"To my mind, there is no doubt of the critical and decisive nature of Dean's holding action outside Taejon. He carried out the maneuver under the worst possible conditions, was forced to feed his green troops piecemeal into the fray, but he succeeded in stopping the Communists. If the Communists had had a clear right of way to Pusan, the war would have ended right there. There is no doubt that this was one of the pivotal points of the war. Personally, I feel that Dean has become one of the truly giant figures among this country's more heroic leaders."

There is no need here to go into the specific exploits which Dean performed on the 19th, 20th, and 21st of July. As he suggests, a capable and courageous sergeant could have fought just as effectively and perhaps more so than General Dean did in the street fighting against North Korean tanks and infantry in Taejon. But no sergeant could have inspired the men of the 19th and 34th Infantry regiments in the way that Dean did, as he fought first beside one group, then beside another. Furthermore, despite his modest suggestion that there were few important command decisions, two were vital to the success of the entire operation.

The first of these was to stay and hold, a decision made unmistakable and unquestioned by the mere presence of the division commander. Then, it should be noted, while he entered personally into the battle with pistol, rifle, and bazooka, he kept in frequent touch with the local situation at the 34th Infantry command post. Only a man on the spot could know when every possible benefit had been obtained from the bitter struggle of the embattled defenders of Taejon. At a time when every minute saved was crucial, but yet when every fighting American soldier was also vital, only an experienced man on the spot could know the exact moment when further efforts would be fruitless in time and wasteful in life. When the moment came, Dean sensed it and gave the order to withdraw. His capture came after he had accomplished his objective.

Dean demonstrated, then, that even in the middle of the twentieth century, personal leadership exercised at the critical point of battle can be decisive. More than any other man, perhaps, Dean saved South Korea and the U.S. Eighth Army by a superlative demonstration of all of the hallmarks of combat leadership "at the risk of his life above and beyond the call of duty."

The Lost Campaign

It is impossible to consider leadership in the Korean War without an assessment of the role of General of the Army Douglas MacArthur. During the ten months that he was Commander in Chief of the United Nations Command in Korea, his forces underwent vicissitudes of defeat and victory, failure and success, without parallel in American military history.

There can be no question that the central figure in these operations was the seventy-year-old General. Supporters and critics alike recognize that he was supported by a competent staff—which made some mistakes. All apparently agree that he made the fundamental operational decisions, and that these decisions were executed by capable field commanders in Korea who displayed a general level of command competence comparable to that demonstrated in World War II. There is equally no doubt that there were serious inadequacies—in numbers, training, indoctrination, and equipment

—in the forces available. But for good or ill, the operations in Korea from July 1, 1950, through April 11, 1951, bear the indelible stamp of Douglas MacArthur. To what extent, then, was he personally responsible for the violent swings in the pendulum of battle fortunes during these months?

His detractors have suggested that the initial setbacks were due to the unreadiness of MacArthur's occupation troops in Japan. They discount the spectacular victory at Inchon as sheer luck, which subsequently deserted him when, despite the warnings of the Joint Chiefs of Staff, he made a similar gamble in his reckless advance to the Yalu. The resulting defeat has been termed the greatest military disaster in American history. Any later successes, his critics insist, were achieved despite MacArthur through the fighting leadership of field commanders such as General Matthew B. Ridgway.

The loyal supporters of MacArthur, on the other hand, maintain that it was only because of the General's consummate skill that certain ejection from South Korea was averted after inept diplomacy invited a Communist invasion of the defenseless country. Such people see clear proof of MacArthur's undiminished military genius in his fateful and perceptive insistence on the Inchon landing, despite the objections of many experienced officers, including the Joint Chiefs of Staff. As to the drive to the Yalu, it is asserted that he had no choice under the terms of his instructions from the United Nations, and from the U.S. Government, but to advance as he did in November, and that such an advance was equally necessary in order to determine Chinese Communist intentions. Scoffing at the suggestion of "disaster," they cite the low casualty rate in the withdrawal from North Korea, and the subsequent success of the UN counteroffensive—initiated before MacArthur was relieved for political reasons—as clear proof that he could have gained a great victory in November and December if the U.S. Government had not forbidden him to attack and destroy the foe's logistic base and lines of communications in the "sanctuary" of Manchuria.

The issues are clear-cut; let's examine them with respect to MacArthur's responsibility and his leadership.

No one was any more aware of the unreadiness of his troops in Japan in the spring of 1950 than was General MacArthur. The state of training of his four divisions was probably no better, and certainly no worse, than was the case of our occupation forces in Germany, or of units in the United States. Despite our far-flung global commitments, and our intense involvement in the Cold War, the total strength of the Army in June 1950 had dwindled to 591,487, including almost 11,000 women; of these troops a scant 100,000 men comprised MacArthur's occupation forces in Japan. Among noncommissioned officers and junior officers in combat units, only a handful were veterans of World War II, the remainder being hardly more experienced than the green teen-agers who comprised the bulk of the fighting troops.

Training was a constant problem. Spread out around Japan, performing occupation tasks at the same time, it was difficult to assemble units for maneuvers, even had there been adequate maneuver space in the overcrowded islands. Weapons and equipment were those that had been brought into Japan by MacArthur's troops in 1945, and were maintained in operating condition only by efforts that used up an inordinate amount of time and manpower. Medium and heavy tanks could not be operated over the light bridges and restricted roads of Japan, and so the few armored units had only light tanks of World War II vintage, which had been inferior to German and Russian tanks in 1944. But the commanders, despite handicaps, did their best to maintain training standards.

Most serious, however, was the numerical weakness of forces which were intended not only to occupy defeated Japan, but to be available for action in any emergency which might arise in the Western Pacific region. In Germany, where occupation forces had also been reduced to about 100,000 men, the commanding general elected to reduce his combat forces to two combat divisions, employing the remainder of his troops in essential occupation and logistical tasks. In Japan, MacArthur, despite prodding from Washington, refused to reduce his structure below four divisions, even though these could be maintained only at two-thirds strength. This meant that each infantry regiment was short one battalion; each infantry and artillery battalion was short a company or battery. Corps and army artillery and equivalent elements of other arms were practically non-existent in Japan, as in Germany.

While MacArthur's decision meant that in his four under-strengthed divisions he probably had available for immediate combat a slightly smaller total of infantry riflemen than there were at the time in Germany, he had at least 30 per cent more heavy infantry weapons and artillery. Furthermore, he had, in existence, with operating headquarters and logistical organization, a skin-and-bones structure of four divisions that could be expanded to full fighting strength by adding individual replacements. There is a serious question whether, with only two divisions, even at full strength, MacArthur would have had the fighting power, and operational flexibility, to hold the Pusan perimeter. He most certainly would not have been able to undertake the Inchon operation in September, and it is doubtful if such an amphibious landing could have been launched before the spring of 1951. When the storm broke, he obtained replacements promptly from the States, and even more quickly by rounding up scattered individual soldiers from commissaries, laundries, occupation teams, and even from the shattered South Korean army (when the 7th Division went ashore at Inchon, two and a half months after the first American ground troops reached Korea, more than a third of its men were South Koreans).

And the key to MacArthur's strategic concept of the Korean War was an early amphibious operation, to bring to bear, as rapidly as possible, U.S. naval and air superiority, as well as the outstanding American advantage in tactical and technical doctrine as developed in World War II. In this way he planned to make up for our inferiority in numbers of ground troops. Even before General Dean began his delaying action with the 24th Division, MacArthur was contemplating a landing near Inchon to take place perhaps within a month. This, of course, was before the full combat power of the North Koreans had been demonstrated, and the initial idea had to be suspended, as MacArthur threw the 24th, 25th and 1st Cavalry Divisions into the Pusan perimeter, and then was forced to commit the 2nd Division and the 1st Provisional Marine Brigade as soon as they arrived from the United States in August.

But MacArthur had no intention of abandoning his concept. He had no doubt that General Walker's Eighth Army could now hold the perimeter, despite the incessant Communist assaults. If he could obtain sufficient additional Marines to give him one amphibious-trained division, he would be able to add his 7th Infantry Division to comprise a corps of two divisions. This he considered would be adequate to make a landing at Inchon, to seize the key road and rail communications center of Seoul, and thus complete a strategic envelopment which would destroy the North Korean army now pounding at Pusan. For psychological reasons, to restore the American prestige in Asia damaged by early North Korean successes, as well as to strike before the Communists built up their strength in the vital, vulnerable Seoul area, he determined to mount the operation as soon as possible.

On August 12 MacArthur directed his staff to plan for an amphibious assault on Inchon on September 15, the earliest date that the tides would be suitable. At this time General Walker's outnumbered Eighth Army was apparently fighting for its very existence on the threshold of Pusan, and MacArthur had no assurances that he would receive the Marines essential to the operation. Even more alarming, to some members of his staff and to the Joint Chiefs of Staff in Washington, was the place he had selected for the landing.

The Inchon beachline had practically every disadvantage conceivable to amphibious experts. The tidal variation of approximately thirty feet would permit the use of the beaches for only three hours of every twelve; long miles of mud flats intervene at other times. The channel was narrow, and dominated by Wolmi Island, which would have to be seized before the main landings. This preliminary landing would jeopardize surprise. Once ashore the troops would face the prospect of costly and time-consuming street fighting. The port facilities were inadequate, and the tidal variation precluded any substantial logistical support over the beaches.

These disadvantages were pointed out to MacArthur on several occasions, both by his own staff, and by high-level messages from Washington. In reply, he insisted that the UN forces could seize the initiative only by an amphibious operation. He pointed out the weak defensive strength in the Inchon-Seoul area, the enemy having committed every available unit to the effort at Pusan. Strategic surprise was almost certain, and the proximity of the communications center of Seoul assured the complete isolation of the Communist armies to the south. These results would not be obtained by a more cautious and conservative landing further south. Victory at Inchon would certainly assure a quick and successful conclusion of the war with North Korea. Since time was of the essence, the General insisted in his replies to Washington, they must send him the additional Marines essential to his plan.

There could be no rebuttal to these arguments; the Marine division, less two battalions which could not arrive on time, was made available; the final increment arrived in Korean waters, from the Mediterranean, on September 12.

They pay off on the scoreboard. Applaud the Inchon decision as bold, condemn it as hazardous, if you will. The fact remains that the landing went off on schedule against little opposition, and by the end of September, 1950, MacArthur had obtained the results he had forcast. By that date the rout of the North Korean Army was complete. Part was cornered in southern Korea, part driven back into the north. As a whole it was so disorganized and depleted that it would not recover in the following years of protracted combat.

Once more a bold, hazardous MacArthur operation had gone according to plan.

But two months later another bold plan was suddenly and unexpectedly wrecked, to initiate a controversy in the United States that will never be satisfactorily settled.

Following the Inchon victory and in accordance with the UN Security Council's directive to "restore international peace and security in the area," the Joint Chiefs of Staff on September 27, 1950, ordered MacArthur "to destroy the North Korean armed forces." He was authorized to operate in any part of Korea to carry out his mission and thus gain the full fruits of his Inchon success.

But there was one important restriction placed upon his operations by the U.S. Government. To avoid the possibility of antagonizing Communist China, no United Nations aircraft, under any circumstances, was to fly north of the Yalu River. Although the remaining enemy forces in the field were able to maintain themselves only by means of arms, supplies, and reinforcements coming openly from Red China's Manchuria, these bases, and their pipelines right down to the Korean side of the river, were out of bounds. And even though Communist China was loudly blustering about intervention, Allied aerial reconnaissance of its gathering troop concentrations north of the Yalu was prohibited.

Promptly, MacArthur moved the Eighth Army up the broad western corridor of Korea, seizing the North Korean capital of Pyongyang. On the eastern side of the great spiny mountain ridges splitting the country from north to south, ROK forces pushed up the coastal highway, while the X Corps, re-embarking at Inchon, was ferried around the peninsula to make an amphibious landing at Wonsan. So complete was the enemy collapse, however, that by the time the X Corps arrived at its objective, Wonsan was already in the hands of ROK troops. Approximately 135,000 enemy soldiers had been captured since the assault on Inchon, some 40 days before.

MacArthur's entire strength (some 175,000 men, half of whom were U.S. troops) was thus progressing northward on a 300-mile front over wild, mountainous terrain. But it was moving in two independent bodies, physically separated from one another by the central mountain mass, over which communications except by radio were extremely difficult; hence immediate mutual support between Eighth Army and X Corps did not exist. The two forces were controlled by MacArthur from Tokyo.

By the first week of November the advance had reached to between thirty and seventy miles south of the Yalu. Some Eighth Army units had penetrated much further, but Walker, discovering that substantial reinforcements of Chinese Communist "volunteers" were bolstering up the enemy on his front, drew his spearheads back and began concentrating his troops from their far-flung and thinly scattered pursuit, the while ensuring that his supply lines caught up with his much-extended army. At the same time he asked guidance from MacArthur on this new development of Chinese Communist reinforcement.

MacArthur was faced with a new decision. Was this appearance of Red Chinese "volunteers" an indication that Peking's threats of intervention would materialize? MacArthur's headquarters doubted it, a doubt shared by the U.S. Government's Central Intelligence Agency. Nevertheless the possibility could not be overlooked, now that an estimated 75,000 Chinese appeared to be already south of the Yalu, with at least 500,000 more gathered just across the river in Manchuria.

MacArthur's mission was to destroy the North Korean forces. Only by overrunning all of North Korea could this be accomplished. The JCS, somewhat perturbed by the Chinese Communist reinforcements, now suggested caution, but in light of CIA's estimate that Red China would not risk a full-scale war, in mid-November they reaffirmed MacArthur's mission. This had the specific approval of the National Security Council and President Truman. It meant, then, that the buck had been passed to the General, who must make the decision.

As MacArthur saw the situation, ground patrols had shown the enemy present in considerable strength, but estimate of specific numbers was impossible. Between the Yalu River and the front, the distance was so short that air reconnaissance did little good. Hundreds of thousands of Chinese soldiery could conceal themselves in that wild, wooded country, within one or two nights' march of the river. And, of course, the final source of information, air reconnaissance of the enemy activities across the border, always a telltale of strength, was prohibited.

Three major courses of action were possible. He could advance boldly to fulfill his mission, maintaining maximum local ground security. This would risk serious danger, should the enemy decide to attack suddenly in great strength.

He could withdraw to the narrow "waist" of Korea and establish a defensive perimeter. This would be in effect an admission of timidity; his mission would be unaccomplished and North Korea enabled to re-establish control of more than half its original area, regardless of Chinese entrance into the struggle. Propaganda-wise, the North Koreans could claim, after such an Allied withdrawal, that they had been victorious. This, and the appearance of timidity in the face of the Chinese Communists' threats, would be interpreted throughout Asia and the rest of the world as evidence of United States weakness and fear of China.

The third course would be to dig in on the line now held. This plan offered all the political and military disadvantages of the others, without offsetting advantage. Not only would the mission remain unaccomplished, but also, from the military viewpoint, the position would be less defensible from a Red Chinese attack than if his troops were disposed along the Yalu itself.

MacArthur, choosing the first course, made in fact the only decision possible under the circumstances. It would have been unthinkable to the American public at that time that we back down in the face of Chinese Communist threats. Hindsight, of course, shows that this decision courted disaster. But the calculated risk was clear at the time to MacArthur, as it was to the Joint Chiefs of Staff, who approved his decision.

It must be remembered, too, that MacArthur felt that should Red China enter the fight, all restrictions upon his air operations against enemy bases and communication lines across the Yalu would be immediately lifted. He was confident, then, that he would be able, under any circumstances, to stabilize the situation in the northern portion of the peninsula. So the advance continued.

On the night of November 25–26, 1950, a massive Chinese Communist offensive coming down both sides of the dorsal mountain chain smashed into MacArthur's troops, rocking them back. Surprise was complete. The blow would have been devastating except for the stamina and local troop leadership which finally enabled Eighth Army on the west, and X Corps on the east, to change probable envelopment and rout into a steady withdrawal.

Detailed tactical analysis of this operation is not for this book. But several salient points must be discussed.

As we know, the government did not see fit to lift the existing restrictions on his air operations. There is no absolute assurance, either, that unrestricted air activities over Manchuria would have altered the ground situation greatly. It is hard to believe, however, that a ground army of 300,000 men, rapidly swelled to over 500,000, could have moved so quickly, so strongly, and so far down the peninsula had their bases been destroyed and their bridges over the Yalu been knocked out. In retrospect there seems little doubt that, having failed to back its initial bet, the government made a grave mistake, the final results of which are still incalculable. If it was not prepared to let him fight without restrictions, MacArthur should not have been permitted to move to the Yalu. But ex post facto criticism is easy. It is not so easy for the political leadership of a democracy to risk precipitating global war, no matter how slight the possibility that the worst will occur. In any event, the government's decision and its possible future implications in other limited wars are of the utmost significance to analysis of military leadership. We shall return to this problem later.

But if MacArthur's strategic decision seems sound, under the circumstances which existed at the time, the tactical execution is open to severe criticism. And if MacArthur deserves the credit when his plans went well, then he must equally bear the responsibility when things went wrong.

In the first place, security was obviously inadequate. MacArthur's headquarters was aware of the presence of large Chinese Communist forces south of the Yalu which, when combined with reinforcements nearby in Manchuria, totaled some 600,000 men. Even if there had been only 75,000 in North Korea, as was estimated, instead of the 300,000 that actually struck on the night of November 25–26, such a force was too large to be ignored by an army spread as thinly as MacArthur's. Yet, so far as the front-line units were concerned, the enemy's potential was apparently ignored. If any grave warnings— any orders for extra security precautions—issued from MacArthur's headquarters, they apparently did not reach the troops. As for Walker, who as we know had already noted evidences of a Chinese Communist build-up in front of him, he, too, seemingly ignored the danger. Misled by the slight opposition his advance elements were encountering, he pushed his troops into the jaws of the trap. There is no excuse for surprise, and no army has ever been more thoroughly surprised than was the Eighth Army that November 25. The blame for any lack of alertness must be shared by Walker and MacArthur, who had the ultimate responsibility.

Next on our hindsight list comes consideration of the advisability of simultaneous advance along the entire broad front. Surely, it would seem, a more cautious probing, confined initially to the western front, was indicated under the circumstances. This portion of the zone included the major Yalu crossings, and the terrain made for more favorable communications. The X Corps, under such conditions, would have become, despite the mountain ridges separating the two forces, a strategic reserve of sorts.

Lastly, one may well question the advisability of an offensive by two independent forces in the same theater of war. Here Mac-Arthur may be criticized for violating the principle of unity of command. True, he was in supreme command, but he was in Tokyo. Walker, commanding Eighth Army and bearing the brunt of the field command in Korea, had no operational jurisdiction over Almond, commanding X Corps.

As it was, in the face of the almost paralyzing surprise blows delivered in overwhelming strength at critical points, United Nations forces could avoid disaster only by a prompt and extensive withdrawal. And disaster *was* averted, to the everlasting credit of the units and their leaders, from lowest to highest. Despite terrific Chinese pressure, the withdrawal was accomplished and was conducted in accordance with a hastily devised plan which resulted in the establishment of a new line. The entire United Nations command took a beating, and some units suffered very heavily indeed. But over-all losses were relatively light; amazingly light, in view of the circumstances, and in comparison with losses of forces of similar sizes under equally fierce combat conditions. Despite undeniable local confusion inevitable in a hasty withdrawal, the operation was creditably performed. What might have been a major disaster became a distressing but revocable misfortune. After having been pushed to the thirty-eighth parallel, and then some fifty miles or more further south, exactly two months after the first shock of the Yalu defeat United Nations troops were launching a successful counteroffensive.

By April 11, when President Truman's fateful decision relieved him of command, MacArthur's troops, in steady, irresistible advance against Red Chinese troops at least three times their number, had recaptured Seoul and were fighting their way north across that artificial thirty-eighth parallel border once more. And though Mac-Arthur cannot escape blame for the defeat of his army on the Yalu, no one can take from him the credit for this amazing resurgence.

But no amount of genius and skill in the high command could have extricated MacArthur's troops from North Korea, nor brought about their marvelous resumption of the offensive, without the splendid leadership of their combat commanders, from army down to squad.

Let's look at one company and two men. This story typifies the thousands of instances of American combat leadership in that drab Korean War.

"We're Good!"

In those grim November days of 1950 Captain Reginald B. Desiderio was commanding Company E—"Easy Company" in soldier jargon—of the 27th (Wolfhounds) Infantry Regiment. Thirty-year-old "Dusty" Desiderio had started soldiering early. At fifteen he had enlisted in the field artillery. A second lieutenant of infantry in World War II, he had garnered, for gallantry in action, the Silver Star and the Bronze Star with three oak-leaf clusters. Now he was back in the Army again.

Ordered to withdraw after the toughest kind of fighting during the night of November 25–26, Easy Company was again engaged in a fight for its life the next night. Wounded twice during the night, the captain kept moving from man to man, dug in on a hill in the path of a main Chinese route of advance, as the foe threw attack after attack at the postion. Sensing the growing desperation of his men, he began shouting "Hold till daylight and you've got it made! Hold till daylight and you've got it made!" The shout was picked up by his men, and repeated again and again, as a cry of defiance, in the face of the unabated assaults.

But it wasn't enough. Shortly before dawn the enemy burst into the perimeter. Some men ran, others wavered; two supporting tanks started to leave. Desiderio ran to the tanks, banged their steel hulls with his rifle, shouting, "Goddammit, we're not quitting!" The tanks stopped, resumed firing, and the captain rushed toward the breach in the perimeter where one of his platoons had cracked. In the gray light of gathering dawn he led another officer in a desperate two-man charge to re-establish the position. Witnesses insisted that the captain, though wounded again by grenade fragments, single-handedly killed at least fifteen Chinese and wounded twelve more with rifle fire and hand grenades, before he was killed. But in those few moments, while Desiderio held the position of a platoon, his example had inspired the beaten men. They dashed back, and this time they stayed. Desiderio had indeed held till daylight.

That was Easy Company in the midst of defeat and withdrawal. Two months later Easy Company would be on the offensive, with another man in Desiderio's shoes.

The action started when the company's first platoon, skidding and scrambling across a frozen rice paddy, was suddenly boxed in by Red Chinese artillery, mortar, and machine-gun fire. The date was February 5, 1951; the place, Korea's abomination of winter desolation not far from Suwon, the gateway to Seoul. Hill 440, its multiridged shoulders dominating the terrain, was a Red strongpoint in that area; the local high-water mark of the Chinese Communist tide that had swept down the peninsula from the Yalu River.

The fight ended two days later with a handful of the same men on another hill, dancing a macabre jig of victory amid sprawling piles of dead Chinese soldiers. That might seem ridiculous to one merely listening to parched, cracked voices, chanting in monotonous rhythm: "We're good! We're good! We're good!" But the men who danced that jig and croaked so childishly were waving bayoneted rifles dripping red. They had killed to the last man the enemies opposing them. They were warriors who had won with cold steel. They *were* good. And they knew it.

Easy Company had been one small element of the American counteroffensive which since January 24 had been prying the enemy from his holds, piece by piece. It was a seasoned combat outfit, this company of the Wolfhounds poking its way in near-zero weather from hill to hill, and from one snow-crusted ridge to another. To the casual observer, however, as the counteroffensive began, it presented one thing unusual at that time in Korea; it went into action with bayonets fixed.

This bayonet business had been going on for more than a month; ever since Massachusetts-born Captain Lewis L. Millett had taken command. A cheerful, rangy, athletic six-footer was this Millett, just passed thirty years. He had a winning smile, twinkling eyes, cocky bearing, an enormous yellow mustache, and a liking for cold steel.

Easy Company had known Millett casually before he took command. A forward observer for the 8th Field Artillery Battalion supporting the Wolfhounds, he had shared their fortunes, good and bad, in front-line action up and down the Korean peninsula. He had been wounded in the same dreadful action in which Captain Desiderio had lost his life.

Rumor in the company had it that Millett had left the hospital before his leg wound had healed; that he'd taken to aerial observation; that he'd insisted on being dropped behind enemy lines to rescue a South African fighter pilot who had crashed, and had waited there alone until the little two-seater could carry the pilot back to safety and return for him.

What the men didn't know was that Millett had transferred into the infantry because he craved combat, and that he had particularly asked to be given Easy Company because he had admired Desiderio and had seen the company perform in battle. They looked him over more closely now. There was no doubt abut his previous combat service. He wore the Silver Star, the Bronze Star, and the Purple Heart, and his World War II African-European service ribbon bore seven campaign stars. Rumor, again correctly, spoke of a battlefield commission won at Anzio while with the 1st Armored Division.

If the men of Easy Company wondered a bit about that M-1 rifle Millett carried, with bayonet fixed, and the hand grenades dangling from his shoulder straps, they soon found out, just as they found him self-confident and quick in decision; an officer who knew what he wanted and who would cut corners to get it. His changes in the company were few but potent.

A new issue of bayonets was drawn immediately (the men of Easy Company, like most of Eighth Army, it seemed, had thrown theirs away). And from then on Easy Company habitually carried its bayonets fixed. Continual bayonet drill went on; no fancy work, just the basic cut-and-thrust which, Millett assured them, they would use in battle.

He made them jab their bayonets into bales of hay or shocks of cornstalks; into soft mudbanks and into convenient trees, at odd times and at all times. And since the issue bayonets were dull (they always are) and whetstones could not be requisitioned, they sharpened their bayonets on the grindstones of Korean farms or any other convenient stones.

Millett also drew hand grenades, loads of them. In Easy Company hand grenades were tossed about as casually as baseballs. The men carried them hung on their bodies and in their pockets; each vehicle carried a quantity of them, too. Finally, the new commander insisted on increased firepower, with two automatic rifles in each squad.

Swinging a bayoneted rifle is not the highest form of entertainment; actually it takes hard physical effort. And sticking that bayonet into every shock of cornstalks one meets may become monotonous, but, in Korean winter at least, it's warming work. So, too, is running full tilt up and down rocky hillsides, another Millett complex. And as for hand grenades, Easy Company had seen sufficient combat to appreciate that they are useful things to have around when need comes.

So Millett's men festooned themselves with grenades, emulated mountain goats on bouldered slopes, brandished their rifles until they could twirl them with the ease of drum majors twirling batons. And they kept their bayonets sharp.

The payoff came that February morning under the frowning, snow-powdered escarpments of Hill 440, with the enemy bunkered in strength along its twisting skyline. The Turkish Brigade had had one go at Hill 440, but even those tough fighters couldn't quite make the grade. Then a battalion of the 35th Infantry got a toehold on one ridge, and the 27th was ordered to hit the other end. Easy Company led the way, on a two-platoon front, the third in support prepared to cover the others by fire.

When the enemy fire dropped on the first platoon struggling in the rice paddy, Millett, jumping out in front of the second, waved his rifle.

"Follow me!" he roared and dashed forward.

The second platoon went driving behind its shouting captain. They were shouting, too, by this time. All reached the base of the hill to crouch in momentary defilade, protected by the slope from the hostile fire. Then Millett jumped upward.

The third platoon's fire, concentrated now on the ridge, lifted as they saw Millett reach the top, standing boldly on the skyline. Screaming and yelling, the men below tore up after him, up and across the ridge and into the cleverly dug bunkers where the Chinese clung. Out of the rice paddy came the first platoon, its own situation forgotten. Then Easy Company was over the top. Bayonets were jabbing, rifle butts were smashing at enemy faces, and the ridge was won.

That was the first episode; there was more to come. In Korea you gained one ridge only to find another one beyond. So, two days later, Easy Company met its second test, on what was called Hill 180.

The company was skirting this hill in its usual formation; first and second platoons abreast, the third on a hill to the right rear, ready to fire when necessary. Some tanks, part of the task force, were snouting along the road.

There was, it seemed, an inordinate amount of foliage still on that ridge, stunted trees and brush. Someone in the third platoon noted this unusual circumstance; noted, too, a flicker of movement here and there, as if heads were peering through at the troops moving by. The captain's attention was called.

Millett looked. Then swinging his two platoons, he led them on the run toward the ridge just as it blossomed with enemy fire. Actually, as they soon found out, the whole area was honeycombed with bunkers and fox holes filled with fighting Chinese soldiers—a human hornet's nest vomiting grenades and small-arms fire.

Millett, topping a saddle in the ridge, gathered the first fourteen of his men to reach him, then charged down the reverse slope, a fifty-yard slide. They crossed the flat below, then up the next rise, with the rest of the company hard behind.

In every pit, behind every boulder it seemed, were Chinese, whose fire took quick, bitter toll as the slashing Americans stumbled through. But the Reds—themselves expert at fearsome noisemaking in combat—were outdone by the shouting doughboys closing in. And they had no defense against those bayonets. Their best just wasn't good enough.

One bunker did hold, momentarily. But one brave soldier—Pfc Victor Cozares—standing on its lip, hurled his own grenades, then turned and catching grenades tossed him by men behind, unpinned and flung them in a steady stream spouting fire and destruction below.

Then the line heaved on.

When it was over, forty-seven of the Chinese defenders were still there, all dead.

Then it was that the punch-drunk victors, bloodied weapons still in hand, went into a shuffling, jigging Indian war dance, while the Korean hillsides reverberated to their chant, reiterated from steaming, frost-rimed lips:

"We're good! We're good! We're good!"

For all of its differences from America's past wars, Korea was a reaffirmation of the leadership lessons of recent and distant past.

With one revolutionary exception.

For the first time in American history, commanders were forbidden to do their utmost to achieve victory—or so it seemed to many military men and to many civilian observers as well. Even when his army was faced with possible destruction, General MacArthur had not been permitted to smash the major sources of enemy strength across the Yalu, though it seemed clear to him and his subordinates that this would have directly affected the course of the battle. And a few months later his successor, General Matthew B. Ridgway, and the fighting commander of the Eighth Army, General James A. Van Fleet (Walker had been killed in December), were to face similar frustrations when, with the foe reeling and beaten, and a stunning ground victory apparently within their grasp, the advance was halted by orders from Washington.

There was no question in the minds of these generals, or of their disconcerted subordinates, as to the extent and pre-eminence of civilian governmental authority over the conduct of war. But it was a new experience to them to have this authority exercised in such a way as to restrain them from seeking victory, or from visiting the greatest possible destruction on the foe, at the least cost to their own forces in terms of American lives. General MacArthur spoke for most American military men, and for a sizable proportion of the nation's civilian population as well when he later asserted: "There is no substitute for victory!"

Yet other thoughtful Americans, paraphrasing Clausewitz, the oracle of most of these same military men, insisted that war is fought only for the purpose of furthering national policy. There are times, they argued, when it is more important to the national interest to keep a war limited in objectives and in scope, than to gain a victory which might cause a desperate enemy to force an expansion of the war. The issues in Korea were such, for instance, as to warrant the risks of a minor war to punish local aggression and to re-establish the status quo. The issues were not great enough, such people insisted, to affect fundamental U.S. interests, and thus to warrant the risk of precipitating World War III and with it the possible devastation of the United States.

This latter view prevailed. But General MacArthur was able to write, after that war ended in stalemate and armistice:

"Certain fundamentals to military success have remained unchanged. Foremost among these is the requisite that there be preserved to the soldier unimpaired the will to win. He must fully understand the national objectives for which his sacrifice is asked. He must be assured that the diplomat, once he has failed to achieve such objectives by the normal process of diplomacy, will not be entrusted with the strategy designed to enforce them by war. He must have full faith that once his country has committed him to battle it will invincibly support him until victory has been won."

The issue, therefore, was not settled by the Korean War. Is there any possible reconciliation of the opposing points of view? Or must the military leader, unable to count on the assurances which General MacArthur has demanded for him, face the grim uncertainties which made Korea a nightmare of leadership?

CHAPTER XIX   ☆ ☆ ☆   *Leadership*
Yesterday, Today, Tomorrow

For almost two centuries of American military history, a pattern of combat leadership, first established during the Revolution, has proved its validity. Not that there has ever been a typical American leader. Some have been austere and aloof; others gregarious showmen. Some have excelled in civil life; other brilliant soldiers were unable to achieve success outside the Army. Some have been models of deportment; others have had a propensity for being in constant hot water in both official and private affairs. While most have had the benefit of education and culture, some were rough-hewn sons of farm, forest, or plain.

Nevertheless, the pattern exists, and clearly visible as its major threads are six definite characteristics which all successful American leaders have shared, to a greater or lesser degree: Professional military competence, an understanding of the human tools of the commander, insistence on high standards of training and discipline, ability to inspire their men, unquestioned personal courage, and consistent perseverance and determination in the face of adversity.

Has the advent of nuclear warfare changed any of these requirements? Is it possible, as some have already asserted, that past concepts of war and battlefield leadership, valid as recently as 1953, may have been ended forever by the new weapons?

One cannot discount the possibility that the devastation and radioactivity of a nuclear conflict will prevent effective battlefield maneuver by either side. Perhaps we shall never know the answer to this, since the very possibility may inhibit the employment of such weapons. Yet the mere fact that the weapons exist must forever affect future warfare. The leaders on both sides in any future war can never forget that the opponent *might* use nuclear weapons.

Whether nuclear weapons are actually employed or not, therefore, their potential effects are such that modern forces must be able to fight effectively even when widely dispersed. Nuclear-age forces must possess great mobility. Units will have to be more self-sufficient than in the past; an obvious result of increased mobility and increased vulnerability. Old methods of supply and communication are obviously inadequate for the kinds of battlefield our military theorists envisage. Movements will be too fast, land lines of communication too vulnerable, to permit the kind of methodical means of administration and support which were employed in World War II and in Korea.

For the Army leader it all adds up to the need for greater versatility, greater self-reliance, and ever-increasing study to maintain adequate professional competence. It is clear that, to the extent combat is feasible under nuclear conditions, the same qualities of alert, resolute leadership, sharpened and improved by the best possible training and improved equipment, are required as in the past.

But the dramatic change in the role of weapons, brought about by the nuclear age, presents an additional problem to leadership. Until recently weapons were but instruments of warfare, which was itself, in turn, an instrument of policy. Now, with relatively unlimited destructive capability, weapons have become determinants of national policy as well as instruments of that policy.

In and out of the government, policy makers and students of policy, military and civilian, have been trying to cope with the incredibly complex new problems which arise from this momentous change in the relationship of weapons to policy. There is general agreement that unlimited nuclear warfare would be an irreparable disaster to all participants. No true victor could emerge, and no nation is likely to embark deliberately on such a war. But this does not mean that nations will not use armed force in support of national interests less vital than the total destruction of the opponent's homeland. In fact, an aggressor might be tempted to embark on such limited actions in the expectation that a potential opponent will be reluctant to risk armed conflict for anything less than a direct threat to its national existence.

Civilian and military scholars conclude, therefore, that limited wars are not only possible in the future, but are more likely to occur than are total, nuclear wars. But the possibility remains that some terrible miscalculation or act of lunacy might precipitate the all-out nuclear war which the world wishes to avoid. Or that a local and limited conflict might get out of hand through a spiral of increased intensity, each side alternately raising the ante to the point where one of them, believing its national security to be directly threatened, strikes an all-out blow against the other's homeland.

This, then, leads directly to the first major problem of military leadership in the nuclear age: effective conduct of a limited war, without precipitating nuclear Armageddon.

History tells us that wars are fought most effectively when a trusted professional military commander is given clear-cut objectives by the top civilian authority, and is then allowed to conduct operations without political interference. Political meddling has always hampered military operations, and frequently it has been disastrous.

But history, as we have seen, proves also that even the greatest general is not infallible. In pre-nuclear times a military failure in a small war could mean at its worst only a lost campaign. In the nuclear age, no matter how small the war, the stakes can be national survival at each roll of the military dice. A nation's political leadership, then, must inevitably feel a need for keeping closer surveillance over military command than in former times.

Political authority must recognize, however, that once having decided to embark on a conflict for reasons of national interest, even the most limited war entails some risk. Military leadership, on the other hand, must recognize why civilian authority must impose a somewhat tighter control than was previously necessary or desirable. More than ever before, there is need for mutual confidence between military commander and civilian authority.

In the light of this somewhat new perspective on limited wars in the nuclear age, it is illuminating to take a fresh look at the top command problems of the Korean War. The United States and

Soviet Russia both possessed nuclear weapons, which for the first time became determinants of policy.

There certainly was not a feeling of mutual confidence between the nation's political authority and General MacArthur. In Washington there was a feeling that MacArthur was willing—indeed, trying—to expand the scope of the war to an extent which would risk a major war with Communist China and the possible involvement of Russia, thus touching off World War III and a nuclear holocaust. MacArthur believed that civilian authority was overestimating both the aims and capabilities of the Communist enemy; that it was allowing itself to be unduly influenced by timorous allies; and that consequent failure to achieve military victory would irreparably damage the American position in the Far East.

Political authority was unquestionably right in principle, but MacArthur's evaluation of enemy aims and capabilities in 1950–1951 was probably more realistic than that of the government. Yet this must forever remain one of the great unanswered questions of history. In any event, the outcome was the only one possible in American military tradition: the supremacy of civilian authority was asserted and accepted. Despite subsequent partisan political wrangling, and widespread doubts as to the wisdom of our strategy in Korea, flouting of civilian authority would have been unthinkable to American soldiers and the American public.

But what of General MacArthur's famous assertion that "there is no substitute for victory"? Was this merely an anachronism uttered by an old soldier unable to keep abreast of the times? Before we decide, it would be well to make sure of what we mean by "victory."

The facts of nuclear-age life require, more than ever before, care and precision in the establishment of limited military objectives carefully tailored to fit limited political aims. Whether or not they can be characterized as "victorious," over-all military results must conform to the predetermined aims and objectives. But there is still a serious question in the minds of many military men as to the extent to which the restrictions of a limited war will affect military leadership below the top echelons.

For instance, an official statement of Army combat doctrine published in 1954 asserts that "victory alone as an aim of war cannot be justified, since in itself victory does not always ensure the realization of national objectives."

Previous to Korea, American military minds had been conditioned to thinking in terms of total wars and total victory. It was probably desirable in 1954 to point out to frustrated Army men that limited wars of the Korean pattern would be more likely in the nuclear age than total wars, and to remind them that objectives in limited wars cannot be unlimited. In such context there was indeed a substitute for total victory.

But was this statement of doctrine intended to mean that it is not necessarily important to gain "victory" in *any* engagement, no matter what size forces may be engaged? If so, its implications cannot be so readily accepted.

Today as in the past, when our forces are engaged in combat, they must conform to restrictions imposed by higher authority. At the same time, soldiers must fight as hard as necessary to carry out their missions.

The nuclear age requires greater precision in the art of fitting military objectives to political aims. In times past it was not necessarily catastrophic if tolerances were loose; the result was merely an unnecessary waste of time, money, and blood. In the nuclear age a poor fit could mean the destruction of civilization. Thus there is an even greater premium upon professional competence at the top levels of nuclear-age leadership. And this need for precision must be reflected also in the decisions of lower-level commanders in assigning objectives to subordinates, and in prescribing limitations on the means to be employed.

But the basic requirements of combat leadership are not affected. Orders must be carried out. No soldier can question the propriety of instructions from higher authority, or decide for himself whether a victory would contribute to national objectives. Every will, effort, and energy must be directed toward success in accomplishing the assigned mission—which some might call "victory."

The increasingly marked tendency in all our society toward conformity and uniformity on the part of all individual members of that society is another stumbling block to leadership. Like all major social characteristics, this development is to a great degree reflected in the armed forces of the society. It is odd, indeed, that military leadership, ever dependent upon discipline, should be threatened by individual tendencies toward conformity.

Some thoughtful Army officers believe that they sense here a paradox between, on the one hand, the increasing need for self-reliant leaders and, on the other, an unmistakable drifting toward uniformity, conformity, and the stifling of initiative.

Is there the possibility that "organization men" are becoming as prevalent in our armed forces as in our society in general? Should we, in the future, expect no more Anthony Waynes, no more Nathan Bedford Forrests, no more Douglas MacArthurs?

Look upon the definition of leadership in the Army's latest manual on combat doctrine:

"Leadership is the art of influencing others to cooperate in the achievement of a common goal. It may be either authoritative or persuasive in nature, or both. Although the military command structure is designed to facilitate authoritative leadership, the persuasive variety is more effective. Persuasive leadership can inspire men to face dangers which are more immediate and grave than the punishment that can be inflicted by authority."

One immediately harks back to General Zachary Taylor, under heavy fire at Resaca de la Palma, barking to Captain May: "Charge, Captain, *nolens volens!*" Or General George Washington reforming the shattered Continentals at Monmouth. Or Colonel Hanes halting the fugitives at the foot of Korea's Bunker Hill.

Persuasive leadership? Not a bit of it; there was no time for persuasion in these cases. But men in great danger, and fearing for their lives, responded instantly to the voice of authority—known, respected, and a bit awesome. Why did they respond? The answer is not so easy, though training, discipline, and soldierly pride played their varying parts in the reactions of each soldier who responded. But most of all, the response came because they were inspired—not persuaded—by the powerful personality as well as the authority of the individual giving the orders.

This definition of leadership quoted above is only one of a number of troubling evidences of the spreading of "organization man" thinking in the Army; to the detriment, some believe, of the old, classic virtues of leadership.

Take, for instance, the Army doctrine of "completed staff work." According to this, a staff officer, given a problem, studies it exhaustively, prepares one or more possible solutions until he finds one that will satisfy all other staff officers having a proper interest in the matter, then he drafts precise and detailed plans which would assure the accomplishment of the solution. The proposed solution, and the plans for "implementation"—military jargon for "getting it done"—are then, and not until then, presented to the commander for approval or rejection. If possible, the matter is condensed on a single sheet of paper so as to save the commander's valuable time.

There are good reasons for this doctrine of completed staff work. Commanders have too many responsibilities to be forced to worry about the details of the myriad matters with which they are concerned. They should be able to rely upon staff officers, when given a job, coming up with complete and thorough solutions, presented in the form of concise, clear-cut recommendations. The commander is then left free to think about broad problems and major issues. But there are dangers in the system not always appreciated by commanders or their staffs.

In the first place, if a commander gives an important problem to his staff, without guidance as to the kind of solution he expects, he will receive as recommendations a concensus of staff opinion. Sometimes this will be good. Frequently, when the issue is controversial, the recommendation will be a watered-down compromise. And compromises, while often desirable in politics, are rarely good in battle.

There have been cases where commanders, relying completely on their staffs for ideas, have developed none of their own. The results have not been inspirational.

By its mere existence, then, a staff, in handling day-to-day problems, can become a decision-making body rather than an advisory group. A commander who acts only on the recommendations set before him by his staff is no leader. He is at best a glorified referee, at worst a rubber stamp.

It would be incorrect to say that our modern staff system has created a form of group leadership in the Army. The relatively recent instance of a MacArthur overriding staff objections to a landing at Inchon, and the splendid results of his unequivocal directive to that staff to produce a plan for the landing, is an example of the traditional relationship between a strong-minded, competent leader and a professional, expert staff.

Yet the trend toward command by consensus does exist, and it is worrisome. We believe it to be extremely dangerous; threatening to self-reliant, decisive, prompt leadership.

What has caused this trend is not clear. It could possibly stem from the system of training and development of our officers, with its understandable need for uniformity in the interests of efficiency, the need for common understanding and acceptance of basic doctrinal concepts, and the inherent tendency of any large organization to knock off the rough edges of all but the most rugged of individuals. Or perhaps this retreat from individualistic leadership is due to a perversion of the military system, since that system still ostensibly admires the qualities of initiative, drive, and aggressiveness. If so, then it would appear that despite itself the military system may be reflecting a general condition of our American society.

Certainly the Army should not try to change society, nor deliberately seek to produce antisocial individuals. But the Army's principal responsibility to society is to produce and maintain military forces whch will best protect and preserve that society.

During the period between World Wars I and II, when the internal-combustion engine was revolutionizing the tactics and techniques of warfare, the Army was equal to the challenge. It prepared the type of leadership the nation might need in war. In a schooling and training system epitomized by the Command and General Staff School at Fort Leavenworth, Kansas, the Army developed the forceful, aggressive leaders who operated so successfully in all parts of the globe in World War II. Although that training and schooling system has been subjected to scrutiny, and has been greatly modified to adapt itself to the revolutionary changes of the atomic age, there may remain in it some complacency about basic concepts and procedures which proved effective in an earlier war. Whether or not this be so, undoubtedly schooling and training should be continually analyzed to make sure that in our concern with the kind of war we may have to fight, we do not overlook the need for developing the kind of leaders necessary to win such wars.

Fundamentally, we see nothing in the development of modern weapons to change the basic pattern of military leadership. So long as humans strive to kill and conquer one another, and regardless of the complexity of motives and of implements, the qualities of the leader must remain those which have been essential since the dawn of history, and which have so clearly demonstrated their validity in this country since the Revolution.

No training system can, of course, instill into an individual those personal qualities of courage, perseverance, and determination in adversity, an understanding of human nature, or the ability to inspire others to fight and work together in the face of dreadful danger. But it can reveal and foster the development of such of those qualities as may be latent to some degree in most of us.

The system must, of course, instill into its potential leaders the basic military knowledge and skill which are vital to successful conduct of military operations, no matter what form these may take in the future. With this professional competence, training methods and standards of discipline can be devised to assure the most effective use of the latest weapons and implements produced by technology.

Military competence, however, will always be threatened by two dangers. The military organization, which will be always more or less representative of the society it protects, must not be allowed to be submerged and emasculated by the society. And military men must never be satisfied with achievements which can become outmoded with the invention of each new weapon.

These dangers can be avoided only by the production of leaders who can understand and be responsive to discipline, while scorning a mere conformity; men who respect the lessons of history as guides for future development, while rejecting the stultifying effects of custom and blind tradition. Even more than in the past, circumstances in rapidly moving modern war cannot be altered to fit preconceived plans; plans must be improvised on the spot by alert, competent, self-reliant leaders, who will have no time to await detailed instructions from higher headquarters.

In short, no matter what the weapons, or what the current mores of society, the nation's military security, and thus its very existence, depends upon producing the same kind of military leaders who have fought for that security from Bunker Hill in Boston Harbor to Bunker Hill in the desolate mountains of Korea.

SELECTED BIBLIOGRAPHY

General

The following works constitute the hard core of reference in all matters pertaining to the United States Army:

American State Papers—Military Affairs. 7 vols. Washington: Gales and Seaton, 1832–1861. (Congressional documents relating to the Army, from March 3, 1789, to March 1, 1838.)

DUPUY, R. ERNEST. *Compact History of the United States Army.* New York: Hawthorn, 1956. (Our army, as an entity, from the Revolution through the Korean War.)

DUPUY, R. ERNEST, and DUPUY, TREVOR N. *Military Heritage of America.* New York: McGraw-Hill, 1956. (A serious and comprehensive analysis of American military history, from the nation's birth, with highlights of the major campaigns; many maps and charts; extensive bibliography.)

GANOE, WILLIAM A. *History of the United States Army.* New York: Appleton-Century, 1942. (An authoritative history up to mid–1942.)

HEITMAN, FRANCIS B. *Historical Register and Dictionary of the United States Army.* Washington: Government Printing Office, 1903. (Indispensable register of commissioned personnel, and gazetter of American battlefields, posts, camps and stations, through the Philippine Insurrection and Boxer Rebellion; outline history of all arms and branches of the Army to 1902.)

MILLIS, WALTER. *Arms and Men.* New York: Putnam, 1956. (A recent study of the development of American military policy.)

SPAULDING, OLIVER L. *The United States Army in War and Peace.* New York: Putnam, 1937. (American military history prior to World War II, by one of the Army's most distinguished historians.)

STEELE, MATTHEW F. *American Campaigns.* Washington: Government Printing Office, 1901; several subsequent editions by Infantry Journal and Combat Forces Press. (The classic military analysis of American operations from the Revolution through the Spanish-American War, with special emphasis on the Civil War.)

UPTON, EMORY. *The Military Policy of the United States.* Washington: Government Printing Office, 1917. (This masterful analysis of American military policy up to, and into, the Civil War, is the most important military work ever published in the United States.)

355

The Wars

For amplified study of specific wars in which the United States has been engaged, the following are recommended:

War of the Revolution

SCHEER, GEORGE F., and RANKIN, HUGH F. *Rebels and Redcoats.* Cleveland: World Publishing Co., 1957.

TREVELYAN, SIR GEORGE O. *The American Revolution.* 4 vols. London: Longmans, 1921. (Authoritative and impartial military analysis.)

WARD, CHRISTOPHER. *The War of the Revolution.* New York: Macmillan, 1952. (Excellent military history.)

War of 1812

ADAMS, HENRY. *The War of 1812,* ed. H. A. DEWEERD. Washington: Combat, 1944.

JACOBS, JAMES R. *The Beginning of the United States Army, 1783–1812.* Princeton: University Press, 1947. (Exhaustive study of the birth and early growth of the Regular Army.)

TUCKER, GLEN. *Poltroons and Patriots.* Indianapolis: Bobbs-Merrill, 1954.

Mexican War

SMITH, JUSTIN H. *The War With Mexico.* New York: Macmillan, 1919. (One of the finest military histories ever written.)

Civil War

ALEXANDER, EDWARD P. *Military Memoirs of a Confederate.* New York: Scribner, 1907. (Absorbing as a narrative, this critical review of the campaigns of the Civil War, by a participant, is most scholarly and scientific. General Alexander was emphatically unbiased in his viewpoint.)

Battles and Leaders of the Civil War. 4 vols. New York: Century, 1884–1887. (The leaders' own stories.)

COMMAGER, HENRY S. *The Blue and the Gray.* 2 vols. Indianapolis: Bobbs-Merrill, 1950. (A fascinating sampling of human documents and state papers, compiled by a leading American historian.)

War of the Rebellion, The; Official Records of the Union and Confederate Armies. 130 vols. including atlas. Washington: Government Printing Office, 1882–1900. (The basic source material for any and all studies of operations in the Civil War.)

WILLIAMS, KENNETH P. *Lincoln Finds a General.* 4 vols. to date. New York: Macmillan, 1949–56. (A thorough and scholarly review of the Civil War, with particular emphasis on command relationships.)

World War I

MCENTEE, GIRARD L. *Military History of the World War.* New York: Scribner, 1937. (Detailed narrative of operations, copiously supplied with maps and charts.)

STAMPS, T. DODSON, and ESPOSITO, VINCENT J., *et al.* A *Short Military History of World War I, with Atlas.* 2 vols. West Point: U.S. Military Academy, 1950. (Excellent concise history of operations, with superlative battle maps.)

World War II

CHURCHILL, SIR WINSTON S. *The Second World War.* 6 vols. Boston: Houghton Mifflin, 1948–1953. (One of the greatest statesmen of his time writes one of the greatest histories of all time, from the viewpoint of one of the principal actors.)

FULLER, J. F. C. *The Second World War.* New York: Duell, Sloan & Pierce, 1949. (A compendium of operations, by Britain's foremost military historian.)

MARSHALL, GEORGE C. *Biennial Reports of the Chief of Staff, 1941–1943* and *1943–1945.* Washington: Government Printing Office, 1943–1945. (Summary of the American military effort in World War II, from the viewpoint of our senior soldier.)

STAMPS, T. DODSON, and ESPOSITO, VINCENT J., *et al.* A *Military History of World War II, with Atlas.* 3 vols. West Point: U.S. Military Academy, 1953. (Concise and accurate the maps are superb.)

United States Army in World War II, The. 38 vols. to date (11 more in preparation). Washington: Government Printing Office, 1947–58. (A massive, brilliant analytic review of American military operations, by a group of professional historians and soldiers in the Office of the Chief of Military History, U.S. Army.)

STAMPS, T. DODSON, and ESPOSITO, VINCENT J., *et al. Operations in Korea.* West Point: U.S. Military Academy, 1954. (Another concise and accurate West Point military history, with the usual splendid maps.)

Specific Chapter References

Chapter I — The Battles of Bunker Hill

1775

FRENCH, ALLEN. *First Year of the Revolution.* Boston: Houghton Mifflin, 1934.

MURDOCK, HAROLD. *Bunker Hill.* Boston: Houghton Mifflin, 1927. (Competent analysis of the operation, including an impartial survey of the long-continued controversy over American command responsibility.)

1951

GUGELER, RUSSEL A. *Combat Actions in Korea.* Washington: Combat, 1954. (Excellent detailed analysis of selected small-unit operations.)

JACOBS, BRUCE. *Soldiers.* New York: Norton, 1958.

Chapter II — Laurels on the Delaware

FREEMAN, DOUGLAS S. *The Life of George Washington.* 6 vols. New York: Scribner, 1948–1954. (Definitive biography of our first great

soldier by one of our most distinguished military historians.)
STRYKER, W. S. *The Battles of Trenton and Princeton*. Boston: Houghton Mifflin, 1898.

Chapter III — Soldiers Three

BOYD, THOMAS A. *Mad Anthony Wayne*. New York: Scribner, 1929.
GRAHAM, JAMES. *The Life of General Daniel Morgan of the Virginia
Line*. Cincinnati: Derby & Jackson, 1856.
PALMER, JOHN McA. *General Von Steuben*. New Haven: Yale Uni-
versity, 1937. (Brilliant analysis.)

Chapter IV — Shadow and Substance

ELLIOTT, CHARLES W. *Winfield Scott, the Soldier and the Man*. New
York: Macmillan, 1937. (Definitive biography of a great soldier.)
JACOBS, JAMES R. *Tarnished Warrior; Major General James Wilkinson*.
New York: Macmillan, 1938.

Chapter V — A Man from Tennessee

CABLE, GEORGE W. *The Creoles of Louisiana*. New York: Scribner,
1901.
COBBETT, WILLIAM. *Life of Andrew Jackson*. New York: Harper, 1837.
JAMES, MARQUIS. *Andrew Jackson, the Border Captain*. Indianapolis:
Bobbs-Merrill, 1933.

Chapter VI — Old Rough and Ready

GRANT, ULYSSES S. *Personal Memoirs of U. S. Grant*. New York: Century,
1895. (Magnificent autobiography of one of our greatest generals.)
HAMILTON, HOLMAN. *Zachary Taylor, Soldier of the Republic*. Indianapolis: Bobbs-Merrill, 1941.

Chapter VII — Without the Loss of a Battle or Skirmish

ELLIOTT, CHARLES W. *Winfield Scott, the Soldier and the Man*. New
York: Macmillan, 1937.
GRANT, ULYSSES S. *Personal Memoirs of U. S. Grant*. New York: Cen-
tury, 1895.
KIRBY SMITH, EPHRAIM. *To Mexico with Scott*. Cambridge: Harvard
University Press, 1917.
SCOTT, WINFIELD. *Memoirs*. New York: Sheldon, 1864.

Chapter VIII — The Seed and the Ground

DUPUY, R. ERNEST. *Where They Have Trod*. New York: Stokes, 1940.
———. *Men of West Point*. New York: Sloane, 1951.

Chapter IX — Bumblers in Blue

HASSLER, WARREN W., JR. *General George B. McClellan, Shield of the
Union*. Baton Rouge: Louisiana State University Press, 1957.
HERBERT, WALTER H. *Fighting Joe Hooker*. Indianapolis: Bobbs-
Merrill, 1944.

McCLELLAN, GEORGE B. *McClellan's Own Story*. New York: Webster, 1897.

WILLIAMS, T. HARRY. *Lincoln and His Generals*. New York: Grosset & Dunlap, 1952.

Chapter X — *The Giants of the Civil War*

CATTON, BRUCE. *Mr. Lincoln's Army*. New York: Doubleday, 1949.

————. *Glory Road*. New York: Doubleday, 1952.

————. *A Stillness at Appomattox*. New York: Doubleday, 1954. (An excellent trilogy, relating the history of the Army of the Potomac.)

FREEMAN, DOUGLAS S. *R. E. Lee, a Biography*. 4 vols; several subsequent editions. New York: Scribner, 1934–1937. (Sound military analysis in a magnificent biography.)

FULLER, J. F. C. *The Generalship of U. S. Grant*. New York: Dodd, Mead, 1929. (One of Britain's greatest military historians analyzes the genius of one of America's greatest soldiers.)

GRANT, ULYSSES S. *Personal Memoirs of U. S. Grant*. New York: Century, 1895.

Chapter XI — *Strong Right Hands*

FREEMAN, DOUGLAS S. *Lee's Lieutenants—A Study in Command*. 3 vols. New York: Scribner, 1942–1944. (Brilliant and exhaustive analysis of the leadership of Lee's subordinate commanders; excellent biography.)

HENDERSON, GEORGE F. R. *Stonewall Jackson and the American Civil War*. London: Longmans, 1898; several subsequent editions. (Classic military study of a great commander.)

LEWIS, LLOYD. *Sherman–Fighting Prophet*. New York: Harcourt, Brace, 1932.

SHERMAN, WILLIAM T. *Personal Memoirs of Gen. W. T. Sherman*. 2 vols. New York: Appleton, 1875.

Chapter XII — *There Were Others*

DENISON, GEORGE T. *A History of Cavalry*. London: Macmillan, 1913.

HENRY, ROBERT. *"First with the Most" Forrest*. Indianapolis: Bobbs-Merrill, 1944.

PULLEN, JOHN J. *The Twentieth Maine*. New York: Lippincott, 1957.

SHERIDAN, PHILIP H. *Personal Memoirs of P. H. Sheridan*. New York: Webster, 1888.

WILSON, JAMES H. *Under the Old Flag*. 2 vols. New York: Appleton, 1912.

WYETH, JOHN A. *Life of General Nathan Bedford Forrest*. New York: Harper, 1899.

Chapter XIII — *From Plains to Tropics*

BOURKE, JOHN G. *On the Border with Crook*. New York: Scribner, 1891.

DOWNEY, FAIRFAX. *Indian-fighting Army*. New York: Scribner, 1941. (By far the most comprehensive and best-written account of the Army's campaigns against the Plains Indians.)

GRAHAM, WILLIAM A. *The Custer Myth*. Harrisburg: Stackpole, 1953.

KING, CHARLES. *Campaigning with Crook, and Stories of Army Life*. New York: Harper, 1890.

HOWARD, HELEN A. *War Chief Joseph*. Caldwell, Idaho: Caxton, 1946.

NYE, W. S. *Carbine and Lance*. Norman, Okla.: University of Oklahoma Press, 1942.

Chapter XIV — Iron Men

DUPUY, R. ERNEST. *Men of West Point*. New York: Sloane, 1951.

HARBORD, JAMES G. *America in the World War*. Boston: Houghton Mifflin, 1933.

———. *The American Army in France*. Boston: Houghton Mifflin, 1936.

PALMER, FREDERICK. *Newton D. Baker, America at War*. New York: Dodd, Mead, 1931.

———. *Bliss, Peacemaker*. New York: Dodd Mead, 1934.

PERSHING, JOHN J. *Final Report of General John J. Pershing*. Washington: Government Printing Office, 1920.

———. *My Experiences in the World War*. Philadelphia: Lippincott; New York: Stokes, 1931.

Chapter XV — A Fumble and Its Consequences

KIMMEL, HUSBAND E. *Admiral Kimmel's Story*. Chicago: Regnery, 1955.

LORD, WALTER. *Day of Infamy*. New York: Holt, 1957. (Blow-by-blow account of the Pearl Harbor attack of Dec. 7, 1941.)

MORTON, LOUIS. "Japan's Decision for War," from unpublished manuscript, *Command Decisions*. Washington: Office Chief of Military History, U.S. Army, 1957.

THEOBALD, ROBERT A. *The Final Secret of Pearl Harbor*. New York: Devin-Adair, 1954.

U. S. ARMY. *Army Pearl Harbor Board Report*. Washington: Adjutant General's Office, U.S. Army, 1944, mimeo. (The War Department's official investigation.)

UNITED STATES CONGRESS. *Hearings of Joint Committee on the Investigation of the Pearl Harbor Attack*. 39 parts. Washington: Government Printing Office, 1946, (Final and exhaustive Congressional investigation.)

Chapter XVI — Two Promises and Their Fulfillment

EICHELBERGER, ROBERT L. *Our Jungle Road to Tokyo*. New York: Viking, 1950.

KRUEGER, WALTER. *From Down Under to Nippon*. Washington: Combat, 1953.

MILLER, JOHN, JR. "MacArthur and the Admiralties," from unpublished manuscript, *Command Decisions*. Washington: Office Chief of Military History, U.S. Army, 1957.

MORTON, LOUIS. *The Fall of the Philippines*. Washington: Government Printing Office, 1953. (A distinguished and scholarly volume from the series: *The United States Army in World War II*, produced by the Office Chief of Military History, U.S. Army, Washington, 1957.)

ROMANUS, CHARLES F., and SUNDERLAND, RILEY. *Stillwell's Mission to China.* 2 vols. (to date). Washington: Government Printing Office, 1953–1955. (Authoritative sub-series of the Army's *The United States Army in World War II.*)

SMITH, ROBERT R. *The Approach to the Philippines.* Washington: Government Printing Office, 1953. (Another in the official Army series.)

Chapter XVII — Decisions Big and Little

BRADLEY, OMAR. *A Soldier's Story.* New York: Holt, 1951. (General Bradley's personal narrative of his experiences in World War II.)

BUTCHER, HARRY C. *My Three Years with Eisenhower.* New York: Simon & Schuster, 1946. (Intimate narrative, based on official war diaries, by General Eisenhower's naval aide de camp; invaluable source material.)

DUPUY, R. ERNEST. *St. Vith—Lion in the Way.* Washington: Combat, 1948. (The northern sector of the Battle of the Bulge, with specific emphasis on the operations of the 106th Infantry Division; a critical military analysis.)

EISENHOWER, DWIGHT D. *Crusade in Europe.* New York: Doubleday, 1948. (The Supreme Commander's personal account.)

HECHLER, KEN. *The Bridge at Remagen.* New York: Ballantine, 1957.

PATTON, GEORGE S., JR. *War as I Knew It.* Boston: Houghton Mifflin, 1947.

POGUE, FORREST C. *The Supreme Command* (ETO), Washington: Government Printing Office, 1954. (Another excellent volume from the official Army series.)

Chapter XVIII — Leaders Unafraid

DEAN, WILLIAM E. (with WILLIAM L. WARDEN). *General Dean's Story.* New York: Viking, 1954.

GUGELER, RUSSEL A. *Combat Actions in Korea.* Washington: Combat, 1954.

JACOBS, BRUCE. *Heroes of the Army.* New York: Norton, 1956. (Recounts the stories of heroism behind the awards of the Medal of Honor in the Korean War.)

MARSHALL, S. L. A. *The River and the Gauntlet.* New York: Morrow, 1953.

RIDGWAY, MATTHEW B. *Soldier.* New York: Harper, 1956.

SCHNABEL, JAMES F. "The Inchon Landing" and "The Drive to the Yalu," from unpublished manuscript, *Command Decisions.* Washington: Office Chief of Military History, U.S. Army, 1957.

Chapter XIX — Leadership Yesterday, Today, Tomorrow

HALLE, LOUIS J. *Choice for Survival.* New York: Harper, 1958.

KISSINGER, HENRY A. *Nuclear Weapons and Foreign Policy.* New York: Harper, 1958. (A distinguished study, published under the auspices of the Council on Foreign Relations.)

KAUFMANN, WILLIAM W. (ed.). *Military Policy and National Security.*

Princeton: University Press, 1956. (A collection of thoughtful studies by Kaufmann, Gordon A. Craig, Roger Hilsman and Klaus Knorr, of the Princeton Center of International Studies.)

MASLAND, JOHN W., and RADWAY, LAURENCE I. *Soldiers and Scholars*. Princeton: University Press, 1957. (A scholarly study of trends in military education in the United States.)

OSGOOD, ROBERT E. *Limited War*. Chicago: Chicago University Press, 1957.

U. S. ARMY. *F.M. 100–5 Field Service Regulations, Operations*. Washington: Government Printing Office, 1954. (Official Army doctrine.)

————. *A Guide to Army Philosophy*. Washington: Headquarters, Department of the Army, 1958. (An expression of top-level Army thinking on major issues of national defense at the dawn of the nuclear-space age.)

INDEX

Dupuy, Richard Ernest, 1887–
  Brave men and great captains ⌐by⌐ R. Ernest Dupuy
and Trevor N. Dupuy. ⌐1st ed.⌐ New York, Harper
⌐1959⌐

378 p. 22 cm.

Includes bibliography.

  1. U. S.—History, Military. 2. Leadership. 3. U. S. Army—Biog.
ɪ. Dupuy, Trevor Nevitt, 1916–   joint author. ɪɪ. Title.

E181.D77   973   58–6147 ⌐

Library of Congress